P

Encyclopédie

Also by Philipp Blom

Enlightening the World

Encyclopédie, The Book That
Changed the Course of History

PHILIPP BLOM

First published in 2005 by
PALGRAVE MACMILLAN™
175 Fifth Avenue, New York, N.Y. 10010 and
Houndmills, Basingstoke, Hampshire, England RG21 6XS
Companies and representatives throughout the world.

PALGRAVE MACMILLAN is the global academic imprint of the Palgrave Macmillan division of St. Martin's Press, LLC and of Palgrave Macmillan Ltd. Macmillan® is a registered trademark in the United States, United Kingdom and other countries. Palgrave is a registered trademark in the European Union and other countries.

ISBN 1–4039–6895–0

Library of Congress Cataloguing-in-Publication Data available from the Library of Congress.

First published in 2004 in Great Britain by Fourth Estate, a division of HarperCollins*Publishers*.

First PALGRAVE MACMILLAN edition: May 2005

10 9 8 7 6 5 4 3

Printed in the United States of America.

For Jon Stallworthy

CONTENTS

ILLUSTRATIONS

Denis Diderot by Jean-Antoine Houdon © Louvre, Paris/RMN; Jean Le Rond d'Alembert by Maurice Quentin de La Tour © Louvre; Jean-Jacques Rousseau by Maurice Quentin de La Tour © Saint-Quentin, Musée Antoine Lécuyer/RMN; Engraving of Baron Friedrich Melchior Grimm by Lecerf, 1769 © Louis Carrogis Carmontelle/Private Collection/Bridgeman Art Library; Madame d'Epinay by Jean-Etienne Liotard © Musée d'Art et d'Histoire (Cabinet des Dessins), Ville de Genève; Francois Marie Arouet de Voltaire by Jean-Antoine Houdon © Giraudon/Bridgeman Art Library; Torture of Robert-François Damiens © Musée de Versailles/Dagli Orti/The Art Archive; Jeanne Poisson the Marquise de Pompadour, 1755 by Maurice Quentin de La Tour © Louvre, Paris/Bridgeman Art Library; Drawing of Denis Diderot by Jean-Baptiste Greuze © Pierpont Morgan Library, New York/Art Resource/Scala.

The pictures integrated in the text on the following pages are all reproductions taken from the first edition of the *Encyclopédie*, Paris, Le Breton, 1750–1776: pp. x, 14, 34, 50, 68, 80, 100, 122, 138, 158, 176, 188, 202, 220, 236, 250, 266, 282, 302.

ENCYCLOPÉDIE,

OU

DICTIONNAIRE RAISONNÉ

DES SCIENCES,

DES ARTS ET DES MÉTIERS,

PAR UNE SOCIÉTÉ DE GENS DE LETTRES.

Mis en ordre & publié par M. *DIDEROT*, de l'Académie Royale des Sciences & des Belles-Lettres de Pruſſe ; & quant à la Partie Mathématique, par M. *D'ALEMBERT*, de l'Académie Royale des Sciences de Paris, de celle de Pruſſe, & de la Société Royale de Londres.

Tantùm ſeries juncturaque pollet,
Tantùm de medio ſumptis accedit honoris ! HORAT.

TOME PREMIER.

A PARIS,

Chez
{
BRIASSON, *rue Saint Jacques, à la Science.*
DAVID l'aîné, *rue Saint Jacques, à la Plume d'or.*
LE BRETON, Imprimeur ordinaire du Roy, *rue de la Harpe.*
DURAND, *rue Saint Jacques, à Saint Landry, & au Griffon.*
}

M. DCC. LI.

AVEC APPROBATION ET PRIVILEGE DU ROY.

ACKNOWLEDGEMENTS

Scaling a literary mountain like the *Encyclopédie* is a daunting expedition, and I was fortunate to have a wonderful early guide. Professor Daniel Roche, foremost authority on the French Enlightenment, was kind enough to help me survey the mountain before the climb began in earnest. I am most grateful to him.

I would also like to thank my agent, Victoria Hobbs, who supported the project enthusiastically from the start, and my editor at Fourth Estate, Mitzi Angel. Thanks are also owing to Leo Hollis, my editor in the early stages of the book. I am grateful, too, to the staff of the following libraries: the Bibliothèque St. Geneviève, the Bibliothèque Nationale de France, the Bibliothèque de l'Histoire de Paris, the Musée Carnavalet in Paris, the British Library, and the Warburg Institute in London. All were an indispensible help to me. I am, as always, indebted to my wife, Veronica, for her continuing encouragement during the writing of the book.

The book is dedicated to Professor Jon Stallworthy, who guided my first steps as a writer with his characteristic kindness, wisdom, and charm.

Philipp Blom
Paris, May 2004

PROLOGUE

PROLOGUE (*Literature*), in dramatic poetry this is a discourse preceding the piece and in which one introduces either a single character or several of them. [...] The prologues of English pieces are almost always occupied by the apology of the dramatic author who has written the play. *See* **EPILOGUE**.

The 'great' *Encyclopédie* by Diderot and d'Alembert is not the largest encyclopedia ever published, neither is it the first, the most authoritative, or the most popular. What makes it the most significant event in the entire intellectual history of the Enlightenment is the particular constellation of politics, economics, stubbornness, heroism, and revolutionary ideas that prevailed, for the first time ever, against the accumulated determination of Church and Crown, of all established forces in France taken together, to become a triumph of free thought, secular principle, and private enterprise. The victory of the *Encyclopédie* presaged not only the Revolution, but the values of the two centuries to come.

History lived, however, is very different from history written, and for the protagonists of this story – the philosophers Denis Diderot and Jean-Jacques Rousseau, the mathematician Jean d'Alembert, the medical scientist Louis de Jaucourt – this triumphant outcome seemed all but impossible for many years. They themselves lived through arrest and imprisonment, threats, attacks and ridicule, confiscation, and exile. Men had been hanged, burned alive, or sent to the galleys for much less than they were now daring to do, and the threat to their very existences hung over their heads every minute of every day.

Mid-eighteenth-century France was not a good place for free-thinkers and critical minds, and the *Encyclopédie* was intended to be a monument to both. Its most important contributors and editors were atheists (a fact they could not even hint at in writing on pain of forfeiting their lives), social and economic reformers, and critical of absolute monarchy (though hardly any of them were republicans and only one was to play an active part in the Revolution). Many of them came from modest backgrounds, most of them were commoners, some Protestants, and several of them authors of the illegal pamphlets sold under the tables of public houses or at dark street corners by furtive colporteurs. The Encyclopedists, as the loose network of people working on the great project came to be called, were the very people who were most feared in Versailles, and most likely to be thrown into the Bastille.

Change was undoubtedly in the air, and with it came insecurity, dissatisfaction, and calls for reform. After a period of decline, the population of the kingdom had grown by ten per cent within one generation (1710 to 1740), and this continued to rise further. Parallel to this, commerce was flourishing, disastrously for the small subsistence farmers unable to keep up with inflation and battered by successive bad harvests. Time and again news of famines and rural misery reached Paris. In 1725, among rumours that the king himself was speculating on grain, there were bread riots in the capital.

With the rise of the economy, the bourgeoisie, the carrier of the country's wealth, was making its political influence felt, not only through the judges and lawyers of provincial high courts, the *Parlements*, which began to make increasing use of their power to refuse royal decrees, but also through education, and in the Church. The rationalist ideas of Spinoza, Descartes, and Locke began asserting themselves at the colleges of the capital, and their rigorous spirit of inquiry did nothing for the strength of the pupils' Catholic faith. New scientific discoveries and philosophical and economic ideas were discussed more and more openly, and in the salons of Paris it had become acceptable for a while openly to declare one's atheism. Even within the faith, however, there were protest movements that, under the cover of theological disagreements, played out the conflict between the bourgeoisie and the nobility, between orthodoxy and rationalism, hierarchy and democracy.

Louis XV, the great-grandson of the Sun King, preferred to leave his ministers to react to these currents as they saw fit. He himself had taken up the reins of power in 1723, after a long period of regency. He hated politics, which tended to distract him from his main occupation, hunting. He was an expert in the pursuit of both stags and young girls, and he kept a special house in his park for the latter, lovingly replenished with nubile recruits by a specially employed *madame*. He also had an official mistress for many years, the infinitely more cultured Mme de Pompadour, as well as several less official ones, while his wife, Polish, pious, and depressive, languished in religious mortification.

Like his predecessor, Louis was a remote monarch, who much preferred Versailles and other castles to his capital, which he only visited if it could not be avoided. As if to emphasize the frivolity of his rule, the centre of the nation which the French firmly regarded as the most civilized in the world, the room right in the middle of the palace of Versailles, was occupied by a lazy and luxurious cat, the king's favourite pet. Here it sat, gazing towards Paris with amber eyes, its master almost as ignorant of the culture and sciences of the city as it was itself.

As a boy, Louis XIV had almost lost his crown and his life at the gates of Paris when nobles rose against him during the Fronde. He had never again trusted the capital or its inhabitants, its writers, colleges, its discussions and pamphlets, and its infinite possibilities for rebellion and revolt. Louis XV, calling himself the 'most Christian king' with his strict Jesuit advisers and confessors, was simply bored by all intellectual pursuits and tended to see them as potential trouble to be kept at bay by a very effective secret police. Dissent and free speech were anathema to him, and were often punished more harshly than violent crime. Voltaire, the hero of many free-thinkers as well as a man with very powerful friends, was living and writing in comfortable exile; but many others had not been so fortunate and were languishing in prison or being worked to death on penal galleys in the Mediterranean. Heretics were still being executed. Those wishing to save their skins had little option but to live and publish in the Netherlands or in Geneva, and have their works smuggled into France.

For the young men who set out to publish an encyclopedia that was to speak the truth as they saw it, these were the worst possible conditions, and it is all the more incredible that the work eventually saw the light of day. Even in sober, numerical terms, though, the Encyclopedist achievement is quite staggering: in a time without computers and databases, what had begun as the translation of a two-volume dictionary grew into a literary juggernaut comprising twenty-eight volumes of which eleven were illustrations, 72,998 articles totalling some twenty million words written by hundreds of contributors. For most of its existence these were edited, collated, and administered by two men only, Denis Diderot and Louis de Jaucourt – the latter alone writing half of the articles for the last ten volumes. At its height (and right under the eyes of an enlightened Chief Censor who had decided to see nothing despite the work's being officially damned and forbidden) the *Encyclopédie* employed a thousand typesetters, printers, and bookbinders and was distributed not only throughout France, but as far as London and St Petersburg.

Encyclopedic endeavours can be traced back to cuneiform tablets in the archives of the kings of Mesopotamia. Assurbanipal (668–627 BC) kept a sizeable palace library (the remnants of which are now in the British Museum), and among the usual trading correspondence, inventories, and legends is a significant number of tablets containing lists of objects and names linked by theme, similarity, word root, or assonance.[1] One of these lists is devoted to different kinds of palm trees and reads like a creation of Jorge Luis Borges, as well as a recitation of vegetal woes:

Palm tree, wild palm tree, young palm tree, palm plant, withered palm tree, dried-out palm tree, dead palm tree, stinking
palm tree, broken palm tree, palm tree eaten by parasites,
palm tree attacked by parasites, cut palm tree, sectioned palm
tree, pruned palm tree, flattened palm tree, broken palm tree,
cloven palm tree, burst palm tree, split palm tree, trunk of a
dead palm tree . . . palm tree with ripe dates . . . core of palm
tree, fibre of palm tree . . .[2]

Among the Greeks and Romans the writing of encyclopedic
works flourished, with great minds such as Aristotle (who advised
Ptolemy I on the foundation of the library in Alexandria and whose
own writings have truly encyclopedic ambitions) and Plato, whose
nephew and successor as head of the academy is known to have
written an encyclopedia as a teaching aid, strongly favouring such
enterprises. Not one of these works has survived, but it appears
that the first work with an ambition to be more than a simple
list or a compilation of other works was written around the year
370 BC. The Roman urge to set the world in order expressed
itself in a variety of grand collections of all knowledge, among
which was Pliny the Elder's *Natural History*, which remained the
authoritative source of worldly knowledge until well into the
sixteenth century.[3]

When it came to comprehensiveness, nobody could equal the
Chinese with their otherworldly cast of administrators, which was
to spawn, in 1726, the largest encyclopedic enterprise of all time,
the *Gujin tushu jicheng* in 745 thick volumes (though it was really an
anthology of other works). Already from the sixth century onwards,
however, a long procession of reference works wound its way
through the libraries, some of which carried fragrant titles such as
*The Prime Turtle of the Record Bureau, Collected Illustrations of the Three
Realms*, and *Blossoms and Flowers of the Literature Garden*. Despite
this blossoming of reference, though, Orient and Occident stayed
resolutely separate and the different encyclopedic cultures would
not meet (with perhaps only one notable exception, the sixteenth-
century Jesuit Matteo Ricci, who was well versed in Renaissance

encyclopedism and brought this knowledge to China[4]) until centuries later.[5]

A culture closer to Europe and whose intellectual life was to revive and revolutionize that of Christianity was Islam, which had assimilated the classical tradition of encyclopedism and led it to new heights under the mighty protection of the Abbasid caliphs of the eighth to the tenth centuries. Stretching from Spain to India, this civilization was living through a period of peace after extensive conquests, and the cultural consolidation of Islam was aided by encyclopedic works. As with all classification systems, the subdivisions of the dictionaries are always revelatory of the minds of those who conceived and were intended to use the works. One Islamic encyclopedia, for example, the ninth-century *Kitab 'uyun al-Akhbar* (The Book of the Best Traditions) was divided into the sections Power, War, Nobility, Character, Learning and Eloquence, Asceticism, Friendship, Prayers, Food, and, lastly, Women. The Islamic world also knew a collective encyclopedic effort, a work written by the 'Brothers of Purity' (*Ihwan as-safa*), and contributions by some of the most able thinkers of their day, such as Ibn Rusteh's *al A'lāq an-nafisa* (The Precious Atoms) and Ibn Sinnah's *Al-Qanun fi l-tibb* (The Canon of Medicine).[6]

The latter two authors were much admired by medieval Christian scholars, who knew them by their Latinized names Averroes and Avicenna. Several Arabic encyclopedias were translated into Latin and many more were written, most famously by Isidore of Seville, a seventh-century bishop and scholar, who has become patron saint not only of encyclopedias, but also of the Internet. His great *Etymologiae* was intended as a sum of all knowledge, under the headings Grammar, Rhetoric and Dialectic, Mathematics (the classical *trivium*), Medicine, Scripture and Liturgy, God and the Angels, the Church, Languages, Men, the Animal and Mineral worlds, and the Works of Man.[7]

In a culture of glosses, commentaries on glosses, and annotations of translations of refutations of commentaries, medieval encyclopedias often owed as much to faith, literal interpretations of the Scriptures, and to visions in the twilight of monastery libraries as to 'book knowledge' and reliable information, a fact witnessed in their often enchanting names: *The Book of the Wonders of the World*, the *Garden of Delights*, the *Breviary of Love*.[8] In one of the first of these, *De Universo* (Of the Universe), the monk Raban Maur (who wrote between 842 and 847) faithfully describes the order of the world, the hierarchy of heavenly beings, the world of animated beings, and inanimate nature in twenty-two books, mirroring the twenty-two books of the Bible.[9] Another German work, the *Imago mundi* by Honorius Inclusus (1090), treated the history of the world from the fall of Satan to the flourishing of German cities. With the systematically minded Scholastic philosophers of the thirteenth and fourteenth century, great compendia of knowledge gained in importance, and entire schools, such as that of the monastery of Saint-Victor near Paris, were devoted to the idea of *Mappemonde*, mapping the world. The head of this movement, Hugo of St Victor, told his monks that they were 'dwarves on giants' shoulders' while working on his great *Didascalion*.[10]

As medieval knowledge and reliance on ancient authors like Pliny no longer seemed enough to grasp and describe a world with rapidly exploding boundaries, the encyclopedic approach played a major role in the great revolution that was the Renaissance. It expressed itself not only through books, but also through collections seeking to gather everything that was new and strange that did not yet have a place in the system – new continents, unknown cultures, animals and plants, with life on the smallest scale visible under ever stronger lenses and heavenly bodies observed through telescopes – while at the same time imposing order through their arrangement, which often followed allegorical programmes. Italian scholars such as Ulisse Aldrovandi and Francesco Calceolari were among the first to assemble such collections, and some of them also wrote reference works about the order of nature and about their discoveries.[11]

During the sixteenth century, the approach to describing all knowledge became at once more empirical and more mystical. The Spanish scholar Raymond Lull attempted to find answers in occult knowledge (and found many followers) while others pursued different paths. In 1587, Christophe de Savigny published *Tableaux accomplis de touts les arts libéraux*, the first vernacular encyclopedia. The word encyclopedia, from the Greek ἐγκύκλιοϛ παιδεία (*enkiklios paideia*, the chain of knowledge) appeared for the first time in writings about the topic, though the first work with this word in the title, Johann Heinrich Alsted's *Encyclopedia septem tomis distincta*, did not appear until 1630.[12] So fashionable were these mighty tomes, that Rabelais's satirical creation Pantagruel (1532), condemned to a thorough course in education, sighed heartily that his teacher had opened to him the 'true chasms and abysses of encyclopedia', i.e. that he had shown him just how arcane knowledge could get, and how many holes there were in his.[13]

With knowledge liberating itself from the iron embrace of Church teaching, there seemed to be no end to the hunger for new works and to the bibliographies and anthologies, the *florilegia* (selections) and compilations and explanations produced and printed, from lists of suicides, patricides, 'effeminate men' and other scandalous people to works of zoology, geography, and guides to ancient literature.

Mere accumulations of fact and supposed fact according to the medieval model, however, were no longer perceived to be enough, and once again some of the most brilliant and original minds of their times applied themselves to the problem of organizing all this knowledge in the most effective and most constructive way possible. In England, Francis Bacon (1561–1626) grappled with this problem, and found a revolutionary answer to it. Previous debates and attempts to unify knowledge and to investigate the final causes of things, he believed, had proved 'sterile and like a virgin consecrated to God, [producing] nothing'. True knowledge therefore had to begin with an investigation of the empire of the senses.[14]

His projected *Great Instauration*, which he never finished, was a kind of Utopian encyclopedia, ordered not according to the neo-Platonist sequence of ideas of the Scholastics, but in much more empirical terms inspired by Pliny. He drew up a tree of all branches of knowledge, which sprang from human faculties and perceptions. Subdivisions were to include Chemistry, Vision and the Visual Arts,

Hearing, Sound and Music, Smell and Smells, Taste and Tastes, Touch and the Objects of Touch (including Physical Love), Pleasure and Pain, and so forth. As Diderot and d'Alembert were to see immediately, this order had the immense advantage of relegating God and theology to one branch out of many. As they were to find to their cost, the Church was acutely aware of this and regarded every step in this direction as dangerous and heretical.

The sudden increase in encyclopedic projects in the late seventeenth and early eighteenth centuries mirrored a social sea change, which expressed itself in terms of secularism and broadening education, rapid population growth, urbanization, and a growing and increasingly self-confident bourgeoisie. As the story of the Encyclopedists is played out in Paris, we need go no further in search of an example. Until the beginning of the seventeenth century, the French capital had been relatively stagnant within its medieval city walls, but now, almost suddenly, things began to move.[15] Both Richelieu and Colbert had pushed city development, enlarging the city walls and signing contracts with developers. Property speculation became a fashion and a plague, with entire streets being built up, bought and resold without ever being inhabited. The famous Place Vêndome was one of these developments, though for a while funds ran out and left mere façades overlooking the grandiose square.

While the beginning of the eighteenth century was dominated by hardship and the terrible famine of the winter of 1709, it still seemed that there was a new economic dynamism. An average of ten thousand people came to Paris to settle there every year, a number augmented by thousands of itinerant and seasonal workers who stayed in the city for a while only. While these new arrivals mainly swelled the ranks of the poor and the illiterate, other migrants (among them Diderot, Jean-Jacques Rousseau, the Baron d'Holbach, and Friedrich Melchior Grimm, four men at the centre of the *Encyclopédie* enterprise) were highly educated, and there was no doubt that the Parisian middle classes (in stark contrast to the poor, whose fortunes were declining rapidly) were becoming increasingly wealthy and self-confident – a phenomenon that was true for other cities in the kingdom.[16]

The newly strengthened middle class, the craftsmen and merchants, the financiers and the rentiers living off property and
bought offices, the many abbés, teachers, administrators, lawyers,
and even courtiers, consisted of people who often had time on
their hands and had some degree of control over their professional
advancement, their education, and their prospects. Many of them
were reading people (book ownership, for instance, increased dramatically between 1700 and 1780, even among servants[17]), and their
education was not only a matter of entertainment, it was instrumen-
tal to their chances of improving their lot and that of their children.

Good schools and universities became part of the bourgeois
repertoire for young men at least, and the Paris colleges counted
some fifty thousand pupils in all, one in ten people living in the
city. With the population growing all across Europe and economies
expanding, this educated middle class was no longer content to
leave exploration, debate, and discovery to a handful of scholars
while limiting their reading to works of edifying piety and classical
legends; and in a world of scholarship that became more complex
and more detailed with every passing day, works of synthesis were
in strong demand. It was the hour of the encyclopedia, and soon
reference books were written in every major language. Between
1674 and 1750 alone, more than thirty of them were published in
English, German, French, and Italian, more than in the previous
two hundred years.[18]

One of the most important and most authoritative encyclopedias
was published in 1697 by an exiled French Huguenot theologian
and writer, Pierre Bayle (1647–1706), who had fled persecution in
his home country and lived in Rotterdam.[19] Clearly written, Bayle's
two-volume *Dictionnaire historique et critique* was a work of truly universal learning. It was also ordered alphabetically, a relative novelty at
the time, and was designed for enquiring minds: only the smaller,
upper part of its pages was taken up with actual definitions, while
the rest was given over to commentaries on the subjects mentioned,
bibliographical remarks, and a careful annotation of sources in the
original languages. This made the dictionary a more serious work
of reference and scholarship, but hardly made it easy to use. Bayle's

own perspective was also clear. Of the approximately two thousand articles, two-thirds were devoted to figures from the sixteenth and seventeenth centuries, many of them involved in the Reformation. There was little information on geography, very little about sciences, the arts, and literature, and of the great scientists, only Kepler was considered worthy of an article. Despite these impracticalities, the dictionary quickly became popular for its meticulous research, its transparency, and its lucid argumentation and it went through eight French editions over fifty years, as well as being translated into German and English.

Seven years later, the antidote to this Protestant abomination was on the march, written by the Jesuits of Trévoux, near Lyon. The *Dictionnaire de Trévoux*, as it was called, was more ambitious in size and grew from three to eight volumes over several editions. When Diderot and friends announced their own project to the reading public, they were to encounter bitter resistance from the Fathers, who obviously regarded the business of encyclopedism in France as their domain. In view of their accusations of plagiarism against Diderot and d'Alembert's *Encyclopédie*, it should be remembered that the *Dictionnaire de Trévoux* was itself an ideologically 'cleansed' version of an earlier work by another Protestant, Antoine Furetière, a fact that was nowhere mentioned.[20]

When it came to size and sheer thoroughness, however, nobody could beat the Germans, who published several encyclopedias during this period. The largest of these, surely the largest ever devised in the West, was the *Oekonomisch-technologische Enzyklopädie, oder allgemeines System der Staats-, Stadt, Haus- und Landwirtschaft*, begun by Johann Georg Krünitz, which ran to 242 volumes between 1773 and 1858. Not quite as gargantuan but every bit as important, as well as being an exact contemporary of the *Encyclopédie*, was Zedler's *Universal Lexicon*, in sixty-four volumes, a project that had to overcome considerable hurdles.[21] Conceived by a Leipzig bookdealer, Johann Heinrich Zedler (1706–60), it was soon opposed by almost the entire book trade of the city, who were afraid the work might become so comprehensive that there would be no longer any need for other books.

Zedler struggled for decades against ill fortune, sabotage, and bankruptcy (at one stage he tried to keep his work afloat by organizing a lottery) – his financial difficulties were such that he himself never possessed a full set of his own dictionary as he was unable to acquire volumes 13 and 14. The work was written by a group of several corresponding editors, one of whom had translated Bayle's *Dictionnaire critique* into German. It was published between 1731 and 1754. As with all reference works, this grand enterprise, which was, on the whole, exceptionally well researched, had its decided strengths. The dictionary is a full compendium of contemporary medical practice and contains recipes for innumerable ointments, elixirs, pills, distillates, and infusions, including about a thousand kinds of vitriol. The article on amputation is detailed enough to allow an ambitious amateur to have a go, and it is even detailed how long it should take to saw through the bones of the lower arm: about as long as it takes to recite the Lord's Prayer.

English Enlightenment dictionary writers had no ambitions to be comprehensive and make their works the last word on every subject under the sun (the *Encyclopedia Britannica*, a Scottish enterprise, was not started until 1768, after the great success of the *Encyclopédie*). Their aims were more pragmatic and attainable. In 1704, the same year as the *Dictionnaire de Trévoux*, John Harris published his *Lexicon technicum; or, An universal English dictionary of the arts and sciences, explaining not only the terms of arts, but the arts themselves*, in one volume, the first work of this kind in English. The arts and sciences represented here were mainly technical and mathematical, and some scientific questions such as physics and astronomy were given limited space.

It was on reading Harris that the globe-maker turned journalist Ephraim Chambers (1680–1740) came to the conclusion that something altogether more ambitious and better planned was necessary to satisfy the demand for reference books, and he set out to fill this gap. His *Cyclopaedia: or, An Universal Dictionary of Arts and Sciences* appeared in 1728 and earned its author membership of the prestigious Royal Society. He had written the work alone, not without misgivings, as his preface makes clear:

'Tis not without some Concern that I put this Work in the
Reader's Hands; a Work so disproportionate to a single
Person's Experience, and which might have employ'd an
Academy. What adds to my Jealousy, is the little measure of
Time allow'd for a Performance to which a Man's whole Life
scarce seems equal. The bare Vocabulary of the Academy della
Crusca was above forty Years in compiling, and the Dictionary
of the French Academy much longer; and yet the present Work
is as much more extensive than either of them in its Nature
and Subject, as it falls short of 'em in number of Years, or of
Persons employ'd.[22]

Despite his 'jealous concerns', Chambers's dictionary had qualities that made it not only immediately attractive to the reading
public (it went through five editions within eighteen years) but
also lastingly influential. The alphabetic order of the entries was
supplemented not only by clear illustrations, but also by elaborate
cross-referencing, making it easy to find related articles. Thus
ACOUSTICS sends one to EAR, HEARING, and PHONICS, and SHELL
to DELUGE, PETRIFACTION, and FOSSIL. Through years of determination, and while barely scraping a living as a book reviewer and
translator, Chambers had created the first modern encyclopedia,
the direct ancestor of all modern works of reference, and the father
of the *Encyclopédie*. This, in fact, began as a translation of Chambers's
Cyclopaedia, but was to grow into the greatest intellectual enterprise
of its century, and to shake France's *ancien régime* to its very foundations.

Coupe du nouvel Opéra de Stuttgardt esquissé pour en voir l'effet sans aucunes regles de Perspective.

Plan ou Projet de la restauration de l'Opéra de Stuttgardt.

de la Guépiérre Del.

Bonard Fecit.

Salles de Spectacles.

GG

PARIS, 1739

PARIS, (*Géog. mod.*) capital city of France, situated on
the Seine, about 90 lieues south east of London, 95 south of
Amsterdam, 260 north east of Vienna ... Long. orient. of
Paris at Notre-Dame, 20d. 21'. 30". lat. 48d.
51'. 20". long. of Paris at the Observatoire, according to
Cassini, 19d. 51'. 30". lat. 48d. 50'. 10".
Paris is an ancient city, one of the biggest, most magnificent
& most populous in the universe. It alone has produced more
grand personages, more scientists and more great minds
than all other cities in France put together. One counts seven
hundred thousand souls in the city, 23 thousand houses,
and a great number of magnificent palaces. Three superb
and distinguished palaces stand out among the others: the
Tuileries, the Louvre and the Luxembourg. The Louvre is
not yet finished. Each king since François I has added a
greater or smaller portion to it. Louis XV may have the
distinction of achieving its final perfection.

First there is the wood in house-high piles, and the boats, and the
gardens. Then, slowly, from the interlacing furrows of streets and
narrow paths and the names laid over its delicate web in copper-
plate lettering, other aspects begin to emerge. One can lose oneself
just looking at this little world, at the façades of tiny houses, at the
bridges, and the barges on the river. Towards the outskirts there is
a belt of gardens, tiny rectangles with the occasional tree. Then,
further still, come the windmills popping out of the ground like
little mushrooms, and the beginnings of the sweeping countryside,
licking at the safety and order of the city like waves of a dangerous

1

sea attempting to engulf the achievements of civilization as soon as it is given half a chance.

This is Paris, the greatest of cities, with its famous palaces and parks, promenades and spectacles, with its splendid elegance, the world capital not only (in the estimation of the French at least) of culture, but also of fashion and *esprit* – the scene on which the entire story of the *Encyclopédie* was played out. All its main protagonists (apart from Voltaire, who lived in Geneva, and Louis XV, who preferred Versailles) lived in these streets and met in its cafés and theatres. The bird's-eye view of the city I am looking at, a huge map in book form, is known as the 1739 *Plan Turgot* – the first all-comprising graphical inventory of the capital, down to the last orchard and tree, detailing every house and naming even the most modest cul-de-sac, commissioned by Michel-Étienne Turgot (1690–1751), one of the ablest administrators the city ever had. Much of this miniature world is familiar to modern eyes, especially in the central area, with the cathedral of Notre Dame on the Île de la Cité, the Louvre just across the river, and the majestic span of the Pont Neuf linking the Left Bank to the Right.

Then, however, another century begins to assert itself. Most of

the bridges are densely built up with houses, the street names are no longer familiar, and the merciless sweep of Baron Haussmann's reimagined city has not yet razed the small lanes and winding thoroughfares. Along the Left Bank of the Seine, on the site of today's Arab Institute and the new university campus, Paris VI and VII, is a whole ghost town of piles of wood, each as high as four-storey houses and as long as the cathedral itself, towering and sombre, composed of whole tree trunks in mighty perpendicular layers. Some of these piles seem to have collapsed at one end and look like gigantic wedges waiting to be driven into the earth. Opposite this wooden quarter, on the Isle Louver, an island that has long since been reclaimed to form part of the Right Bank, is another, smaller tree repository with neat roads between the house-high piles. Others are just a stone's throw away to the north-east, and further downriver opposite the Jardin du Louvre. Paris devoured forests with gluttonous greed, and ten per cent of its surface was covered by wood: wood for building and construction work, wood for cabinet-makers, and, most importantly, wood to warm hundreds of thousands of human bodies during the long winters. The poor had to ration warmth from cheap pinewood that burned up quickly and spat sparks into their dwellings, or from coal that would glower and smoke and cover everything in soot, while the fireplaces of the rich were crackling with fragrant, air-dried hardwood logs.

In the early eighteenth century, Paris was a city of a little over half a million inhabitants,[1] by far the largest in France and by common consensus Europe's most elegant. It had the panache and wealth of modern-day New York, the hygiene of Cairo or Caracas, and was saturated with police spies like Soviet Moscow.

The bustle of life in the streets that so impressed and intimidated many of its visitors can only be inferred from the artificial stillness of the Turgot map with its empty places and deserted roads, but it is vividly evoked in writings of the period. There were a few essential things every newcomer to the city had to know, ordinary, everyday things, like where to eat, where to sleep, where to hire servants, where to buy reliable horses, firewood, furniture, fashionable

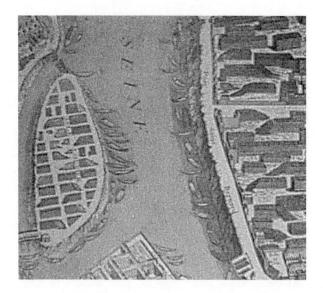

clothes. A 1727 travel guide for young gentlemen on their grand tour who went to spend a few months in the world's most glittering, and, according to the *Encyclopédie* at least, most populated city, gives the following warning: 'I would not advise that one take one's rooms in the rue de boucherie [Butchery Row], as it is narrow and the air is at times strongly infected by the [stench of the] number of animals killed here continually.'[2] Other observers, too, commented on a lack of hygiene remarkable even for its time. Sébastien Mercier, perhaps the first roving reporter the capital had known, and admittedly a man who revelled in picturesque detail, was no more complimentary when thinking about tourist accommodation: 'the furnished rooms are dirty. Nothing is worse for a poor foreigner than to see those filthy beds, windows whistling with all the winds, wallpaper that has almost rotted away, and stairs covered by garbage.'[3]

The 'poor foreigner' would quickly find out that there were many cities contained within the capital, each seemingly with its own rules and customs, so enormous were the differences between rich and poor, so dissimilar the life in the palaces and six- or seven-floor tenement buildings, such a profusion of convents, guilds and under- worlds (the organized beggars, the journeymen fraternities, the paid scandalmongers and police spies), so manifold the jurisdictions. The latter, the world of competing legal competences, may serve as an example of the complex interworking between these spheres. The Hôtel de Ville had authority over the river and everything coming from it, while Châtelet, the medieval city fortress, was responsible for everything on land – a considerable problem in the case of oysters, which came from the water but were a health hazard on land, especially if eaten out of season. Add to this already confused picture the fact that many monasteries and convents held on to their ancient rights to administer, police, and sit in judgement over what happened both within their walls and in their possessions and parishes (borders between jurisdictions at times cut through private houses), and one gets an impression of the despair of the victim of a robbery who has no idea where to turn for justice.

In 1656, some sixty years before the time written about by Mercier, two Dutch travellers had taken rooms in Saint-Germain with a compatriot of theirs, Regine de Hoeve. They quickly fell out with their landlady and found themselves in the street, without their horses, which she had decided to keep in lieu of supposedly unpaid bills. The two travellers sought redress from the Abbot of Saint-Germain-des-Prés, a very wealthy monastery whose authority over the area dated back to its foundation during the sixth century and which was *seigneur*, feudal lord, of the faubourg of Saint-Germain-des-Prés as well as thirty other streets in the city. The Abbot, however, was not interested in the quarrel, more than likely to result in more bother than revenue, and so the tourists had to cross the river and go to the Châtelet, from where they were sent to the house of the police commissioner of Saint-Germain, who finally accompanied them to the inn, only too happy to have an excuse for invading rival legal territory. There, the horses were quickly surrendered.[4]

The offices of judge, police commissioner and bailiff were available for sale. This was not seen as a form of corruption: civil functions like these were openly advertised in the daily papers, while grander positions, that of tax farmer, as well as bishoprics, cardinals' hats, governorships and ministries, were sold by the king or his chancellor directly and formed an important part of the royal revenues. Louis XIV had already made it a habit to create new offices whenever he needed to ameliorate his finances (which was always), and from Overseer of Weights and Measures to Inspector of Pigs' Tongues on the Les Halles market, from Royal Cupbearer to Grand Master of the King's Flowers, offices were acquired, usually not to be exercised, but to derive benefit from the taxation rights, prestige, pensions, and bribes that went with them, leaving the day-to-day running of the affairs to a faceless secretary working away somewhere below stairs.

There was a plethora of intendants, inspectors, directors, magistrates, lieutenants, *procureurs*, and commissaires, and the fact that some of them were redundant and others had wildly overlapping or conflicting competences would have resulted in grave administrative chaos if they had actually been taken seriously. For an ambitious merchant on his way up, this was the way to better himself, second only to entering into the nobility. As often portrayed and caricatured in the literature of the time, it was common practice to try to marry a rich heiress in order to use her dowry to purchase a lucrative office that would enable one to glory in a far-fetched title and set oneself up for life. That some of these positions were actually of some importance for running the administration or for managing the city's food supplies, roads, or justice, for example, was a theme of uncounted and clandestinely printed pamphlets, plays, and novels, as well as the cause of periodic crises. The purchase price was the only qualification necessary for executing almost any office in the land.

'He who buys justice wholesale can sell it retail,'[5] as Richelieu had remarked, and this robustly market-driven conception of public service was widely applied: *La France* was an enormous cake that was carved up by the high aristocracy, had large bites taken out of it by wealthy bourgeois and *nouveaux riches*, and was broken up in lumps jealously guarded by merchants, tradesmen, and rural noblemen. The leftovers then crumbled into myriad hard-edged morsels, too small to fill any stomach, to be squabbled over, stolen, and begged for by those at the bottom of the heap.

One glowing exception to the general rule of staggering incompetence and habitual cynicism was Louis XIV's two Lieutenants of Police, Gabriel Nicolas le Reynie and René Voyer de Paulmy d'Argenson, the latter of whom survived into the reign of Louis XV and became an important figure for the beginnings of the *Encyclopédie*. D'Argenson was that great exception among *ancien-régime* office holders, a conscientious and public-minded man of considerable intelligence who did his best to work for the common good. His office comprised responsibility for almost all aspects of public order, city infrastructure, and planning: the supervision of street cleaning; fire fighting; flood prevention; food supplies; price control; supervision of butchers' stalls; inspection of market places, fairs, hotels, inns, furnished rooms, gaming houses, tobacco shops, and places of ill repute; investigation of illicit assemblies and other sources of disorder; overseeing the guilds; inspection of weights and measures and of the regulations pertaining to the book trade; the enforcement of ordinances against carrying weapons, and more.[6] The Lieutenant of Police was both powerful, and very, very busy. He was aided in his duties by forty-eight *commissaires-enquêteurs-examineurs* at the Châtelet, agents of public security (one of whom rescued the two horseless Dutchmen) who were in practice mainly concerned with profitable tasks such as the sealing of houses of the deceased, taking legal inventories, serving summonses, and imposing fines, from which they, as a perquisite of their job, personally took a cut.

If our two Dutch friends wanted to give their horses a drink, they had to go directly to the muddy and as yet unfortified banks of the Seine, an edge of lawlessness in the heart of the city, where washerwomen, people with cows and horses, bargemen, and beggars mingled into a society of their own, a dangerous but picturesque scene immortalized in many contemporary pictures.

The water situation of the French capital was infamous. Sébastien Mercier wrote: 'the public fountains are so rare and so badly maintained that one has to have recourse to the river. No bourgeois house has ever enough water. Twenty thousand water carriers work from morning to evening, carrying two full buckets from the first

to the seventh floor ... if the carrier is strong, he makes some thirty trips a day. When the river is murky, one drinks murky water, one has no idea what one swallows, but one is obliged to drink regardless.'[7] Being downstream from foundries, tanneries, and butcheries, the water also had very specific qualities, as remarked by the travel writer Nemeitz in his *Séjour de Paris*: 'one uses this water for almost all purposes, drinking, brewing beer, cooking meat; and it is believed to be very healthy for those accustomed to it. Foreigners, however, usually get diarrhoea from it, and the French like to say that this is just a way of paying your dues to this city. The water is sometimes clear, sometimes troubled and like lemonade, so that those who are of a fastidious disposition don't feel very inclined to drink it.'[8]

Visitors lucky enough to have recovered from an upset stomach and to gain entrance into one of the famed salons of Paris society faced another problem: how to get there. The streets of the city were not only lively (and, to the astonishment of many, lit at night by street lamps, introduced in 1697), they were also notorious for being likely to ruin the good clothes and white silk stockings expected to be worn in the elegant houses. The safest way, and socially the only acceptable one, was to hire or buy a carriage with horses and lackeys for the duration of the stay. Nemeitz is quite particular on this point: '*Foreigners of some quality*, like *counts and barons* of the [Holy Roman] Empire who are not trying to enjoy *Paris incognito*, had better *get a carriage directly after their arrival* in the great city.'[9] If funds were insufficient for wheels of one's own, one could hire a cab, and here, too, the guide has useful advice: 'Generally, one should keep to the following maxim: *one must be sweet and accommodating with the coachmen . . . and tell them politely whatever one has to say to them.* These people are usually very coarse and will, if they see fit, throw at one a thousand impertinences and stupidities from which one has nothing but inconvenience and annoyance.'[10]

The least recommended way was the one Mercier thought fit only for beggars and men of genius – on foot. This might have been dignified for a giant of the mind unconcerned with worldly splendour, but it was also dirty and hazardous. Mercier himself was exasperated by this problem: 'why don't people dress more suitably for the mud and the dirt? Why walk in clothes which are good only for people in carriages? Why can't we have pavements, as London does?'[11] Nemeitz was none too impressed with the safety of Paris streets, either. 'One has to be *very much on one's guard on Paris streets during the day.* Apart from the great crowd of those on foot who keep bumping into one another, there is also the incalculable number of coaches . . . and these vehicles don't go gently, but at a thundering gallop, especially if their horses are good.'[12]

If life on the streets was dangerous because of coaches mowing down the pedestrians, it was unpleasant even without them: '*During humid and bad weather, I recommend no one to put on clean clothes.* The least rain makes the streets almost impassable because of the mud they are so full of and which is increasing all the time with those who come and go.'[13] This is the historian's favourite ingredient for local colour: the classic mud of the past (though the particularly slimy black dirt of Paris was famous even for its time), consisting of everything a city without canalization could exhale and accrue, from excrement (animal and human) to dirt, from carcasses to rotten vegetables. 'Nothing is funnier for strangers', wrote Mercier, 'than watching a Parisian cross or jump across this filthy stream [in the middle of the street] with a stately wig, white stockings and a trimmed coat, and run through the terrible roads on tiptoes, only to receive the contents of the gutter [from a high window] on his taffeta parasol.'[14]

True to the enterprising spirit of a large city, however, this omnipresent ill had its equally ubiquitous remedy: 'If one is on foot, one finds *décrotteurs* ['de-shitters'] everywhere, who will flatter you in every imaginable way and clean up your shoes.'[15] Mercier waxed lyrical about the practitioners of this noble profession and their ability to help one avoid a dreadful social *faux pas*: '[a] *décrotteur* attends to you around the corner at every street with a friendly brush and a ready hand. He puts you in a state to present yourself to men of quality and to ladies, for while it is acceptable to arrive with one's clothes a little the worse for wear, or with common linen . . . one must on no account turn up splattered with excrement.'[16]

A sense of the Paris of the *ancien régime* begins to emerge, and the Turgot map with its delicate houses and its river barges now appears to hide more than it reveals.

Consider only the huge wood stores by the Seine. Replenished by tree trunks floated down the rivers from France's still densely forested regions, the *théatres* or *chantiers*, as the wooden cities by the river banks were called, were far from inanimate: they served as breeding places for birds and rats, as hideouts for criminals and runaways, and in their depths rattled the sound of intellectual ferment and dissent. Here clandestine printers of the city set up a secret workshop with small, portable presses turning out satires, pornography, pamphlets, philosophical letters and heretical meditations for a few days, only to vanish again as soon as the police spies were on to them (printing illegal works was punishable by death). Still, the majority of books that appeared during the *ancien régime* were clandestine editions – smuggled into the city in bales of hay and the false bottoms of barrels of salted herring, or printed inside wood piles and on boats, in the alcoves of bourgeois houses and the huts in the gardens around Paris, and hawked in the streets and inns by specialized colporteurs, constantly on the lookout for police.[17]

Some of these were published with tacit permission, effectively the Chief Censor's assurance to look the other way, others were entirely illegal. 'They are a people, or rather a republic,'[18] sighed one observer about the tightknit, fiercely egalitarian brotherhood of the printer-journeymen and their networks reaching far beyond the borders of the kingdom. Their republic existed symbiotically with the republic of letters: the world of cafés and inns, of garrets and cheap, rented rooms, the living quarters of young men from the provinces trying to eke out a livelihood as private tutors, secretaries, or scurrilous writers penning rumours about courtly life, erotic novels featuring the King and his ministers, lascivious bishops, lewd priests and depraved nuns; all while trying to make it as writers, as men of genius in their own right. Many of the later heroes of the *Encyclopédie* belonged to this sphere.

The city of wood on the river banks was mirrored by a second one on the river itself: a profusion of boats and barges carrying everything that could conceivably be carried. In the Turgot map, that pristine filigree metropolis with its streets empty of carts and pedestrians, its houses without inhabitants and smoke, and its large belt around the city of small vegetable gardens in which nobody is digging, planting, or weeding, the river barges alone are peopled with little figures rowing and pulling ropes, shouting from one boat to another, steering and staring at the houses to either side in a faint echo of the constant activity that so astonished contemporary visitors.

It is as if the engravers had been told not to depict any people in the city but somehow considered the river a different territory where they were allowed to exercise their imagination so severely restrained by the repetitive drawing of diminutive façades and tiny trees. Most of these vessels do not have masts, though one single three-masted ship is being towed away from the Pont Neuf, just at the height of the Louvre. Just behind it, the barges are bobbing four deep in the wake of passing vessels so that one could walk, carefully, on wood almost to the middle of the river. Some are

empty, while others have a roof and windows to ferry passengers,
or are laden with wood, large bales of straw, or other cargo covered
with canvas.

Another population hidden from view on the Turgot map, just
next to the market at Les Halles, was that of the Cimetière des
Saints-Innocents. Les Halles itself was Paris at its most medieval: a
huge complex of market stands and shops, partly covered and
partly open air, surrounded by high tenement houses. These were
supplied by thousands of farmers making their way into the heart
of the city from the provinces in the dead of night to sell their
produce at the market and return tired, and most likely drunk, to

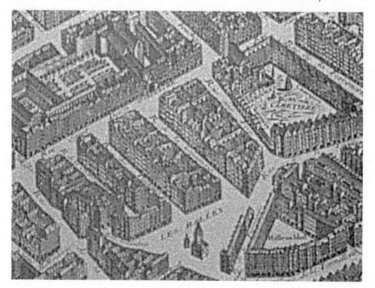

their fields many miles away. The eighteenth century did not seem
to have penetrated into this bucolic scene beloved of contemporary
painters, where the shouts and smells of innumerable stalls laden
with fruit and vegetables, with fish and fresh meat, were dominated
by a curious medieval structure in the middle of the square. A
stone's throw away from the crowds, the market cries, the herring
vats brought in by ox carts, the sides of beef, the dark-smelling
cabbages and ruddy apples, was the Cemetery of the Holy Inno-
cents, even more densely packed, no less odorous, but quieter.

Almost two million Parisians had been buried here since the tenth or eleventh century, and local legend had it that its soil devoured bodies. Burials finally stopped in 1780, after a cellar close to it had caved in, opening what seemed like the gates of hell itself: hundreds of decayed bodies visible in the subterranean blackness, whose stench and substance were poisoning the neighbours.

To the authorities and to the Church, the work that was taking shape in the city under their very eyes must have seemed no less poisonous and much more terrifying than the grinning skulls of their ancestors. The *Encyclopédie des Arts et Métiers* by Diderot and d'Alembert threatened to do more than just upset the neighbours: with its brazen assertions and the conclusions it invited, it was undermining the authority of Pope and King alike.

Fig . 1 .

Fig . 2 .

Fig . 3 .

Fig . 4 .

Prevost Fecit

Dessein, les Ages.

FRIENDSHIP

* **BOHEMIENS**, s. m. pl. (*Hist. mod.*) this is what one calls the vagabonds who are professional soothsayers and palm readers. Their talent is to sing, dance & steal. Pasquier has followed their origins as far as 1427. He tells of twelve penitents, who converted to the Christian faith of lower Egypt, & who, expelled by the Saracens, went to Rome & confessed to the pope, who enjoined them as a penitence to err through the world for seven years, without sleeping in a single bed. Among them were a count, a duke, & ten knights; they were followed by one hundred and twenty persons. Arrived in Paris, they were put up at the Chapelle, where they were gaped at by the crowds. They had silver ear rings, & black & frizzy hair; their women were ugly, thieving & soothsayers. The Bishop of Paris decreed that they were to be shunned & excommunicated those who had consulted them; since that time, the kingdom is infected with vagabonds of the same species.

Being young and poor in the big city has its own mythology, its own literature, its heroes and heroines. Paris has played an immense part in the development of this mythology, more so even than London and New York; but that is the Paris of the nineteenth and twentieth centuries, of *La Bohème* and of the penniless painters of Montmartre – the eighteenth century had another, the original, conception of Bohemians: vagrants, gypsies. Bohemians or not, Louis XV's capital already had its garrets and cheap lodgings full of young men with hopes as great as their incomes were small. Sébastien Mercier knew where the genius of the city was located –

'the attics': 'As in the human machine the most noble part, the thinking organ, is enclosed at the highest point, genius, industry, application and virtue also occupy the most elevated region of the capital. There, the painter is formed in silence, the poet makes his first verse . . . Hardly any famous man who would not have started out in an attic.'[1]

Mercier may have exaggerated a little, as was his wont. In essence, however, he was right: eighteenth-century Paris was already well acquainted with the phenomenon of bright young men who had left their homes and their intended profession to take their chances and live on their wits. The *bohème* of the *ancien régime* differed from that of a century later in being even more linked with the twilight zone between the legal and the forbidden, more closely scrutinized by police spies, and at the same time less controllable. The Bastille, one of several state prisons, was reserved exclusively for recalcitrant noblemen and for writers, hence the symbolic value of its storming during the Revolution.

This is the milieu that Robert Darnton calls Grub Street, after the eponymous place in London's Moorfields (today's Barbican), described by Dr Johnson as 'much inhabited by writers of small histories, dictionaries, and temporary poems'.[2] There was a Grub Street in every major European city. It was made up of talentless hacks and paid inventors of rumours and slander, by embittered poets and obscure revolutionaries, all of whom were spied upon or who spied on others in the service of the police or of a wealthy patron. The young men who entered this world could only hope to find themselves a benefactor, for it was nearly impossible to live on writing alone. Manuscripts were sold for a fixed fee, usually a pittance, and the entire proceeds of sales went to the publisher. The author could hope only to gain an *entrée* to a fashionable salon or a grand house by means of a flattering dedication and some copies given humbly to possible protectors. As long as he was part of the twilight zone of Grub Street, a writer was expendable, without any protection from the police or from poverty; only patronage carried with it a measure of security, perhaps an annuity, the possibility of a state pension, and the greatest prize of all: fame.

One of the many fortune seekers living this precarious life and dreaming of great things was a young man who had wanted to become a Jesuit only a few years earlier: the young abbé Denis Diderot. His new career in Paris alarmed his anxious and respectable parents, who had hoped to see him become a cutler, like his father, or a priest. He had come to the capital to study from Langres in the Champagne, a proud and ancient town of some ten thousand inhabitants, commandingly perched on a hilltop and overlooking the plain below from massive ramparts. The townspeople were pious folk; several members of the boy's family had taken holy orders, and Denis, born in 1713 as the eldest of the four surviving children of Didier and Angélique Diderot, went to the local Jesuit college, almost directly opposite his parents' house in the town square. He was a gifted pupil, but the ease he showed in his Latin translations and verses did not keep him from taking part in battles mounted by rival gangs of boys – he was to carry a scar from a well-aimed slingshot hit on his forehead for life.

When school began to bore the twelve-year-old Denis, he tried his hand as a cutler himself in his father's workshop. According to his own daughter, he ruined every knife, fork, and lancet he touched and soon found the work he was given so mindless that after four or five days he simply got up from his bench, went to his room to fetch his books, and went back to school. The clergy was a natural destination for a clever boy from a pious family, and it seems that as an adolescent he went through a phase of true piety. He chose a career in the Church, was tonsured by the Bishop of Langres in 1726, and was now entitled to call himself an abbé and to wear clerical clothes, complete with soutane, short black mantle, and ecclesiastical collar.

The abbés were a confusing peculiarity of the *ancien régime*; they were neither abbots, i.e. monks, nor priests, but ecclesiastical scholars. Even the steadfast German travel guide Nemeitz confessed an initial moment of bewilderment when confronted with this cast: 'I always thought that in France all those wearing little collars and short mantles were men of the Church. For this reason, I was certain that these saintly men were prostituting their character when I saw

an abbé play at cards with ladies or others in the company
assembled.'[3] He need not have worried: being an abbé did not
necessarily entail a life of religious exercise and lonely self-
chastisement, though those who had assumed the title were not
allowed to marry and usually became teachers, writers, or scientists.

The Jesuits teaching the young Abbé Diderot regarded the boy
as a promising recruit, despite the fact that the family already had
a different path in mind for him: he was to succeed his maternal
uncle, Didier Vigneron, as Canon of Langres Cathedral. When the
cathedral chapter, however, objected to having a canon who was
only fourteen years old foisted upon them, the boy began to follow
the path of his awakening intellect and dreamed of becoming a
Jesuit. Later in life, Diderot looked back at this religious episode
in his intellectual development with some scepticism, as witnessed
by a passage from his novel *Jacques the Fatalist*, which seems to
describe the adolescent abbé at his most pious:

> There comes a moment during which almost every girl or
> boy falls into melancholy; they are tormented by a vague
> inquietude which rests on everything and finds nothing to
> calm it. They seek solitude; they weep; the silence to be found
> in cloisters attracts them; the image of peace that seems to
> reign in religious houses seduces them. They mistake the first
> manifestations of a developing sexual nature for the voice of
> God calling them to Himself; and it is precisely when nature
> is inciting them that they embrace a fashion of life contrary
> to nature's wish.[4]

While happy enough to see their son enter the Church, Diderot's
parents were obviously less keen for him to enter a Jesuit academy
at so young an age. The boy himself, headstrong as he was to
remain, had set his heart on entering the Society of Jesus and was
discovered by his father sneaking out of the house one night with
a bag of clothes. Asked where he was going, he replied that he
was on his way to Paris to become a Jesuit. His parents eventually
resigned themselves to the inevitable, and at fifteen Diderot went

to the capital to continue his education there, probably at the famous Jesuit college Louis-le-Grand.[5]

The young Abbé Diderot, a bright and sensitive lad who had left behind a somewhat dour, provincial town of a few thousand souls, found life in the city far more interesting than he was supposed to. Having been educated within the Church, his newly discovered horizons were initially spiritual in nature, and in all likelihood Diderot soon changed from his prestigious college to the equally famous Collège d'Harcourt. This was no simple swap of schools: the Collège d'Harcourt was an important centre of Jansenism, the great rival movement to the Jesuits. Young Diderot had therefore changed sides.

Such a step was highly significant when the influence of the Church permeated every aspect of public life and power. The Church itself was split between these two rival factions, which can be broadly characterized as a 'centralist' Jesuit block favouring the closest possible adherence to the Pope, and another movement standing for more religious and political independence from Rome, a more 'low-church' ideology, naming itself after the sixteenth-century Flemish theologian Cornelius Jansen (1585–1638).

Unlike the Jesuits, the Jansenists believed that no amount of good works and repentance could assure redemption. Divine grace, Jansen believed, could not be attained through faith or pious works, but had to be bestowed by God himself, and independently of personal merit.[6] All are damned, unless God freely chooses to save each and every one of us. With its moral austerity, its bleakness of tone, and its insistence on study and piety, Jansenism was in many ways similar to Protestant theology. Its core belief, however, was implicitly, and dangerously, democratic: if God bestowed grace freely and independently of ritual and intermission, why was a Church, with its huge apparatus of priests and sacraments, necessary at all?

As a spiritual guardian and as the richest and most powerful estate in the land, the Church could not countenance such a threat to its existence. The Jesuits, the Church's undisputed intellectual avant-garde, were opposed to the new moment from the very start.

Now they did everything in their considerable political power, both at Court and in the Vatican, to thwart its influence.

Jansenism, however, had developed into a natural theological rallying-point against ecclesiastical vice and aristocratic decadence, as democratic as it was sober. The Paris *Parlement*, an elected non-aristocratic chamber that was in its function effectively a French equivalent to the British House of Lords, had long chafed under the yoke of royal domination, and its bourgeois advocates and judges had soon adopted Jansenism, by now a *de facto* kind of Protestantism within Catholicism, as well as a focus of political opposition.

By changing to a Jansenist college, the young Abbé Diderot had done more than simply choose different teachers, and eventually it became clear that it had been a step down the path that led him from intellectual dissatisfaction with the Church to atheism. Jacques-André Naigeon, a friend of Diderot's later years, believed that he stopped wearing his ecclesiastical clothes while at the Jansenist Collège de Harcourt.[7]

In 1732 Diderot was awarded the degree of Master of Arts from the University of Paris – and he vanishes from view for a while. It seems that Diderot's father found him a place with a lawyer, with the aim of having the young man, who had abandoned any intention of becoming a priest, study law. His enthusiasm for this profession, however, was so limited that his employer eventually gave him an ultimatum. Diderot left, saying that he only wanted to study. He then became a private tutor for the children of a rich financier, a good job that he also quit, telling his employer: 'Monsieur, look at me. A lemon is less yellow than my complexion. I am making men of your children, but each day I become a child with them. I am a thousand times *too* rich and *too* well off in your house, but I must leave it. The object of my desires is not to live better, but just not to die.'[8]

Diderot had gained his freedom, but lost his income. He accumulated debts and lived for a while off a monk, Frère Ange, under the pretext that he was settling his worldly affairs in order to enter the monastery, which, of course, he never did. His mother also sent him what she could, and once the aged family maid came to Paris on foot in order to give him not only something from Mme Diderot, but also her own savings. This period of need and uncertainty brought Denis closest to Grub Street and its inhabitants. The tonsured little abbé from the provinces had become a true *bohémien*, unsure whether to choose an academic career or follow his other great love and seek his fortune in the theatre. 'In winter,' he later remembered, 'in the worst sort of weather, I used to recite roles from Molière and Corneille out loud in the solitary walks of the Luxembourg. What did I have in mind? To be applauded? Perhaps. To live on familiar terms with women of the theatre, whom I found infinitely lovable and whom I knew to be of very easy virtue? Assuredly.'[9]

Diderot's transformation from an admirer of celestial virtue to one of easy virtue was to be only a partial journey, for the ideal of difficult, secular virtue was to preoccupy him for his entire life. For the time being, however, he enjoyed his freedom. 'Oh, my good friend,' he would sigh later in a letter to a female correspondent, 'where is the time when I had a great shock of hair fluttering in the breeze? In the morning, when my shirt collar was open and I took off my nightcap, they tumbled down in great, disorderly locks upon shoulders well built and white; my neighbour, who would get up early in the morning from her husband's side, would lift the curtain and gorge her eyes on this sight, and I noticed what was happening. Like this I seduced her across the street. Close to her, we came together in the end; I was forthright and innocent, with a sweet manner, but simple, modest and true. It is all gone: the blond hair, the candour and the innocence.'[10] Meanwhile, Diderot knew better than to let candour and innocence get out of hand. Always looking for a little extra money, and at times for any money at all, the abbé-turned-libertine began to write odd pieces of journalism and even put his theological training to good use by penning a series of sermons, which he sold to a missionary on his way to the Portuguese colonies. Whenever he had the time, he studied: Greek, Latin, English and Italian, as well as mathematics (his first area of competence), philosophy, and the writers of his day; he was, and would remain, insatiable in his intellectual appetite and in his capacity for discussion, for company.

Diderot was in his early twenties, no longer in one world and not yet in another: a walker of parks and frequenter of theatres, a reader who always had Virgil and Homer in his pocket, attracted by the freedom of an artist's life but still flirting with a life as a university theologian, a fugitive, at times, from hunger, and from his family's expectations every day. He drifted into the cafés in which most of the men in his position found themselves sooner or later, to talk and to drink, and to discuss and to brag, to warm themselves around the big stove, to play chess and to read and to write.

It was here, at the Café de la Régence, that he met another young man in much the same situation, who had arrived from Lyon with his great wit and even greater ambitions, and in his bag a new system for notating music. The two quickly became firm friends. The stranger was Jean-Jacques Rousseau (1712 –78), already brilliant, already difficult, and looking to forge his future, a future that was to be more unhappy and more brilliant than he could have feared or hoped, and that would transform him into a European cult, a bestselling author, and a writer more ardently revered than any of his contemporaries.

Jean-Jacques was burning to be recognized. His life up to this point had been peripatetic and restless. Like Diderot, he was the son of a craftsman, a Genevan watchmaker in his case, and like his new friend, he had been apprenticed to his father for a little while. Soon, however, he, too, had fled the confines of the workshop. He had gone to Italy, where he converted to Catholicism. He then lived for eight years with a rich widow, Mme Warens, and spent the time studying, trying to decide, it seems, in which field of endeavour to become famous. After breaking with his protectress and mistress, he had gone to Montpellier and from there to Lyon, where he became a private tutor, only to abandon his position and travel to Paris. Unable to make an impression there, he quickly returned to Lyon, on foot, and attached himself once more to his wealthy lover, who treated him kindly and would later have the dubious pleasure of finding her love affair aired in front of the world in his *Confessions*.

Still unable to settle down, Rousseau had come to Paris a second time in 1742, with the grand sum of fifteen *louis* in his pocket, and taken lodgings in the rue des Cordeliers in the Latin Quarter. He was twenty-nine. He determined to seek his fame in music, and more particularly with the propagation of a new system for writing it, based on the numeric values of notes in the *solfège*, the common method by which musicians memorized and talked about music.

Like his friend Denis, Jean-Jacques was given to walks in the Jardins du Luxembourg with a head full of plans and his pockets full of books. In his *Confessions*, he would later write: 'Diderot . . . was much about my own age. He was fond of music, and knew it theoretically; we conversed together, and he communicated to me some of his literary projects. This soon formed betwixt us a more intimate connection which lasted fifteen years, and which probably would still exist were not I, unfortunately, and by my own fault, of the same profession with himself.'[11] This portent of evil, two friends estranged by their common passion for literature, would indeed come to haunt them.

For the time being, however, their friendship seemed indestructible, even when Diderot began to develop other lasting emotional attachments that put an end to any remaining plans of a respectable academic career. Much later, Diderot would sum up the entire period as follows:

> I was going to take the fur [by obtaining a doctorate in theology] and install myself among the doctors of the Sorbonne. On my way I meet a woman beautiful as an angel; I want to sleep with her, and I do; I have three children by her and am forced to abandon my mathematics, which I loved, my Homer and Virgil, which I always had in my pocket, the theatre, for which I had a taste, and was only too happy to undertake the *Encyclopédie*, to which I devoted twenty-five years of my life.[12]

In truth, things had been considerably less straightforward than these short, factual phrases tend to suggest, though the events serve as an excellent illustration of Diderot's temperament.

The woman 'beautiful as an angel' was Anne-Toinette Champion (1710–96), the daughter of a widow dealing in linen and lace, herself the daughter of a 'gentleman' ruined by speculation. Denis lived in a small room in the same house as these two women, and he was enchanted by his young neighbour. As neither daughter nor mother, both living in pious seclusion, was inclined to welcome him as a suitor, he drew on all his passions – theatre, theology, and literature – for one great introductory performance. He had, he informed them, decided on a religious life and would soon be entering the Seminary of Saint-Nicolas. He would need someone to repair and replace his linen, and he asked the two women to take this into their hands. He found reasons to drop by almost every evening to discuss buttons, seams, fabrics, and other essential matters.

Madame Champion, Toinette's mother, though pious, was certainly no fool. She saw that this bohemian ne'er-do-well was turning the head of her respectable young daughter with his golden tongue and his sweet letters, and she determined to put a stop to the liaison. As for Denis, he found himself faced with similar objections from home, as the girl was not only impecunious but also his elder by two years. This combined resistance made him redouble his efforts, write more secret missives, and try and try again.

During his courtship the former aspiring cleric finally came to spend some time in a monastery, if not entirely of his own volition. He left for his home town, Langres, in early December 1742 to win his parents over to his plan. Initially, things went well, especially as he had chosen to wait for the right moment (which had not yet come) to impart the news, and also because the stagecoach had brought from Paris the proofs of Templey Stanyan's *Grecian History*, which Diderot had been translating from the English for the bookseller David l'âiné. Seeing that their son's seemingly aimless and unproductive drifting in the capital had now resulted in his name appearing in print impressed the parents immensely. Things might have remained harmonious, and his parents might even have been reconciled to their son's career, had Denis not decided to tell them of his marriage plans after Toinette started sending him increasingly bitter and plaintive letters from Paris. The father, who had hoped much more for his elder son, flew into a rage, threatened to disinherit him, and, when that did not have the desired effect, had him imprisoned in a monastery to cool off, not an uncommon procedure for the time. Diderot himself takes up the story in a letter to his beloved written in February 1743:

> My dearest friend
>
> Having undergone unheard-of torments, I am free. What can I tell you? My father carried his harshness to the point of locking me up with the monks, who treated me in every way that maliciousness can dream up. I finally hurled myself out of a window during the night from Sunday to Monday. I have been walking all the way until I reached the stagecoach in Troyes, which will take me the rest of the way. I have no linen. I have walked the thirty lieues [90 miles] in atrocious weather. I have lived badly, because I could not follow the normal routes for fear I might be caught, and I had to rely on villages where I hardly found bread and wine. Luckily I had some money . . . which I had hidden in my shirt . . . I forgot to tell you that they took the useless precaution of shaving half of my head so that I would not be able to save myself.[13]

Denis eventually got his way and was married, in a secret ceremony, on 6 November 1743. His wife was beautiful, a good housekeeper and a good mother – and a woman who shared none of her husband's intellectual interests and who disapproved of most of his activities. Having fallen in love with the young man who had wooed her so imaginatively, she now found that too many sacrifices were asked of her. Her daughter, Angélique, would later tell the story of these early years:

> My father was of too jealous a character to let my mother continue in her commerce which obliged her to receive strangers, and he begged her to abandon her profession. She consented with great difficulty . . . but eventually she thought it would make him happy, and she did it . . . Often, when my

father ate in town, she supped on bread, and it was a great
pleasure to her to imagine that she could make a dinner twice
as good for him the next evening.[14]

Eventually, the former beauty Toinette became bitter and no
longer hesitated to make her disappointment clear. In Angélique's
words: 'Loneliness, the petty domesticities to which poverty condemned her, distress at my father's infidelities and ignorance of
the manners of society had soured her temper; so scolding became
a habit with her.'[15] The marriage lasted for forty-three years and
was copiously unhappy.

On 17 November 1717, an infant boy was laid on the steps of
Saint-Jean-Lerond, a chapel on the outside of Notre Dame, commonly used as a depository for unwanted newborns. The child was
taken in by the local commissaire of police, was baptized and named
Jean-Baptiste Lerond, after the chapel in which he was found. Like
other foundlings, he was sent out of Paris to a wet nurse. Six weeks
later the child was claimed by Dr Molin, *médecin du roi*, a man who
did not usually deal with penniless orphans. A foster mother in
Paris was found for the sickly baby, which was at first rejected by
several nurses who thought it unlikely the child would survive
infancy. Eventually, and despite having a head 'no larger than a
common apple',[16] he was taken in by the wife of a glazier, who took
pity on him. Having received protection from on high, the newborn
Jean-Baptiste Lerond had escaped a home for abandoned children
and been given the chance of a very different sort of life altogether.
     The royal doctor was only one of several near-miraculous inter-
ventions in the young boy's life. He was, in fact, the natural son of
Mme de Tencin, a society lady of acknowledged beauty, whose way
to prominence in literary Paris had led her to the beds of a succession of influential men, most recently the Chevalier Destouches,
a military officer and the boy's father. Mme de Tencin herself had
opened her famous salon as soon as she had sufficiently recovered
from giving birth. This salon was to become one of the great insti-

tutions of Paris literary life. These salons operated according to a simple principle: a lady of standing announced that her house would be open for one or several evenings a week, and that men of letters and amusing hangers-on were welcome to drop by unannounced. She would then hold court at the designated times, using the prerogatives that being a woman in society gave her to guide conversation, make introductions, smooth over quarrels, provoke discussions, neutralize enmities and create new rivalries – all under the protection of being a lady admired, and at times desired, by every man in the room.

The boy Jean Lerond continued to benefit from this distant protection. As one of the very few pupils who was not of noble birth, he was admitted to the Jansenist Collège de Quatre-Nations, and was educated as a young gentleman. His education comprised, apart from sciences and humanities, lessons in dancing, riding, and fencing. The Fathers teaching the boy soon realized his potential. With some special care, they decided, he might be made into a formidable opponent to the Jesuits. As his biographer Joseph Bertrand remarks, their wish was granted, even though they shot past their goal: their old boy became equally hostile to both factions.[17]

As a teenager, he was inscribed in the faculty of arts at Paris University in 1735, though not under the name Jean Le Rond, Jean Lerond, or even Jean Lerond Rousseau but Daremberg, and later Dalenbert. Much has been written about this curious name change (another permutation, the more aristocratic-sounding d'Alembert, was to come), but it is likely that the young man, who showed great talent in mathematics, simply chose an acrostic:

BATISTE LEROND
DALENBERT, SOIT
Batiste Lerond shall be Dalenbert.[18]

Dalenbert, or d'Alembert, read law and medicine, but without enthusiasm. Mathematics, however, fascinated him more and more, and he already showed a trait that he was to exhibit for the rest of his life: a steely and at times opportunist ambition. His father having died, he knew that he would have to make his way on his own and that, despite occasional help from his father's family, there was no powerful protector to smooth his path and buy him honours.

D'Alembert decided to become a member of the Academy of Sciences, a body that admitted promising scientists by election only. It took him several attempts and three years, but in 1742, having written essays in mathematics and mechanics, he was finally made *adjoint pour la section d'astronomie.* He was twenty-four, and his mathematical career, one of the most distinguished of the eighteenth century, was under way. Despite this early achievement, d'Alembert was not content with his new title and was soon involved with the political affairs of the Academy, whose minutes show that he was one of the members of the commission that examined and eventually rejected a system of musical notation submitted and presented by a young composer and harpsichordist, Jean-Jacques Rousseau.

'Diderot, always followed by d'Alembert',[19] writes Flaubert in his *Dictionary of Received Ideas,* and it is true that the *Encyclopédie* has bound their names together. The similarities between them, however, cannot obscure their great differences: Diderot came from solid, respectable, provincial stock but had broken with his family to lead the life and marry the woman he had chosen; d'Alembert still lived with his foster mother (and would do up to her death) and was the illegitimate child of two members of the lower aristocracy. His mother was famous, educated, and influential. Diderot was, and remained, indifferent to all social decorum, hardly ever took a coach (even when he finally had the money) and would usually appear for all but the most formal occasions without a wig; d'Alembert was acutely aware of his appearance and frequented the fashionable salons. Diderot was effervescent and communicative, ebullient and generous, and at times tactless; d'Alembert, a slight man with a high voice, was more at ease in a polite salon than in a café.

One other difference was and remained significant: while d'Alembert, very sensibly, sought his appointment to the Académie des Sciences and Rousseau had accepted a position as secretary to the wealthy Mme Dupin, their friend had actively eschewed all forms of patronage, all useful appointments or rich benefactors, and tried to make his way as a writer, and as a writer alone, no doubt much to the despair of his wife, who did not enjoy virtuous poverty and who was, by early 1744, expecting their first child. Diderot, though, was determined to make his way alone, to make a name for himself with books that would blast a trail of reason through the fogs of superstition and injustice that befuddled France. For the time being, however, he would hide behind a foreign book. The work was a translation of *An Inquiry Concerning Virtue and Merit* by Lord Shaftesbury, an essay that Denis translated with great freedom and spiced with an introduction and extensive footnotes containing his own comments and thoughts. As the translation was anonymous and the book published, ostensibly at least, in Amsterdam, he felt that he could for the first time put his own philosophy in words without fearing censor or Church. In the footnotes of this book of moral philosophy, Diderot is already unmistakably there, with his vivid and immediate writing and his impossible, discursive generosity. One footnote reads, to the dismay of the devout (and, had she read it, of Mme Diderot): 'I love very passionately my God, my king, my country, my parents, my mistress, and myself.'[20]

Other, more daring books were to follow, and Diderot rapidly gained a reputation as an outspoken *philosophe*, a freethinker and man of principle, a dangerous creature. He fairly revelled in this image and in his gift to enchant people with his stream of eloquence. Even his father, not usually a man for radical intellectual inquiry, had to admit with comic despair that he could not honestly say he preferred the strictly religious Didier, his second son, to his wastrel eldest: 'Alas! I have two sons. One will certainly be a saint, and I am very much afraid that the other may be damned. But I cannot live with the saint, and I greatly enjoy the time I spend with the damned one.'[21]

In September, Denis and Toinette Diderot buried their first child, who had not survived infancy. The parish registers describe the father as a 'day labourer'. He was certainly hard at work, for in spring his *Pensées philosophiques* (Philosophical Thoughts) appeared. Having tested the waters by appearing in disguise, he now published under his own name. Despite the fact that many of his ideas are still at a developmental stage, this is already essential Diderot, quite unlike the rigidly rationalist image with which the Enlightenment is associated. The very first of these aphorisms is a defence of passion, followed by an attack on the bigotry of the Church:

> What voices! What cries! What groaning! Who has locked up in these dungeons all these pitiable cadavers? What crimes have these miserable creatures committed? Some beat their chest with stones, others tear at their body with hooks of iron; all have regrets, pain and death in their eyes. Who has condemned them to these torments? – God, whom they have offended. – Who is this God? – The God of Loving Kindness.[22]

Much of the work, written by a man who had a few years earlier seriously considered becoming a priest, wrestled with atheism. Diderot was not yet the out-and-out atheist he would become, and although he stated boldly that 'I believe that superstition is more injurious to God than atheism',[23] he would not make the last step. Another of the *Pensées* shows the young Denis Diderot, just arrived in Paris from the countryside, among the onlookers in the Cemetery of Saint-Médard, a place of popular 'miracle healings', already formulating an important philosophical idea:

> The *faubourg* is reverberating with the cries: the ashes of a man elect produces miracles there like those Jesus Christ himself performed. People run there, people are carried there, and I follow the crowd there. I have just arrived when I already hear them shouting: Miracle! Miracle! I approach, I look, and I see a little lame boy walking with the aid of three or four charitable souls who hold him; and the people gawp and repeat: Miracle! Miracle! Where is the miracle, you imbeciles? Don't you realize that the little cheat has just exchanged one set of crutches for another?[24]

Having religion compared to a pair of crutches was too much for the Paris *Parlement*, which ordered the *Pensées philosophiques* to be torn to shreds and burned by the public hangman on the Place des Grèves, the square in front of the city hall where executions took place. Burning books was a common procedure at the time and the next best thing to doing the same to the author.

If Diderot was making a name for himself, his friend Jean-Jacques Rousseau had no such luck. Having spent a year in Venice as secretary to the French Ambassador, living with the wig-and-brocade set, fancying himself a man of the world and being rowed along the canals in a coloured, ambassadorial gondola, he had quarrelled with his employer, left Italy, and was once more in Paris, a genius smarting from lack of recognition. He had moved in with a housemaid, Thérèse Levasseur, with whom he was to stay for the remainder of his life. It was a curious relationship, and much commented on, since Thérèse could not read and had the greatest trouble even learning how to tell the time. Both Jean-Jacques and his friend Denis had chosen women who were in no way their intellectual equals.

Rousseau had once more taken up employment with his rich patroness, Mme Dupin. Inspired by the music he had heard in Venice, he was now planning to make his name as an opera composer. He presented his work, an opera entitled *Les muses galantes* (The Amorous Muses) to the famous composer Rameau, who told him very bluntly that half of the music was written by a consummate artist, and the other half by a man who had no idea of what music was. Rousseau, who never took criticism lightly, grudgingly accepted that his work might be somewhat uneven.

In 1747, Jean-Jacques wrote an enormous chemical treatise, a 1,200-page manuscript building on his work undertaken during his time with 'Maman' Warens, his erstwhile protectress, as well as on research he had been carrying out for his new and former employers, the Dupin family, before his departure to Venice. He had been paid by the Dupins to be a kind of auxiliary brain, helping father, mother, and son, all of whom had literary or scientific ambitions, excerpting books, taking dictation, and working in the laboratory; but he had not much enjoyed this intellectual subservience, further complicated by his ill-concealed love for the mistress of the house. Her son, Charles Louis Dupin de Franceuil, was the aspiring chemist whose greatest goal in life was to publish a scientific work that might gain him admittance to the Academy of Sciences. While Jean-Jacques had struck up a friendship with him, his parents liked to keep the edgy Genevan at arm's length, a fact that stung particularly as they had one of the most fashionable salons in Paris, studded with all the cultural grandees a good wine cellar could attract. To Rousseau's quiet outrage, however, Mme Dupin, who had already once put him in his place over a love letter she thought quite inappropriate, saw to it that he had his day off when great men called on her, and he could not, for the time being, profit from their exalted connections.

Jean-Jacques did find stimulating company when he began hosting modest weekly dinners at his lodgings close to the opera to which he invited the Abbé de Condillac (1715–80) and Diderot. For Denis these evenings were a welcome escape from domesticity, which by now was hanging around his neck like a millstone. Rousseau remarked: '[They] pleased Diderot in the extreme, for he, who would usually miss all his appointments, never missed a single one of these'.[25] For a while the two friends thought about founding a satirical magazine, but nothing came of it. Diderot showed the draft to d'Alembert and introduced him to Rousseau, who remarked in a less than enthusiastic tone that the two had met once before at the Academy of Sciences. It may have been d'Alembert who advised caution, especially since he and Diderot were already beginning their occasional involvement with the Encyclopédie. Things were going well, and there was no reason to provoke the authorities.

As for himself, d'Alembert was flourishing. He was working steadily and his star was rising, appropriately enough, due to his work in theoretical astronomy. His Treatise on Dynamics, which dealt with mechanical problems, had spread his name throughout Europe's mathematical community, and he divided his life between his mathematical work and socializing in the salons of Mme

Geoffrin and Mme Deffand, or with young writers and scientists. He did not accept any specific position, continuing instead to live very modestly with his adoptive mother in a simple flat over a glazier's workshop. Jean-François Marmontel (1723–99), later an Encyclopedist himself, described this time in the mathematician's life:

> He was the most cheerful, the most animated, and the most amiable of us all. Having devoted the morning to mathematics, he came out of the glazier's house like a schoolboy skipping class and wanted nothing more than to meet someone, and with his pleasing and lively voice and his wit that was at once luminous and firm, he made one forget that he was a scientist and seemed nothing but a lovable man. The source of this enjoyment was a pure soul, free of strong passions, content in itself, and the happiness of discovering every day some new truth that crowned his work.[26]

His mother was displeased that her adored Jean had quit the law for mathematics. 'You will never be anything but a *philosophe*,' she told him, 'and what is a *philosophe*? A fool who torments himself during his life so that people talk about him when he is dead.'

For the three young men, however, this posthumous fame was the only glory worth having.

Pl. VI.

Fig. 19.

Fig. 20.

Fig. 21.

Benard Fecit.

Escrime.

PROJECT

PROJECT, s. m. (*Morale*) a plan which one intends to carry out, but it is a long way from the *project* to the execution, and even further from the execution to success; what crazy projects people have!

WORK, s. m. (*Gramm.*) a daily occupation to which man is condemned by his need & to which he has to pledge at the same time his health, his subsistence, his happiness, his good sense & perhaps his virtue. Mythology considers it an evil and believes it was born of Erebe & of night.

* **EREBE**, s. m. (*Mythol.*) This word means *tenebrae*. *Erebe* is, according to Hesiod, the son of chaos & of night & the father of the day. The ancients also called a part of their hell *erebe*; it is the place for those who have lived well.

The true history of the *Encyclopédie* begins with a fist fight. The blows were dealt out, with some gusto, by a bookseller, André-François Le Breton (1708–79), who was trying to save an investment with his bare knuckles. On the receiving end of 'one punch of the fist to the stomach and two strikes by a cane to the head',[1] which promptly brought him down, was a hapless English literary fortune hunter, sometime translator and later writer on agriculture, John Mills. Le Breton had engaged Mills to translate an English work, the *Cyclopaedia* by Ephraim Chambers, and now found himself lumbered with a collaborator who seemed to be both lazy and incompetent.

The driving force behind the translation had been a German

35

scholar of some reputation, Gottfried Sell (1704?–67), also known by his Latinized name Sellius, in January 1745. He had studied in Marburg and Leyden, both universities of great renown, and was said to have got his start in literary life by marrying a wealthy heiress, and with her a handsome library, a collection of pictures, and a laboratory. His scientific reputation, which ensured his election to the Royal Society, the Academy of *Naturae Curiosorum* in Germany, and finally even to two chairs of law (Göttingen and Halle), was based on a Dutch worm. It was an important if particularly revolting creature which he had described in great detail, the *Teredo navalis*, or ship worm, a maritime mollusk causing great concern in the Netherlands, where it bored into ships' hulls and wooden dykes, precipitaing their destruction and the inundation of many low-lying areas. In later life, the career of the polyglot scholar would seem just as worm-eaten as one of the structures he had studied by the North Sea, so that Louis Petit de Bachaumont would record in 1767: 'Sellius, the savant, known for his grand projects and vast erudition, but above all for the first project which would bring to France, in 1743 [*sic*] the *Encyclopédie*, has died in Charenton, miserable and mad.'[2]

During the early 1740s, Sellius had washed up in Paris, having been forced to sell his library and later to abandon his professorship and leave the country to escape his creditors. He needed a new start, and with the *Cyclopaedia* he believed he'd found it. Despite his scientific credentials, though, his qualifications as an editor and translator were somewhat limited. A contemporary later wrote: 'As he knew our language very well, he translated fluently, at the speed of writing, and showing himself more attentive to the literal words of the author . . . than to making him speak French, which rendered the result incomprehensible [*obscur*].'[3]

Despite this handicap, Sellius was obviously determined to refloat his fortunes with the *Cyclopaedia* and recruited a second translator, John Mills, a much younger man, who had moved to Paris from London and was to leave the French capital soon after having found himself at the wrong end of Le Breton's stick. Sellius managed to persuade the bookseller and furnished some specimen articles as early as 1743, while his partner was introduced as the supposed heir to a considerable fortune who was able to secure the financing of the enterprise. Le Breton took out the requisite *privilège*, the permission to publish granted by the Royal Chancellery, on 25 February 1745. It was registered on 13 April; work on the translation could now begin in earnest.

Mills was part of that literary ferment of young men trying to make it in Paris that was so important for the *Encyclopédie*, for literature in France, and, some forty years later, for the Revolution: writers with ambitions but without money or patronage, out to make a name for themselves and to find a niche somewhere, somehow. Like them, he lived on the little revenue he could make from odd literary jobs translating or writing pamphlets, with the occasional bit of private tutoring. Unlike some of his contemporaries, however, he seems to have been neither very gifted nor terribly eager to work. Charged with doing the lion's share of the translations of the English reference work into French, he gave the appearance of having 'a great part of it translated'[4] and of having gained the support and cooperation of many men of science and letters of the Académie Française and the Académie des Sciences (the promising young M. d'Alembert among them). Mills nevertheless suffered from the considerable handicap of having only a 'mediocre' grasp of French.

Believing the work to be well advanced, Le Breton felt it was time to inform the wider public of his plan and to invite subscriptions. This announcement of an *Encyclopédie, ou Dictionnaire universel des arts & des sciences* was printed around April 1745 (the famous Jesuit *Journal de Trévoux* reviewed it enthusiastically in its May number) and contained translated sample articles from Chambers on 'Atmosphere', 'Fable', Blood', and 'Dyeing'. The fact that the prospectus was successful despite the inadequacy of the translations was because Le Breton had paid an unnamed 'intelligent person' to correct them. This nameless but competent translator seems to have been the young Denis Diderot, the future editor and hero of the *Encyclopédie*.[5]

Mills had not, it seems, translated much apart from the contents of the prospectus: his contemporaries agreed that, even had he wanted to, his French was not proficient enough for him to do what he had been paid to do. This did not prevent him from asking a great deal of money, 1,200 *livres*, from Le Breton in a letter dated 7 August. The return post brought not the desired purse full of *louis d'or*, but the bookseller himself, who had had enough of financial demands and other difficulties. Having called several times while Mills had been out (or hiding behind a curtain), he called again and this time found the Englishman at home. In the ensuing conversation, Le Breton eventually decided that words alone were not enough. Later he would claim that Mills had in fact drawn his sword against him and that he had merely defended himself.

After the violent confrontation, Mills brought a suit against his assailant, and Le Breton contemptuously called his bluff:

> The title *savant* with which Mills decorates himself is not deserved. He is no older than 29 or 30, and his function in Paris is that of junior clerk of a banker, M. Le Chevalier Labert. The contract he has signed with Sellius proves that he was not in charge of the translation from the beginning; had not even started [translating] before the 17 February 1745, and that he was free to work only when his other position permitted; that the men of science eager for the advancement of letters are in fact all reunited in the person of Sellius . . .[6]

Le Breton was exasperated and outraged. Mills did not even possess a copy of Chambers' *Cyclopaedia* to work from and had had to borrow one to start work on the translation. Le Breton, on the other hand, had invested in the project and gone to the trouble of procuring a *privilège*, which was now revoked by Chancellor d'Aguesseau, who took it upon himself to deal with the matter personally. He looked at the dossier of Mills and Sellius and 'quite easily detected their incompetence and their swindling'.[7] Having made up his mind, he seems to have dealt with the matter in a swift and unbureaucratic manner: no damages were awarded against Le Breton, Mills left for Britain soon afterwards, and the bookseller was given to understand that a reinstatement of the *privilège* might only be a question of time if he found the right editors.

After the disappearance of the enormous imaginary inheritance that Mills was supposed to have at his disposal, Le Breton looked for partners to carry the financial risk, and found them in his colleagues Antoine-Claude Briasson (1700–75), Michel-Antoine David (1706?–69), and Laurent Durand (1712?–63), who agreed to take a stake of one sixth each, with Le Breton holding the remaining half of the shares. They signed an agreement on 18 October 1745 and a further one, contracting Le Breton to print 1,625 copies of the work, on 14 November.[8] On 21 January 1746, the project of a translated *Cyclopaedia* was granted a new *privilège*. It was now officially afloat and in search of an editor.

Even before an official agreement was reached, and long before his official involvement, one name appears repeatedly in the account books: on 17 December 1745, the librarians paid 105 *livres* to Jean d'Alembert; another payment, 84 *livres*, was made to him on 31 December. The accounts also show that the librarians had to spend 600 *livres* to buy back manuscripts from Mills, picked up from him (at a cost of 5 *livres*) by carriage. In February, the book-sellers made the first payment (60 *livres*) to Denis Diderot.

The editor who was entrusted with the booksellers' investment was the Abbé Jean-Paul Gua de Malves (1711?–86), a mathematician as gifted as he was eccentric, who taught philosophy at the Collège de France. According to a police spy (the police, after all, kept tabs on all figures in literary life), Gua had the bearing and appearance of a madman. The importance of his involvement with the *Encyclopédie* is not entirely clear. In his eulogy on Gua de Malves, the marquis de Condorcet (1743–94), perhaps the last of the Encyclopedists, portrayed him as the key figure in recasting the scope of the undertaking and transforming it from a mere translation into something altogether more ambitious.[9] Condorcet, however, was only three years old when these events took place; he made these remarks after all the others involved in the affair had already died. Jacques-André Naigeon (1738–1810), who also belonged to the circle of the Encyclopedists and was to write a biography of Diderot, describes the project under Gua's editorship as being limited to a translation 'with some corrections and additions'.[10] Neither of the two positions is backed up by documentation.

Gua's contract with the booksellers offers a modified explanation. It was signed by two witnesses, Denis Diderot and Jean d'Alembert, and stipulated that 'if there are in the already existing translation [by Mills and Sellius] articles which MM. d'Alembert and Diderot believe need to be retranslated, the said booksellers are duty-bound to have them retranslated'.[11] This is the first joint mention of the two names under which the *Encyclopédie* would be known, and proof that both d'Alembert and Diderot were involved, in an advisory capacity, at this early stage. Diderot had already made a name for himself as a translator and needed money; he was therefore an obvious choice. D'Alembert was a mathematician and a colleague of Gua de Malves at the Académie des Sciences. Gua's contract with the booksellers already stipulated that he was to 'extend the part having to do with the arts, preferably, as much as will be possible for him to complete', a brief that left considerable room for manœuvre.[12] For his work he would be paid 18,000 *livres*, of which he promised to pay 1,200 each to his two collaborators. It therefore quite possible that the new conception of the project was not due to Gua alone, but grew out of discussions with Diderot and d'Alembert.[13]

Gua de Malves' editorship was not to last more than thirteen months. The Abbé was not an easy character. In spite of the eulogist's iron maxim *de mortui nihil nisi bene* [speak no ill of the dead], Condorcet later admitted: 'M. l'Abbé de Gua, whom misfortune had made more easily wounded and more inflexible [than most], soon grew disgusted and abandoned this work on the *Encyclopédie*.'[14] The booksellers themselves were not keen to repeat the catastrophic situation with Sellius and Mills and the contract was cancelled on 3 August 1747. The Abbé, who was to ruin himself designing a sand-screening machine for gold prospecting, now bowed out of the story of the *Encyclopédie*.

Once again a project that might have been so wonderfully simple to carry out, the translation of an English encyclopedia, was without an editor, and once more the booksellers found themselves pressed to find a replacement. It is probable that they approached several people, for the contract with the new editors was only signed on 16 October. In the end, the editors chosen were Denis Diderot and Jean d'Alembert, the former of whom was to assume the main responsibility and workload, a fact that was reflected in his pay. While d'Alembert was to receive a total of 2,400 *livres* in monthly instalments of 144 *livres* (roughly £1,150 in today's terms), Diderot was paid a one-off fee of 1,200 *livres* and another 6,000 *livres* at the same rate as his colleague, indicating that the total work on the *Encyclopédie* was projected to last three and a half years.

For Diderot, the new position required him to be in Paris, and the modest salary of 144 *livres* per month allowed him and his wife to move back into town to the popular Faubourg Saint-Marcau on the Left Bank, into the populous parish of Saint-Médard. While Toinette was sitting at home, alone, and struggling with her second child (which like its predecessor was to die in infancy), Diderot enjoyed being in the centre of things once more. He finished his second translation, James's medical dictionary, and amused himself with the close-knit group of friends he had found: Jean d'Alembert, Jean-Jacques Rousseau, and Étienne Condillac.

He also took a mistress, a Mme de Puisieux, and encouraged her to develop a literary career of her own. To launch her on this noble path, and to show her just how easy it was to improvise a spicy work of fiction, he penned an erotic novel, *Les Bijoux indiscrets,* set in a fictitious African kingdom, in which the hero's magic stone had the ability to make the 'jewel' of the female characters of the novel talk, a kind of risqué romp through a pre-Freudian unconscious. Thomas Carlyle, obviously no lover of the erotic novel, called this effort 'the beastliest of all past, present, or future dull novels'.[15] This Victorian tongue-lashing is surely undeserved, for the novel is inventive, often funny, and, of its type, quite successful – so much so, indeed, that its author (to whom posterity would be a growing concern) was later to remark ruefully that he would gladly cut off a finger if he could make it disappear, so much was his name still associated with it.

Diderot was certainly beginning to be known, if only by the police. In June 1747, the parish priest of Saint-Médard, Hardy de Levaré, had taken it upon himself to denounce his parishioner and to paint him in the blackest colours as a man who stopped at nothing (and who obviously had visitors or a maid, or a charwoman, ready to tell all):

> M. Diderot is a young man who passed his early years in debauchery. Eventually he attached himself to a young woman without money but of the same social position as his, and he married her without the knowledge of his father. To conceal this so-called marriage he has taken lodgings in my parish at the house of M. Guillotte; his wife goes under her maiden name ... The remarks that Diderot sometimes makes in his household clearly prove that he is a deist, if not worse. He utters blasphemies against Jesus Christ and the Holy Virgin that I would not venture to put into writing ... it is true that I have never spoken to this young man and do not know him personally, but I am told that he has a great deal of wit and that his conversation is very amusing. In one of his conversations he admitted being the author of one of the two works condemned by the *Parlement* and burned about two years ago. I have been informed that for more than a year he has been working on another work still more dangerous to religion.[16]

The report had the desired effect, for the 'dangerous' work M. Diderot was working on, the *Promenade d'un sceptique* (A Sceptic's Walk), was not published until 1772, and Diderot's daughter relates that a police agent searched Diderot's house and impounded the offending manuscript.

Still set on building up a solid intellectual reputation independent of the publication of the *Encyclopédie*, Diderot had to start again. In June the following year, no doubt inspired by d'Alembert's record, he published a work that was unlikely to get him into any kind of trouble, a collection of mathematical essays on acoustics, a new design for an organ, wind resistance, and mechanics, a very competent work that was well received in the scientific community.

So much safety, however, was out of character for a man who needed to communicate, to talk, to provoke, and to exchange ideas about everything that moved him. He needed to write something else, something more ambitous and likely to get him noticed beyond scientific circles. First of all, though, he and his young family needed to move away from the prying priest to the rue de la Vieille Estrapade, where their address on all correspondence was: Nr. 3, second floor, at widow Chatel's.

Meanwhile, the preparations for the publication of the *Encyclopédie* were going at full steam. The workload was staggering: if the *Encyclopédie* really was to circumscribe the entire knowledge of the period, it was necessary to decide in advance which keywords were to be admitted and according to which criteria they were to be chosen. One important decision made at the beginning was to follow Chambers in adopting an alphabetical order. This would occasion a good deal of criticism; indeed the re-editing of the *Encyclopédie* by Pancoucke that was to capitalize on the original enterprise grouped the articles by subjects, with only the subsections arranged alphabetically.[17]

An alphabetical order had seductive advantages: it democratized all forms of knowledge and avoided from the beginning the necessity to devote entire sections to subjects like theology. It also conformed with the fundamental ambition of the Encyclopedists to order the world according to rational criteria alone. It did, however, require a great deal of additional work. While thematic volumes could be planned one by one, an alphabetic encyclopedia had to be planned (at least in theory) down to the last entry. Not only did the great themes have to be laid out: in a work that dealt with crafts and industrial processes, every single craftsman's name for a specific tool, every last chisel and dovetail joint, carving knife, and journeyman's term had to be registered, explained, and integrated before even the first volume could be written. Cross-references had to be agreed upon as well, binding the articles together in a network of interrelations; and then they had to be noted and remembered, making certain that a reference in a word beginning with 'A' to one beginning with 'Z' would not point to a nonexistent entry (inevitably, it did at times, as enraged subscribers were to point out).

The entire conceptual work of the *Encyclopédie* had to be done before selected authors could be asked to contribute articles, and the entire sequence of volumes had to be planned out, in principle at least, before even a single article had been committed to paper. Then authors had to be found and approached, juggling competences, ideological affiliations, and personal vanities. It is worth remembering that everything had to be written and filed by hand: tens of thousands of key words for projected articles, correspondence with authors, and, eventually, their essays, which had to be edited, filed, and ordered, corrected again in galley form, and finally committed to print.

It fell to Diderot, d'Alembert, and a few close co-workers to write most of the articles for the first volume. Diderot himself contributed nearly two thousand articles on subjects from crafts to metaphysics, and from philology to botany. D'Alembert was responsible mainly for mathematics, geometry, and astronomy, Rousseau for music. Among the other collaborators, the indefatigable Abbé Edmé-François Mallet wrote most of the articles dealing with theology (a very delicate subject indeed) and ancient history. Two other abbés, Yvon and Pestre, also contributed significant numbers of articles.

Rousseau gives a glimpse of the early stages of the work by Diderot and d'Alembert:

> These two authors had just been working on a *Dictionnaire Encyclopédique* [*sic*], which was initially supposed to be nothing more than a translation of Chambers, similar to that of the *Dictionnaire de Médecine* by James, which Diderot had just translated. He wanted me to contribute something to this second enterprise, and he offered me the musical articles, which I accepted, and which I executed in a great hurry and very badly

during the three months he had given me and all the other
authors who were supposed to work on the enterprise, but I
was the only one who had finished in the agreed time. I sent
him my manuscript, which I had copied by a lackey of M. de
Franceuil, who was called Dupont, who wrote very well, and
to whom I paid ten *écus*, out of my pocket, for which I was
never reimbursed. Diderot had promised to pay me back on
behalf of the booksellers, but never mentioned it again, and
neither did I.[18]

Rousseau's remarks make clear that, having decided on key words
and authors, the editors would offer them an area and ask them
to write as many articles as they could, starting with 'A'. What they
do not make clear, incidentally, is that Diderot's wish for his friend
to contribute something would have been a great advance, intellectually and financially, on Rousseau's usual main source of income
at the period, copying music.

All but a few scraps of the official materials documenting the
work on the *Encyclopédie* have been lost. Notes quickly scribbled to
contributors and editors were simply thrown away, as were other
papers. Most of the manuscripts were destroyed, and so the day-to-
day functioning of this gigantic operation can only be reconstructed
from tiny scraps of evidence.

Much of Diderot's time was taken up with the *description des arts
et métiers*, industry and artisanship, which he considered such an
important part of the new *Encyclopédie*. His ambition was nothing
less than to give a complete picture of all manufacturing processes
in France at the time, from silk weaving to ship building, from the
construction of bridges to the manufacture of pins. Nothing of this
magnitude had ever been attempted. There were monographs on
individual crafts intended for scientists and the Paris Académie des
Sciences had long been ruminating over a similar project for the
benefit of experts, but a survey of manual work undertaken for the
general reader was unheard of. It was not only new: a work that
was to contain every workman's tool but very little information on
kings, ruling houses, great battles, or saints was also revolutionary.

By implicitly shifting the balance away from the nobility and the lives of the great towards humble, often anonymous, manual work, Diderot, the son of a cutler, and d'Alembert, adopted by a glazier, intended to declare boldly, if not loudly, what was really important in the world.

Researching the articles and the plates dealing with the *arts et métiers* meant visiting dozens if not hundreds of tradesmen and master craftsmen in their workshops, observing them during their work and taking notes, asking questions, having their tools drawn and the working processes described and sketched, and then comparing representation and reality, correcting, refining. The draughtsmen had to be supervised, their designs corrected and then sent to be etched in plates that were to accompany and accommodate the text and which were to be grouped in chapters and equipped with descriptions of their own.

The *Encyclopédie*'s main draughtsman, Louis-Jacques Goussier (1722–99), also contributed articles, notably PAPETERIE, which he had written, in exemplary fashion, after spending several weeks drawing, studying, and listening to workers in a paper mill near Montargis. His main occupation, though, was the production of thousands of careful drawings from life, which were then scaled down before being passed on to the etchers who would prepare the plates.[19] Several states of these plates would then be submitted to Diderot, who would study them for their realism and level of detail. Finally, one of them would be marked by his hand *bon à tirer*, suitable for printing.

Goussier was a fascinatingly anarchic character and one of the very few Encyclopedists to come from a genuinely humble background: in 1759, his sister was employed as a maid, and one of his cousins was a coachman. Louis-Jacques himself was Paris-born. He lived the same bohemian existence as Diderot had done, supporting himself by teaching mathematics and helping scholars and researchers with their projects. It is possible that he had known Diderot as early as 1744: they moved in the same circles and had several acquaintances in common. In 1747 Goussier's involvement with the *Encyclopédie* became official. Diderot would send him on trips to the provinces to observe manufacturing processes and to draw and describe them.

One of the main problems of this painstaking process was that the objects of this enquiry were not always willing to cooperate, believing that those who were keen to learn all their secrets and see all their tools and workplaces must be there on other than encyclopedic business. Anyone writing an article on the mechanical arts, Diderot wrote despairingly,

> will learn, after having for some time gone from workshop to workshop with cash in his hand and after having paid dearly for the most preposterous misinformation, what sort of people craftsmen are, especially those at Paris, where the fear of taxes makes them perpetually suspicious, and where they look upon any person who interrogates them with any curiosity as an emissary of the tax farmers, or as a worker who wants to open shop.

As the *Encyclopédie* had no permanent office, Diderot's apartment became the main port of call for manuscripts, which now began to arrive by the hundred from all corners of France to be edited, corrected, and sent to the printers. The galley proofs would then be returned to be corrected.

At some point soon after his involvement with the project began, Diderot had an interview with the Chancellor Henri François D'Aguesseau (1668–1751) that was to influence the fate of the entire enterprise. This visit is attested to on the excellent authority of the later Chief Censor, Chrétien-Guillaume Lamoignon de Males-herbes (1721–94), who was to write forty years after the event:

> The plan [of the *Encyclopédie*] was concerted with the most virtuous and enlightened of magistrates, the Chancellor d'Aguesseau. M. Diderot was presented to him as that one of the authors who would have the greatest share in the work.
>
> This author was already marked, by many of the pious, for

his freedom of thought. However, the pious M. d'Aguesseau
wished to confer with him, and I know that he was enchanted
by certain marks of genius that shone forth in the conversation.[20]

This account indicates that the Chancellor met Diderot when he
was already the main editor, and it is therefore possible that, as the
project was growing, it was becoming apparent that the existing
privilège of 1746 authorizing the printing of an encyclopedia 'translated from the English Dictionary of Chambers and of Harris, with
some additions'[21] was no longer sufficient, and that the booksellers
would have to apply for a new one recognizing the scale of the
work. The visit would therefore have taken place just before the
granting of a second, modified *privilège* on 30 April 1748. The very
same Malesherbes, though, states elsewhere: 'The late Chancellor
had cognizance of this project [the *Encyclopédie*]. Not only did he
approve it, but he corrected it, reformed it, and chose M. Diderot
to be the principal editor of it.'[22]

This second statement suggests that it was d'Aguesseau who determined that the young Diderot should become the new editor, and
that the Chancellor himself – a stern man and a Jansenist of the
old school, but an excellent and principled administrator – decided
to widen the scope of what had been presented to him as nothing
more than an improved translation, and to give it into the hands
of the young nobody whose enthusiasm and intelligence had conquered him. This would mean that Diderot came to visit him before
signing his contract with the booksellers, and that d'Aguesseau
must be considered one of the fathers, albeit an unlikely one, of
the *Encyclopédie*. Diderot himself later went on record with a remark
that is as intriguing as it is cryptic: 'I protest that undertaking the
Encyclopédie was not of my choosing; that a word of honour, very
adroitly extracted and very unwisely granted, bound me over, hand
and foot, to this enormous task and to all the afflictions that have
accompanied it.'[23]

Perhaps Diderot did not really want to edit the *Encyclopédie*. It
is possible that the Chancellor, seeing before him a man of un-

deniable gifts, but one who in all likelihood had already been brought to his attention by his spies (literary Paris was small), pushed Diderot in a direction that the young writer, wanting to be an author, not an editor, did not want to take, but felt duty-bound to pursue in view of his young family. Diderot's remark was made in later life, when he saw in the *Encyclopédie* nothing but a multi-volume millstone around his artistic neck, and considering his emphatic manner of communicating it is very possible that the dramatic impetus of the sentence got the better of him. It is also possible that the 'word of honour' had less to do with editing the *Encyclopédie* than with not getting into trouble by penning any works of his own. Whatever happened in d'Aguesseau's office, and whatever promises were extracted from the young writer, Diderot was to be the Encyclopedist charged with publication until the last volume of plates appeared in 1771.

Benard Direx.

Antiquites, Catacombes de Naples.

PRISON

PRISON (*Hist. mod.*), this is what one calls a place for locking up people who are guilty or accused of a crime.

These places have probably been used since the origin of cities for maintaining order & for shutting away those who have caused trouble.

As the bishops have their own legal authority and a court of justice which is called the *officialité*, they also have *prisons* of the *officialité* for locking up clerics who are guilty or accused of a crime. One can distinguish various kinds among the secular *prisons*. There are those intended for imprisoning debtors like the Fort-l'Evêque in Paris, then there are those where one keeps thieves and murderers, like the Conciergerie, la Tournelle, the grand and the petit Châtelet in Paris, Newgate in London, &c. Finally there are state *prisons*, like the Bastille, Vincennes, Pierre Encisse, the castle of the Seven Towers in Constantinople, the Tower of London ...

On the morning of 24 July 1749, at half past seven in the morning, two police officers clambered up the narrow steps of the house in the rue de la Vieille Estrapade. They proceeded to search the house for manuscripts (of which there were many) and informed Diderot that he was under arrest. After having ransacked his study, they took him away in a hired coach. Denis tried to pretend to Toinette that he was merely being called away on business, but when she looked out of the window and saw him being escorted into the coach, she knew otherwise.

Diderot had been arrested by a *Lettre de cachet*, a particularly pernicious instrument of *ancien-régime* justice: a warrant signed by one of the King's ministers authorizing detention without stated reason, trial, or term. They were a formidably frightening and demoralizing institution, used especially against those who were making a nuisance of themselves, and it was rumoured that it was also possible to procure signed warrants with the names left blank, a very useful piece of paper to have in one's drawer. In Diderot's case, though, everything had gone through the proper channels. His nemesis had been once again Hardy de Levaré, the same curate of Saint-Médard who had denounced him earlier. This time, the Count d'Argenson, the Minister of War and Director of Publications (effectively the Censor-in-Chief), had written to the Lieutenant-General of Police asking him 'to give orders for putting M. Didrot [*sic*], author of the book on the Blind Man, in Vincennes'. Good as his information was in substance, the Count had only a vague idea not only of the spelling of the prisoner's name but also of his works, of which he cited not only the *Lettre sur les aveugles* (Letter on the Blind) but also the *Avenue of Ideas*, i.e. the *Sceptic's Walk*. It therefore seems safe to assume that he had not bothered to read either of them.

Meanwhile, Diderot was rattling out of Paris in a stagecoach, across the river, past the Bastille, and down the long rue Faubourg Saint-Antoine towards the medieval darkness of the Château de Vincennes, where he was handed over to the governor, François-Bernard du Châtelet, and promptly put into a cell in the central keep. The Château de Vincennes, now in a suburb of Paris, has lost little of its menacing air over the last centuries: a formidable fortress with a deep moat, a narrow drawbridge, and a forbidding keep rising high above the walls. It was later enlarged by a slightly less sinister structure with nine defensive towers rising above the surrounding forest, a veritable fortified town that served as royal residence, state dungeon, and military barracks. On the December folio of the Duc de Berry's famous *Très riches heures*, the Château is depicted as a graceful corona of towers rising proudly above the already leafless trees of a winter landscape in which hunters watch their dogs tearing into a wild boar; but even in the heat of July the keep looked anything but ornamental to its prisoners. To the young man in solitary confinement at its very heart, it soon became a living nightmare.

Diderot had brought this misery upon himself, as his father was quick to point out in a letter to his imprisoned son, adding that from now on he should pray to God and obey the King if he wanted to live a happy and contented life. It was true that Diderot had not prayed for a long time, and that it was his very opposition to religion that had brought him into his present situation.

With publication of the first volume of the *Encyclopédie* imminent, Diderot had had to face up to the fact that his name was going to look pitifully bare next to that of his co-editor on the title-page. D'Alembert was a member of the Académie des Sciences, was of noble birth (which mattered, even if on the wrong side of the blanket), and, the world agreed, a young scholar of immense promise, already author not only of the work on mechanics, but also, more recently, of a monograph on the causes of air currents and winds, which had won him an affiliate membership of the Prussian Academy in Berlin, the capital city of Voltaire's friend the 'Philosopher King', Frederick the Great.

Diderot himself was nobody and had nothing. He had published a few translations, an amusing and indecent novel, and a series of philosophical reflections, both anonymously, and a clutch of mathematical essays, which, though competent, had not exactly caused a sensation. His most recent effort to publish something of value, his *Sceptic's Walk*, had been impounded by the authorities and he had been warned that he was being watched. He was a member of no Academy, and was known only to his friends and the police.

Something must be done, he had felt, and done quickly. It is a testament to Diderot's determination that, aside from writing articles for the *Encyclopédie* and soliciting and editing others, from spending time in workshops and with his friends, he had still found time to write a philosophical work that, though short, was considered and well informed, his first coherent statement as a *philosophe*. In view of his experiences with censorship and denunciation, he had retreated to an area he thought safe from such intrusions: science. The result of this new approach was his *Lettre sur les aveugles* (Letter on the Blind). It was to make him famous, or infamous.

The occasion for this work was the case of a young girl, born blind, whose cataracts had been operated on by a Prussian physician and whose bandages were removed in front of invited guests, who marvelled at the spectacle of the girl seeing for the first time in her life. Diderot had requested to be present at the occasion, but had been refused. In his philosophical essay, he used the case to speculate on the perception of the world blind people have. He had also, he claimed, visited a man who was blind from birth and had discussed this problem with him. The blind man describes his 'view' of the world, a conception in which optical terms and metaphors have no meaning. A mirror is 'a machine . . . which puts things in relief far away from themselves, if they are placed in a convenient relationship with it';[1] when asked whether he would like to have his sight restored, the man, who has no real idea what this might mean, says that he would just as soon have longer arms with which to 'see' the world his way.

Diderot's work is, in Arthur Wilson's words, a 'steeplechase', and the reader, allowing himself to be led on 'over most of the various metaphysical jumps, finally gets himself soaked in the water hole called "Does God Exist?"'[2] Addressing the case of a blind Cambridge professor, Nicholas Saunderson, who taught optics, the young philosopher goes further and further into the labyrinth of philosophical implications of a world without vision. A blind person would evidently not have any instinctive shame of being naked, as he has never seen others without clothes, nor felt their glances upon him. What other differences might his inner world, his moral sense, have from that of sighted people? How can someone used to verifying the things around him by seeing them 'with his skin' accept the existence of anything as abstract as God? 'If you want me to believe in God, you must make me touch him,'[3] Diderot has Saunderson say.

The blind man become a metaphor for radical empiricism, for rational thought, obscured, paradoxically, by the dazzling world of vision, and the deceptively simple, conversational work makes a clear case for people who are in touch with a world of facts, and acknowledge that speculation on metaphysical matters outside the realm of their senses is just so much talk. Its author announced himself as a man who had read not only the important philosophers of his day, especially Descartes and Locke, but also scientists such as Newton and Saunderson (who was not yet translated) and who could write with equal ease about metaphysics, mathematics, physics, and theology. The book was published in 1749.

The first immediate consequence was a letter from Voltaire, to whom Denis had sent an advance copy. This was proof positive that he was being noticed by the right people, especially as an epistle from the exiled master was something of a semi-public act of blessing, even if it contained remonstrances about the all too radical way his young colleague had chosen. It also, however, lavished upon Denis a great deal of flattery, and an invitation to a 'philosophical luncheon'. Tasting at last the recognition he had so long craved, he responded effusively and at length, writing: 'the moment at which I received your letter was one of the sweetest of my life'.[4] The letter also contains a sudden, slightly rhetorical sigh, revealing something about its writer's state of mind: 'Oh, philosophy, philosophy: what are you good for, if you can neither soften the pricks of pain and annoyances, nor the sting of passion?'[5] It seems safe to say that the former applied to both his work and his domestic situation, while the latter was a reference to his still hotly felt infatuation with his mistress, Mme de Puisieux.

The second consequence of Diderot's philosophical daring was his incarceration. There was no escaping the mountainous walls of the medieval keep of the Château de Vincennes, and if Denis had thought that he would soon leave by other means he was forced to reconsider. All prisoners received two candles daily, and after two weeks in his vaulted, octagonal prison room, he had accumulated a considerable supply of them that he tried to return to his jailer. 'Keep them, keep them,' was the answer, 'you may have too many now, but they will be very useful in the winter!' It was early August, and the prisoner suddenly saw himself confronted with the possibility of indefinite incarceration without trial or sentence.

At a first interrogation, Denis learned from Berryer, the Lieuten-ant-General of Police, that the *Lettre sur les aveugles* was not the only work he had been arrested for and that he was suspected of having penned a whole raft of impious, immoral, and generally seditious works. Used to talking himself out of holes, he denied everything. His jailers, however, had a powerful argument against which even his famous wit and eloquence were powerless: time.

Diderot, the endlessly and effusively communicative and talkative Diderot, who was always out with his friends debating and dis-cussing, dining, seeing his mistress, or watching chess players in the cafés, quickly despaired of the isolation of his solitary confine-ment. His spirit, which later proved so indomitable while editing the *Encyclopédie* in the direst of circumstances, was crushed by the silence of the surrounding walls and by the perspective of indefinite imprisonment; indeed, Condorcet later related that his friend was almost driven crazy. He began writing letters to Berryer and to Count d'Argenson, masterworks of grovelling that also bespeak real fear:

> Monseigneur
>
> An honourable man who has had the misfortune to incur the disgrace of the ministry implores your clemency and your protection. From the Château de Vincennes, where he has been held for twenty days, and where he is dying of physical pain and misery of the mind, he throws himself at your feet and asks for his freedom. He is despairing of the mistakes he has made and quite resolved never to make others. A few instances of men-tal intemperance are all he can be accused of.[6]

Having spent sufficient time at the minister's boots, the eloquent prisoner then appeals to the lofty realms of his mind, promising to put his every effort into finishing the *Encyclopédie*, on which, he writes, he has been working 'for three entire years'. He then turns bargainer and offers the only bribe a writer can – eternity:

> Alas, Monseigneur, when he was driven to this prison, he was at the point of publishing the prospectus and of soliciting of

Your Grandeur the permission to publish under his auspices
this work undertaken for the glory of France and the shame
of England, worthy, perhaps, at least from this point of view,
of being offered to a minister and protector of letters and
those who cultivate them.[7]

Denis was not the only one working for his freedom. His friends
were writing letters to people in high places, and the booksellers
did their utmost to protect their investment. On 24 July, the day
of the arrest itself, the account book of the syndicate lists: 'For
carriage fees in the morning and after dinner in order to solicit
for M. Diderot, 7 [*livres*] 7 [*sous*].'[8] On the same day, they sent a
letter to Argenson:

We take the liberty to put ourselves under the protection of
Your Grandeur and to present to you the misfortune into which
we are plunged by the detention of M. Diderot, driven this
morning to Vincennes on the King's orders. This man of letters
is of recognized merit and probity, and for almost five years
now he has been charged by us with the edition of a *Dictionnaire
universel des sciences, des arts et métiers*. This work, which will cost
us at least two hundred and fifty thousand *livres* and on which
we have already spent some eighty thousand *livres*, was at the
point of being announced to the public. The detention of M.
Diderot, the only man of letters we know capable of such a vast
enterprise and the possessor of the key to the entire operation,
could result in our ruin.[9]

The booksellers were not exaggerating. The sum of 250,000 *livres* is
equivalent to roughly two million pounds sterling in today's money.
Historical comparisons of financial value are always difficult
because the purchase power was very different in a very different
economy; but for the sake of illustration, the sum of eighty thousand
livres that the booksellers claimed to have laid out already was the
equivalent of the annual income of eight hundred farms.

Eventually, the *Encyclopédie* was to become more expensive, and
much more lucrative, than the booksellers had thought. At its high

point, it was to employ a thousand printers, etchers, draughtsmen, bookbinders, and others, meaning that almost one out of every hundred Parisians benefited from the enterprise financially, directly or indirectly. As correction of the galleys of the first volume, which appeared exactly two years later, was already under way when the booksellers wrote to d'Argenson (Diderot had been approached by a messenger boy with proof sheets as he was hustled into the carriage that took him to Vincennes), it seems fair to say that at least part of this magnitude was already visible. The Director of Publications would have understood that the *Encyclopédie* had not only ideological ramifications for Church and State, but also economic ones for the French, and more specifically the Parisian, book trade. Prisoner Diderot was therefore more than a mere hack to be silenced.

While his friends were petitioning on his behalf, Denis himself was so worn down by his imprisonment that he decided to confess everything. On 13 August, only three days after his letters to Berryer and d'Argenson in which he avoided admitting to anything specific, he wrote to the Lieutenant-General again:

Monsieur

My pains have been pushed as far as possible. The body is exhausted, the spirit crushed, the soul penetrated by suffering. . . . I will therefore cede to the high opinion I and the entire Enlightened world have conceived of you, to the ascendant which you always take over other minds by virtue of your superior talents and the singular qualities of your heart and your mind . . . and to the extreme confidence I have in the word of honour which you gave me that you would not be insensible to my remorse and to the sincere promise I am making you now never again to publish anything without having submitted it to your judgment first . . .

I therefore admit to my worthy protector something that the long days of a prison and all imaginable tortures could never have made me tell a judge: that the *Pensées*, the *Indiscreet Jewels*, and the *Letter on the Blind* are moments of intemperance of the spirit that have escaped me . . .[10]

In the same letter he also claimed that another minor work of his, *L'Oiseau blanc, contre bleu,* was in fact not by him but by a lady whom his feeling of honour forbade him to name, and that he had merely corrected it.

The confession had an immediate effect. Within a week, Beyrrer had ordered the Marquis du Châtelet, the prison governor, that Diderot was to be released from the keep itself and given the freedom of the larger enclosure.

> His Majesty also saw fit, in view of the editing work with which he is charged, to allow him freely to communicate by writing or orally in the château, with the customary precautions, with persons from the outside who come there either for that purpose or for his domestic affairs . . . You will have the goodness to have assigned to him in the château one or two commodious rooms for sleeping and working, with a bed and such other furniture as you customarily furnish to prisoners in the keep, and nothing more, reserving for him to procure greater conveniences at his own expense if he desires them.[11]

Diderot signed a declaration promising not to leave the château and enclosure, on pain of being incarcerated for the rest of his life. After one month, the ordeal of solitary confinement without visits had come to an end, but at a price. Not only had he admitted to authorship of forbidden works, which the police had never doubted in any case, he had also promised the Chief of Police never again to publish anything without submitting it to censorship or else gladly submit himself to indefinite imprisonment. Diderot had decades to repent at leisure this promise he had given in haste, and for the rest of his career he worked under the shadow of the knowledge that somewhere in the drawers of His Majesty's Government was a piece of paper that could be used against him at any moment; that he could never again write freely without having to fear a repeat of his solitary terrors, this time without any hope of release. Before even having embarked on any of the ambitious philosophical works he had wanted to write, he now found himself condemned to silence.

While Denis saw his future as a writer in grave peril, his life at Vincennes improved considerably. Du Châtelet (a relative of Voltaire's mistress, Mme du Châtelet, who may have put in a word for the young freethinker) seemed glad to have animated company and had given him rooms in his own residence. He often invited his prisoner to dine with him. Friends came to sympathize, and work on the *Encyclopédie* could continue. Toinette often visited and may even have stayed with her husband for some of the time. A note from du Châtelet to Berryer shows that his prisoner was kept in every possible comfort: 'He has gone out three times in the evenings for an hour with his wife in the park. He is well. Many people come to work with him, but I believe he is unable to get much done here.'[12]

Among the stream of visitors, friends, well-wishers, collaborators on the *Encyclopédie*, printers, and others, was Diderot's closest friend at the time, Jean-Jacques Rousseau. 'Nothing can ever describe the anguish that my friend's misfortune made me feel. My dark imaginings, which always lead me from bad to worse, sent me into a state of panic. I believed he was to stay there for the rest of his life.'[13]

Jean-Jacques took to visiting his friend regularly, and his long walks to Vincennes (he could not afford a carriage) were to assume a significance all of their own. He had been active over the past few months and had collected a considerable circle of powerful acquaintances, first and foremost the rich Mme Dupin, for whom he was working as a secretary and who introduced him to the Prince of Saxe-Gotha, and other aristocrats. Diderot had remained intentionally and obstinately aloof from society (in his letters to d'Argenson he lists as people who can vouch for him several who were famous in intellectual circles, such as the naturalist de Buffon, d'Alembert, the philosopher Helvétius, and Voltaire, but no one of great social cachet and not one member of the high aristocracy). D'Alembert accepted it all as his birthright. But Rousseau, though he would not have admitted it, worked society with all his might.

On hearing that Diderot was no longer held in the dungeons and was now allowed to receive visitors, Rousseau immediately set out on his way. D'Alembert and a local cleric were with Denis, and Jean-Jacques found his friend very marked by the experience of the past weeks: 'The dungeon had left a terrible impression on him, and despite the fact that he had very agreeable rooms in the château and was allowed even to go for walks in the park [of Vincennes] which is not enclosed, he needed the company of his friends so that he would not fall into black moods.'[14] The first meeting was an occasion of great joy for both friends, and Rousseau, never less than demonstrative, did nothing to conceal his emotion: 'When I entered, I saw only him, and I leapt towards him, cried out, and pressed my face to his, embraced him closely, without speaking to him with anything but my tears and my sobs.' If Jean-Jacques, however, was all emotion, Diderot's first thought, according to Rousseau's *Confessions* at least, was not his friend, but the world at large; when released from the embrace, 'he turned to the cleric and told him "You see, monsieur, how my friends love me!"'[15]

Jean-Jacques was amply rewarded for the hardship of his long walks. He found the real key to future greatness on the dusty road to Vincennes, and not in the salons he had frequented so eagerly. It was somewhere between Paris and the prison that he was walking one stifling summer's day, alone in the heat of the afternoon and almost fainting with fatigue. He sat down by the roadside to rest and began to read a newspaper he had taken with him (perhaps for Denis), the *Mercure de France*. In it he found a prize question for an essay, proposed by the Academy of Sciences in Dijon. The question was: 'Do the Sciences and the Arts Contribute to Corrupting or to Improving Morals?' It was obviously the question the young Rousseau needed to be asked: 'Within an instant of reading this,' he remembered later, 'I saw another universe and became another man.' Rousseau had found the passion that was to dictate the remainder of his intellectual life and that was to make him one of the spiritual fathers of Romanticism: the destructive influence of civilization on every human being. In his *Confessions*, he finds a curious way of both crediting and blaming Diderot for this: 'I remember distinctly that I arrived at Vincennes in a state of great agitation, almost delirium. Diderot noticed this; I told him the

reason and he . . . exhorted me to let my ideas soar and to compete
for the prize. I did this, and from this moment I was lost. The
entire remainder of my life and my unhappiness was the inevitable
effect of this moment of ecstasy.'[16] This 'moment of ecstasy' was,
in a way, Jean-Jacques's rebirth. The famous *Correspondance Litteraire*,
written by Rousseau's friend, Friedrich Melchior Grimm, summar-
izes his career up to this point as follows:

> M. Rousseau had come back to Paris, indigent, unknown,
> ignorant of his talents and his resources . . . He took up music
> and verse. He published a dissertation on how to note down
> music in ciphers. Nobody was interested and it was not read
> by anyone. He then composed the words and the music of an
> opera, *les Muses galantes*, which could never be performed
> . . . [and he] also wrote very bad poems, some of which were
> published in the *Mercure*. He wrote comedies, of which most
> never saw the light of day. He also tried to build a machine
> which, he thought, would allow him to fly, but without
> success . . .[17]

It was obvious that Rousseau's plans had been taking flight only in
his dreams. He was already in his forties, and his friends agreed
that his true vocation still eluded him. The theme of the Dijon
competition, however, seemed to have galvanized him. He wrote
an impassioned essay on the topic and sent it off. He was awarded
the first prize on 9 July 1750. From total obscurity and destitution,
M. Rousseau had suddenly become someone much talked about
in intellectual circles, one of the great hopes of literary Paris. He
revelled in the attention, and, typically for a man who was never
anything but contrary, he quit his position with his patroness, Mme
Dupin, to live entirely off copying sheet music. His friend Grimm
joked that he should become a lemonade seller at the Place du
Palais-Royal: 'This idea amused us for quite a while, and it was no
more extravagant than his own'.[18] Rousseau, however, preferred
the elevation of a garret to a life among the crowds.

While Rousseau was all exaltation and contradiction, d'Alembert,
who was now effectively managing editor of the *Encyclopédie*, took

a surprisingly cool stance in the face of Diderot's imprisonment. His reaction to this first setback makes it likely that he was never an active participant in the actual editing process of the *Encyclopédie*, and that he was already feeling ambivalent towards it. His scientific career, after all, was taking him in different directions. He was at the peak of his intellectual productivity and was working on differential equations and on problems of physical astronomy, as well as corresponding with the best mathematicians of his day and writing on epistemology. A pugnacious man who had quickly discovered that politics and polemic could be useful tools in mathematical research, much of his energy was taken up with scientific quarrels with mathematical colleagues, notably Alexis Claude Clairaut, a rival at the Academy, with whom d'Alembert traded insults in the scientific papers of the day. The *Encyclopédie* was certainly important to him, but only as part of a wider range of activities, and he made it abundantly clear that he would do little more than write articles and have his name associated with the project:

> I have never really had much of an inclination to meddle in anything concerning [the *Encyclopédie*] apart from the mathematical and astronomical sections; I am not able to do anything but this, and I have not the least intention of condemning myself to six years' worth of boredom bound in 7 or 8 folios. I rely on the fact that as soon as M. Diderot is freed (which seems to be quite soon by all appearances), we will work on the prospectus and will put it on the printing press soon afterwards.[19]

As d'Alembert felt disinclined to perform the thousand little tasks his co-editor had been fulfilling for the last four years, the operation was practically in abeyance, with only a small portion of the work being done by Diderot at Vincennes. He could no longer visit workshops or go and talk to contributors. This, as the booksellers remarked in their letter to d'Argenson, was a considerable handicap. More than that, the sheer complexity of the enterprise simply required the main editor's presence. Their letter gives a good impression of Diderot's now dormant day-to-day editing work:

> The articles which are sent in demand at least his presence in Paris, in reach of their authors. His work here is mainly the revision and the comparison of different parts of the work. . . . If sieur Diderot is obliged to work at Vincennes, he will be deprived of the necessary means, especially as men of letters find it difficult to move about and it would be necessary to agree eventual changes by correspondence – an endless affair . . .

Apart from the quotidian drudgery of receiving texts of varying quality and having to call on the authors to convince, flatter, or threaten them into accepting changes, there was the even greater problem that many of the articles (though the booksellers may not even have known this themselves) were not yet written at all.

The illustrations proved a herculean labour. Their sheer number, and their thousands of tiny details, required a constant trade-off of space against clarity. The printers had to be constantly supervised, especially when it came to subjects they did not know themselves – which was most of them:

> Sieur Diderot has an intelligent draughtsman come to Vincennes, Goussier. They wanted to work together on the reduction [to scale] of the designs, but as they did not have the objects in front of their eyes, they did not know which size to accord to them on the page. When it comes to explaining the illustrations the situation is even more difficult, as many of the tools look alike, and it is necessary to have them in front of one, otherwise it would be very easy to mistake one for another and to get lost in a labyrinth of very gross errors . . .

The booksellers were aware that the greatest challenge lay in the scale and nature of the *Encyclopédie* itself. Not only was the conception, despite or because of its underlying alphabetical simplicity, extraordinarily complex to put into practice. If the work had to be edited elsewhere, it would have been necessary to move Diderot's study, and that would almost certainly have been impossible in view of tens of thousands of pieces of paper and hundreds of books, a chaos of information comprehensible only to its owner, constantly at risk of being jumbled up and becoming entirely useless – and, most of all, impossible to transport to Vincennes in its entirety.

While the booksellers were trying to argue Diderot out of his arrest, his friends, too, did their utmost. Jean-Jacques Rousseau even wrote to the King's mistress, Mme de Pompadour, but his letter remained unanswered. Denis himself had, for the time being, established a relatively convenient working routine in the enforced idyll of the governor's residence. As he was kicking his heels with Toinette and their little son François-Jacques-Denis (who was to die a year later), his legend began to grow. During his first month of imprisonment in the castle keep, he had not been allowed writing materials and had improvised a pen with a toothpick and ink out of wine and soot, both of which he had used to compose an 'Apology of Socrates' into the margins of Milton's *Works*, which he had with him. The image of the *philosophe* languishing in the dungeons, a true Socrates, cast out from society and yet pursuing his calling against all odds, spread quickly throughout France and beyond. Voltaire, more than two hundred miles away, wrote about the case only a few days after Diderot's imprisonment, and all of Paris was talking about it, from the literary circles and the cafés right up to princes and ministers. The hard-working editor of the *Encyclopédie* was experiencing an apotheosis and becoming more than a famous man: he was becoming a symbol.

His incarceration was not, in fact, any more arbitrary or more unjust than that of other writers at the time. During the very month of his arrest, several Jansenists had been exiled or sent to the Bastille for criticizing the corruption of the Church; the writer Jacques le Blanc was arrested for publishing a deist work of philosophy, *Le Tombeau des préjugés*; and the young Pidansat de Mairobert was thrown into prison on 27 June for the sole reason of having complained a little too loudly at the Café Procope (also an Encyclopedist haunt) about the recent military reforms – he, too, was to remain imprisoned for a year.[20] Somehow, though, undoubtedly aided by the intervention of people like d'Alembert and Voltaire, it was Diderot's case that struck a chord with the public imagination, while the others were forgotten, or even went unnoticed.

Diderot's imprisonment made his name and, almost overnight, transformed a young writer into a figurehead of the French Enlightenment, a Socrates who was seen to suffer for his convictions. The price he had paid for his fame, however, was enormous: in the drawers of the Minister of War was his assurance never again to write anything contentious, on pain of being locked up for the rest of his life.

Denis was to keep this promise not to publish an important work of philosophy or literature in his lifetime, and he would suffer from it. By making it, he had destroyed his career of choice. He could have gone abroad of course (as Voltaire had done, and dozens of other writers), but there was his obligation to the booksellers, and there were his family, his friends, and Paris with its theatres, cafés, and life. Leaving all this would have been too much. When he was released, therefore, on 3 November after only six months of imprisonment – an outcome that he almost certainly owed to his position as editor of a commercially valuable enterprise – he went back to the rue de la Vieille Estrapade, to an office where shelves and desk were groaning under the weight of countless sheets of paper. The *Encyclopédie* was about to swallow up every minute of his time.

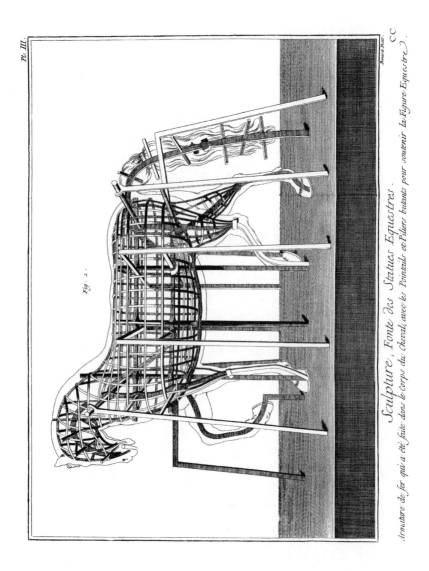

Pl. III.

Fig. 1.

Sculpture, Fonte des Statues Equestres.

Armature de fer qui a été faite dans le corps du cheval, avec les Printaux et Piliers butants pour soutenir la Figure Equestre.

Benard Fecit.

PHILOSOPHE

PHILOSOPHE, s. m. Nothing is easier nowadays than to be called a *philosophe*; a life lived in obscurity, a few profound utterances, a little reading are enough to fool those who bestow this name on people who do not merit it.

For others, freedom of thought has taken the place of reasoning, and they think themselves the only true *philosophes* as they have dared to throw off the sacred ties of religion and have broken the shackles with which faith constricts reason. Proud of having rid themselves of the prejudices of their religious education, they disdain others as weak souls, servile geniuses, lily-livered minds, who let themselves be frightened by the results of irreligion and do not dare to step out of the circle of established wisdom, walk new paths, & who finally fall asleep under the yoke of superstition.

But one has to form a fairer assessment of the *philosophe*, and this is the character we ourselves ascribe to him:

Other people are determined to act and to feel and not to know the causes of their movement, or even to dream of them. The *philosophe*, however, disentangles things as far as possible, & foresees them & submits himself knowingly: he is, so to say, a watch that sometimes winds itself up on its own . . . other men are carried by their passions, without their actions being preceded by reflection; they walk in the shadows of torment. The *philosophe* acts not out of his passions, but after reflection; he travels at night, but a flame precedes him.

While Diderot was trying to direct the encyclopedic enterprise from the enforced rural idyll of Vincennes, a young German, one of many who came to Paris to make their fortune or to gain a cultural polish that their own, more rural country could not offer them, was beginning to find his way around the streets of the capital. As yet unknown to Diderot, the young Friedrich Melchior Grimm (1723–1807) was to become not only his most intimate friend but also the propagandist of the *Encyclopédie*, as well as an enigmatic and elusive critic, journalist, and diplomatic entrepreneur.

The son of a Protestant pastor in Regensburg, in southern Germany, Grimm had come to Paris in late 1748 or early 1749 in the service of his childhood friend, the Count of Schomberg. He had changed employer and was now living as secretary of another German count and had been introduced to Rousseau at a garden party. They discovered their shared taste for Italian music and soon became firm friends, meeting frequently to discuss music and sing Italian arias with Grimm or Rousseau at the cembalo.

In the summer of 1750 Jean-Jacques was the talk of the town after having been awarded the essay prize by the Dijon Academy. It was about this time that he quit the employment of Mme Dupin to glory in his new-found independence, which he celebrated by selling his watch (he would never again have to wonder about the time, he said) and by exchanging his courtly attire of white stockings, brocaded coat, and powdered wig for more workmanlike clothes and a wig without a pigtail, as worn by abbés. He was no stranger to somewhat radical decisions when it came to making time for his writing, as he himself relates in the *Confessions*: 'My third child was therefore put into the orphanage, as had been the two first and as would be the two after it, as I had five in all. This arrangement seemed to me so good, so reasonable, so legitimate, that I would have boasted of it openly, were it not for respect towards their mother.'[1] According to his own testimony, though, he did take it upon himself to inform all his closest friends proudly of having found a progressive solution to being kept awake by crying babies. Later, when he made his name as a philosopher of education and described the ideal harmony between a good father and his daughter in his famous novel *Émile*, this boast would come back to haunt him. His friend Denis Diderot, a father three times over, though to his sadness and that of Toinette all three had died, could little understand such an attitude.

While Rousseau was rearranging his family and delighting in throwing off the yoke of servitude for a life of honest, if slightly engineered, simplicity, his new friend Grimm took the opposite route and discovered Parisian fashions with great enthusiasm. His fondness for white, perfumed face powder earned him the nickname *tyran le blanc* (the White Tyrant) among his friends, who had borrowed it from a fifteenth-century Catalonian poem recently translated into French in which one of the characters was Tirant lo Blanch. Grimm took to the sophisticated life of Paris society with its salons, antechambers, and ballrooms like a fish to perfumed water, certainly helped by his astounding proficiency in French. A generation later, Goethe, then a student in Strasbourg, would be informed that 'all endeavours by a foreigner to speak French were doomed to failure. One is tolerated, but is never received into the bosom of the only church of language. Only a few exceptions were granted. They named to us a Herr von Grimm.'[2] Herr von Grimm (the 'von' being a later addition) would eventually write one of the most influential French publications of the time and would give up writing German altogether.

Jean-Jacques took it upon himself to introduce his German friend to his own friends and to Paris society, to which he had only recently gained access himself, very probably as one of the curious hangers-on tolerated by the rich to provide amusement and occasional opportunities for charity. Rewriting the events after his rupture with the Encyclopedists, Rousseau's account of this introduction into society already bears subversive traits, one of them being his characterization of Grimm's socializing: 'All my friends became his, that was very simple, but none of his ever became mine, which was less straightforward.'[3]

Grimm, the calculating White Tyrant, unleashed a storm of affection in Denis Diderot. A close friendship between a man who detested the world of the high aristocracy and one who made his career out of serving it seems strange, but their characters are not as easily summarized as that. Grimm especially was a complex man, and later his profession as a freelance ambassador for German princes (and, eventually, the Tsarina, Catherine the Great) did not hinder him from holding and articulating very forthright and enlightened opinions to his friends, and even to his employers, indicating to all that true nobility was of the mind. He was also a very witty man ('How dare this Bohemian have more wit than we do?' demanded Voltaire after reading one of his essays) whose literary judgement was feared and appreciated in equal measure and whose views were often far ahead of his time. A lifelong bachelor who spent some years living with a talented writer, Louise d'Épinay, he wrote of the fate of women:

> All the faults one can reproach them of are the work of men, and of society, especially of a misconceived education. Should one really be surprised to see them artificial, hypocritical, and deceitful, if all our efforts are directed towards nourishing in them the very sentiments which the unjust laws of a chimaera-like propriety command them to hide? Always oscillating between emotions authorized by nature and the conventions which bizarre traditions have elevated into duties, how are they expected to escape that labyrinth where all that is real and natural is sacrificed to what is imaginary and constructed? . . . Just out of the convent [where they are indoctrinated] they find themselves on the arm of a stranger with whom, they are informed, their destiny is linked by eternal and unbreakable bonds . . . and the victim is immolated on the man's desires.[4]

With convictions like this, Grimm would not have been out of place among the more forward-thinking writers of the 1970s.

Grimm, a servant and counsellor to the nobility, may have furnished 'rather elaborate proof that he knew which side his bread was buttered on'[5] in later life, but in a time when patronage was the only way out for a bright young man who had the misfortune not to be born a nobleman, this may be forgiven, and he must be credited with always maintaining an ironic perspective on his own work and with always using his influence to promote and defend the interests of his less well connected friends.

Diderot found in this very different character a kindred spirit –
more than that: 'I love Grimm,' he wrote to his later mistress and
soulmate, Sophie Volland, when Grimm was in Geneva. 'In other
circumstances my heart would be enveloped in one thought: to
find him and to embrace him. With what impatience have I been
waiting for this man, so dear to me! Now, however, I hardly think
of it. You are the only person occupying my mind.'[6] A few days
later, after Grimm had returned, Denis wrote again to Sophie:

> What a pleasure it was to find him back! With what warmth
> we hugged each other! My heart was quite adrift. I could not
> speak, and neither could he. We kissed without saying a word,
> and I wept. We had not waited [for him]. We had already been
> at dessert, when the message came: 'It's Monsieur Grimm –
> It's Monsieur Grimm!' I myself shouted these words, leapt up
> and ran towards him, and was already around his neck. He sat
> down. He ate badly, I think. As for me, I could no longer get
> my teeth apart, neither for talking nor for eating. He was close
> to me. I held his hand and looked at him.[7]

Despite all the reflexes of our own time, there is no evidence at all
that Grimm and Diderot were lovers; in his expansive soul his
mistress and confidante occupied the same place as his best male
friend, and his demonstrations of affection were as overwhelmingly
generous (and jealous) towards him as they were towards her, with
the one difference that Sophie and Denis also shared a bed.

Denis had taken up the reigns of his old life, and of the *Encyclopédie*. There were enormous amounts of work to catch up with, articles
and correspondence, as well as the preparation of the *Prospectus*,
which was finally to announce the work to the public and to invite
subscriptions. All this still left time for friends, for writing, for a
thousand things. Grimm later commented on this personal and
intellectual profligacy:

> M. Diderot's genius resembled one of those sons of a rich
> family who, raised in the bosom of the greatest opulence,
> believe the fountain of their wealth to be inexhaustible and

thus impose no limit whatsoever on their fantasies, no order
on their expense. There would have been no height of excel-
lence to which this genius could not have risen, no enterprise
too great for its forces if he had only directed it towards a
single object and reserved for the perfection of his own works
all the efforts expended ceaselessly for whoever came asking
him for his help, or his advice, or his expertise![8]

Less extravagantly talented than his close friend, but wiser and
more methodical in his own career, the White Tyrant could only
watch as Diderot seemed to squander his endowments, to invest
them in the smallest details of the *Encyclopédie*, in day-long visits to
workshops and descriptions of the humblest and most humdrum
things, in correspondences, meddling with other people's affairs
and arranging this and that for friends (it was he who saw to it
that Rousseau's essay appeared in print) and in seemingly quixotic
projects not worthy of his mind.

The enlarged circle of friends, Diderot, Rousseau, Grimm, and
also the literary journalist Abbé Raynal and the rich and ebullient
anti-religious writer Baron d'Holbach (another German), would
meet, usually *chez* Jean-Jacques, to talk, to drink, to play the harpsichord and sing, and to talk more, until morning broke and they
heard the peasant carts returning from their deliveries of fruit and
vegetables to the great market at Les Halles, close to Rousseau's
lodgings at the Palais-Royal. It was a curious group: the editor of a
dictionary who had been in prison for his literary ambitions, a
failed musician who had just published an attack on a society he
had rejected with a grand gesture and whose adoration he craved,
a somewhat foppish German secretary of some count or other, a
journalist, and a robust atheist and amateur philosopher who could
have bought them all out a hundred times over. D'Alembert was
missing at the table – he was the star of Mme Geoffrin's salon and
increasingly less a part of the social circle around Diderot, whose
warmth and eloquent effervescence made him the natural centre
of every assembly.

More and more often the friends would meet at Baron d'Holbach's grand house in the rue Royale Saint-Roche, and also in the houses of the German aristocrats Count Friese (Grimm's employer), Count Schomberg, the Prince of Saxe-Gotha, and others, who had come to Paris to gain the *mondaine* elegance and polish their provincial courts could not afford them. Their entertainments were not only intellectual and musical: once they visited the preceptor and chaplain of the Prince of Saxe-Gotha, a certain Klüppfel, who happened to live with a prostitute – this was Paris, after all – and who insisted that both Rousseau and Grimm partake of her professional and private charms. Grimm, though no stranger to the whorehouses of the suburbs, was taken aback and later told his friends that he had gone in and shared a bed with the girl to keep up appearances, but that nothing had happened between them.

Meanwhile, preparations for the *Prospectus* were progressing apace, and in November 1750 Diderot, d'Alembert, and the associated booksellers could finally announce to the world at large the forthcoming publication of the great work, projected to run to ten volumes, to be published at intervals of six months, paid by subscriptions of 60 *livres* on account and then a further 36 *livres* for the first volume, 24 for numbers ii to viii, and 40 *livres* for the last two volumes consisting of some 600 illustrations and their explanations; 280 *livres* in all (equivalent to some £2,250), payable over five years. When, more than a quarter century later, a disgruntled subscriber, Luneau de Boisgermain, sued the booksellers for breach of contract, he could point out to them that by then the work, in twenty-eight volumes instead of ten, and published over a much longer period, had cost him and the other subscribers 980 *livres*.

The *Prospectus* was printed with an enormously large run of 8,000, and began, as the historian John Lough writes, with a 'whopping lie':[9] 'The work we are announcing is no longer a work to be done. The manuscript and the drawings are complete.' Considering that the articles for volumes viii to xvii were not ready for press until 1765, this was stretching credulity a little. The statement of editorial policy, however, drew readers in with its astonishing breadth and ambition. The work, it claimed, would have no less an aim than that of

> indicating the connections, both remote and near, of the beings that compose Nature and which have occupied the attention of mankind; of showing, by interlacing of the roots and branches, the impossibility of knowing well any parts of this whole without ascending or descending to many others; of forming a general picture of the efforts of the human mind in all fields and every century; of presenting these objects with clarity; of giving to each of them its appropriate length, and, if possible of substantiating by our success our epigraph:
>
>> So great is the power of order and arrangement;
>> So much Grace may be imparted to a common theme.[10]

The *Encyclopédie* had come a long way from a simple translation. From the general, the author of the *Prospectus*, Diderot himself, went proudly to the particular, and to what he considered one of the strongest points of the work, the *arts et métiers*:

> Everything accordingly impelled us to have recourse to the workers themselves. We went to the cleverest ones in Paris and in the kingdom. We took the pains of going into their workshops, of questioning them, of writing under their dictation, of developing their thoughts, of educing from them the terms peculiar to their profession, of drawing up tables of such terms, of defining them, of conversing with those persons from whom we had obtained memoranda and (an almost indispensable precaution) of rectifying, in long and frequent conversations with some, what others had imperfectly, obscurely, or unfaithfully explained.[11]

The accompanying sample article, ÂME (Soul), slyly drew the attention of closer readers to the actual purpose of the *Encyclopédie*, as well as to one of the strategies it would employ. The article itself was written by Abbé Yvon and was a rather orthodox explanation of concepts of the human soul, proceeding with plodding precision to give a selection of philosophical opinions:

> **SOUL,** s. f. *Ord. encycl. Entend. Rais. Philos. or Science of spirits, of God, of the Angels, of the Soul.* One means by *soul* a given principle of knowledge [connaissance] & of sentiment. Several questions have to be discussed here: 1. what is its origin: 2. what is its nature: 3. what is its destiny: 4. which are the beings in which it resides.

No doctor of theology could object to any of this; it was all good practice as taught at the Sorbonne and at every theological seminary. The following article, or rather dissertation (20,000 words in all), might have been mildly problematic in that it placed too great an emphasis on the differing opinions of Greek and Roman philosophers as well as the Church Fathers. But all the arguments proffered were accepted and acceptable, apart from perhaps a worryingly thorough explication of the Spinozan conception of the soul, though at least this confirmed deist and converted Jew, a suspect individual indeed, was called 'the all-too-famous' Spinoza. There might also be rather too much about heathen conceptions of the soul; but it was, after all, an encyclopedia with a certain obligation not only to impart dogma, but also information. It might have quoted not only Plato, Aristotle, and St Augustine but also objectionable characters such as Epicurus, Hobbes, and Spinoza, but it ended up refuting them.

Then, however, came the cheeky asterisk, marking, as it does throughout the first seven volumes of the *Encyclopédie*, a contribution by Diderot, who added to the already lengthy investigation a consideration of the important question of where in the body the soul might be located, a subject that had much exercised the Scholastic philosophers in the Middle Ages. After letting several hypotheses and wildly unlikely locations pass by the reader's increasingly bewildered eye, he employs a ruse that had served him well in the *Lettre sur les aveugles*, and gives a case study describing a peasant who had received a heavy blow on the head and had lost part of his brain but not his reason, indicating that the soul does not reside in the brain. He also proves that Descartes must have been wrong in thinking that the pineal gland was the seat of the immortal soul by citing a case of a man who had lost his, and lived.

Another case recounted the story of a young man hit on his parietal bone, on the side of the skull, who subsequently lost his senses and suffered terribly (not least at the hands of the doctors treating him) until an abscess was removed that had formed on top of his brain. The young man recovered completely, but would lose his reason again as soon as another substance or object was introduced where the abscess had been between brain and skull. From this Diderot draws the following conclusion:

> Here we have it: the soul is installed in the bony matter, until some other experiment comes along and displaces it once again, in which case the physiologists would once more be reduced to not knowing where to put it. In the meantime, consider how its functions are dependent on tiny things: some disturbed tissue; a drop of blood spilled; a light inflammation; a fall; a concussion; & *adieu* judgement, reason, & all those qualities of which men are so proud, for all this pride depends on a filament placed well or badly, healthy or diseased.[12]

For those with eyes to see (and with the patience to plough through to this point), all was open, all was in question; the existence and nature of the human soul itself, which people had to take holy communion in order to save, the opinions of the philosophers and, by implication, the teaching of the Church itself, were rendered irrelevant by a simple blood clot.

France was in no way prepared for this. This was the *ancien régime* at its most *ancien.* A young metropolitan intellectual who stuck his head above the parapet to doubt publicly the existence of the human soul could only do so, and remain at large with his head safely on his shoulders, if he either did it from abroad or did it so skilfully and so obliquely that most of his readers would miss it altogether.

The *Encyclopédie* promised great things, quite apart from its already implied irreverence, and there was a decided flutter of excitement throughout educated France. Literary journals wrote at length about the project and printed excerpts from the *Prospectus*, and six months later, when the first volume appeared, more than a thousand subscribers had committed themselves to the associated booksellers. At the end of 1751, the number of subscribers had risen to 2,619, and would continue to rise.

In the anonymous article PHILOSOPHE, the author, probably Diderot himself, would write: 'The *philosophe* acts not out of his passions, but after reflection; he travels at night, but a flame precedes him.' Another of his writings completes the metaphor: 'Wandering in a vast forest at night, I have only a faint light to guide me. A stranger appears and says to me: "My friend, you should blow out your candle in order to find your way more clearly." This stranger is a theologian.'[13]

Diderot had constructed a huge engine to fight superstition, bigotry, the Church, everything hated by himself and by his friends, everything that had circumscribed his life as a young abbé only ten years earlier. Now it was time to go to war.

Benard Direx.

Antiquités, Apothéose d'Homere.

B

CONTROVERSY

---

* **CONTROVERSE**, s. f. a dispute, in writing or *viva voce*, about religious matters. We read in the dictionnaire de Trévoux that there is no reason to fear that the peace of Christianity be disturbed by these disputes, and that nothing is more conducive to turn those who are on the wrong way back to the true faith: two truths we feel obliged to honour in our own work. One might add that for a *controversy* to produce beneficial effects it is necessary that is should be held freely on both sides ...

The 28 June 1751 edition of the *Annonces, Affices et Avis divers*, the semi-official paper of the Paris area, lists all the usual news. There were houses to sell: a *seigneurie*, a large farm, with grounds, 36 *lieues* from Paris; another one in the village of Nerville, in the parish of Prestes, with a new house, a large garden with a house for the gardener, a hundred acres of arable land, an orchard, and a wood, two rental houses, all bringing a total of 1,800 *livres* income a year, sold by M. Bordier, Procureur au Châtelet, rue du Roi de Sicile, close to rue Tiron. A 'large and beautiful house' in the rue Royal was advertised with true estate agent's patter:

> Comprising large living quarters between court and garden, with a great vestibule, dining room, living room, kitchen and offices on the ground floor, four rooms and a cabinet on the first and as much on the second, a large interior court, store rooms, stables, sheds, cellars, porter's lodge, garden shed, and a small, mature wooded area at the bottom of the garden. Well

81

decorated and in good condition. *Please apply to M. Cazaubon,
rue d'Argenteuil, close to the little gate S. Roch*[1]

Among the official announcements is a reminder that opening
shops on Sundays and holidays was illegal, and that market traders
were forbidden 'to draw their swords, to blaspheme, to swear by
the name of Our Lord, and to carry prohibited weapons, etc.'.
There is the notice of the sale of the estate of Mademoiselle de la
Roche-sur-Yon, consisting of wall hangings, a bed cover, a canapé,
easy chairs and other furniture, decorated with embroidery and
gilding, and other sales of private effects. M. Caziot is to be inter-
viewed for the vacant chair of Law at Paris University, and, on
20 June, a gentleman lost at the opera 'a box decorated with
diamonds, sapphires, and emeralds, with a parrot in *émail* on the
top and a clasp in black onyx representing the head of a woman',
though it is not documented whether he ever got it back. Ships
arriving in Bordeaux and Calais are listed for the benefit of
merchants and anxious relatives. Demoiselle Marie-Magdeleine
Piquant, the widow of M. Varney, Esq., has died in the rue des
Vieux Augustins, and the Académie Royale de Musique will give a
performance of Rameau's *Les Indes Galantes* on the 29th.

A selection of new books is presented to the reader: a Russian
atlas with Latin and French explanations and seven maps of the
environs of St Petersburg; a dissertation about the campaigns of
the Roman armies in Germany, published in Berlin; a book entitled
Delights of Country Life, or Remarks about Gardening, published in
Amsterdam; and the following announcement:

> The gentlemen Briasson, David l'âiné, Le Breton, & Durand,
> booksellers in Paris, give notice that on the first of July they will
> deliver the first volume of the *Encyclopédie*, and that, after the
> closure of the subscription list, several persons have presented
> themselves who had to be turned away and that there were others
> who wanted to see the 1ˢᵗ volume before committing themselves.
> The above-mentioned booksellers will therefore allow subscrip-
> tion for another 3 months; but the first payment will now not
> be 6ol. but 84l. This augmentation of 24l. on the total is only

> just with regard to the first subscribers & will leave the possibil-
> ity for 3 months of procuring the work well under its eventual
> price. The volumes will not be sold separately, and only the
> subscribers will be sent them as they appear.

It was done: the first volume was printed and bound and lying in
the warehouse in large, orderly piles of tall, stately spines, embossed
with gold and smelling sweetly of leather and good paper.

Diderot & Co. had already had a taste of the opposition they
were to encounter. The attack had come from the *Journal de Trévoux*,
the learned Jesuit periodical edited by a certain Father Berthier.
Berthier had taken issue with a chart of human knowledge in the
Prospectus depicting all the fields of knowledge as branches and
sub-branches and illustrating their interdependences and relationships. The *Journal de Trévoux* had pointed out that this chart largely
followed the one designed by Francis Bacon, and this accusation of
plagiarism could have been extremely damaging to the *Encyclopédie*,
which was yet to appear. Diderot immediately penned a response,
all the more indignant for the fact that the text of the *Prospectus*
had made explicit reference to Bacon and to the debt owed to
him. Alluding to the fact that the *Journal* had excerpted famous
works by other writers and that large parts of text from the *Encyclopédie*, which Berthier obviously detested, had appeared in his own
publication, Diderot wrote to the Abbé in a heavily ironic open
letter: 'The mass of these modest authors cannot be led to immortality except through your good offices. I hope therefore that you
will be, to use your own words, "the carriage taking them there".
I wish you a good journey.'[2]

The enmity was now well publicized, but hardly new. The Jesuits,
it was rumoured, had taken umbrage at never having been asked
to contribute to the *Encyclopédie*, especially on the subject of theology. They had decided that there were two options: to destroy it
altogether, or to weaken it so much that they could eventually take
it over. Berthier's accusations were no more than a shot across the
bows. The journey had begun, with the Encyclopedists, Berthier
and his *Journal*, and many others all in one cramped carriage.

Berthier was not to be silenced by a little irony – he was a sharp writer himself – and so Diderot found himself reading in the next issue of the *Journal*: 'Several of these gentlemen of the *Encyclopédie* are known to us; we hold them in high esteem; they have competence, politeness, morals, and religion. M. Diderot has given a singular proof of his modesty by not naming them after him in the frontispiece of the *Prospectus*. Their names would have shed a great lustre upon his.'[3] Diderot replied in kind, but the dispute only heightened public interest in the *Encyclopédie* itself.

The tree of knowledge, which had so enraged the Abbé, had been planted expressly to undermine the foundations of the Church. Its dangerous character lay in its subtle adoption of Bacon's model, rather than the simple fact of its use. The result looked innocent enough: a family tree of all branches of human sciences and arts, beginning with Understanding and then branching off into Memory, Reason, and Imagination, and into countless subdivisions. The division *Reason*, for instance, was subdivided into Metaphysics and other philosophical disciplines, Theology, and Psychology, and, next to it, Knowledge of Man, and Knowledge of Nature. Knowledge of Nature branched out into Mathematics and Physics and their various sub-disciplines, right down to Hygiene, Cosmetics, and Hydraulics, while Knowledge of Man described a similar course from Communication to Rhetoric, and from there to Pantomime and Heraldry.

It is always said of the devil that he likes details, and here he led unsuspecting readers a merry dance. To have Heraldry, the science of the coats of arms of noble families, next to Pantomime was one thing; but in the division Knowledge of God, Theology found itself relegated to a withered and unproductive branch, leading directly to Divination and Black Magic, no larger visually than the Manufacture and Uses of Iron. While Bacon had given great importance to Ecclesiastical History and its many subdivisions, Diderot and d'Alembert had replaced it with Natural History; and while Theology was an independent branch in Bacon, for Diderot and d'Alembert it was a branch of Philosophy, subject to reason, not to faith, revelation, or to the Jansenists' obsession, grace. The strict application of this structure held some surprises: that Reason begot Philosophy and General Metaphysics seems only just; that Gardening, Falconry, and Athletics are sitting on its last twigs seems more peculiar, as does the fact that Complete History and Antiquities were thought no more important than Monstrous Vegetables and Unusual Meteors.

The idea of the 'chain of knowledge' was further developed in the *Discours Préliminaire* preceding the first volume of the *Encyclopédie*, which laid out a grand conception of what human knowledge is and can be, and which set out in a systematic manner what would later be fragmented into thousands of articles. While the articles extrapolated principles from individual circumstances, the *Discours Préliminaire* painted with great brush strokes the world as seen by the Encyclopedists: an organized world, a world in which everything had its place and its value, all according to its usefulness in promoting humanity through knowledge, justice, and progress.

The author of the *Discours* was d'Alembert, and this text of 48,000 words was to remain his largest contribution to the *Encyclopédie* and to Enlightenment literature. Like the *Encyclopédie* itself, it was a programmatic and polemic work and began by laying out a very uncompromising, Lockean epistemology, declaring that everything we know must have come to us through sensory impressions and was not, by implication, already present in our God-given soul. Stopping short of affronting the Church on the very first pages of the long-awaited work, d'Alembert then makes the volte-face that Descartes had made a century earlier in his famous aphorism, 'I think therefore I am'. Human beings, d'Alembert writes, may effectively be automata that can be explained without recourse to a higher power; but the very fact that they are aware of their own imperfection in an imperfect world implies the pre-existence of the idea of perfection and thus of 'an all-powerful intelligence to whom we owe our existence'.[4]

As d'Alembert had almost certainly studied the Scholastic philosophers at the Collège des Quatres-Nations, where he had been regarded as a great philosophical hope for the Jansenist movement, he would also have been aware of the fact that this proof of God's

existence, the so-called ontological argument, had already been
refuted during the Middle Ages. Anselm of Canterbury had set out
to convince the biblical 'fool' who says 'There is no God' of the
creator's existence.[5] Anselm's relentless logic decreed that if a greatest conceivable being can be conceived of, then it must also exist
in reality, as otherwise another, even greater being would supplant
the idea in the human mind. This beautifully simple idea had been
demolished by a monk named Gaunilo, who had replied on behalf
of 'the fool', saying that if Anselm was right, and everything the
human mind could conceive of must also exist, then a largest conceivable island must also be waiting to be discovered somewhere
in the ocean.[6] Anselm could not counter this *reductio ad absurdum.*
D'Alembert would not have been unaware of this famous controversy, and so the palliative he gave to pious readers after his
materialist exposition of the human mind may have been designed
to choke them once they had swallowed it, unsuspectingly.

The *Discours* then goes on methodically to build up a panorama
of human endeavours and the genealogy of scientific and philosophical discoveries, beginning with the Renaissance – the implicit
assumption being that medieval thought was so infested with
dogma, superstition, and obscurantism that nothing of any value
had been written or thought at all during the long first millennium
of Christian civilization. 'The masterworks the ancients have left us
in almost all areas,' wrote d'Alembert, 'were forgotten for twelve
centuries.'[7] Later philosophers had rescued Europe from the darkness of the mind: Bacon, Leibniz, Descartes, Newton, and Locke,
as well as several scientists, and they all receive homage in this
account of a collective march towards the light.

For all the structure imposed on this history and organization of
human knowledge, the Encyclopedists were by no means naïvely
convinced by the idea of inexorable progress and the absolute rule
of reason. Diderot was in many ways quite a Romantic thinker, a
philosopher and writer for whom impulses and what would later
come to be called the subconscious are a constant presence. Even
the coolly scientific d'Alembert wrote in the *Discours*: 'Barbarism
lasts centuries, it seems that it is our element. Reason and good

taste are only passing episodes.'[8] There may have been a march towards Enlightenment, but the Encyclopedists knew that its flame could be snuffed out by the sharp draft hissing at them through every church door.

Unsurprisingly, the hissing started at once. The *Journal des Sçavants* [Scholars' Journal] reviewed the *Discours* very unfavourably. D'Alembert, not to be intimidated, launched into a blustering counterattack. He would abandon the project altogether, he wrote, fully aware of the prestige his name and association lent to it, 'unless the *Journal des Sçavants* makes me an authenticated apology, just as I dictate it'. This in itself would have been extraordinary enough, but d'Alembert wanted total immunity from all criticism:

> There shall be given to us enlightened and reasonable censors, and not brute beasts in [theologian's] fur, sold out to our enemies . . . There shall be allowed to us the sustaining of all opinions not contrary to religion or government, such as the one that all ideas come from the senses, which our illustrious Sorbonne would like to make a heresy of, and an infinity of others . . . It shall be forbidden to the Jesuits, our enemies, to write against this work, to say either good or ill of it, or else it shall be permissible for us to engage in reprisals.[9]

D'Alembert was not, in fact, in a position to dictate anything. His haughtiness exasperated Diderot, as did other aspects of the day-to-day editing, notably the sloppiness of the printers. A note of his to the bookseller and publisher Le Breton, dating from February 1751, illustrates one of the many problems of having to compose and edit a large and complex book in a bid to meet increasing public expectations: 'Monsieur, I implore you to tell the typesetters, once and for all, that they must not put any letters where there are none, to set only those I have marked, and not any others.'[10]

In the end, the publication of the first volume was to surmount all the obstacles, from Diderot's imprisonment to the carelessness of the typesetters; even the new Chief Censor of France, the Director of the Book Trade, had given it his blessing.

The new Censor was a figure of particular importance for the Encyclopedists. He was the son of the newly appointed Chancellor of France, Guillaume de Lamoignon, and had just taken over the job from the ageing d'Aguesseau in the winter of 1750. A member of one of the most prominent families of Paris, the 29-year-old Chrétien-Guillaume de Lamoignon de Malesherbes (1721–94), advocate at the *Parlement* of Paris, had been appointed by his father. Without Malesherbes' protection, the *Encyclopédie* would have died an unnoticed and early death. An educated and worldly man, a member of the Academy of Sciences and an active sympathizer of the Encyclopedists and other progressive thinkers, he did everything he could to allow Diderot and his collaborators the greatest possible freedom. He considered it his task to be an arbiter rather than a censor, adjudicating in libel cases and intervening only when absolutely necessary. Courageous, moderate and principled throughout his life, he later defended Louis XVI before the Revolutionary Tribunal and was himself arrested and guillotined, together with his daughter and granddaughter, on 22 April 1794.

Malesherbes was pragmatic and liberal, had grown up among the intellectual vanguard of the capital, and had taken up his post, which tore him away from his reading, somewhat reluctantly. 'For many years I have concerned myself exclusively with literature,' he was to write later to Abbé Morellet, one of the Encyclopedists, 'and lived only in the company of men of letters. When I found myself led by unforeseen circumstances – and possibly against my will – into a different sphere, I wanted nothing more than to be able to render service to those with whom I had lived my life. I thought I had found the occasion of doing so when I was put in charge of the book trade, since I found myself in a position to procure for them the liberty of writing that I had always seen them sigh for.'[11]

Now, in early 1751, having just obtained his post, Malesherbes had to decide what to do with the new *Encyclopédie*. He had two options, reflecting the arbitrariness of the legal system of his time: he could accord the work a Royal Privilege, which was strictly speaking a necessity for every published work, and the eighteenth-century equivalent to copyright. This, however, also entailed the explicit

consent of his office and thus, by proxy, of the King himself. Malesherbes also had a second possibility, a Tacit Permission, an official
promise to look the other way, no less recognized and a way of
nodding through things that might fail the standards of censorship
but which were still thought to be of some value. The censor in
charge, Abbé Sallier, who was to become Royal Librarian, had the
unenviable task of trawling through the entire first volume for
ideological admissibility. He made his feelings quite clear in a letter
to his superior:

28 December 1750

I already examined the book which you do me the honour of
sending me by order of M. le Chancelier D'Aguesseau [Males-
herbes's predecessor] ... and I would never have given it my
approbation for being printed in France, as there are some
reprehensible parts in it.

These ... mostly regard the Catholic Church and the
received doctrine, but on the other hand there are in the new
Dictionnaire such an immense learning and such an array of
useful knowledge which neither injure nor even interest
religion, that I think it would be advisable to have it printed
under a simple permission of tolerance ... The trade has to
see large sums go to Holland for the acquisition of books
printed there [which did not pass French censorship]. If one
tolerates a work that does not openly attack morals or religion,
one renders a service to the state, I believe.[12]

Malesherbes consulted other censors and finally decided to allow
the *Encyclopédie* to be printed with full Royal Privilege, a fact that
gave added protection and prestige to the enterprise, though at
the cost of both risking the Chief Censor's own professional reputation and limiting the freedom of the work. The first volume was
duly authorized and appeared with the following, splendid title:

ENCYCLOPÉDIE, OU DICTIONNAIRE RAISONNÉ DES
SCIENCES, DES ARTS ET DES MÉTIERS, *PAR UNE
SOCIETÉ DE GENS DE LETTRES.*

Mis en ordre & publié par M. *DIDEROT,* de l'Académie
Royale des Sciences & des Belles-Lettres de Prusse; & quant
à la Partie Mathématique, par M. *D'ALEMBERT,* de
l'Académie Royale des Sciences de Paris, de celle de Prusse,
& de la Société Royale de Londres.

*Tantùm series juncturaque pollet, Tantùm de medio sumptis accedit
honoris !* Horat.

TOME PREMIER.

A PARIS,
Chez BRIASSON, *rue Saint Jacques, à la Science.*
DAVID l'aîné, *rue Saint Jacques, à la Plume d'or.*

LE BRETON, Imprimeur ordinaire du Roy, *rue de la Harpe.*
DURAND, *rue Saint Jacques, à Saint Landry, & au Griffon.*
M. DCC. LI.
AVEC APPROBATION ET PRIVILEGE DU ROY.

On this title-page, a very pleased Diderot was able to introduce
himself to the public as a Fellow of the Royal Academy of Sciences
and Literature in Berlin, to which he had been elected just in time
for printing, the first and almost the last academic honour he was
to receive in his lifetime.

The stately tome that now made its way to subscribers throughout France, spanning A–AZYMITES, was a document that had to
be read with the greatest care, for it deployed its subtle, and sometimes not so subtle, editorial policy of attacking the Church and
the authorities to considerable effect, though modern readers
may be surprised not to find barnstorming revolutionary oratory.
Most of the articles were concerned to impart the most accurate
information available on very everyday topics of eighteenth-century
life: pragmatic and useful facts about ABEILLE (Bee), ACCELERA-
TION, AIR, AMPUTATION, ARBRE (Tree), ALSACE, ACIER (Steel),
and ARIAS. Hidden between the straightforward and sometimes
even dull articles, not all of them very distinguished and not all
of them accurate, were wild and highly personal polemical esca-
pades, while other texts quietly aimed to convince the reader of

something he or she had not opened the book to be convinced about.

The boisterous generosity and wit of Diderot's voice dominate the first volume. He appears, very much as himself, as contributor on everything from mythology to botany, from geography to philology, and whenever the opportunity arises he throws off the yoke of dry definitions to impart to the reader some of his own convictions, or indeed some point that has nothing to do with the theme of the article. Writing on botanical subjects, he shows himself particularly enraged about the mixture of vague travellers' accounts and legends that often passed for scientific information. In the article on ACO, a mysterious fish described during the Renaissance, he gives the one and a half lines of information on what was known about the creature and then comments: 'Now go and find out what an *aco* is.' In another article, editorial decorum deserts him altogether:

> * **AGUAXIMA**, (*Hist. nat. bot.*) a plant growing in Brazil and the islands of middle America. This is all we are told; & I would like to ask for whom descriptions like this are made at all. It cannot be for the natives of the country, who obviously know more characteristics of the *aguuaxima* than this description contains & who have no need of being informed that it grows in their own country; it would be like saying that the pear tree grows in France & in Germany. It is also not made for us; for what does it matter if there is in Brazil a tree that is called *aguaxima* of which we know nothing but the name? To whom is this name useful? It leaves ignorant those who were ignorant in the first place; it teaches nothing to anyone; & if I mention this plant, & several others equally badly described, it is to oblige those readers who prefer finding nothing in an article of the Dictionnaire, or even finding a stupidity, than not finding an article at all.

In a time when a great deal of knowledge was no more than hearsay, spread on bad authority or, worse, on the authority of a theologian, bad definitions were obviously something worth

fighting against. In AMPHIPHON, Diderot reflects on what exactly
the editor of a dictionary should be doing in the first place:

> * **AMPHIPHON**, (*Mythol.*) a cake made in honour of Diana
> & which was surrounded by little flames. This is all we know.
> Those who wrote about it fall into a strange contradiction:
> they all knew that their works would be passed on to pos-
> terity, but most of them spoke about things in a way only
> comprehensible to their contemporaries. I know that there
> are a great number of works in which good taste does not
> permit details, that one should not expect from a poet who
> mentions a weapon or an ostrich feather to give a thorough
> description of it, but this is not the case for all authors.
> Those writing dictionaries do not have this excuse, on the
> contrary, if they are well made, I think they should also
> serve as commentary to all other works ... there have been
> so many dictionaries, but one still remains to be written: one
> in which all the obscure passages in the works of good
> authors are explained.

The main articles on religious matters, such as ABSOLUTION,
ÂME, ANGE, APOCALYPSE, and ASSUMPTION, are quite as orthodox as any censor could have wished. The obscurer subjects, however, can spring genuine surprises on the unsuspecting reader.
Religious customs in general are ridiculed if they happen not to
be Catholic – the cult of the bullock of APIS, for instance ('Only
women were accorded the honour of visiting and serving him; they
presented themselves naked, a fact which the priests were in a
better position to appreciate than the god'), or ANAETIS, which
portrays an annual procession with the statue of a goddess as an
absurd superstition, a sly comment on devotees of the Holy Virgin.
In AIGLE (Eagle), Diderot slips in the following ancient Roman
custom, with a disingenuous ode to the religion of rationalism:

> The eagle was depicted with Jupiter ... & seen as the bird of
> God, of the heavens and of the air & given a bolt of lightning
> to carry ... superstition has the most extravagant and the most
> vulgar visions. These visions are then consecrated by time &
> popular credulity, and woe to him who, without having been

called by God to the great and perilous vocation of missionary, loves his own peace so little and knows people so badly that he charges himself with instructing them. If one lets a ray of light into the owl's nest, one will only hurt their eyes & provoke their cries. A hundred times happier are those people whose religion contains nothing but things that are true, sublime & holy & that imitates only virtue; this is our religion, and philosophy must only follow its reasoning to arrive at the feet of our altar.

In a country filled with religious images showing the Holy Spirit as a dove fluttering above or in front of God the Father, this was not difficult to read, and the effect was only heightened by the bombastic praise for the Church. At the same time, Diderot could cast himself in the light of the man who loved his own peace so little and knew so little of his fellow men that he had taken it upon himself to enlighten them even against their will – a heroic role indeed.

Diderot was, however, not content to remain abstract. In ASCHARIOUNS, dealing with a Muslim scholar and the sect he had founded, he gave a well-aimed slap across the face to Jansen and his followers by pointing out that morals become meaningless if God decides the fates of individuals in advance. As for the Jesuits, the first volume of the *Encyclopédie* is not directed against them, though Diderot cannot resist inserting the following remark into his article on ARISTOTELISM: 'We will not discuss [the great Jesuit theologians] at length here, for if there were great men among them, there are others who made it their exclusive business to praise them. This society has an opinion on everything, and never yet has a Jesuit of merit remained unknown.'

While most of the *Encyclopédie* dealt with less controversial matters and many articles toed the ideological line of the time to perfection, Diderot's articles undermined the seeming orthodoxy. ACHOR, the Cyrenian god of flies, becomes an agent of subversion in the editor's hands. Pliny had reported on this cult in some detail, noting that all flies died as soon as the god had received his sacrifice. Diderot comments:

A modern scholar might remark that Pliny could have added, in the name of truth, that this was the vulgar opinion; it therefore seems to me that one should not expect a dangerous truth from an author who has been accused of lying so often when there was no consequence to be feared & that Pliny obviously did not believe in the divinity of the fly-killing god, but that he wanted to instruct us on the prejudice of the inhabitants of Cyrene and could not express himself differently without compromising his own safety. This, I believe, is one of the instances in which one cannot draw any conclusion from an author's testimony against himself, or from what he writes about.

Read my articles, the editor advises, but I have a family to look after, so you should believe me only when I am writing as a *philosophe*. If Diderot was struggling to hide his convictions behind discussions of obscure gods, other contributors were just as sly. Pierre Tarin, an anatomist who contributed about 350 articles to the early volumes of the *Encyclopédie*, writes in his article ABEILLE (Bee) a seemingly straightforward and exhaustive scientific text:

The drones are smaller than the queen, but larger than the worker bees; they have a rounder head; they live off nothing but honey, while the workers eat raw wax. With the rising of the sun the latter part for a day's toil, while the drones go out much later; then only to frolic around the hive, without working. They come back in before the calm & cool evening; they have neither stings nor claws, nor prominent teeth as do the workers ... The only usefulness of the drones is to impregnate the queen. As soon as this is done, the workers hunt them down and kill them.

For eighteenth-century eyes, it would have been hard to ignore the similarity between drones and the aristocracy. As to the fate of the drones, it was, after all, a fact of nature. While the *Encyclopédie* did not advocate revolution, passages like these are open to interpretation.

The first volume of the *Encyclopédie* could not yet draw on the network of writers that the editors later had at their disposal: 1,984 of the approximately 4,000 articles in the volume were written by Diderot, 199 by d'Alembert, and, among the named contributors, a substantial number each by a good dozen other writers. Only twenty had been written by Rousseau. After Diderot, the most prolific author of all, with 484 articles to his name, was the Abbé Edme Mallet (1713–55), one of the most obscure and probably most underestimated of all the Encyclopedists. Mallet's reputation is that of a droning, boorish and brainless reactionary who was assigned religious articles to maintain a veneer of religious respectability.

It is true that Mallet's articles are at times deadeningly plodding, exploring every last nook and forgotten cranny of ancient theological debates, and his life was certainly that of a good man of the Church. First a preceptor of the children of the *fermier général* Lalive de Bellegarde d'Épinay, he later became a doctor of theology and was appointed Royal Professor of Theology at Navarre. He was certainly a strange choice as an important contributor to the *Encyclopédie* and it has been suggested that he had a powerful protector and that Diderot simply could not afford to refuse to take him on. But if Mallet was a tedious and long-winded writer, he was also, perversely, a brilliant choice, since he managed to kill every religious sentiment he touched.

Writing about gospels in ÉVANGELIE, he helpfully pointed out that there were not only four but actually another thirty-nine apocryphal ones, which he then proceeded to name and describe in a particularly long contribution. In ENFER, he collected all historically sanctioned speculations about the precise location of hell (possible candidates: Australia, the environs of Rome, or a comet, or the sun itself), its exact capacity and size, and the precise duration of a stay there. In a remarkably well-informed article on the intellectual history of ancient Egypt, the author comments that Moses was a pupil of Egyptian priests and that during a religious dispute between the followers of rival cults of 'cats and onions' the eaters of beans were condemned to be burned as heretics – displaying an implicitly sceptical turn of mind for a man so supposedly orthodox. Other articles of his conjecture as to what variety of fruit the forbidden Tree of Knowledge bore (a cherry tree was favoured by some authorities, others maintained the apple tradition) and about the physics of the Ascension.

Intellectual resistance to the *ancien régime* could take many guises. Consider the most famous article by the Abbé, dealing with Noah's Ark, a long and serious dissertation, beginning just as one would expect:

> **ARK OF NOAH** means, in the language of the Scripture, a kind of boat or a gigantic, floating building constructed by Noah in order to preserve from the deluge the diverse species of animals which God commanded the patriarch to take into it. *See* **DELUGE**.
> The Naturalists & Critics have conducted diverse enquiries & imagined different systems about the *ark of Noah*, its form, its size, its capacity, the materials employed in its construction, the time it took to build it, & the place where it landed when the deluge receded. We will follow all these points within the limits of the present work.

So far, so perfectly obvious. Mallet then goes on to do just what he has promised, outlining the current scholarly consensus that Noah took one hundred years to build the ark, from 1555 to 1656 after the Creation, but noting that some authorities disagree, notably the Jewish *Tanchumah* (Mallet is well up on his rabbinic sources), which allots only fifty-two. It is probable, writes Mallet, that the patriarch was aided in his task by his three sons, though according to some chronologies they had not been born at the time of its completion. The Abbé then analyzes the variety of wood and the size of the ark, coming to the conclusion that the latter in particular raises certain questions. The biblical measurements, 300 × 50 × 30 ells, are clearly insufficient to allow all known animals space within the vessel. The solution seems to be, according to the Renaissance scientist Athanasius Kircher, to assume that Egyptian ells were used as the unit of measurement, which would give the ark a size and length similar to St Paul's cathedral; but an obvious problem presents itself, for, if the ells are used consistently throughout the account, Noah and the animals would also be of gigantic size, thus renewing the original conundrum. Mallet addresses himself to recent zoological research to ascertain exactly how many species of animals there are on earth, how much space each animal would need, and consequently how many stables the ark would have to have contained. This allows him to calculate the amount of fodder the ark would have to have taken on board, on the assumption that, following calculations published by the English bishop and scientist John Wilkins (1614–72) – a man who wrote on everything from the design of submarines to the possibilities of travel to the moon – the carnivores would have eaten no more than would twenty-seven wolves (a very conservative estimate, it appears) and the herbivores no more than 208 head of cattle. He concluded that 109,500 cubic ells (47,085 cubic metres) of hay and 1,825 sheep (as well as hay for them, one might add) should have sufficed for the year, as well as 31,174 *muids* (363,489 hectolitres) of fresh water as ballast in the bottom of the ark. Needless to say, other authorities had different estimates and had therefore come to different conclusions. The buoyancy and stability of the vessel were major and constant concerns, especially regarding its box-like form. The distribution of animals and fodder throughout the ark turns out to be an act worthy of a professional engineer, as relative weight, the logistics of feeding, airing, and mucking out all of animal creation, and the character and mutual compatibility of the animals, all have to be taken into account. For reasons of balance, incidentally, Noah and his family would have to have stayed with the birds on the third floor. Despite these estimates, even Bishop Wilkins had to admit that the true number of animals having to enter the ark might have been much larger, as much of the earth, and therefore many species of animals, had still to be discovered.

Was the Abbé Mallet really so learned and yet so bone-headed, so profoundly well read in several languages and yet so incredibly naïve to submit reams of articles like this, which destroy the very subject they purportedly treat with such reverence by making them crumble to dust in the reader's imagination?

It is difficult to decide which version is less likely: the traditional

one, that Mallet was a phenomenal bore and that Diderot maliciously shovelled pre-selected theological topics in his direction to
have them ground to bits by the millstone of his dull mind; or the
alternative, that Mallet, while beyond reproach in the eyes of his
contemporaries, was really possessed by an all-destructive rage
against Catholicism and that, when asked to contribute to the *Encyclopédie*, saw the opportunity to create his life's work in a series
of devastatingly subversive but unassailable dissertations. It seems
probable that in Abbé Mallet the *Encyclopédie* had one of its most
effective, if quietest contributors, submitting article after article that
was absolutely incontrovertible from a theological point of view but
which, at the same time, exposed the myriad cracks and fissures, all
the inconsistencies and feeble-minded squabbles, of the Christian
tradition.

If the Abbé was a subtle doubter, he remained misunderstood.
On the other hand, D'Alembert's haughty self-righteousness and
the patently false protestations of fidelity made by Diderot, a man
who had already been imprisoned and had had one of his works
lacerated and burned by the public hangman, were easy to see
through. Mallet's strategy of disorienting the reader by giving too
much information for any faith to bear was so well concealed that
his reputation never recovered from it.

Before long, everybody in literary circles had an opinion on the
Encyclopédie, its merits, and its shortcomings. Unsurprisingly, the
Jesuits made it their special business to discredit the work, pointing
out its many typographical errors, its frequent failures to give accurate sources or acknowledge quotations, and making it clear that
they had not remained blind to the methods of the work's editors:
'The names of kings, savants, saints, etc., are excluded from the
Encyclopédie, yet those of pagan divinities are admitted,'[13] they stated
with piously raised eyebrows, and, taking a leaf out of the Encyclopedist fondness for natural metaphors, they added, referring to
the often all too generous and at times downright plagiaristic
borrowings in the volume: 'One may harvest the way bees do . . .

but the thievery of the ant, which walks off with the whole thing, ought never to be imitated.'[14]

But the complaints of the Jesuit fathers were not enough to discredit a work so eagerly expected and so passionately discussed. The high-minded feared it might be used as a shortcut to culture, others criticized the variable quality of the work; but everyone seemed to be talking about it in one way or another, and the prevailing view was summed up by a Genevan journalist, who wrote: 'With his vagrant as well as scientific imagination, M. Diderot would inundate us with words and sentences. This is the complaint of the public against his first volume, which appeared a little while ago. But an infinitely copious background of material and a fine taste of sound philosophy, which gives value to it, compensate for these superfluities.'[15] Having received the first volume with great interest, the public was ready for more. The declared enemies of the enterprise, churchmen and particularly the Jesuits, had not succeeded in dragging it down at the first opportunity. Their next chance, which almost ended the *Encyclopédie*, was handed to them by the editors themselves.

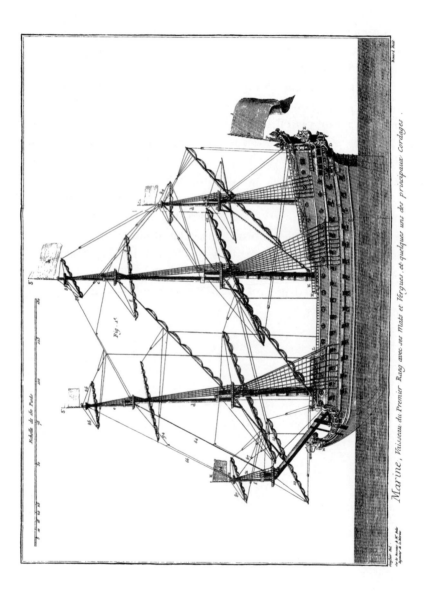

Marine, Vaisseau du Premier Rang avec ses Mats et Vergues, et quelques uns des principaux Cordages.

PLAY OF NATURE

JEU DE LA NATURE [PLAY OF NATURE] (*Anat. Physiol.*).
One means by *jeu de la nature*, in the human body, a [strange]
formation of single or multiple solids, other than that one
might call *natural*, as it happens ordinarily.

When dissecting corpses, says M. de Fontenelle, the singu-
larities of the *jeux de la nature* become more common, the
different structures better known & in consequence the
assumptions less frequent. Perhaps, with time, one could
gain significant insights into these formations in general by
looking at the particular ones.

I will not examine, whether all conclusions are equally
correct; it suffices to remark here that one can assemble very
remarkable observations about the *jeux de la nature* in all its
curious expressions. I myself had collected a great amount
of data on this subject, which I regret having lost, as they
have perished in a shipwreck.

Chevalier de Jaucourt

The Chevalier de Jaucourt was a medical man, but the irony of the
term *jeu de la nature* cannot have been lost on him, for it was through
a seemingly senselessly cruel game of fate that he himself became
washed up on the shores of the *Encyclopédie*. Indeed, there would
have been no *Encyclopédie* but for the Chevalier de Jaucourt. In its
latter stages, when most of the authors were too scared or too
exhausted to carry on and when Diderot himself only grudgingly
did his duty as a literary 'galley slave', it was the unassuming
Chevalier who researched and wrote 40,000 articles – half the
entries in the last ten volumes – and he did so dependably and

swiftly enough for the enterprise to be achieved when the time was right.

He was never compensated for his quiet heroism – not by Diderot, who praised him in the prefaces to the *Encyclopédie* but was personally cool towards him and belittled his efforts behind his back; not by the booksellers, who never paid him more than a few books, while he had to sell a house to pay the secretaries he had employed to do his research; and not by historians, who remember the heroic figures of Diderot and d'Alembert but have swallowed Diderot's bait and dismissed the Chevalier as a mediocre and pedantic scribbler, a man simply too boring to stop working for a moment while the ink was drying and look at the world around him. How wrong they are.

Louis de Jaucourt (1704–79) had, in fact, seen quite a lot of the world. While Diderot had not yet been beyond Paris and his home town of Langres, and d'Alembert had never left the capital at all, the young Chevalier had been educated in Geneva and (to the utter bewilderment of his aristocratic mother) had studied medicine in Leyden and Cambridge. The Jaucourts were not used to having a doctor in their ranks. A Burgundian family that could be traced back to the early thirteenth century, they had been functionaries at the court of the Prince de Condé and had converted to Protestantism during the sixteenth century.[1] After the horrors of St Bartholemew's Night, during which thousands of Huguenots had been slaughtered, they had ostensibly converted back to Catholicism. Despite being part of a persecuted minority, the Jaucourts were widely respected and had among their acquaintances some of the most influential noblemen of France, such as Lamoignon-Malesherbes (the Chancellor and father of the Director of the Book Trade), the Minister of War d'Argenson (who had imprisoned and then freed Diderot and to whom the first volume of the *Encyclopédie* had been dedicated), and the Duc d'Orléans.

Louis was born in Paris but soon sent to Geneva for his education, an indication that the family still had strong Protestant sympathies. In order not to endanger them by indicating disloyalty to the Church, the boy would live there under an adopted name, Louis de Neufville, for many years. In Geneva, he attended the Academy that had been founded by Calvin and stayed with a rich and highly educated great-uncle, who prided himself on his art collection and his library. In 1727, having finished his studies in Geneva, Louis announced to his parents that he was accompanying his brother-in-law to London 'to see a little of the many curiosities of that city'.[2] He seems to have liked England and decided to stay in Cambridge to continue his studies and learn English, which proved far more difficult than he had anticipated: 'I have been here 7 weeks without making any substantial progress. This language is so abundant, so difficult to pronounce, and so great for a Frenchman who has not been here at least since the age of 10, that I defy the most able person ever to be able to find the right tone.'[3]

The university was not much more to his liking: 'the masters [the dons] make a living by extracting as much as possible out of their students and then not bothering with them much. They throw parties and all they seem to do all day long is drinking and smoking.' Louis noted that the students did not seem to mind that the dons were lazy and ignorant, as they knew that they would get a degree after a certain period whether or not they did any work: it was all just a question of money, of which most of them seemed to have enough. In any case, Cambridge and its students bored the young Chevalier, who stated that 'a Frenchman who is not good at their language, who cannot really get fired up about their Whigism and Toryism, and who does not know the art of drinking and smoking is thought of very little at this university'.[4] While the university failed to impress him, he greatly admired other aspects of English culture, whose intellectual life and system of government were in stark contrast to the climate in France, from which his family was continuing to suffer and which had made him an exile. In his first printed work, a life of the philosopher Leibniz, de Jaucourt would write:

> He took the first opportunity to see England, that happy island where vast commerce creates abundance, and the love of free-dom forms the distinctive character of the inhabitants, where the sciences flourish, where all the arts are honoured and duly

compensated, where people think for themselves, and where one can speak without fear. He went to the universities and stayed principally in London, that immense city, at the same time the equal and the superior of Paris, where the best geniuses of the kingdom are assembled . . .[5]

It is easy to see the young Louis de Neufville in the shoes of his intellectual hero. Louis made good use of his time. Together with his distant Genevan cousin, Théodore Tronchin, he was admitted to London society, as Théodore had a powerful protector: Henry St John, Lord Bolingbroke (1688–1766), former British Prime Minister, man of letters and friend of Voltaire, and who had, as a supporter of the Jacobites, spent some years in France after the accession of George I. Dr Johnson gruffly savaged Bolingbroke, calling him 'a scoundrel, and a coward',[6] but his Uxbridge estate was nevertheless a focal point for some of London's finest writers (with the notable exception of Johnson himself). Pope and Swift were frequent guests, and it is possible that Louis, who would quote both of them in the *Encyclopédie*, met them there.

One man the young Chevalier and his cousin certainly met was Sir Hans Sloane (1660–1753), the doctor, explorer, President of the Royal Society and, most notably, collector of immense appetite and curiosity, whose 200,000-item collection, comprising everything from rare stones, dried fruits and leaves, and stuffed and preserved animals, to gems and medals, medieval manuscripts, and Greek sculpture, was a magnet for all travellers, especially those with scientific interests. The two young visitors obviously made an impression, for they became sufficiently friendly with Sloane for him to send them a copy of his famous work *A Voyage to the Islands Madera, Barbados, Nieves, S. Christopher's and Jamaica, with the Natural History of the Herbs and Trees, Four-footed Beasts, Fishes, Birds, Insects, Reptiles, &c.* to Leyden five years after their visit, a present for which they thanked him in a long and florid Latin letter. Voltaire, too, was in Britain at this time (1726–9), and it is possible that Louis was introduced to him by Lord Bolingbroke. What is certain is that Voltaire knew Jaucourt and wrote to him as to a friend.

Abandoning an earlier idea of becoming a Protestant pastor, a notion that had shocked his family, who already found it difficult enough to keep up Catholic appearances, Louis de Neufville, as he still was, metamorphosed into a serious young natural scientist. For the study of natural sciences, however, there was one place in the Protestant world, and possibly in Europe, whose reputation was unequalled: the little university town of Leyden near Amsterdam, the birthplace of Rembrandt and home to one of the greatest medical scientists of the eighteenth century, Herman Boerhaave (1668–1738).

On their arrival in Leyden, the two students were greeted with a surprise. They had received a letter of recommendation from a Cambridge don, which they duly took to its recipient, Professor Peter Burmann, a famous but affable man, who read the letter, turned a furious shade of red, and proceeded to chase the young men out of his room with a large stick. Louis and Théodore assumed that he had gone mad, but it later transpired that the letter they had been given had been an orgy of invective and insults against Burmann, a little exercise in British humour. On 13 September 1728, 'Neuvil de Jaucourt, Gallus. 23, M.' inscribed himself in the university register. It was the first time he used his family name in any document.

Louis worked hard, reading, attending dissections and other lectures, writing his first publications. His family were bewildered – aristocrats simply did not work – but benevolent; his mother, trying to come to terms with sniggering acquaintances, wrote to his sister that being 'a professor of medicine may be ridiculous, but it is not really a vice'.[7] Meanwhile, Louis' scholarly inclinations were getting the better of his will to practise medicine. He had already helped with the publication of a complete catalogue of the famous cabinet of Albert Seba (1665–1736), a collection similar in ambition and scope to Sloane's but almost exclusively containing objects of scientific (as opposed to historical or ethnographic) interest.

The collection had seen two incarnations: one had been bought in its entirety by the visiting Tsar Peter the Great in 1716; the

second one, partly financed by Peter's purchase price, had since
grown to outshine the earlier version, but the experience may have
contributed to Seba's decision to commission a catalogue illustrating every last humble shell and stone in his possession as the only
way of ensuring the immortality of the ensemble in its entirety.
This project was similar to the later work on the *Encyclopédie*: a
collaboration of various scholars and scientists, contributions were
edited in one magnificently illustrated and produced work of eight
volumes, published over a period of thirty-six years, the appropriately grand *Locupletissimi rerum naturalium thesauri accurata descriptio,
et iconibus artificiosissimis expressio, per universam physices historiam.* Two
editions were printed: one in Dutch and Latin, one in French and
Latin. Only twenty-eight and already involved in one of the most
important scientific publishing projects of the time alongside men
of the stature of Boerhaave himself, Louis was eminently unim-
pressed with himself. He wrote to a Genevan friend, another
member of the Tronchin family:

> I have been living in this country for four years, continually
> pursuing various studies, but particularly that of medicine,
> which takes up the greatest part of my time; I pass the rest of
> my time amusing myself with reading books of all kinds and
> waste my time in this way, ruining my health in the process,
> which interests me little, and after all this work I always find
> myself in the same circle of ignorance.[8]

Louis de Jaucourt liked this life, and when family business called
him back to France in 1733 he went reluctantly and retained a
room in Amsterdam. With the death of his father three years later,
however, his stay in France became permanent. The inheritance
was complex and presented considerable legal problems, so his
presence was a necessity. Still, in 1737 he was once again in Amsterdam, as witnessed by a letter from Voltaire, who had visited the city
but had not found the time to see the scholar, excusing himself
for 'having profited so little from the honour of knowing you'. In
a later letter he added, by way of consolation: 'If you come to

France, believe me, Monsieur, execute your project of coming to Cirey [where Voltaire lived at the time]. You will find there a person who desires to see you and esteems you. The lady of the château [Voltaire's mistress, Mme du Châtelet] also asks you to come.'[9] After his return to Paris, a friend of the family wrote: 'In Holland he was always called Neuville and I have seen his life of Leibniz. He is a young man who is as amiable in character as he is ugly to look at, but his knowledge is exact and extensive.'[10] This unflattering thumbnail sketch is the closest thing to a portrait surviving of de Jaucourt's physical appearance. No paintings are known, and the only miniature purporting to depict him is in a series of portraits of Encyclopedists, most of which are totally unrecognizable.

When the problems surrounding the inheritance had been solved, Louis de Jaucourt, as he now called himself again, was a man of independent wealth; not rich, but in a position to pursue his passion, scientific research and writing, without having to worry about his income. He had received a substantial sum of money, 75,000 *livres* (around £600,000), as well as income from several estates and a house in Paris. Not in the least interested in becoming a man about town, and noticeably reluctant to establish himself in France as a scientist – his Huguenot background would have made this very difficult – he decided to make use of his freedom by living partly in Paris, where he could find books and company, and partly in the quiet of his family's country seat, working on a medical dictionary.

A specialized reference work projected to run to six folio volumes, this took him almost twenty years to complete. Finally, in the summer of 1750, the Chevalier once again travelled to the Netherlands, this time with a very specific project in mind: to prepare publication and negotiate terms with a publisher. Amsterdam was, after all, one of the best places to publish, and he still had contacts with booksellers and printers. On his return to France, he had the manuscript boxed and transported to Rouen and from there by sea to Amsterdam.

The vessel sank somewhere off the Dutch coast, and with it the manuscript, the only copy. It is difficult to imagine the reaction to such an event, the loss of half a lifetime's hard work, and of all hopes of belated scientific recognition in his own country. Now, however, Louis was forty-seven years old; it was too late to start again, and so he decided instead to approach the editors of the *Encyclopédie* and to offer them his collaboration and the exploitation of whatever notes and articles he still had available. He sent some specimens to the bookseller David l'âiné, whom he might have known as a scientific publisher. David handed them on to Diderot, who promptly responded:

> To Monsieur the Chevalier de Jaucourt
> Rue de Grenelle
> 20 September 1751
>
> I owe you, monsieur, particular thanks for the article *Anatomie*;
> I will gladly use the articles Mr David passed on to me, as well
> as those that you may still want to communicate to me, and I
> am not unaware that our Dictionary will gain by it. I would be
> charmed to have the honour of receiving you in my house,
> but permit me that I pay you a visit. We will be able to talk
> more easily at your house, and I would like to profit from this
> conversation for the perfection of our work. I will present
> myself Sunday morning, between nine and ten. Meanwhile, I
> am with all esteem and respect due to a man of your merit,
> Monsieur
> Your very humble
> And very obedient servant
> Diderot
>
> If the day and hour I have mentioned are not convenient to
> you, please indicate others.

A storm somewhere off Holland made the Chevalier de Jaucourt an Encyclopedist. This was the *jeu de la nature*, the play of nature, he so ruefully described in the *Encyclopédie*. The advertisement to the second volume also carried another echo of the tragedy when his articles were introduced as 'the precious debris of an immense work, perished in a shipwreck, & of which he wanted to make sure that at least the little that was left would be of some use to his country'.

When, during the eighteenth century, Swedish scientists discovered slight alterations in the Baltic coastline, theologians immediately made representations to the Government in Stockholm, demanding that this discovery should be condemned as it was not consistent with Genesis. The Government, however, answered that, as God had made both Genesis and the Baltic, if there was an inconsistency, then it must be in the copies of the Bible and not in the Baltic, which was the original.[11]

In Catholic France, theologians could not be spoken to as firmly as their Swedish colleagues when they demanded that the first volume *Encyclopédie* should be condemned. Somehow, everybody agreed that the project was important; everybody saw in it a powerful means of possibly furthering their own goals; but nobody was actually content with it. The Abbé Raynal, a friend of several of the Encyclopedists, complained that there were too many useless articles in it and that 'several authors write in a barbarous style, several in a precious manner, and many possess nothing but prolixity'.[12] Both of the important scholarly journals of the time, the *Journal des Sçavants* and the *Journal de Trévoux*, published review articles containing harsh criticisms. The former concentrated on d'Alembert's *Discours Preliminaire*, and unsurprisingly singled out the Lockean orientation of the article:

> The system of Locke is dangerous for religion, although one has no objections to make when those who adopt it do not draw noxious conclusions from it. M. d'Alembert is one of this number; he recognizes rather eloquently the spirituality of the soul and the existence of God, but he is so brief on each of these subjects, concerning which there are so many things to say, and he is so copious on others that the reader has a right to demand the reason for the distinction . . .[13]

The Jesuit *Journal de Trévoux*, still smarting from the fact that no invitation to participate in the *Encyclopédie* had been forthcoming, was sharper in its reading. Its main editor, Father Berthier, who had already crossed swords with Diderot over the *Prospectus*, pointed out that the Encyclopedists had a somewhat cavalier attitude to their sources, especially in the gastronomical articles, which were at times lifted word for word from a famous cookery book of the time. He chose to ignore the history of the Jesuit *Dictionnaire*, which was a case of wholesale literary theft, and took great delight in quoting and revealing other examples of unacknowledged borrowings, especially when the source author was a Jesuit.

This was not the kind of publicity the *Encyclopédie* was looking for; but despite the splutterings of disapproval from several sides, the booksellers found that it had been worth the risk of printing not the originally intended 1,625 copies, but more than 2,000. The *Encyclopédie* sold well, and subscriptions were still coming in. The work soon received a form of flattery on which no author is keen (but of which the Encyclopedists were at times guilty themselves): imitation, or, to be precise, piracy. A consortium of London booksellers announced, in the beautifully florid language of the period, an unauthorized edition of the *Encyclopédie*:

> The first volume of the French encyclopedia, herewith published, is printed verbatim from the Paris edition, and was carefully corrected by two ingenious Gentlemen, Natives of France. The Proprietors have engaged in a Design of Reprinting the whole at London, with a view to serve their Country, by encouraging Arts, Manufactures, and Trades; and keeping large sums at Home, that would otherwise be sent Abroad. They offer their Work at half the Price of the Paris Edition; and hereby promise, in case they meet with no Discouragement, to proceed regularly in printing the subsequent Volumes. But, if they should be obliged to stop short, it is hoped that no Blame will fall upon them, for declining to sacrifice their private Fortunes, upon finding too few to join them in their real Design of promoting the Public good.[14]

The 'discouragement' of this public-spirited initiative came in the shape of two of the four Paris booksellers, who travelled to London specifically to negotiate with their London colleagues, as there were no copyright laws to prevent the enterprise. The result of this visit is mysterious: according to their account books, the booksellers paid 20 *livres* to London, the first volume came out in London in 1752 (and was duly acknowledged by the *London Magazine*), but no trace of it survives and no further volumes were pirated.

The second volume of the *Encyclopédie*, covering B–CEZIMBRA, appeared on 25 January 1752, on time and, by common consent, was better than the first. The subversion of the censors by means of bamboozling them with rhetoric, or lulling them to sleep with theology, had worked beautifully – the Encyclopedists, after all, were well aware of the work of censors: fifteen of them were or had been working in this capacity themselves.[15] The editorial work finally settled into a comfortable routine and the editorial team was working efficiently under Diderot's direction. Its new member, de Jaucourt, was introduced with some flourish in the preface to the work: 'M. le Chevalier de JAUCOURT, who has become dear to all men of letters by virtue of his quiet industry and the variety of his knowledge, & who applied himself with distinction to Physics and Natural History, has communicated to us numerous and extensive articles, written with all possible care.' For the time being, his contributions numbered only eight, though the following volume would carry ninety-nine. The reason for the fact that so few articles by him had been accepted can be discerned in their headings: BYSSE (a fabric mentioned in the Old Testament), CACHOU (a lozenge to sweeten the breath), CALEBASSIER (the calebasse plant), CANNELLE (cinnamon), CARACTÈRE, CAROUBIER (Carob Tree), CARPE and CASSIS OU CASSIER: he had simply got in touch with Diderot when most of the sheets containing the letter 'B' had already been printed.

Unbeknown to the Encyclopedists, the very day they had chosen to publish the second volume was also the date of another, less

public event. In the Sorbonne, the theological faculty of Paris
University, the assembled doctors had decided to condemn the
dissertation of an abbé named Martin de Prades. The entire story
is an academic farce of the kind that still circulates today. De Prades
had written a dissertation on the Heavenly Jerusalem, an innocent
enough topic. It was a brief essay that, as required by the rules, was
posted for all to read in the Sorbonne. It seemed that nobody,
including his examiners, bothered to read it, not even the Revd
Luke Joseph Hooke, an Irishman who was the thesis supervisor,
and who was busy at the time correcting the proofs of his own
book.

On 18 November, Prades's viva voce examination, which went
on for some seven hours, was deemed a triumph. He was awarded
the title of *doctor theologiae* and was looking forward to an academic
career. Then rumours began to fly. The small print of the Abbé's
argument had subsequently been scrutinized and the work was
found to be 'blasphemous, heretical, erroneous, favourable to
materialism, contrary to the authority and integrality of the laws of
Moses, subversive of the foundations of the Christian religion, and
impiously calling into question the veracity and divinity of the
miracles of Jesus Christ'.[16] It was all very embarrassing for the
university, a pillar of the Church, which seemed to have inducted
a heretic into the higher academic orders. It was also tainted by
the corrosive influence of the band of nihilists who had published
the *Encyclopédie*, a work that seemed bent on doing just what de
Prades had done: favouring materialism, subverting the foundations of Christianity, and calling into question the veracity of the
Miracles.

Soon everyone had read the dissertation and had found that
it was, in fact, very similar in orientation to the Lockean ideas
propounded by d'Alembert in the *Discours Préliminaire*. De Prades
had allowed himself to use psychology in his analysis of religious
questions, to declare that natural religion was preferable to revealed
religion, that chronological inconsistencies in the five books of
Moses meant that they contained later inventions, and that Christ's
own miracles were no more astonishing than the healings per-

formed by the legendary Greek sage Aesculapius. The Sorbonne was up in arms against Prades and, no doubt, against his examiners who at the very least had shown implicit sympathy with his ideas. Far from taking it all as a small embarrassment, the affair was treated very seriously indeed: the Irish professor lost his post, the Bishop of Paris and even the Pope condemned the thesis, and the Bishop of Montauban wrote a pastoral letter in which he declared in apocalyptic tones:

> Hell has vomited its venom, so to speak, drop by drop. Today there are torrents of errors and impieties which tend toward nothing less than the submerging of Faith, Religion, Virtues, the Church, Subordination, the Laws, and Reason. Past centuries have witnessed the birth of sects that, while attacking some Dogmas, have respected a great number of them; it was reserved to ours to see impiety forming a system that overturns all of them at one and the same time.[17]

De Prades hurriedly left for Berlin, just in time to escape a *lettre de cachet* already made out in his name. While he had saved himself from imprisonment and the possibility of being sent to the galleys, in Paris the affair entered a second stage. The dissertation, it began to be stated with increasing confidence, had in fact been nothing but a trick by the Encyclopedists to undermine and ridicule the Sorbonne and its doctors and to threaten the authority of the Church. Illegal pamphlets, the currency of free speech at the time, appeared in great numbers and written by authors of very different philosophical and theological persuasions; but even the Jansenists, who despised the Sorbonne as a Jesuit stronghold, believed that 'the thesis of M. de Prades was the result of a conspiracy formed by some would-be freethinkers in order to insinuate their monstrous errors into the Faculty of Theology'.[18]

The indications seemed indeed to speak against the Encyclopedists, though it is unlikely that they had plotted all of this: d'Alembert had mentioned de Prades and his distinguished theological work (though not the dissertation) in his *Discours Préliminaire*, and

de Prades himself had contributed an important article, CERTI-
TUDE, to the second volume of the *Encyclopédie*, which appeared
just as the uproar about his thesis was at its height. He was also a
housemate and friend of two of the most devoted contributors on
theology and other philosophical and historical questions, the
abbés Claude Yvon, a decidedly progressive writer, and Edme Mallet
(another indication, incidentally, that Mallet is very unlikely to have
been the orthodox oaf for whom history has taken him). Jean-Martin
de Prades was, it seemed, at the very heart of the Encyclopedist
group, and it was therefore against them that the wrath of the
authorities now turned.

The consequences seemed dire indeed. D'Argenson, the former
Minister of War, noted down in early February:

> This morning appeared an *arrêt du conseil* which had not been
> foreseen: it suppressed the *Dictionnaire encyclopédique*, with some
> appalling allegations, such as revolt against God and the royal
> authority, corruption of morals . . . etc. It is said on this score
> that the authors of this dictionary, of which only two volumes
> have appeared, consequently must shortly be put to death, that
> there is no way of preventing their being hunted down and
> informed against.'[19]

D'Argenson, who had until the previous year served at the very
centre of power, was not making any idle claims: people had been
executed for much less in Louis XV's France, and the authorities
were especially merciless when it came to matters of religion.

Until now, the Jesuits had been on the sidelines, sniping at the
Encyclopédie in the *Journal de Trévoux* but unable to either stop it or
to gain control over it. Now they scented blood and promptly moved
in to give their prey the *coup de grâce*. They had friends in high
places, and it was their strategy to let others speak for them. It was
widely accepted that it had been through Jesuit intervention that
the Sorbonne had suddenly taken note of the Abbé de Prades's
thesis[20] and that they were speaking, to use the colourful image
from Edmond Barbier's diary, 'without moving [from] behind the

curtain' through the 'carcass, skeleton and old bones' of the venerable Sorbonne and its doctors.[21]

The Jesuits now pushed hard to eliminate their enemies and to
crown their campaign by usurping their project. One of their most
devoted friends was Jean-François Boyer, Bishop of Mirepoix and
preceptor of the Dauphin, the 'most ardent enemy of the *Encyclopédie*'[22] and of the Jansenists. Soon after the de Prades affair, Mirepoix
came into the King's presence with tears in his eyes, telling him in
the most dramatic terms possible that he could no longer conceal
from him that religion was going to be destroyed in the kingdom,
and that *la France* would lose its soul. The sovereign, who usually
regarded affairs of state as an unfortunate encumbrance, had at odd
times of personal crisis sought solace in religion and was appalled to
see a man of the Church reduced to such a condition. He was also
shocked to hear that the order of his kingdom itself appeared to
be at stake and that, by implication, he might be forced to occupy
himself with matters of state. He ordered that action was to be
taken.

Here the story of the *Encyclopédie* would have ended along the
lines sketched out by D'Argenson, had the enterprise not had one
crucial if unlikely friend and protector: the Censor Malesherbes.
On the advice of his father, he went to Bishop Boyer to negotiate.
The Bishop made it clear that he was not hoodwinked by the strat-
egems of the Encyclopedists, claiming that 'they had fooled the
censors appointed by d'Aguesseau by inserting into articles on
medicine, physics, and other secular sciences, errors which could
have been spotted only by a theologian'.[23]

Malesherbes suggested a compromise. Instead of ruining an
enterprise that did, after all, also have considerable economic implications as well as furthering the name of France abroad, would the
Bishop be satisfied if he could appoint his own censors, who could
control all areas of the *Encyclopédie*? The Bishop was delighted, and
was to get what he wanted: for the next four volumes, every single
article had to be given the blessing of one of his censors, the abbés
Tamponnet, Millet, and Cotterel, the two former of whom were
declared enemies of the *Encyclopédie*. Tamponnet was one of the

Sorbonne doctors who had not bothered to read the thesis by de Prades and no doubt took his appointment as a welcome opportunity to wash himself clean of the embarrassment. Millet, who had already censored the second volume and had found nothing in it that was against Holy Doctrine, had been quick to change his tune and to convince the Bishop of Mirepoix of the subversive nature of the work.

While already working behind the scenes to save the project, Malesherbes decreed on 7 February that any further distribution or sale of the *Encyclopédie* was illegal. The royal *arrêt de conseil* demonstrates that not even the authorities were blind to the ruses used by Diderot and friends: 'His Majesty has found that in these two volumes a point has been made of inserting several maxims tending to destroy the royal authority, to establish a spirit of independence and revolt, and, under cover of obscure and ambiguous terminology, to build the foundations of error, of moral corruption, of irreligion, and of disbelief.'[24] Rumours were flying thick and fast: D'Argenson believed that a *lettre de cachet* had been made out in Diderot's name but that the writer had fled before he could be arrested, the diarist Barbier reported that Diderot was 'afraid of being put a second time in the Bastille',[25] and all manuscripts pertaining to the projected future volumes of the *Encyclopédie* were confiscated by the authorities. Barbier, a judicious observer as well as a wise man, commented on the entire affair:

> This book, the *Encyclopédie*, is despite all rare, valuable, lofty, and cannot be appreciated by anybody but by people of spirit and lovers of science; their number is small. Why, therefore, putting out an episcopal letter which makes all the faithful curious about it? . . . This seems imprudent . . . There are many more people capable of reading this document of thirty pages than of leafing through seven folio volumes.[26]

While Diderot's arrest seemed imminent, the future of the *Encyclopédie* itself seemed to be assured, as D'Argenson noted: 'It is not doubted that the Jesuits will take the enterprise over and continue it.' To do so, they only had to apply for a release of the manuscripts. Even Grimm, Diderot's best friend, gives a very black, if bemused, account:

> The papers had already been taken from M. Diderot, and the Jesuits believed that they had carried off an encyclopedia that was all but finished . . . [and to have to do nothing but to] arrange and order the articles which were, they thought, ready for publication. But they had forgotten to take the head and the genius of the philosopher as well, and to ask from him the key for many of the articles which they could not understand and tried in vain to decipher.[27]

Appealing as this version is, it is also very unlikely to be correct. The Jesuits had among their numbers some extremely capable writers, and their own *Dictionnaire de Trévoux* demonstrated that the editing of a large encyclopedia was by no means beyond them, even if Diderot's handwriting and the general state of his notes and materials may not have lent themselves to quick and easy publication. At worst, they could have rewritten parts of the work themselves, which, in view of some of the material contained in the later volumes, they would have had to do in any case. It is therefore far more probable that the Jesuits' frustration at being deprived of control of the *Encyclopédie* once again came from a different quarter: Mme de Pompadour (1721–64), the King's mistress and patroness of the arts.

La Pompadour came from exactly the kind of rather modest, bourgeois Parisian house in which traditionally sympathies for Jansenism were high and Jesuits were hated. She had maintained intact her violent dislike of the Society of Jesus, and with it the Bishop of Mirepoix and other, demonstratively pious figures at court. Interested in literature, in music, and the arts, she was a consistent advocate of progressive ideas at court; Maurice Quentin de La Tour's wonderful pastel portrait of her shows a ravishingly graceful young woman sitting at a table and reading a musical score. On the table itself are several books, a selection of etchings, and a globe, all attributes of learning, usually to be found in the portrait of a scholar, not a mistress. Behind her are a few books ranged along the wall. The spine of the largest one reads: ENCYCLOPEDIE TOME IV.

In later years, Mme de Pompadour would welcome Diderot and members of his circle to informal suppers and discussions in her apartments, but she seems to have established contact with the Encyclopedists as early as 1752. D'Argenson, who followed the entire affair as an interested observer, remarked on 7 May: 'Mme de Pompadour and some ministers have had d'Alembert and Diderot solicited to devote themselves again to the work of the *Encyclopédie*, while practising the requisite resistance to any temptation to touch upon religion or authority.'[28] For the time being, at least, the work was safe.

The crisis brought home to Diderot not only the fragility of the project and of his own situation, but also the volatile temperament of his co-editor, who had earlier made clear that he would brook no criticism and for whom, it appears, the entreaties of Mme de Pompadour were not enough. D'Alembert felt himself slighted and insulted, and he threatened not to continue his collaboration if all parties concerned did not apologize to him personally. In a letter to Voltaire, who had mentioned the *Encyclopédie* with approval in one of his own works, he presented his view of events. 'I suspected that after having maltreated us as they did, they would come around to begging us to continue, and this has not failed to come about. For six months I refused, I shouted like Homer's Mars, and I may say that I gave in only because of the public eagerness.'[29] The mathematician, who had nothing to do with the quotidian job of editing the *Encyclopédie*, and whose name appeared on the title-page only in connection with the mathematical section, presented himself to Voltaire as the man responsible for the work, and in his idyllic remoteness Voltaire was not disabused of this notion until Mme d'Épinay visited him in 1757. Even a visit by d'Alembert himself the year before had done nothing to dissuade Voltaire from believing that he was speaking to the editor in charge. In fact, the name d'Alembert had last appeared in the booksellers' account books in 1749, an indication that his active involvement was indeed minimal. In the text, too, d'Alembert had the mark 'O' after his articles, much like other contributors, while Diderot's contributions were identified, if they were identified at all, by an asterisk before the text, marking them, as it were, as editorials.

Meanwhile, the official stance towards the *Encyclopédie* was becoming confused: the censor's request that the work be continued had been issued before any such continuation was legally authorized, and certainly before Diderot was given back his materials. A compromise had to be worked out that would allow all parties, at Court at least, to save face. D'Alembert, who evidently liked the heroic stance adopted in the letters to Voltaire, must have thought the legal device allowing the continuation of the work ridiculously inappropriate: the *arrêt du conseil* outlawing the *Encyclopédie* was quietly lifted, or rather substantially modified. The first two volumes, declared dangerous and blasphemous, remained illegal, which, strictly speaking, was no tragedy as they had been sold already. All further volumes were to be published with tacit permission and after having been subjected to thorough censorial scrutiny. The Jesuits had to admit defeat, if only for the time being. D'Alembert put the grandest appearance on the whole matter, writing to a friend:

> The affaire of the *Encyclopédie* is concluded. I have consented, after having resisted for six months, to giving my mathematical essays, on condition that I do not have to be concerned with the rest, that I get total satisfaction from the *Journal des sçavants,* and absolute liberty as to what I want to say, or at the very least a censor whom I deem acceptable. I thought I owed it to my public to take back my original refusal, as they are already avenging that harassment to which we were subjected.[30]

Diderot meanwhile, restored to his position, proved that his passion for discussion was a good deal stronger than his prudence. On 12 October he published, anonymously and clandestinely, the *Suite de l'apologie de M. l'abbé de Prades* (Continuation of the Apology

of M. the Abbé Prades), despite the fact that the first two parts had
not even appeared. In this booklet, purportedly written by de
Prades, Diderot played off a Jansenist bishop against the Sorbonne,
and both of them against the doctrines of the Church, which the
former abbé remembered only too well from his Jesuit college. The
work ends with a flourish:

> I will give myself without respite to that grand work which I
> have undertaken to carry out, and in a way that will one day
> make all my persecutors blush ... my enemies will be con-
> founded and good men will bless the Providence which has
> taken my by the hand at the time at which my uncertain steps
> were erring, and which has led me to a land where persecution
> does not follow me.[31]

This is the voice of the Encyclopedist, of a man whose life had
been threatened only a short time before, and who knew that police
spies were still posted around the corner.

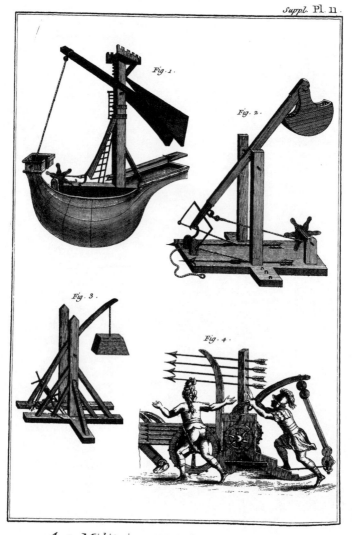

Fig. 1.

Fig. 2.

Fig. 3.

Fig. 4.

Art Militaire, Armes et Machines de Guerre.

THE WAR OF FOOLS

RÉCITATIVE, s. m. *in Music*, is a way of singing very much like talking; a musical declamation, during which the musician strives to imitate, as much as this is possible, the inflections of the voice of the actor . . .

The Italian language is sweet, flexible, & composed of words that are easy to pronounce, & allows the *recitative* all the rapidity of declamation. They insist, though, that nothing foreign should mingle into the simplicity of the *recitative* & that ornaments spoil it. The French, on the other hand, put in as many as they possibly can. Their language, more laden with consonants, harsher, & more difficult to pronounce, demands slower tempi, & it is on these slowed-down notes that they use accents, *portamenti*, and even trills . . . Foreigners therefore can never distinguish in our operas what is recitative and what is aria.

(*S*)

The Encyclopedists spent much of the summer of 1753 in the luxurious rooms of their constant host, Baron d'Holbach. Here they would assemble every Thursday and Sunday to enjoy the freedom of speaking their own minds and being in the company of people like themselves. It was the place of the Encyclopedists at play, with Diderot and Holbach effectively monopolizing the discussions for much of the time. Ten years younger than Diderot, Paul Henri Thiry d'Holbach (1723–89) had been baptized Paul Heinrich Dietrich in the Palatinate and had come to Paris at the age of twelve. He was that rare and wonderful creature, a wealthy man who was generous as well as modest. Like de Jaucourt, he had studied in

Leyden and, like him, he was well-travelled but ultimately devoted only to friends and books. Having inherited a large fortune that brought him around 60,000 *livres* (equivalent to £550,000) of rent per year, he was happy to put this at the disposal of entertaining, buying books and works of art, and financing the endeavours of artists and authors, as well as translating and writing himself.

Holbach's house became one of the main intellectual meeting points of progressive minds far beyond the borders of France. Among his foreign friends and visitors were Laurence Sterne, David Hume, David Garrick, Benjamin Franklin, a scattering of enlightened princes and other noblemen, and other passing luminaries. The salon became a fixed stopover on the intellectual grand tour. Discussions would begin in the afternoon and would stretch, lubricated by the contents of a well-stocked cellar, into the evening: 'This was the place to hear the best and most enlightened conversation there ever was,' enthused the Abbé Morellet, one of the *Encyclopédie*'s stalwarts, 'every conceivable argument, political and religious, was disputed there with the utmost subtlety and intelligence'.[1] The regulars set the tone: boisterous, worldly, intellectually acute, and often mischievous, with Denis and the baron himself as the focus of attention. 'Whatever was the subject under discussion among the friends,' wrote the baron's literary agent Naigeon, '[Holbach] effortlessly inspired such an enthusiasm in those listening to him talking about the arts or sciences, that one could not leave him without regretting the fact that one had not cultivated this particular branch of knowledge.'[2]

Similar characteristics were attributed to Diderot, who was a tireless talker and encourager of others. The Abbé Morellet had profited from this: 'The conversation of that extraordinary man Diderot . . . had great power and great charm; his style of discussion was vivid, supremely honest, subtle without being obscure, varied in its forms, speaking with imagination, overflowing with ideas and stimulating ideas in others . . . There was never a more easy-going and indulgent man than Diderot; he lent, indeed he positively made a gift of, wit to others.'[3]

The Abbé Raynal, another regular guest and a voluble man himself, watched the two literary stars with undisguised envy and was particularly irritated by Diderot's uninterruptible stream of words. 'If he so much as spits or coughs or blows his nose, he's lost,' the Abbé predicted darkly, without seemingly finding an opportunity to capitalize on this. The witty Abbé Galiani found a solution for breaking their unstoppable and scandalous talk. 'Messieurs, messieurs,' he interjected late one night in comic despair, '*messieurs les philosophes*, you're racing. I begin by telling you that, if I were the Pope, I would drag you in front of the Inquisition, and if I were the King of France, I'd have you thrown into the Bastille. But as I'm luckily neither one nor the other, I will come back next Thursday and you will listen to me as I have had the patience to listen to you.'[4]

In later years, while Holbach's salon remained one of the intellectual crucibles of Europe, his study would become the scene of a veritable one-man industry of atheist and materialist pamphlets and books, some of which he translated while writing others himself, usually anonymously. His greatest work, *Le Système de la nature*, created a sensation when it appeared in 1770 and contained many of the thoughts formulated, eighty-nine years later, in Darwin's *Origin of Species*. The Abbé Galiani was not totally convinced by the society's demonstrative atheism, and he enjoyed the sport of discussion too much to leave the floor to the atheists so easily. After having got the assembly's ear by threatening to have them all incarcerated, he came back the next Thursday as promised, bringing with him three dice. He asked Diderot to bet some money on the outcome and threw sixes twelve times in a row. Diderot, who had seen the spectacle with mounting impatience, and mounting losses, exclaimed 'but the dice are loaded and this is a cut-throat game!' Galiani calmly replied:

> Ah, *philosophe*! How that? Just because ten or twelve throws have come out so as to make you lose six francs you firmly believe that this is the consequence of an adroit manœuvre, an artificial combination, and a well-concealed trickery, and seeing in our universe a prodigious number of combinations

thousands and thousands of times more difficult and complicated and more useful, you do not assume that the dice of
nature are also loaded, and that up there is a great trickster
who makes a game of catching you?[5]

Galiani may have found an ingenious way of tripping up his
friend Diderot's intellectual complacency, but his wit did nothing
to change the atheist convictions shared by Denis and Holbach:
the latter would eventually express them in philosophical works as
well as in hundreds of articles for the *Encyclopédie*, while Denis,
debarred from writing philosophy at any rate, would later seek to
articulate them through novels, stories, and literary essays. While
Holbach hit the nail on the head and would not stop hitting it,
Diderot made it his speciality to smuggle his ideas past the vigilance
of censor and reader by adopting a hundred charming and fascinating guises. Their friendship was to last over more than two decades,
and Diderot spent many happy summers working, dining, and
going for long walks on Holbach's country estate. Toinette, who
had never forgiven her husband's initial treatment of her and had
never got over the fact that she had married a scandalous and
impious man who kept bad company, stayed in Paris, which seemed
to suit them both.

Holbach's fellow countryman and frequent guest Friedrich Melchior Grimm, meanwhile, had also begun to make a name for
himself in Paris, if not quite in the way he might have anticipated.
Grimm's initial claim to fame in the capital had nothing to do with
the grand diplomacy and literary criticism at which he would later
excel; he simply fell in love, desperately and unhappily, with an
opera singer, Mlle Fel, who could not be moved to show any interest
in him. Seeing all his overtures rejected, the young German unwill-
ingly performed an act worthy of Goethe's arch-romantic lover
Werther (whose story was not written until twenty-five years later):
he took to his bed and fell into a deep, seemingly fatal trance from
which nothing could stir him. A shocked and bemused Jean-Jacques
Rousseau was there to care for him:

He spent the days and nights in a continuous lethargy, the
eyes wide open, the pulse beating, but without talking, without
eating or moving, seemingly at times understanding what was
said to him but never answering, lying there without agitation,
without pain and without fever, just as if he were already dead
. . . The invalid stayed immobile for several days without eating
even bouillon or anything else except the candied cherries
which I put on his tongue from time to time and which he
swallowed well. One morning, he got up, got dressed, and took
up his normal life without ever talking about the episode . . .[6]

The news of the fashionable young man who had almost died for
love spread throughout Paris like wildfire, and Grimm was now
regarded with a flutter of female admiration, and sideways glances
of male distrust.

Already a sentimental starlet, the White Tyrant Grimm was soon
to become a literary star. The occasion was the long-awaited première of the Italian opera troupe in Paris, which took place on
1 August 1753. Diderot, Rousseau, and Grimm had been brought
together by their common passion for Italian music, which they
thought much more exciting and melodious than the overwrought
courtly creations of the great French composers, Lully (who actually
was Italian by birth) and Rameau. Jean-Jacques, who was still trying
to make a career as a musician, had made himself a champion of
this cause. In the months leading up to the musicians' arrival,
Grimm had already stirred up a debate by publishing a pamphlet
in the form of a letter, the *Letter on Omphale*, in which he attacked
a lyrical tragedy by the dramatist Philippe Néricault, known as
Destouches, and tried to prove the superiority of foreign music
over French, which, Grimm wrote, was enslaved to the words in
both recitative and arias. An exchange of letter-pamphlets had
developed, and it was still going on when the Italian musicians
came to perform in Paris. Now the musical friends were to have
their views put to the test, and expectations were high for the
première of Pergolesi's *La serva padrona* at the Comédie-Française,
performed by the Italians.

The first performance was not a musical triumph. The orchestra was dreadful, and few of the singers were up to the task. The music itself, however, was everything the friends had been hoping for. The Italian ensemble had brought with them a whole season's worth of comic operas, *opere buffe*, and the ensuing controversy over their style of composition and performance became know as the *querelle des bouffons*, the quarrel of the buffoons. Rousseau, Diderot and friends listened to the music from beneath the Queen's box, where the more progressively minded members of the audience huddled together, showered with scathing remarks (and at times not only remarks) from the society members higher up and from the 'other place', the partisans of French opera underneath the King's box. Called the Queen's Corner and the King's Corner, the two poles of opinion made the ensuing controversy sound like a boxing match. Rousseau, a manifestly partisan observer, describes the two sides:

> All of Paris was divided in two camps, and tempers were more heated than they could have been for an affair of state or of religion. The first, more powerful, more numerous, composed of grand people, the rich, and women, supported French music; the other one, more lively, more proud, more enthusiastic, was made up of true connoisseurs, men of talent and of genius.[7]

For once, historians agree with Rousseau: wit and talent were on one side, apoplectic rage and accusations of treason on the other.

The affair was hotly debated in the literary salons. It was much more than a question of taste and, much like the controversy between the Jansenists and Jesuits, it became a surrogate topic for a political discussion that could not, on pain of imprisonment, be held in the open. A debate that hardly ever explicitly mentioned anything but music, its participants were really talking not about arias and accompaniment, quavers and crotchets, but about social change and the arrogance of power.

French opera – whose greatest living exponent was Jean-Philippe Rameau (1683–1764) – was essentially a courtly art form, much loved by Louis XIV, who had liked to act himself, appearing in ever more outlandishly grand and allegorical garbs and dancing, passably, before a public commanded to attend. The operas dealt with mythological subjects and did not always require great vocal artistry from the singers, no doubt partly because some of the roles had often been taken by members of the Court. It was sophisticated, with dances and ballets, long and ornate recitatives, and stunning stage effects: flying gods, landscapes, parks, palaces, and naval battles – all accompanied by hundreds of candles, fireworks, and fantastically elaborate costumes. The music had to be content with a supporting role, so much so that the Italian stage writer Goldoni said that French opera was 'heaven for the eyes and hell for the ears', particularly for foreign ears unused to the musical declamations in grand dramatic style that in French opera replaced the more elegant, and certainly more easily comprehensible, *recitativo*.

The Italian operatic tradition, which Rousseau had first experienced in Venice, was almost diametrically opposed to this approach. The operas performed by the troupe of Maestro Eustachio Bambini were works by Pergolesi, Domenico Scarlatti, and other Italian composers. Their titles already showed the very different social orientation of the libretti: *Il giocatore* (The Gambler), *Il maestro di musica* (The Music Master), *La finta cameriera* (The False Chambermaid), *La donna superba* (The Superb Woman), *Il medico ignorante* (The Quack), and the greatest box-office success, *La serva padrona* (The Maid as Mistress). Whereas French opera depicted gods or kings, this was almost social realism, realistic comedy at the very least. Not many people had met Castor and Pollux, Zoroaster, or Anacreon (all subjects of Rameau operas), but everyone knew all about bad doctors and cheeky maidservants and could relate to dramas set, not in the Elysian Fields or on Mount Olympus, but in a drawing-room or a small draughty castle. The choice of topic was mirrored by the musical style, with its distinctly hummable tunes and often simple accompaniments, its recitatives with keyboard and cello, and its occasional bursts of vocal glory. Here the spectacle was not in the stagecraft, but in the drama and the music.

There were, of course, dangerous undertones of rebellion in

preferring this popular Italian style over the heritage of the Sun King. It also offered a possibility of siding with a cause that, whilst it attacked aspects of life at Court, was clearly not religious in character, and was certainly not tainted by the dour moralism of the Jansenists, who were the usual rallying-point for the more bourgeois and democratically minded parts of the population. Italian opera became an alternative to the otherwise enforced religious choice, just as the *Encyclopédie* was becoming.

It was in this controversy that the White Tyrant, Grimm, saw a chance of becoming known not as a sentimental fool, but as a wit and a representative of the progressive cause. He wrote a small satire poking fun not only at France's musical life, but also at the all too serious conventions of ideological – that is, usually religious – controversy, a little book entitled *Le Petit Prophète de Boehmischbroda*, published in early 1753. The little prophet, the hero of this mock-biblical tale, sits in his bohemian attic playing the violin when a heavenly voice begins to speak and he is transported through the air to the Paris Opéra. He describes what he sees there in some detail:

> And I saw a man who was holding a stick, and I believed he was going to castigate the bad violins for I heard many of them, among the others that were good and were not many. And he made a noise as if he were splitting wood, and I was astonished that he did not dislocate his shoulder, and the vigour of his arm terrified me . . .
>
> And I beheld that they called this 'beating the time,' and although it was beaten most forcibly, the musicians were never together.[8]

With its mock naïvety, the pamphlet might have been no more than a little amusement, but it had a remarkable effect. Amid the responses, some indignant, some learned, everybody had taken note of the young German who was trying to make his way in Paris, just as the little prophet was astonished to learn that in Paris a dissonant and bizarre spectacle of the sort he had witnessed was called an opera – a French opera, of course.

For the Encyclopedists, the *querelle des bouffons* was a moment of great solidarity; they all rallied around the ensign of Italian music, and its implications. D'Alembert, caustic as usual and more willing than most to expose the undercurrents of the debate, gave some advice to their opponents:

> I am astonished in a century where so many authors busy themselves writing about freedom of trade, freedom of marriage, freedom of the press and freedom of art, that nobody has so far written about freedom in music . . . for freedom in music implies freedom to feel, and freedom to feel implies freedom to act, and freedom to act means the ruin of states; so let us keep the French opera as it is if we wish to preserve the kingdom – and let us put a brake on singing if we do not wish to have liberty in speaking to follow soon afterwards.[9]

While d'Alembert was pitching in to aid both his allies and the progressive cause, Rousseau involved himself in the debate with an essay far more damning and less lightfooted than Grimm's. It was entitled *Lettre sur la musique française*, and it roundly denies the existence of any French music worthy of the name. French being a guttural, heavy, and unattractive language, Rousseau argues, it cannot be set to music easily, and generations of composers have had to seek refuge in subterfuge: 'In the absence of real beauties they have provided fictitious "style" . . . in place of good music, they have invented a scholarly music; to make up for the lack of song, they have multiplied accompaniments . . . to disguise the insipidity of their work they have increased the confusion. They believe they are making music; but they are only making noise.'[10]

Rousseau's war cry against French music came at a crucial time for him, and was all the more paradoxical because he himself had written a French opera, though in the Italian style, which was being rehearsed at the Paris Opera and would soon be premièred in front of the King himself. The work, *Le Devin de village* (The Village Soothsayer), had been submitted anonymously to the theatre directors, but Rousseau feared they might still remember the terrible

flop of his previous venture into the genre and might still be smarting from, or smirking about, the scene of Rameau humiliating his
young colleague in front of the orchestra. After a successful first
rehearsal, however, the veil of secrecy was lifted, and the piece
was judged excellent by M. de Cury, His Majesty's entertainment
secretary. A performance at Fontainebleau was arranged. Rousseau
attended the dress rehearsal, 'bashful as a schoolboy' amid the grand
and sophisticated courtiers (whilst despising them at the same time),
and then retreated to the anonymity of a café the following day, only
to hear an army officer regaling his comrades with stories and
reenactments of the composer's comportment during the performance. Rousseau fled, 'flushed and with lowered eyes', believing that
he had been recognized. 'On the street I noticed that I was
drenched in sweat . . . and that they saw in me the shame and the
embarrassment of a guilty man,'[11] a sentiment more indicative of
his state of mind than of the situation.

Rousseau's psychological and physical sufferings were acute and
do much to explain his behaviour, and possibly even some of his
moral and social philosophy – great intellectual edifices are often
built on the most mundane of foundations, personal or physical
flaws among them. Rousseau, the lover of solitude and nature,
despiser of women, and idealizer of 'innocent', primeval society,
suffered from a crippling and (probably) congenital urinary
complaint, which meant that he could only pass water drop by
drop and lived constantly with the urgent pain and anxiety of a
full bladder. He had consulted numerous physicians and surgeons,
had attended healing spas, and tried everything that might bring
relief, but had never been able to rid himself of this affliction,
which was not only painful, but also acutely embarrassing, especially
as he was never in absolute control of his bladder, as he himself
explained in his testament. He had to be very careful as to when
and for how long he was seen in society, and he would not receive
ladies at all, or be in a closed room with them. Like Nietzsche and
Schopenhauer after him, he would turn his shyness and perceived
inadequacy into a tower of sublimated heroism and violent ambivalence towards the other sex.

Because most people were not let in on this undignified secret, Rousseau's behaviour at Court must have seemed most peculiar. As it was, it probably ruined his chances of advancement. The fact that he had appeared at the première, on 18 October 1752, held in the presence of the King, in simple and rather grubby worker's clothes, with a shaggy beard, a badly kept wig and a rough shirt, was bewildering to the courtiers, who had no idea that his good shirts had recently been stolen and who might have been unaware of a music copyist's wages. Rousseau tried to make himself believe that his appearance in this costume was tantamount to a philosophical manifesto, but this was far removed from the man who had fancied himself a diplomat in Venice only a few years earlier. His music, after all, bore the clear imprint of his Venetian experiences, and the vigorous overture and graceful airs ('the first piece really is of a most touching naïvety', he himself remarks approvingly in the *Confessions*) must have awakened memories of idyllic evenings on the Grand Canal.

While Rousseau's score recalled Italian influences, the libretto, also by him, was pastoral and as profoundly conservative as Italy's *opera buffa* tradition is subversive. In Pergolesi's success *La serva padrona*, the maidservant ends up marrying her master, but Jean-Jacques offered a different vision, much more calculated to please a King: a shepherdess falls in love with the local lord, and her lover has to engage the village soothsayer to make her see the error of her ways, regain her affections, and restore feudal order, a surprising plot from a man who professed to despise social distinction. The opera was a great success, despite the composer's unkempt appearance. The King, who did not usually care for such entertainments, personally commanded its author to appear in front of him the following day, indicating that he intended to bestow upon the bearded genius a royal pension, which would mean the end of all of his financial worries, to allow him to compose at leisure.

But Jean-Jacques took a coach back to Paris early in the morning and refused to go back to Fontainebleau. His friends entreated him to reconsider. The producer of the opera, a M. Jelyotte, wrote to him, saying: 'You were wrong, Monsieur, to have left in the midst

of your triumphs. You would have enjoyed the greatest success that
has ever been witnessed in this place. The whole Court is enchanted
with your work. The King, who, as you know, does not like music,
sings your airs all day with the worst voice in the Kingdom, and he
has asked for a second performance within a week.'[12] Jean-Jacques's
mind was made up. He was unable to master his 'damned shyness',
and he was terrified of sitting in an antechamber full of grandees
for hours on end suffering torments from his bladder, only to be
finally admitted into the King's presence and reduced to a stammer-
ing idiot or, worse, wetting his breeches.

Rousseau decided that he would not take the royal yoke ('adieu
truth, freedom and courage') and that the honest métier of a music
copyist was a hundred times better than becoming a royal parasite.
Two days after his hasty retreat, he went to dine with his patron
Mme d'Épinay, only to find a carriage waiting in front of the house
and a figure in the shady interior beckoning him to come inside.
It was Diderot, who wanted to talk to him. Never a man to seek
advancement and positions for himself, Diderot had seen his friend
suffer enough deprivation and humiliation, and knew enough
about his talents to warn him against throwing away such a singular
opportunity. He tried to change his mind, to convince him of his
responsibility towards his gift, and towards his mistress. But Jean-
Jacques refused to listen. Denis, inveterate meddler that he was,
insisted, and the two quarrelled for the first time in their lives.

From this day on, Rousseau harboured suspicions against
Diderot, against Grimm, against all his friends. They looked at him
differently, they spoke of him behind his back; they were obviously
envious of his success at Court. The paranoia that was to divide
Rousseau from all his friends had begun to work its poison. The
first evident change happened at Holbach's house. Rousseau had
always been a reluctant attendee, snobbishly describing the baron
as 'the son of a parvenu' who did not have any 'nobility of race'.
Theirs was already a troubled relationship: 'a natural repugnance
long prevented my responding to his invitations', a lofty Jean-
Jacques relates. 'One day [Holbach] asked me why, and I replied
"You are too rich." He persisted, though, and in the end I was

conquered. It has always been my greatest unhappiness that I could not resist the marks of esteem others showed me.'[13]

Holbach's gracious decision not to take any notice of his friend's shows of arrogance, and his understanding that this bravado barely covered up a terrible shyness, did nothing, however, to prevent Rousseau from deciding that he was no longer a welcome guest. His great success after decades of obscurity (*Le Devin de village* now played to full houses at the Opéra) had a powerful effect on Rousseau, who was now forty. He had always been too timid to interject himself into the waves of oratory rolling back and forth between the baron and Diderot, and had shone only when allowed to sing some of his arias at the harpsichord. The others, for their part, had learned to treat him 'like a beautiful woman, capricious and vain'. Marmontel, one of the regular members of the circle, saw in him clear signs of distrust: 'He followed the maxim *Live with your friends as if they will one day become your enemies,*'[14] a motto which, in the event, became a self-fulfilling prophecy.

Jean-Jacques was beginning to see enemies everywhere, to hear whispering as soon as his back was turned, to search every work written by his friends for hidden sneers, to see a spy or a mocking face in every *décrotteur.* He no longer had any doubt:

> Since the success [of the opera] I no longer saw that cordiality, that frankness, that pleasure to see me that I had seen until now in either Grimm, or Diderot, or in other men of letters. When I entered the baron's salon, the conversation ceased to be general. They assembled in little groups, whispering into one another's ears, and I remained alone without talking to them . . . finally I was so repulsed by this disgraceful treatment that I left, resolved never to return.[15]

Rousseau's suspicions erupted one evening at Holbach's salon. Diderot had been bothered for a while by a country curate believing himself to be a poet of some consequence. He had been introduced to the *philosophe* in the Jardins du Luxembourg and had pressed Diderot to give his opinion on a poem of seven hundred verses he had written. Even for Diderot, who was always willing to help, to facilitate, and to give advice, this was too much and he advised the curate not to waste time on poetry but to write a tragedy instead. Inevitably, the curate returned, not only with the play, but also with a long discourse on theatrical composition included by way of a preface. Half irritated and half amused, Diderot invited him to read the work to the assembled guests at Holbach's salon, which the curé promptly did, believing that this was the beginning of fame and fortune in the capital. But the work was so bad that the *philosophes* found it very difficult to stifle their laughter.

Suddenly Rousseau, who had watched the proceedings with mounting impatience, jumped to his feet, charged at the curé, wrestled the manuscript from his hands, threw it to the ground and shouted at the author, who was beside himself with fright, 'Your play is worthless, your dissertation an absurdity, all these gentlemen are making fun of you. Leave here, and go back to do curate's duty in your village!' The embarrassed would-be poet, however, far from being grateful, showered his unbidden rescuer with insults most unbecoming for a man of the cloth and would have proceeded to beat him up had he not been restrained by the others. 'Rousseau left in a rage,' Holbach recalled, 'which I believed to be temporary, but which has never ceased and which has done nothing but increase since that time.'[16]

In the midst of these upheavals, the publication of the third volume of the *Encyclopédie*, CHA–CONSÉCRATION, in November 1753 went almost unnoticed. The publishers, though, could be highly satisfied. The work had new contributors, had weathered the storm of the de Prades affair, and had emerged triumphant. Most importantly of all, from a commercial point of view, it had almost doubled its original print run, with 3,000 copies coming off the presses.

Pl. XV.

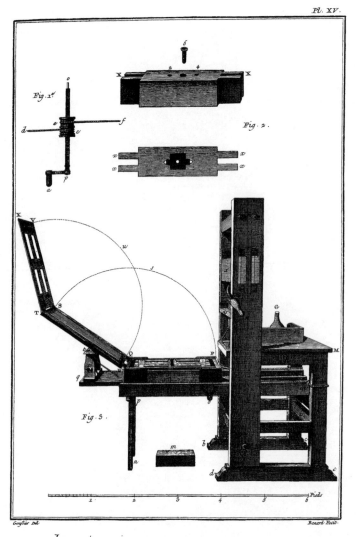

Fig. 1.

Fig. 2.

Fig. 3.

Pieds

Gouffier Del.

Benard Fecit.

Imprimerie, Presse vue par le côté du dehors.

ENCYCLOPÉDIE

ENCYCLOPÉDIE, s. f. (*Philosoph.*) This word means *linking of areas of knowledge* [*enchaînement de connoissances*], it is composed of the Greek preposition *en* and the substantives *circle* and *knowledge.*

The goal of an *Encyclopédie* is to assemble all the knowledge scattered on the surface of the earth, to demonstrate the general system to the people with whom we live, & to transmit it to the people who will come after us, so that the work of centuries past is not useless to the centuries which follow, that our descendants, by becoming more learned, may become more virtuous & happier, & that we do not die without having merited being part of the human race.

Volumes iv, v and vi of the *Encyclopédie,* CONSEIL–DIZIER, *Saint;* DO–ESMYNETE; and ET–FNÉ, appeared in October 1754, November 1755, and October 1756 respectively – a solid annual rhythm, though not quite the six-month interval originally promised to the subscribers. These tomes are probably the best of the *Encyclopédie,* judged by the number and celebrity of the contributors as well as by the quality of the writing contained in them, and give a good impression of the intentions and scope of the project as it was designed.

Responding to criticism from various sides, volume iii had already carried an *avertissement* by d'Alembert that served as a restatement of editorial policy. After having given short shrift to the idea of introducing even more lengthy articles on Church doctrine, an idea several critics had advocated, the author set out the aims of the project in his usual, pugilistic tone:

> One will find in this work . . . neither the *life of the Saints* . . . nor the *genealogy of noble houses,* but the genealogy of sciences, more precious for those who can think . . . not the *conquerors* who laid waste the earth, but the immortal geniuses who have enlightened it . . . for this *Encyclopédie* owes everything to talents, nothing to titles, everything to the history of the human mind, and nothing to the vanity of men.

Not only was the sheer survival of the *Encyclopédie* a victory against its enemies, it could boast other success. For instance, the great Voltaire himself had agreed to contribute articles, among them ELÉGANCE, ESPRIT, FANTASIE, and FAUSSETÉ (Falseness), although Diderot never quite trusted him – wisely as it would turn out – and gave him subjects that had limited political significance.

Other well-known scientists and writers had also been attracted to the cause: César Chesneau Dumarsais (1676–1756), a scholar from a previous generation and a humanist of great renown, wrote widely respected articles on grammar; the naturalist Louis-Jean-Marie Daubenton (1716–1800) wrote on botanical, mineral, and zoological topics; medical articles and others on chemistry were contributed by Gabriel-François Venel (1723–75) of the famous medical faculty in Montpellier; Jean-Baptiste Le Roy (1701–1800) wrote on watchmaking; the librettist Louis de Cahusac (1706–59) on music and opera; the cartographer Nicholas Bellin (1703–72) contributed naval articles; the royal councillor Antoine-Joseph Dezallier d'Argenville (1680–1765) articles on hydraulics and gardening; Louis-Guillaume Le Monnier (1717–99) on electricity and magnetism; Guillaume Le Blond (1704–1781), who gloried in the title *professor de mathématiques des pages de la grande écurie du roi* and who was tutor to the King's own children, wrote on fortifications and military questions; the famous architect Jacques-François Blondel (1704–74) wrote on his speciality; the eminent legal scholar Antoine-Gaspard Boucher d'Argis (1708–91) on legal and constitutional matters; the *Encyclopédie*'s draughtsman Goussier wrote on stone cutting, and mechanical instruments, as well as contributing a large number of drawings and being one of Diderot's main assistants for the description of crafts.

In addition to these named contributors, Holbach wrote numerous anonymous pieces on mineralogy and subjects across the board, and the Chevalier de Jaucourt was carrying an ever increasing workload of articles on all issues under the sun. Always keen to appropriate great names, the editors also inserted a fragment written by Charles de Secondat, Baron de Montesquieu (1689–1755), one of the most illustrious minds of his time. The piece, GOÛT (Taste), was a fragment that had not actually been written for the *Encyclopédie*, but it was printed and garnished with remarks that made sure no reader could overlook its author's association with the work.

While their enemies were growing increasingly irritated with the Encyclopedists, whom they held responsible for many of the ills of the time, it was very difficult for them to name exactly who they were. One might spontaneously think that they were a young, bourgeois, and irreligious rabble of mischievous abbés and atheists, people with most to gain and least to lose from change – people like Denis Diderot, in fact; but that was far from true for the majority of the contributors.

The *avertissements* to the different volumes of the *Encyclopédie*, in which collaborators are introduced and thanked, name 143 of them.[1] Even among the regular contributors, there were considerable differences in social origin, profession, income, and outlook. Diderot was the only Encyclopedist who lived from writing alone, and one of the very few to come from an artisan family; d'Alembert was a foundling in name only, but his career was unthinkable without the protection of his aristocratic parents. Rousseau, whose collaboration was brief, also came from an artisan background.

The clutch of abbés working for the *Encyclopédie*, Mallet, Morellet, de Pestré, de Prades and Yvon, were a different group. Edme Mallet was a theologian, a professor, and practising curate. The *avertissement* to volume six carried a special homage to him: he had died in 1755, depriving Diderot of one of his most cunning and assiduous contributors. The sharp-tongued André Morellet (1727–1819), who earned himself the nickname *mords-les* – 'bite 'em' – because of his ability to savage his opponents, was an economist, the eldest of fourteen children of a paper merchant. Martin de Prades, on the other hand, who had caused such great offence with his Sorbonne dissertation and who had taken refuge in Berlin, came from the *noblesse d'epée*, an old aristocratic family who had gained their title by fighting for the King. The backgrounds of de Pestré and Claude Yvon, who also had to flee in the wake of the de Prades affair, are almost entirely unknown.

Later, it became too dangerous for abbés to be associated with the *Encyclopédie*, and their work was absorbed entirely by Louis de Jaucourt. Another land-owning aristocrat, though, as Rousseau had been quick to point out, one of a more recent vintage, was Holbach, whose contribution was substantial. There were few other contributing noblemen: the Comte d'Hérouville de Claye, the Comte de Tressan, and Turgot were exceptions, and often their titles were not mentioned in the *avertissment*, true to d'Alembert's egalitarian creed.

As already mentioned, there was a significant number of doctors and professors of medicine and chemistry,* men with positions at court,† senior civil servants and office holders,‡ some members of the *Parlement* in Paris and from provincial government,§ a handful of army officers,¶ as well as an engineer of roads and bridges (Nicolas-Antoine Boulanger), an engraver (Jean-Baptiste Papillon),

---

* Gabriel-François Venel, Paul-Jacques Malouin, Antoine Louis, Jean Bouillet, Jean-Henri Nicolas, Théophile de Bordeu, and the anatomist Paul-Joseph Barthez.

† Antoine-Joseph d'Argenville, Charles Georges Le Roy, and Adrien Cuyret de Margency.

‡ The *fermier général* Perrinet d'Orval, Étienne-François Turgot, the brothers Nicolas and Claude Durival, and Claude-Henri Watelet.

§ Antoine-Gaspard Boucher d'Argis, Louis de Cahusac, Charles de Brosses, and Jean-Joseph Rallier des Ourmes.

¶ Antoine de Ricouart d'Herouville, Nicolas Liébault, Antoine Eidous, the musketeer, veterinarian and equine specialist Claude Bourgelat, and the cavalry tactician Charles-Louis des Amourettes d'Authville.

the Royal Historiographer (Charles Pinot Duclos), a draughtsman (Charles-Nicolas Cochin the younger), a banker (Louis Necker de Germagny), a steelworks engineer (Étienne Jean Bouchu), and several economists (including François Véron de Forbonnais and François Quesnay). Several manufacturers had written articles about their own areas of expertise, such as the silk manufacturer Buisson and the brewer Longchamp. Among the writers and poets were such well-known names as Jean-François Marmontel and the Marquis de Saint-Lambert.

No women authors are named in the *Encyclopédie*, though the Marquise de Jaucourt, the sister-in-law of the Chevalier, was probably responsible for at least two articles, FALBALA and FONTAGE. It is also possible that Mme d'Épinay, who was later to play an important role in Grimm's *Correspondance littéraire*, may have provided some contributions anonymously.

The list, like every list, is interesting for its omissions: the most glaring of these are the Jesuits, who were usually well represented in areas of intellectual endeavour. The higher clergy, too, was understandably not in evidence. The *societé des gens de lettres* responsible for the work consisted, for the time being at least, exclusively of French writers or those (Rousseau and Holbach) who had made France their primary residence. Despite their progressive ideas, their anticlericalism, and their criticism of official politics, very few of the Encyclopedists went on to play an active role in the Revolution, with the notable exception of Alexandre Deleyre, who would vote for Louis XVI's death. This was partly for generational reasons – most of them would be in their sixties and seventies when the Revolution broke out – but it was also a question of orientation. The Encyclopedists sought evolution, not revolution.

Considering the fanfares about the importance of the mechanical arts and the genius residing in the crafts and *métiers*, one might have expected the *Encyclopédie* to give pride of place to the men and women who worked in these crafts; but in fact they remain largely anonymous. Of the multitude of artisan activities described in the work and of the hundreds of informants who gave up their secrets, only ten were rewarded with a mention in the *avertissements*, and none were prevailed upon to write about their craft, though there were some, especially among the more refined crafts, who were no doubt capable of doing so.[2] The world of crafts in the *Encyclopédie* remains as it is depicted in the accompanying plates: an impersonal, ideal world, peopled by graceful men and women adopting classical poses in clean and sunny environments, without either disorder or sweat to upset the reader's enlightened sensibilities.

The Encyclopedists were right to claim that their work had achieved a breadth and depth never seen before, with many articles written by leading experts in their field. As d'Alembert had made clear, the work intentionally left out (or almost so) historical persons (they were later to be admitted through a back door by de Jaucourt), great kings, famous battles, Church Fathers, favourite saints, or historical essays. On human genius and ingenuity, however, and on economic and scientific questions, the *Encyclopédie* was thorough and often thought-provoking, frequently authoritative, and usually engagingly opinionated.

One example is a large dissertation on a small object, Alexandre Deleyre's learned 5,000-word analysis ÉPINGLE, dealing with the modest pin and its fabrication. This was encyclopedic ambrosia: a tiny object handled by every seamstress in the kingdom, each individual pin had undergone a long and sophisticated process of manufacture that illustrated not only methods of production, but also questions of national economy, a fact that was not lost on the author:

> Of all mechanical works, the pin is the leanest, the most common, the least precious, & at the same time one of those which demand perhaps most combinations [of work processes]: consequently, art as well as nature demonstrate their marvels in these tiny objects & that industry is at the same time limited in its approach and admirable in its resources; for a *pin* undergoes eighteen operations before it gets into the shops.

Deleyre then follows the pin's progress, from the rolls of wire arriving from Hamburg or Sweden 'all black from the foundry' to the cleaning and stretching of the metal, the sharpening of the points, the turning, cutting, rounding off, and broadening of the heads, to the polishing of the metal, the placing of the pins in cardboard, and the wrapping of the pin cards in paper. Three meticulously drawn and engraved illustrations (published later in the volumes of plates) served to clarify the text.

Articles like these had the immense advantage of being calmly and unpolemically informative, as well as ideologically progressive. When Adam Smith published his *Wealth of Nations* (1776), he chose a pin factory as his example of the beneficial effects of the division of labour.

It had been Diderot's editorial policy from the very beginning to allow dissent between different articles of the *Encyclopédie*. Nevertheless, the first six volumes give a clear indication of an editorial line, roughly indicative of the consensus in the salon of Baron d'Holbach or other fashionable Paris hosts. There was, of course, no area of debate on which State and Church did not claim a monopoly of righteousness, and the Encyclopedists had to be careful to tread a delicate line between being dishonestly conformist, and being thrown into the Bastille.

The political thinking of the *Encyclopédie* was a case in point. By far the most famous political article in the entire work is Rousseau's ÉCONOMIE (*Morale et Politique*), which marks an important step in the development of his philosophical ideas but is not, perhaps, typical of those of the editors or authors of the encyclopedia as a whole. At the time, political contributions by Diderot himself, AUTORITÉ POLITIQUE (Political Authority) and DROIT NATUREL (Natural Law) caused considerably more interest, and outrage. His essay on political authority begins with a blast for freedom:

> No man has received from nature the right to command others. Liberty is a present from the heavens, and every individual of the same species has the right to enjoy it, as much as he enjoys reason. If nature has established *authority*, it is the father's power, but this power has limits; & in nature it ceases as soon as the children are in a state to look after themselves.

All other authority comes from another origin than nature. If one examines them, one always returns to the same two sources: either force & violence exercised by the strong; or the common consent of those who submit themselves to it by a contract made and agreed between themselves & the one to whom they cede the *authority*.

This conception of contractual authority may leave open a possibility of living in a monarchy (if a more limited, constitutional one than the French); but any idea of rule by divine right was implicitly denied, despite the fact that the text was peppered with Scriptural references in order to make it more palatable, and despite the final sentences, which were full of the most sugary monarchist piety.

One common strategy was to hide progressive opinions behind established authorities, particularly the constitutional ideas of Montesquieu and his hugely influential *magnum opus*, *De l'esprit des lois* (1748), and those of two other luminaries, the Dutch humanist and natural rights theorist Hugo Grotius (1583–1645) and Samuel von Pufendorf (1632–94), a Lutheran, who developed the ideas of Grotius and Hobbes. By using much of this material (not always acknowledged), the authors, especially Diderot and de Jaucourt, were able to develop a theory of natural law, equality and constitutional monarchy without going beyond what was already established and accepted.[3]

Scattered through miscellaneous articles there were little rumblings of political critique, nothing systematic, but enough to stimulate readers to draw connections of their own. In GALANTERIE (*Morale*), Diderot smuggles in the following consideration:

Under a government where one single individual is charged with the affairs of all, the idle citizen, placed in a situation he cannot change, will try to make it at least livable; & from this necessity is born a broader form of society. Women will have more liberty in it; men will make it their habit to please themselves; & one will see the formation of an art which is that of *galanterie*. This *galanterie* will taint everything, from the manners of a society to all of its productions; they will lose their greatness and force, but they will gain in sweetness and all kinds of agreeable aspects, which other peoples will then try to imitate, which makes them seem gauche and ridiculous.

While Diderot muses on morals and pleasure, de Jaucourt, in FRANCE, compares his country to Rome before the fall of the Republic, and Saint-Lambert remarks in FASTE (Pomp) that a country should not be judged by the excessive luxury and displays of wealth at court, but by the state of its provinces, its commerce, and its army. D'Alembert is more direct in his article on COURTISAN (Courtier), which reads: 'We use this as an adjective, and one must not confuse this with a *man of the Court*, for this epithet is given to the kind of people who have been placed by the unhappiness of kings and their people between the kings and the truth, in order to prevent that the truth reaches them, even if they are explicitly meant to make it known to their ruler.' In COUR (Court), Diderot, taking cover behind Montesquieu, quotes the venerable thinker in defining the air or manner at Court as follows: 'It is the seductive varnish under which are hidden idle ambition, low pride, the desire to get rich without doing any work, an aversion to the truth, flattery, treason, perfidy, the abandonment of all involvement [in public affairs] and deep disdain for the duties of a citizen.'

While they had to be careful with politics, the editors could go further in the economics articles, which did not necessarily touch either Church or Crown directly. One of the century's most distinguished economists and economic reformers, Étienne-François Turgot, later to become *contrôleur général des finances*, was given a free hand to articulate his thinking on political economy. His articles on FOIRE (Market) and FONDATION (Foundation), both published in volume seven, strongly advocated the then fashionable idea of *laissez-faire*, or economic liberalism. Writing about the markets and fairs that were such an important engine of commerce at the time, Turgot rejected the idea of regulation: 'While the natural course of commerce is sufficient for the establishment of markets, we are now faced with the unhappy principle of ... the mania for controlling & regulating everything & never serving people's true interests'. In FONDATION, he lays out the arguments, familiar today, against social welfare through charitable foundations: 'Making a great number of people live for nothing is sustaining idleness & all the disorders that stem from it; is to make the condition of the lazy preferable to that of the working man.'

While Turgot preached the gospel of *laissez-faire*, other authors argued similarly modern ideas. Joachim Faiguet de Villeneuve (1705–80) attacked the guild system that was such a profoundly conservative force in French and European manufacturing. The system controlled professional training and production of most goods and put all power in the hands of a small number of masters, who often ran their guilds on dynastic lines. The answer to the problems this produced – an inherent hostility to innovation, lack of flexibility, and the tendency to criminalize those outside the system – was clear: free competition. Faiguet, a schoolteacher, outlined his ideas in a long and closely argued article on ÉPARGNE (Thrift), and his values were very much those of a man used to working hard and saving a little here and a little there. In his strong work ethic and disgust at public taverns, in his wish to free up working time by abolishing religious holidays and his hope that someone might encourage French youth on the path of righteousness by instituting a prize for thrift and frugality, he is already a man of a different age. He is, as Arthur Wilson writes, 'the disembodied voice of an upthrusting bourgeoisie'.[4] The next century would belong to him.

Perhaps the most important author on economic issues was Dr François Quesnay (1694–1774), a doctor and surgeon as well as an economist, whose ideas created a new theory, the Physiocratic movement, and who had signed the articles FERMIERS and GRAINS. Reacting against the Mercantilists, whose economic theory had given primacy to government, the axiom of all Physiocratic thinking was that the wealth of an economy was to be sought in its agriculture and that land ownership, not manufacturing or the ownership of the means of production (factories and machines), was the most important economic lever of power. Only in agriculture could the 'produced wealth' exceed the 'consumed wealth'; all other branches of the economy were occupied with nothing but mixing and adding, thus forming a 'sterile class'. This economic conception was to be made redundant within two or three decades by the advance of industry, which demonstrated overwhelmingly that factories, machines, and technological innovation were the true forces behind economic and social change, while land ownership and agriculture were quickly being consigned to a supporting role. The Physiocratic theory may have placed the *Encyclopédie* at the cutting edge of contemporary debate, but its inclusion also exposed the considerable limitation of an economic school (and an editorial policy) completely unaware of the industrial revolution that was already taking its first tentative steps.

Despite its emphasis on land owning, which implicitly favoured the aristocracy, the Physiocratic doctrine was also critical of a restrictive government policy that had left agricultural production in tatters for much of the first half of the eighteenth century. (Poverty in the countryside was endemic: in 1707, Sébastien Vauban had estimated: 'Of every ten men one is a beggar, five are too poor to give him alms, three more are ill at ease, embarrassed by debts and lawsuits.'[5]) Diderot's own economic ideas were close to those of the Physiocrats, as is clear from his article HOMME (*Politique*), which begins with the rousing declaration: 'There are no true riches other than man & the earth. Man is worth nothing without the earth, the earth nothing without man.'

While Diderot agreed with Physiocratic ideas himself, he also ensured that a measure of debate was introduced into the *Encyclopédie*. François-Louis Véron-Duverger De Forbonnais (1722–1800), who was a declared opponent of the Physiocrats, supplied the articles on CHANGE, COMMERCE, and COLONIE, which were an argumentative counterpoint to total economic liberalism, advocating a more classical (and, as it happens, more adaptable) balance between raw materials and industry, trade and regulation.[6]

Although there is much distinguished scholarship in the articles, it cannot be overlooked that the quality of some individual contributions were often wildly uneven. While some pieces had been written by leading experts, others had been cobbled together rather hastily and published anonymously – many by correspondents whose enthusiasm for seeing their work published was considerably greater than their competence. Even Diderot himself was occasionally guilty of doing the very opposite of what the *Encyclopédie* had set out to achieve, piecing together various half-truths and prejudices and letting them pass for informed judgement. His article HUMAINE, ESPÈCE is riddled with extremely shaky information and is certainly one of the least well informed in the entire work. 'All ugly peoples are crude, superstitious, and stupid,' the *philosophe* wrote, apparently with great authority.

> The Lapps and the Danes venerate a fat, black cat. The Swedes call the devil with a drum. They run on wooden shoes on the snow with such speed that they catch the lightest animals ... They have almost no idea of God or religion. They offer their wives and daughters to strangers. They live under the ground ... their women are dressed in reindeer hides in winter and in bird skins in summer.

Diderot further wrote that the Chinese were 'soft, peaceful, indolent, superstitious, submissive, slavish, & ceremonious'; that the inhabitants of Yeço (Yangzu, a province of China) were 'fat, brutal, without morals & without arts, with short and fat bodies and long, unkempt hair'; the Egyptians, by contrast, were 'tall & their women short'. Unsurprisingly, the peoples of Europe were 'the most beautiful & the best proportioned' on earth. Some contradictions worried Diderot: 'People are more chaste in cold countries than in warmer climes. They are less amorous in Sweden than in Spain or Portugal, & yet the Swedes produce more children.'

Remarkably, this stew of misinformation and rumour was not overly tainted by malice, or by dogmas of racial or religious superiority. Diderot was a man of his time, writing that 'while in general the Negroes have little intelligence [*esprit*] they do not lack feeling', but he did not deduce from this the right to subjugate other races: 'We have reduced them not to the condition of slaves, but to that of beasts of burden; & we are reasonable! & we are Christians!'

Diderot did not think the Europeans inherently more valuable than other races, nor did he propagate other common stereotypes. In describing the 'people of Judea' he eschewed any anti-Semitic ideas, writing merely that they 'resemble the Turks'.

One of the reasons the *Encyclopédie* is remarkable to readers today is its very Gallic asymmetry, an irredeemably French intermingling of high organization and occasional total anarchy. At times subjects of considerable importance were dealt with within a few lines, while seemingly trivial matters had many columns and pages devoted to them; articles purporting to be about a certain subject suddenly veered off into a different direction never to return, and if Diderot thought a contribution not expressive enough, or if he was taken with the idea, he added his own commentary underneath, often contradicting what the article itself said, or undermining its meaning. If his immense courage, learning, and easy friendship made the work possible, his eclectic character made it what it is. Indeed, his long and wonderfully discursive article ECLECTICISME makes the point by following as many tangents as Sterne's *Tristram Shandy*, a novel Diderot admired hugely. What made the *Encyclopédie* so fascinating was the fact that Diderot had neither the ambition nor the systematic mind of a collector of facts: he was, instead, an artist. The work was a vehicle for his ideas; it gave him an income, and was to make his name, and it dignified subjects that had never before graced the printed page; but systematic, all-embracing meticulousness was not among his interests.

Conservative critics who had pointed this out, and who wondered increasingly loudly about the true purpose of the work, found in volume five an article that confirmed their misgivings. The article *ENCYCLOPÉDIE*, some 35,000 words long, is perhaps the most important in all the twenty-eight volumes of the work: it is at once a manual on how to compile and write an encyclopedia and, just as important, how to read one; a treatise on language and an ode to liberty; a surprisingly frank admission of all the faults in the *Encyclopédie*, and a rousing invocation of its ambitions. It is a document of luminous humanity, as well as exasperating vanity.

The piece begins relatively innocuously. An encyclopedia,

Diderot writes, cannot be compiled by a single person or a formal institution but by a loose association of experts. Typically for Diderot, the article goes on to oscillate between analytical and political statements, between reason and revolution: 'Today, as philosophy is advancing with great steps; as it subjugates to its empire all the objects within its reach; as its tone is dominant, & as people start to throw off the yoke of authority & of [traditional] ways to obey the laws of reason, there is hardly an elementary & dogmatic work that could satisfy entirely.' It is close to a miracle that the theological censor let sentences like this one slip through the net.

Diderot's reflections on the principles of classification and ordering of the articles also allow him to write about things far beyond those he is ostensibly addressing. The alphabetical order, he writes, has been chosen because it seems the most logical and least intrusive method, communicating the fact that all branches of knowledge are interlinked: analysis and contemplation of each given detail can lead to an understanding of the whole:

> Generally, the description of a machine can be begun by any of its parts. The greater and more complicated the machine is, the more its parts will be interlinked, and the less obvious these links will be. A general plan is therefore very necessary. What would happen, then, if the machine were in fact to be infinite in every sense; if it is a question of the real & the intelligible universe, or of a work that is like their mirror image? The universe, real or intelligible, can be represented from an infinite number of perspectives, & the number of possible systems of human knowledge is as large as the number of these perspectives.

Only a system able to accommodate the infinity of the subject matter can do it justice, and the alphabetical order, which allows ever new additions, is ideally suited to the task, especially since it has at its centre the human mind, able to grasp every possible subject with equal ease. For Diderot, that most sociable of thinkers, it is the human mind that makes the world what it is: 'If one banned man and the Thinking and Contemplating Being from the surface of the earth, the sublime and moving spectacle of nature would become nothing more than a sad and mute scene.'

Having decided on the alphabetical order, the second question is how much weight and length should be apportioned to the individual articles and the subjects they deal with. Here Diderot is pragmatic. He is dealing with dozens of writers of different tastes and abilities, and, short of writing everything himself, he cannot possibly impose a uniformity of style and depth. Experience has taught him that nobody can be relied upon to submit just what was promised, and that even famous contributors sometimes hand in 'a few lines without exactness, without style, and without ideas, with the humiliating admission *that he did not know any better*', forcing the editor to write the article himself after all. The *Encyclopédie* therefore is anything but perfect, and its faults are enumerated with all the gusto of a writer let off the leash and an editor subjected to years of frustration:

> The proof can be found in a hundred places in the work. Here we are swollen and exorbitant, there meagre, small, paltry, and emaciated. In another place we look like skeletons; in another, we have appeared inflated; we are alternatively dwarfs & giants, colossi & pygmies; straight, well-proportioned; humpbacked, limping, & malformed. Add to all these grotesque forms a discourse that is now abstract, obscure or far-fetched; but more often sloppy, long-winded & slack; & you have to compare us to the monsters appearing in poetry, if not to something more hideous. But these faults are inseparable from a first attempt . . . and later centuries will correct them.

Posterity, he admits, might find this quite a task as even basic errors cannot be avoided in an undertaking of this size, especially as many of the craftsmen prove often very reluctant to supply accurate information to the authors, taking them for undercover tax inspectors or competitors: 'Some gross gaffes have slipped in (*see the article* BRIQUE), & there are entire articles which contain not even a shadow of common sense (*see the article* BLANCHISSERIE DE TOILES).' These, Diderot suggests, are the necessary side effects of such projects, but a bad *Encyclopédie* is still better than none at all. Chambers, he adds, may have produced articles that are accurate, orderly, and well judged, but 'his are regular; but empty. Ours are full, but irregular.' The methods individual authors choose is their concern, as long as they are committed to furthering knowledge and to 'showing truths; unveiling errors; adroitly discrediting prejudices; teaching people to doubt & to be patient'.

The organization of different entries under the same heading could also usefully be made to work in favour of progressive opinion. Readers wanting to inform themselves about dukes first found under the headword DUC 'a great bird that feeds only at night and has on its head feathers in the form of ears', and only then did the article deal with a member of the high nobility. In this way the encyclopaedic order re-established natural law rather than reinforcing social convention. Similarly, under ROI (King) one read first about a 'bird of the approximate size of a female turkey' before being given a dissertation on the kings of France.

There was another secret weapon in Diderot's arsenal, which he now happily showed off: the cross-references, 'the most important part of this *Encyclopédie*'. In a work conceived like a chain in which every link is connected to all the others, cross-references were obviously valuable in that they supported and broadened a subject. They did, however, have another, less obvious purpose: 'When necessary, they produce the opposite effect; they oppose notions; they contrast principles; they attack, undermine, and secretly reverse ridiculous opinions which one would not dare to attack openly'. The Encyclopedists made liberal use of this possibility. ANTHROPOPHAGES (Cannibals) was surreptitiously commented on by the addition '*See: Eucharist, Communion*'. Similarly, LIBERTÉ DE PENSER (Freedom of Thought) had as a contrasting reference '*See: Intolerance & Jesus Christ*'; while OFFICE (reminding everyone of the positions bought by incompetent courtiers for tax exemptions, pensions, and bribes) was accompanied by '*See: Morals, Morality, and Ethics*'. 'It is the art of tacitly deducing the most powerful consequences', as the editor himself commented. Going one step further, he admitted that some of the articles had been written altogether ironically and were not to be taken seriously:

> The last sort of cross-reference is . . . intentionally satirical or epigrammatic; one of these, for example, finds itself at the end of one of our articles, or follows a pompous eulogy, where one reads: *See: Capuchon*. This burlesque *capuchon*, & what one finds in the article *capuchon*, can lead one to the suspicion that the pompous eulogy is only ironic; & that one has to read the article with care & think of it in all possible ways.

This warning to the reader made clear once more that the authors were not always free to write what they pleased, and that the entire *Encyclopédie* had to be read not with pinches, but with handfuls of salt.

The constraints of censorship (which seems to have failed singularly in this article, as the censors were still appointed by the anti-Encyclopedist Bishop Beaumont) meant that the *Encyclopédie* had to operate with subterfuge if it was to express anything but official piety. By now, Diderot and his colleagues seemed quite comfortable with this, and the editor made no effort to hide the fact:

> There should be great scope for ingenuity and infinite advantage for the authors of this . . . sort of cross-reference. The entire work will acquire an internal force and secret unity, which will necessarily become more obvious with the passage of time. Whenever, for example, a national prejudice demands respect, it will be discussed respectfully & with all its apparel of probability and seduction: but by introducing a cross-reference to articles where solid principles support truths that are diametrically opposed, the entire mud edifice will crumble into a vain heap of dust.

'A bizarre mixture of sublime qualities & shameful blunders', the *Encyclopédie* is nevertheless a historic necessity, a child of the philosophic century, which alone has produced the 'daring of spirit' to bring forth such a work. Its purpose – and once again Diderot leaves no doubt on this point – is an intellectual revolution: 'The old puerilities have to be trampled underfoot; we must tear down the barriers not erected by reason; [and] give Science and the Arts the liberty which is so precious to them.'

Diderot was always inclined to praise virtue where he saw it most, which was usually very close by. One has to praise virtue in order to give a good example, he writes, and proceeds to do just that: 'O Rousseau, my dear and worthy friend, I will never have the strength to abstain from praising you: and in doing so I have felt my taste for the truth and my love of virtue grow. Why all those funeral orations, if there are so few hymns of praise to the living?' Having lampooned his enemies and praised his friends, Diderot finally slipped in a portrait of the ideal editor. Such a person must be 'neither a genius nor an imbecile', but somone 'gifted with great common sense, celebrated for the breadth of his knowledge, the elevation of his sentiment & of his ideas, & his love of his work: a man loved & respected for his character in private & in public; never zealous, if not for truth, for virtue, & for humanity.' That man, implicitly set before the reader's admiring eye, was Denis Diderot himself.

Antiquités.

Benard Direx.

A

LOVE OF THE SEXES

AMOUR DES SEXES. *Love*, wherever it is, is always master. It forms the soul, the heart, and the mind according to its nature. It does not adapt to the size of the heart or mind it fills, but has its own size; & it seems truly that to the soul of a person in love, love is as important as his body is to his soul. . . . As one is never free to love or to stop loving, the lover has no right to complain about the faithlessness of his mistress, nor she of his inconstancy. . . . There is only one kind of love, but a thousand different copies. Most people believe love to be physical desire. But examine your sentiments in all honesty, & find out which of these two passions rules your attachment; look in the eyes of the person holding you in chains. If her presence makes you timid and induces respectful submission, you love her. True *love* forbids you even to think of sensual ideas . . . but if the charms of the person make more of an impression on your senses than on your soul, that is not *love*, it is physical appetite.

All that we have been saying here shows that true *love* is very rare. It is like a ghostly apparition: everybody talks about it, but hardly anyone has seen one.

Maximes de la Rochefoucauld [from the *Encyclopédie*]

By the mid-1750s, political pressure on the enterprise was, for the first time in the history of the *Encyclopédie*, sufficiently relaxed to allow Diderot and his circle to turn their attention to their personal lives. It was a period in which Rousseau decided to retreat into picturesque solitude and Diderot himself took courage and made peace with his family; in which journeys were made, friendships deepened, affairs blossomed, and things began to look as if they could continue in this way for many years to come. This calmer period centred not only on Baron d'Holbach's *palais*, but also on a country house to the north of Paris, the seat of Mme d'Épinay (1725–83), the only woman to maintain a place in the Encyclopedist circle.

While a man's path to becoming a *philosophe* often led through cafés, garret rooms, and, occasionally, prison cells, for women it was very different. Louise d'Épinay's life took her through a humiliating childhood, the marriage bed, the slow and painful realization of the reality of life as a wife and mother, and the awakening of an independent and courageous spirit. Born Louise-Florence Pétronville Tardieu d'Esclavelles, she was brought up by a wealthy Parisian aunt as a poor relative in a grand house. She later chronicled her humiliations in an autobiographical novel, *Mémoires de Madame de Montbrillant*, the closest French equivalent to the works of Richardson, whom Diderot was to admire so much. It was published posthumously and became a considerable sensation in literary Paris.

As an aristocratic child without any income, little Louise first had to do the rounds at Versailles so that royal or noble favour might bestow on her some kind of pension, position, or prospective engagement. Her literary alter ego, Émilie, describes the day in a letter to her mother:

> This morning, my mother presented me to M. le prince de S***, to M. le maréchal de P*** and to M. le maréchal de M***, with whom we also dined. After this, he took us to Versailles, and presented us to the minister; I no longer recall his name, I saw so many people, but it was the minister to whom my father was always writing. On the way there, I was told to throw myself at his knees and to say to him that I came to ask bread. I asked whether that was all he would give us for supper, and M. le maréchal found this very funny . . .[1]

The minister, the former regent to Louis XV and now cabinet chief, Cardinal de Fleury, may have been the first to call the eleven-year-old girl a *philosophe*, but he was not to be the last. To merit this distinction, though, she would have to wait many years. Her education did nothing to help her attain it: 'When I was a child it was not the custom to teach girls anything. They were more or less indoctrinated with their religious duties . . . they were given a very good dancing master, a very poor music teacher, and in rare cases a mediocre teacher of drawing. Add to this a bit of history and geography . . . no more than memorizing names and dates. Above all, we were never taught to think; and any study of science was scrupulously avoided as being inappropriate to our sex.'[2] Her education was then continued in a convent, where she was further instructed to dampen the first stirrings of her mind in holy water and pious precepts.

In 1745, at nineteen, Louise married a distant cousin whom she had loved for years, a rich young man whose father had procured him the position of *fermier général*, or manager of the royal tax funds, one of the most prestigious and lucrative offices in the kingdom. Now a member of the first society and married to a man she loved, Louise was relieved to find that her precarious existence as a hanger-on was a thing of the past. She was ready to invest herself in her marriage and to live for her husband's happiness and for that of her son. She was soon to find out, however, that her husband had a very different idea of marriage, that his passion for her had been temporary, and that she was by no means the only woman who seemed to have a claim on his time and affection. Denis-Joseph d'Épinay was a confirmed libertine who quickly tired of his wife and began looking for excitement elsewhere. Louise found herself abandoned as well as infected with venereal disease. When he and one of his comrades came into her bedroom drunk from a night on the town and she found herself offered to the stranger for sex, she woke up the house with her cries for help, and finally came to understand that neither quiet acceptance nor attempts at character reform would make her husband into the man she had once believed he was.

Louise, now a mother in her early twenties, without education, and in a situation more precarious than ever, initially thought that she could still find contentment in her role as a mother. Already bored with the empty conventionality of the life thought suitable for a woman of the nobility, she preferred a more direct, more emotional approach to motherhood than farming out her baby son to a wet nurse in order to have more children and attend endless receptions.

She decided to breastfeed the child herself. The protagonist of her autobiographical novel has to clear the hurdle of obtaining her husband's consent to this. The response to her maternal longings is prompt, unambiguous, and terribly predictable: 'One more of those crazy ideas which sometimes go through the head of my poor little wife! You feed your own child? I almost died laughing. Dear friend, whatever the doctors say, forget this project immediately . . . What the devil can be so satisfying about feeding a child?'[3] Despite her clamours, the infant was sent away, the mother left abandoned.

Despite her husband's constant affairs and frighteningly expensive habits, Louise, held on a budget that did not even allow her to pay the tailor, still tried to keep up appearances. After having been infected by her husband, she demanded an end to their sexual relations, to which he mockingly replied that they might now both go their own ways in business and pleasure. In order to be able to pay the household expenses, she finally and successfully applied for a *séparation des biens*, a return of her dowry. The fact that her father-in-law was entirely on her side, and even arranged for part of his son's allowance to be paid directly to her, is an indication of her husband's conduct.

Mme d'Épinay now had a degree of independence and spent most of her time at the family's country seat, La Chevrette, simmering in a broth of boredom and discontent. A portrait painted some five years later shows her looking over her shoulder, amused and thoughtful, with 'large, black eyes' that Voltaire would admire, a captivating young woman, all the more attractive for not being conventionally beautiful. 'I am not pretty,' she would write later, 'but I am not ugly. I am *petite*, thin, very beautifully made. I have a youthful look, but without freshness: noble, sweet, lively, spirited and interesting.'[4]

Soon she attracted a circle of admirers and intellectuals to La

Chevrette. Louise entered into the spirit of things by taking a lover, Charles Dupin de Franceuil, by whom she had a child. Franceuil also succeeded in drawing out her artistic and intellectual interests, which had been buried beneath piety and convention since early girlhood. His father was a *fermier général*, like her own husband, and the social links between the two families were strong. Urban and cultured, Franceuil opened new horizons for her. She accompanied him to what she came to call her 'university', the dinners held by the former actress Mlle Quinault of the Comédie-Française, who invited the capital's leading intellectuals, Diderot among them, to converse freely on daring topics such as primitive sexuality and the origins of Christianity.

Louise found a new world in these conversations, and with Franceuil's encouragement she also converted the orangerie at La Chevrette into a theatre where assembled family and friends would perform plays to an audience of servants and peasants – the only people left on the estate who were not on stage. These new endeavours also brought her in contact with Mme Dupin, Franceuil's mother, and her secretary, a brilliant but tortured Genevan composer and occasional poet who had written one of the plays performed at the orangerie. In Louise's *Mémoires de Madame de Montbrillant* this man is introduced as 'a poor devil of an author, poor as Job himself, but with spirit and vanity for four'.[5] Louise's own alter ego is captivated by this strange figure: 'He is a singular man . . . flattering without being polite, or at least without seeming to be so. He has none of the ways of society, but it is easy to see that he has plenty of *esprit*. His complexion is very dark, and eyes full of fire animate his face.'[6] He was none other than Jean-Jacques Rousseau.

Meeting Mme d'Épinay and attracting her patronage finally allowed Jean-Jacques, a sloppy music copyist anyway, to concentrate totally on his writing. And it was through Rousseau that Louise met the man in whom she would find her real soulmate – Diderot's beloved Grimm, who appears in her autobiographical novel (under the guise of 'Mr Volx') with a dramatic *éclat* worthy of a life-changing encounter.

The scene we are invited to imagine is grandly romantic. Moon-light reflects off white shirts and elegant, cold steel, as two figures furiously exchange blows until both of them stagger away, their blood making dark stains on their linen:

> Good God! What have I heard? Monsieur, come quickly, I entreat you. M. Volx has fought a duel; he is hurt, and I am the cause. This is terrible. This was the one thing that had not yet arrived to make me miserable!
>
> I know no detail; perhaps he is dangerously hurt, and I dare not ask for accurate information or send someone over.[7]

The quarrel immortalized by Mme d'Épinay had apparently broken out during a dinner given by Grimm's employer, the Comte de Friese. One of the dinner guests, a young baron, thought it amusing to say that he had it on good authority that the lady had stolen letters pertaining to one of her husband's numberless debts from the writing desk of her recently deceased sister-in-law. Grimm, d'Épinay's heroine recounts, sprang to her defence, and when the young man, who had had too much to drink, refused to recant, the White Tyrant felt obliged to challenge him to a duel there and then, in the garden behind the house in the rue Basse-du-Rempart. They exchanged a few thrusts – awkward ones, no doubt, for the baron was drunk and Grimm himself was more used to holding a quill – and then separated after each was slightly wounded.

Did this duel really take place? Mme d'Épinay is the only person to testify to it; no other author, diarist, or memorialist of the time even mentions it, though Diderot's extant letters from the period, usually an excellent source of information, are few and far between. It is always difficult to disentangle fact and fiction, reshaped memories and manipulated pasts, when people and groups wrote intensely about their own lives, and the lives of those close to them. Rarely has the art of fictionalized autobiography been carried further: as well as Louise d'Épinay's autobiographical novel, there are Rousseau's *Confessions*, Grimm's *Correspondance littéraire*, which often carries literary gossip, Voltaire's immensely voluminous correspondence and that of Diderot, as well as his and his friends' numerous thinly disguised appearances in novels and essays. People on the margins of the group, Malesherbes, d'Argenson, Abbé Mor- ellet, and Barbier, contributed to the memoirs and diaries dealing with the *Encyclopédie* and with those who wrote it. In fact, Holbach and Jaucourt are the only members of the group not to have left a substantial corpus of autobiographical writings.[8]

Grimm's stature had changed, and not only in Mme d'Épinay's eyes; he had finally managed to acquire a means of making a name for himself that was ideally suited to his talents. The Abbé Raynal, a member of the Holbach circle who had helped to nurse Grimm through his bout of love sickness for Mademoiselle Fel, had for some time written a literary newsletter, the *Nouvelles littéraires*, that was sent to private subscribers outside France. Overtaken by other projects, he had ceased publication in December 1751, but the demand for the journal remained and Raynal suggested to Grimm that he take it up himself.[9] Grimm jumped at the chance and the first issue was published, under the new name of *Correspondance littéraire*, on 15 May 1753. The immense attraction of a work that was not publicly available but was sent to subscribers abroad was of course that it was not subject to the French censors, so enabling writers to express exactly what they thought about books, the lives of literary figures, and the gossip in the *salons*, without any great delicacy towards either the authorities or to literary vanities. Both Raynal and later Grimm made the fullest use of this privilege.

Raynal, who published his books in Amsterdam to avoid having to apply for a royal privilege, had already enjoyed himself a good deal writing without the constraint of the ever-watchful eye of the Directorate of the Book Trade. In November 1750 he had written about one historian: 'We have not yet recovered from the boredom inflicted on us by his last work, the *History of the Arabs*, when a second one comes along, the *History of Revolutions in the Arab Empire*. Revolutions always make good reading ... but despite this, one could not read anything drier, more badly written.'[10] A little later, in a theatre review, he writes: 'There is a new actress at the Comédie Française, who calls herself Mlle Oliva. She certainly is a true Italian, for she does not know a word of French.' The journal is a curious mélange of serious reviews, scientific news, long literary excerpts, and scurrilous stories (including one about the death of an enormously obese Englishman in Essex whose corpse could only be extracted from his bedroom by cutting a hole in the ceiling – hardly something that had a great deal of relevance for French literary life). As the work was not read in Paris, Raynal could write sarcastically even about his friends, and the *Encyclopédie* comes in for some justified criticism:

> The *Encyclopédie* has begun to give rise to violent disputes. Often one finds in it what one is not, in fact, looking for, and one looks vainly for what one ought to find easily. Several of the authors write in a barbaric manner, some preciously, and much of what is contained in it is nothing but verbiage. Here is an epigram addressed to the principal editor, M. Diderot, a good writer and bad believer:
> > I am a good Encyclopedist
> > I know the evil and the good
> > I am Diderot through and through,
> > I know everything, and believe in nothing.[11]

Raynal makes it a point of honour to follow every turn of the *Encyclopédie*'s story (he himself rather mysteriously appeared on the payroll of the associated booksellers, but never contributed a single article). In September 1751 he writes laconically: 'The first volume of the *Encyclopédie* was initially a great success, but is now generally pooh-poohed. One finds revolutions like this one only in France.'[12]

After Grimm took over as editor of Raynal's journal, its tone became more cautious, understandably so, since the author was still finding his voice. This measured tone, however, quickly gave way to a more confident, more ironic reviewing style. Just as Grimm later become the Parisian representative of foreign monarchs, the *Correspondance littéraire* made him the foreign ministry of the Encyclopedists, whom he praised at every available opportunity. The subscribers, who received the hand-copied journal every month by diplomatic post, were initially a number of European aristocrats of

Denis Diderot, the main editor of the *Encyclopédie*. His expression reveals the humane scepticism that marks his works. Bust by Jean-Antoine Houdon

The mathematician Jean Le Rond d'Alembert, the original co-editor of the *Encyclopédie*, who abandoned the enterprise after the first seven volumes. Pastel drawing by Maurice Quentin de La Tour.

Jean-Jacques Rousseau in the simple clothes and Abbé's wig he
adopted after winning the essay prize of the Dijon Academy.
Originally a contributor to the *Encyclopédie* and a personal friend
of the editors, he became a sworn enemy of almost all
Encyclopedists. Pastel by Maurice Quentin de La Tour

Louise d'Epinay was one of the few women believed to have contributed to the *Encyclopédie.* She was the patroness of Jean-Jacques Rousseau and the mistress of Baron Grimm. Pastel by Jean-Etienne Liotard

Friedrich Melchior Grimm, later Baron Grimm, Diderot's closest friend. An ambitious man, a freelance diplomat and journalist, he was held to be 'one of the very few Germans ever to have learned French properly'. Engraving by Lecerf

Voltaire, the secular 'patron saint' of the Enlightenment, contributed several articles to the *Encyclopédie* and could not resist meddling in times of crisis. Diderot remained sceptical of his motives and kept him at a distance. Bust by Jean-Antoine Houdon

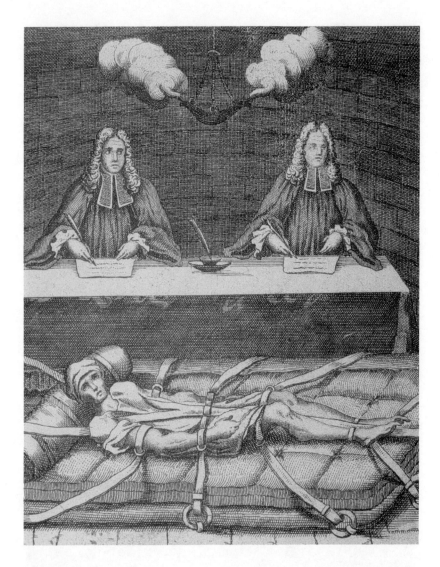

Robert-François Damiens's knife attack against Louis XV was used as
an excuse for brutal repression of critical opinion, and particularly
of the *Encyclopédie*. Damiens himself, though clearly insane, was
publicly tortured and executed.

Mme de Pompadour, Louis XV's official mistress, protected the Encyclopedists against attacks from the King's Jesuit confessor and the reactionary influence of the Church. In this pastel by Maurice Quentin de La Tour, volume IV of the *Encyclopédie*, as well as several other progressive books, can be seen behind her.

This 1766 profile by Jean-Baptiste Greuze shows a weary Diderot during the 'hidden' period of the *Encyclopédie*. Characteristically, Diderot chose to be depicted without his wig, wearing the clothes of a simple artisan.

whom only the Duchess of Saxe-Gotha is known. Eventually, the select group of those who got to read Grimm's uncensored musings on France and all things French comprised some of the most powerful and enlightened rulers, including the Tsarina Catherine the Great, the King of Sweden, Frederick the Great of Prussia, the princes of the Palatinate, of Brunswick-Wolfenbüttel, and of Hesse-Darmstadt, a sprinkling of counts and barons, and several interested persons thought worthy of the honour, among whom, for some time at least, were Horace Walpole and Wolfgang Amadeus Mozart, a special protégé of Grimm's. Through him, the Encyclopedist adventure gained European currency, and the names of Diderot, d'Alembert, and Rousseau became as familiar in the salons of Moscow, Berlin, and Stockholm as they were in the neo-classical splendour *chez* Mme Geoffrin.

With renewed confidence, and benefiting from a growing reputation, Grimm now cut a different figure. But suddenly his livelihood and status as the secretary of the Comte de Friese were threatened by the death of his employer. The Comte, a man known mostly 'for the refinement of his depravity',[13] died on 29 March 1755, probably from syphilis. His death deprived Grimm not only of company and of an opportunity to meet the rich and famous, but, more tangibly, of his lodgings, salary, and social credentials. With the benefit of venomous hindsight, Rousseau gave little credence to his friend's demonstrations of grief, believing that Grimm only made such gestures for his own advantage, especially when he visited the Marquis de Castries, who, he hoped, might become his next protector:

> All Paris heard of his despair after the death of the Comte de Friese. It was necessary to keep up the reputation he had acquired after the rigours of Mademoiselle Fel, which I, more than any other person, should have seen to have been false, had I been less blind. He had to be dragged to the Hôtel de Castries where he worthily played his part, abandoned to the most mortal affliction. There, every morning, he went into the garden to weep at his ease, holding before his eyes his handkerchief bathed in tears, as long as he was in sight of the *palais*, but at the turning of a certain alley, people of whom

he thought little saw him instantly put his handkerchief in his
pocket and take out a book.[14]

Whether or not the young secretary and journalist kept a strategi-
cally moistened handkerchief in his pocket, the Comte's death
meant that he would urgently have to find a new protector, or else
leave the city, unable as he was to support himself there for long
from his writing alone.

For the next four years, however, Grimm seems not to have held
any position. Eventually, he would be employed by the Duc d'Orléans, but it is likely that he lived during this first period from the
modest revenues of the *Correspondance littéraire*, probably aided by
aristocrats such as de Castries and d'Orléans himself, whom, Rousseau alleged, Grimm 'courted' for a considerable time. Freedom,
though, meant financial and social insecurity, and the White Tyrant
seems not to have enjoyed it. But at least being without a position
allowed Grimm to pursue his interest in Mme d'Épinay. Soon the
two outsiders in literary Paris, an impecunious German and an
ambitious woman who lived separated from her husband and who
had recently given birth to her previous lover's child, found that
the precariousness of their respective situations and their shared
tastes created strong bonds between them.

Louise had been touched when Grimm had paid her mother a
visit, his arm still in a sling because of the wound he had received
in the duel – 'My child, embrace your gallant knight', the mother
had said[15] – and had quickly grown attached to him. Now, nothing
seemed to stand in the way of an even closer relationship, especially
as Grimm began to involve himself in Louise's difficulties with her
husband. 'I am suffused by esteem and tenderness for him,' the
fictional Mme de Montbrillant would later write about her lover,
Volx,[16] and like those of his literary counterpart, Grimm's visits to
her house became more frequent and longer, so much so that it
seemed to many outsiders that they were living as a couple.

Another domestic change was to make a great difference in Mme
d'Épinay's life. Not only had she acquired Grimm as a permanent
house guest at La Chevrette; the Hermitage, one of the follies in

the surrounding park, was also inhabited in 1756 by a guest who gave every indication of staying there indefinitely, far from civilization and accompanied only by his mistress and her mother. Jean-Jacques Rousseau, infuriated and disoriented by city life and still suffering from his often agonizing, antisocial illness, had adopted the life of a literary hermit and now, from a safe distance, was able to scoff at city life. This new life away from the crowd brought about a psychological transformation of Nietzschean proportions in Rousseau:

> I was no longer that timid man, more bashful than modest, who did not dare either to introduce himself or to talk in company; who was disconcerted by a single jocular remark, and who would blush whenever a woman looked at him. Audacious, proud, intrepid, I now carried everywhere the firmest assurance ... The disdain which my profound meditations had inspired in me for the manners and maxims and prejudices of my century, had made me insensible to the ramblings of those who were still their captives, and I crushed their little witticisms with my pronouncements, just as I would crush an insect between my fingers.[17]

The Promethean hero in the cottage was indeed happier than he had ever been, going for long walks, writing, and consenting occasionally to call upon Louise and Grimm for dinner or an afternoon's music. On one such occasion, Grimm imprudently laughed about some copying faults Jean-Jacques had made in a score, telling him that he should only write down what was there already and not recompose it, a humiliation for which he was not forgiven.

Uncompromising and searching as ever, Rousseau had spent part of 1754 in Geneva, where he abjured his conversion to Catholicism and where he had apparently intended to stay. When he returned to Paris, however, ostensibly to arrange his affairs before his return, he found it impossible to leave again. The citizen of Geneva, as he now proudly referred to himself, remained in the French capital, where he hoped to repeat the success of his prize-winning discourse on the sciences with a second prize essay, this time on a topic that seemed to have been set just for him: the reasons for inequality between men and its relationship with natural law. The Rousseau of the *Discourse on the Origins of Inequality* is the author at his most radical, and parallels with later thinkers (from Nietzsche's *Zarathustra* to Hegel's philosophy of law, from Schopenhauer's ethics to Feuerbach and Marx) are inescapable. At a time when people clung either to the Church's teachings or to the all-healing power of Reason, Rousseau proclaimed a third way of thinking that was to reverberate throughout European culture and make him one of its most influential authors.

Society is unequal, he wrote, not because of an unfair distribution of abilities, but because of wealth, pride, and greed, all of which are the fruits of a civilization that has removed healthy, savage man from his primitive life in harmony with nature and placed him in the bondage of privilege, position, or poverty. The first beginnings of civilization, of language, art, and refined sentiment, were also the beginning of humanity's ruin, as they led to inequality, to the existence of the clever and the stupid, the haves and the have-nots, the powerful and the helpless, the master and the serf. Looking through the tissue of lies that has been tied over people's eyes, Rousseau asks: 'Is there a man who is so much stronger than me, and who is moreover depraved enough, lazy enough and fierce enough to make me work for his subsistence while he sits idle? If there is, he must make up his mind not to lose sight of me for a single instant . . . for fear that I should escape or kill him.'[18] This being the natural state of affairs in eighteenth-century Europe, it is understandable that his readers were disquieted.

Rousseau, the Promethean, now felt that he had left behind his friends, who continued to live in the city, seemingly unaware of the webs of oppression and tyranny all around them. Diderot, on the other hand, regarded his friend's bearish stance as simply the current favourite among his charades, after the footman, the lover, the diplomat, the scientist, the secretary, the clerk, the Encyclopedist, the composer, and the honest music copyist. As a man who had spent his only time alone when in solitary confinement (a particular agony for him), Diderot could not imagine that anybody might choose to shut himself away from human company. He was wrong. The 'bear' (as Rousseau's hostess had dubbed him) was real and would not change his coat. For the time being, this difference of opinion did not result in open argument.

Rousseau's own thinking is surprisingly close to Diderot's more optimistic vision of human nature. In the article on DROIT NATUREL, Diderot had outlined an idea of natural law based on a conception of general will, a notion that has earned its author the reputation of having a 'totalitarian tinge', though this is to state the case too strongly.[19] Diderot wanted to found his ethical thought on something other than religion, and his notion of a general will turns out to be very similar to another product of eighteenth-century ethical thought, Kant's 'categorical imperative', though it does not entertain the fiction of an individual as an isolated, rational entity.[20] Instead, he began from an almost existentialist, compassionate perspective that is very characteristic of him: 'We lead an existence that is poor, contentious, and full of anxiety. We have passions & needs. We want to be happy; & all the while the unjust man makes others do what he does not want to do himself.'

This social notion of manipulation is similar to Rousseau's, but, unlike Rousseau, Diderot does not dream himself back into a state in which happy savages lived without destructive passions. Instead, he appeals to the soul of the community itself, a worryingly im-precise concept, but one that is typical of a man who could only picture himself as a friend among friends. From the same idea, the inequality of man and the distress caused by it, Diderot and Rous-seau had thought themselves apart, one taking the route into the woods, the other remaining with both feet firmly planted in the hub of life.

No doubt the absence of Jean-Jacques was made less painful for Diderot by the presence of a new person in his life, a woman who is one of literature's great unknowns: the love of his life, the recipi-ent of hundreds of glowingly tender letters, his muse, his mistress and his soulmate for three decades: Sophie Volland. This descrip-tion makes things sound much simpler than they were, for Sophie is most remarkable by her complete absence, like a character invented by a magical realist. All that exists of her is a shadow left in her lover's handwriting, for we have neither a portrait of her nor a single letter by her own hand, neither a description nor any surviving correspondence. Even her name was not Sophie, but Louise-Henriette.

She came from a family of civil servants, well-to-do though not rich, and was about forty years old when Diderot met her. She was not married, perhaps because no suitor had presented himself, perhaps because she had wanted none, preferring instead the liberty of spinsterhood. It was Diderot who called her Sophie, or wisdom, in honour of her mind and her character, which he admired greatly. For posterity, she only exists through the prism of Diderot's letters to her, an extraordinary, rich, and (to us) entirely one-sided correspondence. When he could not see her, he pined for her and wrote to her daily, sometimes twice a day, stalking the servants, the postilions, and the go-betweens to get his hands on her letters, for which he waited with burning impatience. From his letters to her (all of her responses were destroyed), we know that she used to wear reading glasses. The only other hint about her appearance comes from a tender letter her lover wrote to her: 'Adieu, my friend, I kiss your forehead, your eyes, your mouth and your dry little hand, which pleases me quite as much as a plump one.'[21] A dry little hand is all that remains of the appearance of Louise-Henriette Volland.

The long-suffering Mme Diderot apparently accepted this new attachment of her husband's with the sour forbearance that seems to have become her main response to his life, of which she could not approve. A woman who never even learned to spell *Encyclopédie*, she insisted that little Marie-Angélique, their beloved only surviving child, be educated with all the piety the house could muster, while Denis would try to sneak past his wife some lessons in philosophy.

In November 1754 Diderot visited his home tome of Langres to see his family for the first time since he had fled from the monastery a little over ten years earlier. Now editor of a work that was read and discussed throughout France, he felt that he could finally face his past and make peace with them. Toinette had already paid a

visit, and father Diderot had reconciled himself to the marriage
his son had made. Denis came back not so much as a prodigal son,
but as a married man engaged on a famous and grand endeavour,
eager to renew the links of family and friendship he had so long
neglected.

There is a rustic quality to Diderot: in his defence of the crafts
and trades, his readiness to help simple folk, his pose as a man of
the people, his disdain for courtly etiquette, formality, and powdered wigs. Now aged forty-one, he enjoyed partaking in the life
of his family, a life rather more modest than he had become accustomed to in the grand salons of the metropolis. Having always
equally adored and disobeyed his father, Denis now particularly
relished his conversations with him. He found him much aged, a
veritable town patriarch, respected by all, and dispensing charity
and advice with equally Christian firmness and grace. Diderot's
sister, whose good humour contrasted markedly with his wife's
character, now became a close friend; she would remain so for the
rest of his life.

How much he loved and admired what he found at Langres, and
how much the urban *philosophe* was still rooted in traditional values,
may be seen from the fact that he arranged for his little daughter
to be betrothed to the nine-year-old son of a family friend. (The
marriage eventually took place and was apparently remarkably
happy.) Denis also agreed to become godfather to the boy's newborn brother, indicating that he was still trusted by his Langres
friends as a man who respected Christian ideals. Obviously Diderot,
the materialist thinker and destroyer of 'national prejudices', still
thought it possible, and not unduly hypocritical, to accept this role,
which after all required a church ceremony.

The atmosphere of exuberance and contentment Diderot felt
during his visit can still be savoured in a long letter of thanks to
everyone at Langres sent from Paris on 6 January 1755. It is a letter
of bumptious humour and good sense, containing anecdotes about
his journey home, and the promise (made by a proud son) to
send his father, along with the letter, 'a case, containing the fourth
volume of the *Encyclopédie*, leather bound . . .'. He must have hoped

that his father, who only a few years earlier had sent a letter to
Vincennes earnestly admonishing him to ask God for forgiveness,
to live as a good Christian, and to obey the King, would never read
the magnificent tome he now sent him, and that he would content
himself with admiring the workmanship of the binding and his son's
name on the title-page. The son then addressed himself directly to
his ageing parent (whom he would never see again), who had been
hurt by his firstborn's long absence and infrequent correspondence: 'So there! Dear father, are you still angry? Have I not made
good the lost time, and don't you think that this letter is worth a
dozen? I will try to be more diligent in future.'

While in Langres, Diderot had obviously complained about the
yoke of the *Encyclopédie* and had received not only sympathy but
also practical advice from a Monsieur Dubois, a local notary, who
told him that the contract with the booksellers was as unfair as the
payment stipulated in it was inadequate. On his return to Paris,
therefore, Diderot threw himself into negotiating a new contract.
The booksellers eventually caved in and granted him more favourable conditions, but for some time they thought it best to let him
wait, and his irritation at being treated in this way was clear in a
letter to his parents:

> My wife, who sometimes gives good advice, has persuaded me
> that it is best to affect the greatest disinterest regarding the
> conclusion [of the negotiations]. They [the booksellers] for
> their part believed that it would be best for them to employ
> the same strategy and neither of us made a single move for
> fifteen days. I don't know why, during this time, impatience
> did not grip me sufficiently to send them all to the devil, them,
> the *Encyclopédie*, their papers, and their contract. If I had had
> a little more confidence in the probity of my colleague, I would
> have done it.[22]

The colleague mistrusted by Diderot is obviously d'Alembert.
This was the first time that Diderot had voiced his mounting irritation with d'Alembert and with the *Encyclopédie* itself. The relationship between the two editors, never an easy friendship, had cooled

considerably. The philosopher Jean-François Marmontel noticed the change in d'Alembert's attitude: 'I have never known very well why d'Alembert held himself aloof from the society of which I speak. He and Diderot, associates in exertion and in glory in the enterprise of the *Encyclopédie*, had at first been cordially united, but they were no longer.'[23]

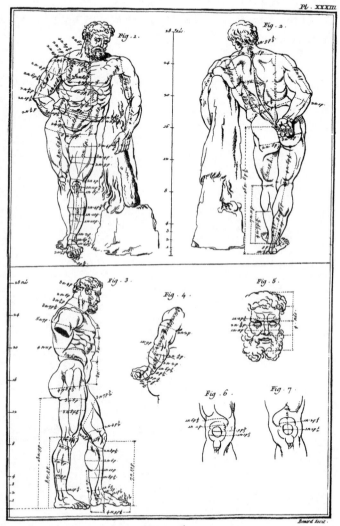

Pl. XXXIII

Dessein,
Proportions de l'Hercule Farnese.

Benard Fecit.

VIRTUE

POESIE DU VERS, (*Poésie*) *see* **VERS,** *Poésie du*; as the letter *P* is already full to bursting point, one has to be allowed this sort of cross-reference, assuming it is not neglected to honour it later. (*D. J.*)

VERTU [VIRTUE]. (*Ord. encyclop. Mor. Polit.*) It is more reliable to know *virtue* as a sentiment than to indulge in reasonings about its nature. If there is an unfortunate person on earth who has never felt it, who has never experienced the sweet pleasure of doing good, all our discussions on this point would be absurd & useless, just like describing to a blind man the beauties of a painting or the charms of a view. A sentiment is known only through sentiment; you want to know what humanity is? Close your books & see those who are unhappy; reader, whoever you may be, if you have never tasted the charms of *virtue*, go into yourself, its definition is in your heart . . .

Let us finish this article, no doubt too long for what it is, but too short for what it should be. *See* **VICE,** *article by M.* **ROMILLY** *the younger.*

[Denis Diderot]

Verse and virtue, poetry and passion, often go together. Diderot, trying to avoid being buried under his editorial tasks, now turned to verse in an attempt to make a new beginning as a dramatist and an original writer; for Louise d'Épinay, her lover Grimm, and her cantankerous hermit Rousseau, poetry and passion took a more immediate form, leading to emotional scenes and Rousseau's final rupture with his friends.

Increasingly disillusioned with the *Encyclopédie*, for which he was writing fewer and fewer articles, Diderot was only too conscious of the fact that, at forty-four, he had not realized a single one of his literary dreams and was known to the world almost exclusively as the editor of a reference work. His friends had all embarked on original literary endeavours: Rousseau, Grimm, Louise d'Épinay, and Thiry d'Holbach were all writing works that, he must have felt, would survive as their legacy and would stand for something in the world.

All he himself could claim as his creations were a handful of philosophical tracts, an erotic novel he now shuddered to think about, and encyclopedic articles that did nothing to establish him as an author in his own right. Posterity (an increasing preoccupation) would remember him, if at all, for an ingenious treatment of selected arts and crafts (including lengthy dissertations on the art of making *émail*, steel production, and the production and uses of wood), some cheeky pieces on mythology, and a book-length article on the purposes of an encyclopedia. None of these were worthy of a true *philosophe*, especially one who was increasingly seen as the figurehead of the movement in France. It was time, Diderot felt, that his merit caught up with his reputation.

He took some time off from working on the *Encyclopédie* (volume seven contains 203 named articles by Diderot, many of which are no longer than one or two sentences) and produced a work worthy of the full scale of his ambition. It was prefaced by an essay on the art of theatre in general, written in prose, a revolutionary thing to do at the time, and purported to tell the story of a man the author had met on his recent journey to Langres, a literary mask characteristic of Diderot's love of mystification.

The outcome, *Le Fils naturel* (The Natural Son), is an interestingly awful play, full of elevated sentiment, long monologues about virtue, and fabulously unlikely coincidences. What makes it interesting, as opposed to simply bad, is that Diderot had not only chosen to write about a virtuous father, when he had just returned from his own family, but he was also blessed with a wonderful ear for dialogue and loved writing in this form. In the novels he was to write, the conversations often seem to jump off the page, and much of his fiction (particularly *Le Neveu de Rameau* [Rameau's Nephew]) is written in the form of immensely engaging dialogues and monologues. The academic structure of the play indicates that Diderot was writing for a specific audience, and his contemporaries were aware of this. The critic Élie-Catherine Fréron (1718–76), one of the chief enemies of the *Encyclopédie*, remarked immediately in a letter to Malesherbes: 'One does not need to be particularly prescient to see that M. Diderot is aiming at the Académie Française, and that ... his *Fils naturel*, the only work he has written in the Academy's line, is a detestable play.'[1]

An academy membership was indeed just what the editor of the *Encyclopédie* needed – the Prussian Academy, it seemed, was not enough. D'Alembert had already been made a member. Perhaps Diderot had even been given to understand that he simply needed to write something that made him eligible for membership, something uplifting, moral, worthy of an Academician.

If Diderot had aimed for the Académie Française, his hopes were dashed when it was pointed out that the play closely resembled a work by Carlo Goldoni, *Il vero amico*, first seen in Venice seven years earlier. Far from being admired as a dramatist, Diderot now had to defend himself against accusations of plagiarism. Another, graver, consequence of the play's publication was equally self-inflicted. 'The good man lives in society, only a wicked man lives alone', Diderot had put into the mouth of one of his characters, seemingly apropos of nothing. He had made sure to send a copy of the play to Rousseau, who was perceptive to the point of paranoia when it came to insults and slights and needed no encouragement to interpret this as an implicit criticism, even a rejection, of himself and his chosen life.

The entire passage of the *Confessions* dealing with this period is dedicated to his friends' dark plots and conspiracies, apparently designed to ruin his life and drive away whatever remaining few faithful friends he might have retained. Rousseau casts himself in the role of a man simply too good, too humane to understand the intrigues of the 'Holbach gang' until it was too late, and who is finally forced to accept the sad truth that he has been betrayed out of spite and pettiness.

The truth was more complicated. There is no doubt that his friends were exasperated by Rousseau's righteous posturing. The 'bear' had gone too far, and it was time for him to come back and rejoin their circle. Paris was, after all, the centre of the civilized universe, and only Voltaire (who had the excellent excuse of being exiled) could afford to live elsewhere. It was in this spirit of irritated friendship that they tried to tease him out of his cave. To Jean-Jacques himself, this behaviour was tantamount to a scornful dismissal of his deeply held beliefs, a choice of life that was to him the only way of living honourably. That this honourable life of rustic simplicity was lived rent free on the estate of an aristocratic friend, conveniently close to an elegant drawing-room should he feel the need of one; that his lover Thérèse did not like the calm of the countryside and that her mother, who had also accompanied him into his poetic solitude, detested it – paying for it with ferocious bouts of indigestion for which no doctor could be fetched and which left her believing her end was nigh – all these were details. He was no more inclined to entertain them seriously than he had seen anything wrong with sending Thérèse's children to the foundlings' house.

Rousseau was deeply hurt when he read in *Le Fils naturel* what he could only interpret as a personal attack. His irritation with his old friend was already at a height, as he wrote later, citing a catalogue of woes:

> I was exasperated at his indefatigable obstinacy in eternally contradicting me regarding my tastes, my likes, my way of living, and everything that concerned only myself; revolted at seeing a man younger than myself wanting at any price to govern me like a child; repelled by his ease of making promises and his negligence in keeping them; worn out by so many meetings agreed and missed by him, and by his mania of making eternally new ones, only to miss them yet again . . .[2]

The meetings missed were not only in Paris. Ever since Rousseau had moved out to La Chevrette he had hoped to see his friend, who despite his promise had not yet come to visit him. In view of the fact that it was a good four hours on foot one way (Diderot could rarely afford to take coaches) and that Rousseau himself had made it very clear that he refused to come to Paris, it seems understandable that Diderot did not feel unduly inclined to make this journey, especially when his editorial duties, and other commitments, awaited his return. In a letter (which is lost), Rousseau gave vent to his feelings of being wronged and slighted, an impression that must have become all the more acute on receipt of the reply, an uncharacteristically short missive, in which Diderot wrote with breezy indifference that he could not come: the bad weather and his daughter's cough precluded any thought of it. In any case, he continued, with an irony that was certain not to be appreciated, 'I am glad that my work touched you.' He then went on to remark that Rousseau was surely the only laudable hermit, but that Citizen Rousseau (who had taken to signing himself 'Citizen of Geneva') was a strange sort of citizen, hidden away in the woods.

Rousseau wrote again, with more reproaches. Though this letter has not survived either, one can gain an impression of the sentiments likely to have been expressed in it from a letter written to Mme d'Épinay that was full of accusations and bitterness. Diderot, he said, had written a letter 'that has pierced me to the soul' and had accused him of being a criminal who was endangering the life of an old woman (Thérèse's octogenarian mother) with his recklessness, that he was abusing her (she kept house for him), and that Grimm was out to steal 'all the friends I have found for him'. It ended with a great flourish:

> Forgive me, my dear Friend; my heart is overborne with sorrows and my eyes full of unshed tears. If I could see you for a moment and weep, I would be consoled. But I will never set foot in Paris again; that is decided for good.
>
> I forgot to say that there are even jokes in the *philosophe*'s [Diderot's] letter. He is becoming a barbarian, cheerfully; he

is growing *civilized* [the worst insult in Rousseau's vocabulary],
it would appear.[3]

Diderot was obviously taken aback by his friend's reaction, for
his reply this time was conciliatory and no longer noncommittal. It
did, however, show another reason for the continuing estrangement
between the two:

> It is true that for fifteen years I have had a wife, a child, a
> servant, no money, and my life is so full of problems and pains
> that often I have no more than a few hours of happiness and
> relief to look forward to. In this my friends, according to their
> character, are elements of pleasure, or of injury . . .
> You refuse to come to Paris. So be it! Saturday morning I
> will set off for the Hermitage, and if it takes me all day to get
> there. I will go by foot; my troubles have not allowed me to
> come earlier. My fortune does not permit me to come any
> other way, and I have to take revenge for all the injury you
> have inflicted upon me over the last four years.
> However much pain my letter might have caused you, I am
> not sorry for having written it. You are too content with your
> own response.
> You do not reproach the heavens for having given you
> friends; may the heavens pardon you for not having used them
> better . . .[4]

Again, Rousseau took grave offence and wrote back informing his
friend not to bother coming, as otherwise 'it might well be the last
interview'.

At this point Rousseau, already in confessional mode, sent the
entire correspondence to Mme d'Épinay, requesting her to judge
for herself and to forward his last letter. On reading the exchanges,
she had no doubt that the fault was on Rousseau's side and that,
instead of provoking a humiliating scene at the Hermitage and
risking the end of an old friendship, a little lie would be preferable.
She therefore sent her son to Diderot with the message that Jean-
Jacques himself was going to come to Paris and it was therefore

not worth Diderot's while to walk all the way to the hermit's cottage. The Saturday arrived, and an expectant Diderot waited all day for his friend's visit. As evening came he understood what must have happened and wrote once more, this time with great vehemence: 'Oh! Rousseau, you are becoming wicked, unjust, cruel, ferocious, and it makes me weep with pain.'

Another, even more extreme letter from Rousseau oscillated between utter rejection and pleas for reconciliation; finally, Diderot went to see his friend at the Hermitage, where he was received with embraces and tears of emotion. The friendship, it seemed, had survived, but only just, a grave crisis born from a banal misunderstanding. It would later become clear that Rousseau's conviction that there were conspiracies against him everywhere was as intractable as Diderot's inability to understand that his friend had changed beyond recognition. This meeting was to be among their last.

Rousseau continued to drive away even his most devoted friends, losing his lodgings in the process. His relationship with Mme d'Épinay had always been cordial. She might have been a little too attentive to his needs, and her relationship with Grimm, whom Rousseau had begun to see as his chief enemy, compromised her in his eyes; but they continued to see each other regularly, to play chess and dine together, and to send each other little notes enquiring after each other's wellbeing. Their friendship intensified when Grimm was invited by the Duc d'Orléans to join him in Germany as a liaison officer and secretary in the French army fighting Prussia and its allies, an opportunity for Grimm finally to gain a post with the Duke, and thus achieve the financial security he had been lacking since the death of the Comte de Friese. With heavy heart and considerable reservations, the White Tyrant departed, leaving his mistress to fret for his safety and to await his return.

In this situation, the friendship with Rousseau became even more important to her, though she did her best to respect his need for solitude and undisturbed work. She would write to him regularly, and Rousseau's notes to her, as far as one can judge from those reproduced in the *Mémoires de Mme de Montbrillant*, were usually models of good-humoured gallantry.

Rousseau, however, had something to hide from his hostess. He was in love with Mme d'Épinay's sister-in-law, the Comtesse Sophie d'Houdetot, who was intrigued by him and, it appears, found in him a friend, a beautiful soul, and a sympathetic audience for her effusions about her love for another man. A contemporary illustration shows her with a simple, large hat and cascading, auburn locks, dressed dashingly in mannish riding clothes with breeches, high boots and coat, as she drops in on the bewigged philosopher who sits by his desk, looking a little more portly than in real life. She was flattered by the famous author's attentions and dropped in often, much to the annoyance of Thérèse, who saw in her a rival. She was right. Jean-Jacques sent the Comtesse a steady stream of passionate love notes, hidden in tree trunks, or delivered to her by, of all people, his mistress Thérèse.

Rousseau's erotic reveries about his new idol were at times so intense that, on his way to a rendezvous, 'my head clouded over, vertigo blinded me, my knees trembled and I could not stand upright . . . my entire machine was in inconceivable uproar and I was close to fainting', and he arrived 'weak, exhausted, worn out, and hardly able to carry myself'.[5] The Comtesse had asked him to their meeting place, and he had come.

The liaison with the Comtesse, however, made Rousseau uncomfortable, and not because of Thérèse. As a 'man of honour', he thought it unacceptable to keep meeting Sophie while her official lover, the Marquis de Saint-Lambert (also an Encyclopedist), was in the field fighting for France. Saint-Lambert was not an old-fashioned man – after all, he had been the lover of Voltaire's mistress, the late Mme de Châtelet, who had died delivering his child – but Rousseau's conscience might have been burdened further by the fact that the world of the Paris salons was small and word was bound to get to Saint-Lambert sooner or later, making Jean-Jacques look a villain and a fool. There had already been moments of high drama when it seemed that the liaison had been discovered; but finally Sophie told her ardent admirer that it would be too risky to continue seeing him.

Rousseau was shaken. Sophie had inspired him to write a roman-

tic novel (the *Nouvelle Héloïse*); but, more than that, his entire sentimental life was now bound up in her. In June 1757, forgetting his
vow never to return to Paris, he went to pay a short visit to Diderot
to consult him over the affair. The *philosophe*'s answer was clear: the
only acceptable course of action was to write a full and frank
account of the relationship in a dignified letter to Saint-Lambert,
convincing him that Mme d'Houdetot had not been betraying him,
but was merely using Rousseau as a canvas on which to paint glowing
images of her undying love for himself. Rousseau, who had neglected to mention to Diderot that he was passionately in love with
the Comtesse and had told her so, declared that this was an excellent idea and proceeded to write to Saint-Lambert. He informed
him that his friend Sophie had become inexplicably cold towards
him and that he suspected Saint-Lambert had warned her off him
because he suspected Rousseau of wanting to separate them – for
moral reasons. 'It is true,' he continued, without apparent irony,
'I cannot approve of your illicit connection, but a love such as yours
deserves some consideration, and the good that comes from it
makes it less culpable.' To interfere with it would be a crime against
their friendship. Friendship, after all, was sacred. 'No, no,' he continued, in one of the finer moments in the history of literary hypoc-
risy, 'the bosom of Jean-Jacques Rousseau does not enclose the
heart of a traitor.'[6] Saint-Lambert sent back a courteous and friendly
reply, acknowledging that he had indeed been wondering about
Rousseau's motives but that he could be assured of his friendship.
True to the tenor of his letter, Rousseau now began indeed to
remonstrate with the Comtesse (who had not made good her threat
to break off their one-sided relationship) about her affair with
Saint-Lambert.

The denouement of this sordid interlude was as inevitable as it
was comically dramatic. It is not clear what happened exactly, but
it seems that, possibly fuelled by feelings of guilt, Rousseau's suspicions had reached fever pitch and he had confronted his own
mistress, Thérèse, accusing her of being part of a conspiracy against
him and trying to drive away the Comtesse d'Houdetot. However,
according to Rousseau himself, Thérèse swore that she was innocent

and told him further that Mme d'Épinay had spied on his every move and had forced her lodger's mistress to show her all of his intimate correspondence. Ever ready to think the worst about those who actually wished him well, Jean-Jacques believed Thérèse and immediately decided that his hostess was a manipulative, lonely, and monstrously jealous woman who had been plotting to thwart his happiness from her solitude in the mansion of La Chevrette.

A note from her, one of the regular missives she sent to the Hermitage, finally confirmed his imaginations (and may have caused him to question his mistress), though to the outsider it looks innocent enough:

> Why am I no longer seeing you, my dear friend? I am worried about you. You promised to visit me! I do not want to impose, but that was eight days ago. Had I not been told that you are quite well, I would have thought you sick. I waited for you yesterday, and the day before, and you did not appear. My God! What is wrong with you? You have no business to conduct, and you have no worries, as I flatter myself you would have come to confide in me. So you are ill! Release me from this uncertainty, I beg you. Adieu, my dear friend, and may this adieu become a bonjour to you.[7]

The reply came quickly:

> I cannot tell you anything yet. I wait until I am better informed, which I will be, sooner or later. Until then, you may rest assured that accused innocence will be defended so ardently that the accusers will repent, whoever they may be.

Eventually, and after an exchange of notes that alternated between compassionate incomprehension and self-righteous fury, Rousseau went to the mansion to confront Mme d'Épinay with her wrongdoing. She was horrified to find out what he believed her to have done and told him that none of it was true. He took her at her word, or so he claimed, and the two seemed reconciled. To Louise, however, this breach of trust was profoundly shocking, and she found it difficult to forgive him.

The situation Louise d'Épinay found herself in was doubly difficult. She was openly living with a man, a fact that was certain to raise eyebrows even in Paris; this man, however, was currently away on military service in Germany, and it was at this very time that her other close male confidant, Jean-Jacques Rousseau, chose to end their friendship in the most dramatic fashion. She had few people to turn to, especially since her lover's friend, Denis Diderot, had so far refused even to meet her, possibly because of the very scandal that had led Grimm to defend her honour in the first place.

In her loneliness, Louise took to writing the epistolary novel that was to become the *Mémoires de Madame de Montbrillant*. She told Grimm that it had been Rousseau's writing that had encouraged her to attempt authorship for herself. When she finally sent Grimm the first part of the novel, she promptly received a letter full of compliments and loving reproaches for the strain she might have placed on her delicate health:

> Truly, I am so angry that I cannot restrain myself. I have read the two thick notebooks of your novel, both written in your own hand. Are you absolutely determined to kill yourself, O most adorable of all possible and impossible friends? . . . I must admit, however, that since their arrival yesterday my anger has been giving way to the admiration that your writing deserves. Really, it is charming. I was very tired, very harassed, when the bundle came I glanced at it – and could not put it down. At two this morning I was still reading it. If you keep this up, you will certainly produce something unique.[8]

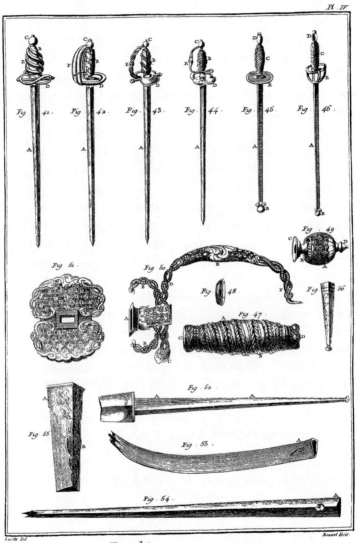

Pl. IV

Fig. 41.   Fig. 42.   Fig. 43.   Fig. 44.   Fig. 45.   Fig. 46.

Fig. 49.

Fig. 51.   Fig. 50.   Fig. 48.   Fig. 56.

Fig. 47.

Fig. 52.

Fig. 55.   Fig. 53.

Fig. 54.

Lucotte Del.   Benard Fecit.

Fourbisseur, Armes Modernes.

REGICIDE

CANIF [Penknife], s. f. *writer's tool*; this is a kind of small knife made of steel, very sharp, with a blade with pyramidal shape; it serves to sharpen quills; there is another kind & of which the upper part of the handle resembles that of a knife, but its lower part is pointed. This point is used to split the quill when one shapes it. There are also *canifs*, which sharpen the quill by themselves, but they do not work well.

REGICIDE, s. m. (*Hist. & Politics*) this is what one calls an attack depriving the king of his life. Ancient and modern history furnish all too many examples of sovereigns slain by their furious subjects. France will always shudder faced with the crime which robbed the life of Henri IV, one of the greatest & best of her kings. The tears shed by the French over a more recent attack will take a long time to dry . . .

During the past century, England has mounted, to an astonished universe, the dreadful spectacle of a king judged and put to death by his rebellious subjects . . . Let us tremble at these excesses of ambition, especially if accompanied by fanaticism and superstition.

SUPPLICE [Torture], s. m. (*Governm.*) corporal punishment, more or less painful, more or less atrocious.

A dictionary of various *tortures*, practices by different peoples around the world would make nature itself shiver; it is an inexplicable phenomenon that exceeds any barbaric and cruel practice one could imagine. (*D. J.*)

The year 1757 was to upset the entire encyclopedic project, the lives of those involved with it, and the very fabric of pre-revolutionary France.

The story begins on a domestic note: a father visiting his sick child. The father in question was Louis XV, who had left his winter refuge, the Trianon palace, on a perishingly cold and inhospitable January day to return to the drafty and unheatable royal apartments at Versailles. He wanted to pay a visit to his favourite daughter, Madame Victoire, who was nursing a cold, and he set off late in the afternoon. It was already dark, and the courtyard of the château was lit by the torches of a row of hussars lining the staircase in the icy wind. The King began to walk down the stairs and towards the waiting coach, accompanied by the Dauphin and several noblemen, the first and second equerry, and a guardsman.

The group reached the bottom of the staircase, and a footman readied the step leading into the coach. Suddenly, a figure dressed in a riding coat and hat pushed his way through the group, broke through the cordon of bodyguards, swept aside an officer of the One Hundred Swiss, seized the King by the shoulder, and plunged a knife into the right side of his chest. A moment of confusion followed, the King shouting 'Duc d'Ayen, I have been hit!', and the courtiers seemingly quite at a loss how to respond to the situation. The only quiet figure was that of the assailant, who stood still next to the waiting coach and, according to court testimony, 'kept his eyes fixed on the King, and resembled a drunken mad-man'.[1] 'Who is this who does not uncover his head in front of the King?' shouted one of the guards, throwing the stranger's hat to the ground.

The King, meanwhile, had made his way towards the coach. 'Was that a needle that has stung me?' he now asked, about to board. He felt his chest and withdrew a bloodied hand. The valet standing by the door saw this, and cried out 'The King has been hurt!'; the monarch himself turned around, pointed at his attacker, and said: 'It was that man there. Arrest him, but don't kill him, guard him well!' The Dauphin and one of the bodyguards now threw them-selves at the shadowy figure, who offered no resistance. They took him by the collar, hit him repeatedly, shouting: 'It's you, It's you ... Why have you done it?' 'Yes, it's me,' answered the man. 'I did it for God and for the people.' 'What do you mean?' 'I understand that the people are perishing. Is it not true that all France is dying?'

The man was searched, and in one of his pockets one of the valets discovered a penknife with a handle made of deer horn. 'Did you try to kill the King with this?' he demanded. 'I did not try to kill the King,' was the answer. 'If I had wanted him dead, I would have used the large blade, but I stabbed him with the little blade to warn him, and to hurt him only slightly.' Apart from the knife, the objects found on the body of the unknown man were a religious book, *Prières et instructions chrétiennes* (Christian Instructions and Prayers, a Jansenist book), some small scissors, and thirty-five *louis d'or*, a sum that was taken for his wages as a paid assassin. Beating him, his capturers demanded the names of his accomplices, only to be told that he had acted alone and on his own behalf.

The assailant was taken to the guardroom, where he was undressed and his hands were tied behind his back. A servant appeared and demanded that he reveal whether the knife was poisoned. 'No, by my soul, I swear it is not!' he responded. Meanwhile, the Seal Bearer (Jean-Baptiste Machault), the Chancellor (Guillaume de Lamoignon, father of Malesherbes, the Director of the Book Trade), and the Minister of War (Comte d'Argenson) arrived in the guardroom. The latter ordered that the suspect was to be questioned immediately with red-hot pincers, but then changed his mind and ordered the guards to 'warm the suspect's feet' in the guard-room fire, which they promptly did by applying red-hot irons to his ankles. Surrounded by the stench of his own burning skin, the prisoner was now questioned, again and again: 'Who gave you this idea? Who instigated this? The Jansenists? The Jesuits? The *Parlement*? The clergy? Perhaps the English?' The man continued to affirm that he and he alone had carried out the attack, unaided, and at nobody's bidding. Losing his patience, Machault ordered two guardsmen to go and seek bundles of tinder and throw them into the fire together with the obstinate suspect; only the

Lieutenant General of the Hôtel du Roi, who had also arrived, prevented this being carried out.

The King himself, meanwhile, was convinced that his last hour had struck. His household was mortified at the thought that the sovereign might have to die in dirty sheets, for most of the bed linen had already been sent to the washerwomen. The royal surgeon was absent, and so it fell to the Dauphin's personal surgeon, Prudent Hévin, to attend to the wound, which he promptly did by bleeding Louis. Weakened, and melodramatic as was his wont, he designated the Dauphin Lieutenant General, and apologized to the Queen and his daughters in deepest contrition for the wanton, scandalous, and immoral private life he had led.

When the King's personal physician, François Quesnay, arrived (the author of the article FERMIER in the *Encyclopédie*), he judged that the three-inch-deep wound 'would not have prevented another man from attending a ball'[2] and told the King that he would not die. The King, however, obviously enjoying the diversion of lingering momentarily at death's door, was not to be persuaded until the arrival of the Marquis de Landsmath, a professional soldier and the commandant of the King's venery, who was known for his robust approach to ceremonial and who now swept aside the footmen and valets hanging about the gilded doors of the royal apartments, where he found Louis languishing and surrounded by his weeping family. 'Get the mourners out of here,' he bellowed with commando voice, then proceeded to seize a chamber pot, and command Louis to 'piss, cough and spit', in that order. Having satisfied himself that these royal functions were still intact, he informed his monarch that his wound was 'nothing' and that they would soon be out hunting again.

The shock in France was profound at the news of the King's presumed assassination. Rumours spread throughout Paris, each with a different version of whether or not the sovereign had been killed, how, and by whom. Edmond Barbier, the great diarist of his time, reflected the general confusion about the motivation and outcome of the attack, when he noted down: 'On 5 January 1757, the King was assassinated by an unhappy fanatic, animated by the bishop's refusal to give the sacraments to worthy (Jansenist) priests, and against the King, because he had not listened favourably to the remonstrances of the *Parlement*, against the archbishop and the clergy . . .'[3]

The sorry tale of the king's attacker reached London within a matter of days. His story is told in a 'Letter from a Gentleman in Paris to His Friend in London', published there later the same year:

> The name of this enthusiastical assassin is *Robert Francis Damien* [Damiens], born in *St Catherine's* suburb in the city of *Arras*; he is 42 years of age, and about five feet seven inches high. He had lived in the service of several families, but was turned off by all of them with the character of a loose profligate. His occupation of late has been to sell balls to take spots out of cloaths; and yet from this mean and contemptible station in life hath this lunatic dared to walk forth, and attempt to deprive a whole nation of their sovereign's life.[4]

The anonymous pamphleteer had a clear idea that only Catholic priests could be so dastardly as to assassinate a king (whose own indubitable Catholicity did not deter the argument):

> He was a very superstitious enthusiastical sort of a man, and therefore a very proper tool or cat's-paw for the Romish priests to work upon. What horrid crimes are committed under the sanction of religion! The artful popish clergy had worked him up to such a pitch of enthusiasm; that, faint-like, he was proud to die in so glorious a cause, imagining his meritorious sufferings would certainly procure him a residence in heaven.

Damiens, the man who had committed the crime upon the royal person, was a former valet and a drifter, and he puzzled his interrogators by alternating between brazen arrogance and deep dejection, and was obviously not always in control of his faculties.

Damiens's life and career were meticulously reconstructed. If fate had set out to create a symbol of all that was foul in the kingdom of France around the middle of the eighteenth century, it could hardly have come up with a more perfect creature. Born into rural poverty in war-torn Flanders as the son of a small farmer during the height of the agricultural crisis that had gripped the country in the first quarter of the century, the boy Robert-François grew up in an atmosphere of hunger, brutal deprivation, and near fanatical piety. Trying to escape this life, he became an apprentice wig-maker, worked in an inn, and finally, at sixteen, became valet to an officer who happened to be staying in the inn on the way to his regiment. On campaigns, he followed his master to the Rhine, into the Grand Duchy of Baden, and he took part in the siege of Philippsburg in 1734.

Three years later, the war was over and Damiens, at twenty-two, was without work. Domestic service seemed his only choice and so he went to Paris, where he was to work in a succession of houses and at the Collège Louis-le-Grand. He secretly married a chambermaid named Elisabeth and had two children with her, the first of whom died at birth. Despite the fact that he sometimes found it difficult to control his temper, he lived like thousands of other domestic servants in Paris and was in no way remarkable. Gradually, however, he became more temperamental, less reliable, changed employers (several of them members of the *Parlement* and Jansenists, like himself), had fits of rage, and began to neglect his wife and child.

In July 1756, his precarious life suddenly disintegrated. Having stolen 240 *louis d'or* from his last employer, Robert-François began a sentimental journey through France (well reconstructed in the court records), first to Arras, his home town, where he unsuccessfully attempted to claim an inheritance, then to Saint-Omer, to visit his brother, to whom he made a large present of wool for his workshop, then to his sister, to whom he also gave money. He visited his old father, attended mass with him, and afterwards went to an inn. Hearing that he was from Paris, a local asked him whether it was true that Jansenists were refused the sacraments, which Damiens confirmed, adding that the only solution would be to hang several clerics. He then returned to Saint-Omer, where he noticed that he had lost his penknife and bought a new one, model 'Namur', with a black horn grip, for 24 *sous*. He then bought other presents for members of his family, assuring the astonished recipients that he had won the lottery. The next day, 13 July, his family, alerted to the fact that Robert-François was wanted by the police, tried to persuade him to give himself up. He tried to kill himself by swallowing arsenic, but vomited up the poison. He told his family that he feared not death, but their dishonour.

His brother having persuaded him to seek refuge in a monastery and to sort out the affair from there, Damiens found that the abbot refused to admit him. He now admitted to his brother that he was haunted by terrible forebodings of murder and bloodshed. While judicial permission to enter the monastery was sought, Robert-François expressed the wish to see the sea, and set off to Dunkerque together with his brother. On the beach, he ran into the sea to drown himself, but was rescued. Despairing and unable to remain in France, Damiens sought refuge in Flanders, near Ypres.

From his exile, 'Pierre Guillemant', as he called himself, followed the goings-on in Paris and became even more embittered. His boarding-house room-mate, Nicolas Playoust, would later testify that Damiens was obviously disturbed, murmuring prayers over and over. He 'talked to himself the whole night long without his [Playoust's] being able to distinguish a single word',[5] slept very little and often only with the aid of poppy juice, and made violent verbal outbursts against the King, whose stance towards the *Parlement* embittered him deeply. 'To get at the King [*toucher le roi*]' and 'becoming the arm of God' are two phrases that remained vividly in Playoust's memory. Some days, his fellow lodger would remember, Damiens stayed in bed refusing to get up, while on others he would walk around the local church six or seven times. On one occasion, he barricaded himself in the room and was 'very agitated'.

Damiens soon returned to France, where he told an acquaintance, 'I have left a bad state of affairs in Paris, but I have to go back. All is lost, the whole kingdom of France is ruined. As for me, I too am lost, for ever. But people will speak of me.' On 20 December, he visited a doctor, who stated that the patient suffered from 'seething blood'; he bled him to calm him down and gave him grains of opium and poppy tea as sleeping aids. But

Damiens's distress was not alleviated by bloodletting. He told his godfather: 'The people are plunged into misery. My poor wife is lost, my daughter's life is forfeit; soon they will all die of hunger.'

Having attended midnight mass on Christmas Eve, Damiens set off for the capital on 28 December, leaving all his luggage behind at the inn. The journey took four days, and he immediately called on his brother Jacques-Louis and then on his wife, whom he had not seen for six months. The next day, 3 January, he took his leave, telling them he was returning to Flanders. His journey, though, only took him to Versailles, where he rented a room in the rue de Satory. On Wednesday 5 January, at ten o'clock in the morning, he asked to be bled by a doctor, but then changed his mind. He walked through the park of the palace alone, until in the early evening he met a poor inventor who was waiting for an opportunity to present a machine of his devising to the Comte de Noailles. The man told Damiens that the King was at Versailles, visiting his daughter. Unchallenged, Robert-François entered the courtyard, chatted to the guards and then remained among the group of soldiers and servants waiting for the King, who appeared punctually at half-past five.

Transferred from Versailles to the Conciergerie prison in Paris by a whole cavalcade of armed cavalry and coaches, Damiens, who expected to be pardoned by a grateful King, was treated like a prisoner of state, with a permanent watch of a hundred soldiers and four sergeants, two doctors, and food sent from Versailles to eliminate the risk of his being poisoned by his supposed co-conspirators. In his cell, he remained chained to a rack in order to prevent him from committing suicide. The two doctors charged with preserving him intact for his execution noticed that 'since the last interrogation . . . he has fallen into a kind of discouragement and melancholy whose persistence alone is remarkable, it being rather common for him to pass alternatively from one of these states to another'.[6]

Beyond the prison, meanwhile, a veritable clandestine propaganda war was unfolding. Overnight, walls were daubed with the slogan: 'Decree by the Royal Mint: a Louis badly struck must be struck a second time' [*arrêt de la Cour des Monnaies: un louis mal frappé sera frappé une seconde fois*], and Jansenist and Jesuit pamphleteers wrote themselves into a frenzy trying to pin the attack on each other, a battle that left the Jansenists looking decidedly weaker, as Damiens had been sympathetic to their cause, had worked for members of the Paris *Parlement*, had declared his intention to avenge Jansenists dying without the last rites, and had been found in possession of a Jansenist devotional book.

The weight of evidence against Damiens was also used to further political, as well as religious, interests. Mme de Pompadour used the attack as a welcome opportunity to rid herself of an old enemy: the Comte d'Argenson, Minister of War, responsible for security in the royal household, was sent into exile by *lettre de cachet*. It was judged convenient by those close to the royal mistress to attach blame for Damiens's attack to a party, preferably the Jesuits, not just to the perpetrator himself. But Damiens remained unwaveringly firm in his assertion that he and he alone had carried out the attack and that nobody had instigated it or paid him for it.

The trial began on 26 March in front of five princes of the blood, twenty-two peers of the realm, twelve presidents, seven honorary councillors, two additional councillors, and sixteen ordinary councillors. The accused maintained remarkable courage, as if he were either not aware of what was happening, or long past caring. He joked with the judges, asked one of them whether his white silk stockings were not too cold for the time of year, and praised another one for his eloquence. He had an answer for every one of his interrogators' questions, repeating again and again: 'No accomplices, no conspiracy. Only I.'

The judges did not take long to reach a verdict, and the entire trial was over in a matter of hours. They decided that Damiens should be punished even more cruelly than the infamous Ravaillac, the murderer of France's great king, Henri IV. The judgment reads:

> The said Damiens is sentenced to pay for his crime in front
> of the main gate of the Church of Paris. He will be taken there

in a cart naked and will hold a burning wax torch weighing two pounds. There, on his knees, he will say and declare that he had committed a very mean, very terrible and very dreadful parricide, and that he had hurt the King ... He will repent and ask God, the King and Justice to forgive him. When this will be done, he will be taken in the same cart to the Place de Grève and will be put on a scaffold. Then his breasts, arms, thighs, and legs will be tortured. While holding the knife with which he committed the said parricide, his right hand will be burnt. On his tortured body parts, melted lead, boiling oil, burning pitch, and melted wax and sulphur will be cast. Then four horses will pull him apart until he is dismembered. His limbs will be thrown on the stake, and his ashes will be spread. All his belongings, furniture, housings, wherever they are, will be confiscated and given to the King. Before the execution, the said Damiens will be asked to tell the names of his accomplices. His house will not be demolished, but nothing will be allowed to be built on this same spot.[7]

Damiens's entire family was condemned to 'leave the realm with the injunction never to return on pain of hanging and strangulation without formality or trial'. Not for centuries had such a medievally bestial sentence been passed. And yet it was not enough. In a last effort to squeeze from Damiens's deranged mind and his already weakened body the confession the court wished, and which Mme de Pompadour wanted particularly, the authorities transported from Avignon a newly invented torture machine, the 'diamond' (a large, sharp cone onto which the suspended prisoner would slowly be lowered), which was said to be not lethal but which imparted unbearable suffering. The doctors counselled against its use, fearing for their patient's life before the execution. A more traditional method was chosen and scheduled for the morning of the execution, the 'torture of the boots', in which the accused had his legs slowly crushed between wooden planks with the aid of eight wedges, hammered in one by one, every quarter of an hour. Damiens's only comment on being informed of the ordeal he was to endure was: '*La journée sera rude*' [It will be a tough day].

On the day of the execution, the Place de Grèves, in front of the hôtel de ville, the city hall, was surrounded by spectators. Society gentlemen and a surprising number of ladies had rented rooms overlooking the scene and were clustered in the windows, as closely as their enormous skirt hoops would permit, overlooking the crowd with lorgnettes more commonly used at the opera. A window at the first or second floor cost 100 *livres*; some of them were even sub-let. The papers later reported, maliciously no doubt, that not one woman closed her eyes or left her window place during the following hours.

Sixteen executioners dressed in ceremonial robes and convened from all over France were ready at the orders of their chief, the Paris *exécuteur des hautes oeuvres*, Gabriel Sanson. At three o'clock in the afternoon, the condemned man was undressed and attached to a scaffold specially constructed for the occasion, rising about three feet above the ground. As Sanson approached, the first scene was one of confusion. The torturer Soubise was drunk and had forgotten to buy the necessary lead, sulphur, wax, and resin, and the wood of the stake was wet and difficult to light. The crowd began to get restless and started abusing the executioners. Sanson started to tear his hair out in a display of impotent rage: what was arguably the high point of his professional career was now in danger of becoming overwhelmed by the crowd's ridicule. Servants sent out to buy the missing materials found themselves hard pressed to find merchants willing to sell them what they required, for much of the working population, unlike the higher ranks of society, felt sympathy towards Damiens. It took an hour to arrange everything, but finally an infernal mixture of sulphur, wax, lead, and resin was melted in cauldrons while pincers were heated in the embers.

It is not necessary to describe what happened afterwards or to quote the meticulous witness reports collected with the help of detached interest and good binoculars. Suffice it to say that the condemned's tendons proved so strong that after sixty unsuccessful attempts at quartering him with four horses and one change of horses, permission was finally given by President Molé and the councillors Severs and Pasquier to cut through the soft tissue of

Damiens's shoulders and thighs with knives so that the equine workload might be lighter. 'Ah, the poor animals, how I feel for them!' cried the niece of a famous financier, Bouret, on seeing the horses sweating in their harness.[8] The condemned man watched every stage of the procedure 'with great attention . . . showed great firmness and proffered not a single judgement'.[9] The public screamed and groaned almost as much as Damiens himself. Night had fallen by then, and when the sentence had finally been carried out, a relieved crowd applauded warmly. It took four hours for the bleeding rump to burn to ashes, which were 'cast to the four winds'. It was generally agreed that the spectators had had their money's worth.[10] The King himself did not attend the execution, preferring instead to pray in the chapel at Versailles. He took great pleasure, though, in hearing about it in great detail the next day, and gloated in front of foreign ambassadors, repeating the accounts he had been given, omitting no detail.

The brutal execution of a man who was mentally disturbed even in the eyes of the time (in today's parlance, Damiens's would be a case of acute psychosis with religious delusions),[11] a man who had tried to commit suicide twice, who was tortured by visions and who ceaselessly muttered prayers, who did not sleep, who roamed graveyards, who had no conception of danger, and who had already given himself up for dead, was shocking even to people used to a system of violent justice. The authorities responded to the popular consternation by attempting to stifle any discussion of the case; anyone who was heard so much as mentioning Damiens in an inn or a café could be imprisoned in the Bastille.[12]

Royal power had never been weaker since the Fronde, and perhaps the court wanted to avoid finding too much proof of a general atmosphere of discontent that made Damiens not the monster he was portrayed as in contemporary literature, but a perfect representative of what many French thought at the time, perhaps even a figurehead for revolt.

As it was, the Damiens affair had significant political consequences.

Mme de Pompadour, who had insisted on trying to implicate the
Jesuits, lost influence; France lost its Minister of War and its highly
competent Seal Bearer (and consequently sank into debt even more
quickly than before), both of whom were sent into exile; the Paris
Parlement, having successfully escaped being blamed for the deed
of their unbidden defender Damiens, became assertive once more,
while at the same time following a political line far less tolerant of
dissent; and the mood in the inns and on market squares, everywhere where people congregated to discuss and debate, was more
violent than ever.

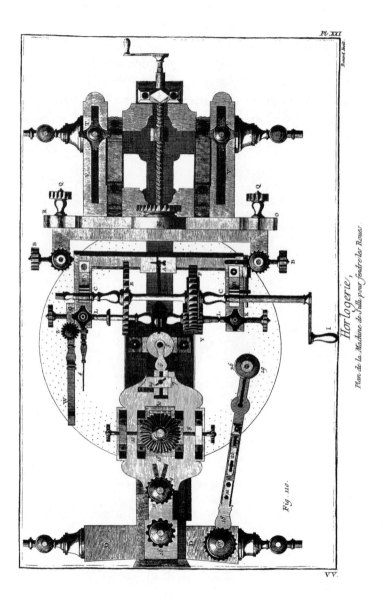

Pl. XXI

Bonard fecit.

Horlogerie,
Plan de la Machine de Sully pour fendre les Roues.

Fig. 110.

GENEVA

GENÈVE, (*Hist. & Politiq.*) ... Theatre is not tolerated in Geneva; it is not that the citizens disapprove of the performances themselves, but it is feared, they say, that the troupes of actors will further among the young a taste for finery, for dissipation and loose morals. Still, would it not be possible to counter this effect through severe laws about the conduct of actors? In this way, Geneva would have theatre and morals ... & Geneva would unite the wisdom of Lacedemonia and the politeness of Athens ...

We still have to talk about religion in Geneva; the part of the article which is perhaps of most interest to the *philosophes* ... Many of the pastors of Geneva have no other religion than perfect Socianism; they reject all mysteries & imagine that it is the first principle of religion not to impose anything that would harm reason. Also, if pressed on the necessity of revelation, that dogma so essential for Christianity, many of them substitute the term necessity which seems better to them; these latter ones may not be orthodox, but at least they are firm in their principles. *See* **SOCIANISME**

(*O*)

CENSURE *of books or propositions,* a note or a qualification of everything that hurts truth ... [which is], so to speak, a delicate flower, which one cannot touch or alter without ruining it ... An opinion is called *dangerous* if it so embarrasses the Catholic dogma with the incertitudes of the theological system, that this opinion would bring with it the ruin of the dogma and the system. Nothing is more dangerous, for faith, than to make it depend on human opinion, subjected to the inquiry of the reason of everyone wishing to attack it. *See* **NOTE & QUALIFICATION.**

(*X*)

The Encyclopedists had followed the Damiens affair, but their lives, for the time being at least, seemed very distant from the political upheaval surrounding them. Voltaire, in his enlightened blindness to all things human, considered Robert-François Damiens to be 'a domestic servant who could not even spell, a fanatic who dishonours his century'.[1] Mme d'Épinay, in some two and a half thousand pages of chronicle, did not find space to mention Damiens at all, whilst to the 'bear' Jean-Jacques Rousseau living in her park, these worldly matters had long since lost all interest.

In the edition dated 15 January of his *Correspondance littéraire*, Grimm briefly mentioned the presumed assassination but it took him until May to take up the issue again, though without any consideration for Damiens himself. He may have had to observe a certain discretion concerning his own feelings: while his letters were not censored in France, they were nevertheless intended for a public unlikely to be enthusiastic about effusions of sympathy towards Damiens.

Diderot took a more humane approach, although he mentioned the affair in only one letter, in which he imagined the horrors of the execution, admired the condemned man's courage, and then took refuge in classical allusion: 'That very instant, I imagine that next to me is breathing a soul of the stamp of Regulus [a Roman who had chosen torture over treason].' To Diderot at least, the humbly born Robert-François Damiens was a breathing soul, a living being worthy of pity.

Volume seven of the *Encyclopédie*, FOANG–GYTHIUM, appeared on 15 November 1757, a good seven months after the Damiens execution, in an atmosphere of great political tension. The Seven Years War into which France had been drawn by the first great demonstration of Prussian hunger for power and territory, was going badly for Louis XV. Only ten days earlier, the royal forces had lost an important battle near the German town of Rossbach. It was seen by many as a national humiliation and as a worrying symbol of France's decadence. Internal criticism was stifled with all the means at the government's disposal until there was no more room in the Bastille. By royal decree, all writers of material that tended to attack religion and authority, and generally 'to upset minds', were to be treated with the utmost severity.

Away from the political arena, the Encyclopedists were still enmeshed in their personal problems. There were tensions between d'Alembert and Diderot, between Diderot and Rousseau, and between Rousseau and all of them. The absence in the field of Grimm, who had often absorbed Diderot's energies and smoothed over possible ruptures, was also felt. Another important star in the Encyclopedist firmament was missing: Mme d'Épinay, who was ill with consumption and about to travel to Geneva to consult the famous Dr Tronchin, a journey that would almost cost her her life. Her imminent departure had created new tensions between Rousseau and Diderot: the latter believed that, after all she had done for him, the very least Rousseau could do was to accompany her on her painful and dangerous journey, a suggestion that had come from Mme d'Épinay herself but that had been shrugged off by him immediately. Rousseau saw his friend's intercession as yet another instance of his moralizing meddling, and, worse, as proof positive of a conspiracy. Diderot's letter ran as follows:

> I am made for loving you and for giving you trouble. I hear that Mme d'Épinay is going to Geneva, but I do not hear it being said that you are accompanying her. My friend, if you are satisfied at Mme d'Épinay's you have to go with her, if you are dissatisfied there, you have to part much more quickly. Are you not already overburdened with obligations towards her? This is a possibility to discharge them at least in part and to free yourself. Will you find another occasion in your life to give her evidence of your gratefulness? She is going to a country where she will be quite helpless. She is ill, she will have need of amusement and distraction. . . . Are you not afraid that your conduct will be misinterpreted? You will be thought of as ungrateful, or of having another, secret, motive.
>
> I know very well that, whatever you do, you will have your own, clear conscience; but is this in itself enough? Is it permissible to neglect those of others? I am writing you this note out of obligation to you. If you don't like it, throw it into the

fire, and we will treat the matter as if it had never been written.
I salute you, I love you, and I embrace you.[2]

Rousseau, in his *Confessions*, described his reaction: 'Trembling in
my rage and dizzy with fury I could hardly finish the letter, but I
still noted that Diderot affected a sweeter tone, more tender, more
honest, than in other letters.'[3] This, of course, seemed part of his
friend's dastardly deception, and as soon as his anger permitted
him to hold a quill, Jean-Jacques was swift to draft a reply, pointing
out that Diderot had no business judging him and that, anyway, it
was very clear that this advice did not come from Diderot himself.
He then plucked up his courage, scampered over to La Chevrette,
burst in on Mme d'Épinay and Grimm, who was on leave, and
confronted the two with both letters. 'At this unexpected audacity
from a man normally so timid, they were both bowled over, stunned,
and not able to respond with a single word; especially that arrogant
man [Grimm] stared at the ground and did not dare to confront
the fire in my eyes. That very instant, in the depths of his heart,
he swore my ruin.'

Rousseau's patroness and her lover were indeed bewildered by
this scene, if not for the reasons postulated by him. Asked for one
favour in return for years of kindness, he was now making a scene
about conspiracies and injured virtue. He himself knew how his
imagination was wont to get the better of him. On another occasion,
when a publisher had delayed sending proofs to him and Rousseau
had been convinced they had been handed to the Jesuits, Malesherbes intervened and a ruefully emphatic Rousseau wrote back to
him: 'Oh! Monsieur, I have done an abominable thing . . . Nothing
has changed since the day before yesterday, yet everything now
takes on in my sight a different complexion, and where I thought
I saw the clearest proofs I now see only some very ambiguous
indications. Oh! How cruel it is for a sick and melancholy man,
living alone, to have an unregulated imagination.'[4]

This time, however, his imagination had firm hold on his reason,
and he shot off a furious letter to Grimm in which he acknowledged
no moral debt whatever towards his hostess, calling his time at the

Hermitage his 'two years of slavery' and wishing that he had never allowed himself to be 'dragged' there in the first place.[5] Grimm, who had been jealous of the place Rousseau obviously had in Mme d'Épinay's life, especially now that he himself was not there to help or accompany her, decided that this ingratitude was too monstrous to be tolerated, and sent his former friend a letter that sealed his depiction as the Machiavellian White Tyrant in the *Confessions*: 'I shall never in my life see you again, and I shall deem myself fortunate if I can banish from my mind the recollection of your behaviour.'[6] The bands of friendship between the Encyclopedists, their greatest source of strength, were fraying badly.

Slowly, pressure from the outside was also mounting. An article, '*Premier mémoire sur les Cacouacs par l'abbé Odet Giry de Saint Cyr, de l'Académie française*' (First Memoir of the Cacouacs, by Abbé Odet Giry of the Académie Française) appeared in the *Mercure de France*. It had a thin, a very thin, ethnological veneer which readily showed what was underneath: 'In the region of the forty-eighth degree of northern latitude [which passes between Paris and Orléans] one has found a new nation of savages, more ferocious and more fearsome than any Caribbean tribe.'[7]

This tribe, the Cacouacs, is described as looking quite civilized: 'They carry neither arrows nor clubs, their hair is artfully arranged, their clothes brilliant with gold, silver, and a thousand colours, making them look like spectacular flowers, or like birds with the most awe-inspiring plumage.' These birds, it seems, had been fluffing up their rainbow tails so much of late, and had ruffled so many feathers, that it was time for them to be plucked themselves, and the anonymous author (one Nicolas Moreau, who was paid by the Government) had set himself to do just that.

The chief weapon of the savages, the delighted readers of the *Mercure de France* discovered, was poison hidden under the tongue, expelled with every word they spoke. Being intrinsically malignant, the Cacouacs made a social outcast of everyone they sprayed with their poison, and were no kinder to each other, spitting venom 'on those whose friendship and good offices they have experienced', an indication, perhaps, that Rousseau's recent antics had not gone unnoticed by the all-seeing eyes of literary gossip-mongers.

This article was followed a month later by a second, longer one in which the vicious Cacouacs were described by a would-be ethnologist who had actually lived among them, and could therefore give a first-hand account of their life and customs. In the spirit of Jonathan Swift's *Gulliver's Travels*, the author writes that the tribe, far from being savage, is polite and cultured. Their race, he believes 'goes back to the Titans who wanted to climb the heavens'.[8] They have made it their goal to enlighten the beasts of the woods, and they are great talkers: 'Their language has something sublime and unintelligible that inspires respect and admiration. Everything they say is ruled by image, sentiment, and passion.'[9]

In an initiation rite, the author is presented with the great Cacouac treasure: 'There were seven coffers [seven volumes of the *Encyclopédie* had appeared], a foot long, half a foot wide, and one hand thick. They were covered in blue morocco leather and were indistinguishable but for the first seven letters of the alphabet, one of which formed a little diamond clasp on each of them.'[10] The leader of the tribe, 'a universal mind and the most industrious of all of them', is working on amassing records of strange cults similar to the Christian religion, in order to make it look ridiculous. Initiated into the cult, the author finds himself regarding the rest of nature and mankind as mere ignorant insects and sees the world with new eyes (usually through cheeky quotations from Diderot and Rousseau). When the powder that was blown into his eyes finally loses its power, he leaves the tribe and returns to his previous state.

The pin-pricks of satire, however, were as nothing compared to the storm brewing on the horizon, a storm caused by a single ill-judged article but strong enough to threaten the entire encyclopaedic enterprise. The article in question, GENEVA, had been written by d'Alembert and was full of extremely outspoken opinions about the city republic, its laws, and religious practices. The republic was outraged to have its Christian credentials called into question and to have a French mathematician lecture them on local political issues. Neither an introduction describing a pretty city set in idyllic countryside nor praise for the city's democracy could dispel their anger; indeed, they must have felt that much of what the French critic told them was simply none of his business. Like a disapproving nanny, d'Alembert had pointed out to the Genevans that they had no right to retain a part of their coat of arms, that the inscription on the city hall had to go, that the singing in their churches was in bad taste, and the verses sung even worse.

The pastors of the city saw that more had been challenged than their taste in poetry: the allegation that they were Socinians – believers in a single God, who denied the Holy Trinity – was severe indeed, even if d'Alembert might, rather naïvely, have intended it as a compliment. They drafted a Declaration of Orthodoxy (printed in Paris by Fréron's *Année Littéraire* in February 1758) and debated the possibility of a formal protest to the French government. It fell to the secretary of the committee to write to d'Alembert first, asking him to apologize and retract. He was none other than Dr Theodore Tronchin, the very doctor attending to the ailing Mme d'Épinay himself, a contributor to the *Encyclopédie*, a great champion of vaccination against smallpox, and a doctor of European renown, as well as being the lifelong friend of de Jaucourt (with whom he had studied in Leyden). Ironically, he had also received personal praise in the disputed article.

D'Alembert, intellectual pugilist that he was, would have none of it, and gave the pastors to understand that their protest was so much wasted paper. In his own reply to Dr Tronchin, Diderot chose a very different tone. He had met the doctor two years earlier when Tronchin had been in France to inoculate the children of the Duc d'Orléans against smallpox, a spectacular and highly controversial event. The two had become friends, and Diderot obviously felt that he could write to the Genevan emissary in some confidence, though with great care as the letter was also likely to be read by others. D'Alembert and he, Diderot wrote, were co-editors and solely responsible for their own articles, even if the other disagreed, 'which was the case with GENEVA'.[11] But d'Alembert's blunder, he went on, was surely no more than that, especially as d'Alembert had been so enthusiastic about the city after a recent visit. In any case, Diderot was happy to offer his own apology, substituting it for his colleague's, and accepting the blame as main editor.

Diderot's letter was politically motivated, and was written to diffuse a potentially serious crisis; but it nevertheless seems honest, especially in his opposition to the article. Entries in the *Encyclopédie* relating to cities and countries were usually very brief – the article FRANCE in the same volume was a fifth of the length of d'Alembert's piece on Geneva – and it must have been obvious to all that the article was particularly clumsy. It was likely to offend the French, who had Geneva waved in front of them as a shining example of integrity; the Genevans, who found themselves hectored by a Frenchman; the Protestants, who were designated unmelodious heretics; and the Catholic Church, which was infuriated by everything in the *Encyclopédie*, especially an article that presumed to tell it how to train its priests. It is likely, therefore, that Diderot advised against publication but that d'Alembert's stubbornness prevailed.

Voltaire was behind this mischief. During his recent visit to Geneva, d'Alembert had stayed with the old fox, and this personal connection would have done much to strengthen the Encyclopedist cause had not Voltaire, according to contemporary gossip at least, encouraged his admirer to mention in the *Encyclopédie* article that it was a shame Geneva did not allow the performance of good, tasteful plays such as his own. The article was also a good opportunity to reprimand the Genevans for other aspects of city life that had come to gall Voltaire in his self-imposed exile, as well as to laud them for others he had come to admire. With remarkable gullibility (or, worse, indifference), d'Alembert had taken up the suggestion and written the disputed article, reason enough for sharp-tongued contemporaries to claim that what was to grow into the great crisis in the life of the *Encyclopédie* was caused by Voltaire's wish to admire his own plays in performance, and to see others admiring him.[12]

In the climate of late 1757, a few months after the Damiens affair and just after the French army had been defeated humiliatingly by

Prussia, the *Encyclopédie* looked suspect enough without attracting additional publicity: it bore, after all, on every one of its title-pages, the proud legend 'of the Prussian Academy' after the names of both of its chief editors, who had wasted no opportunity to praise Voltaire's friend the Philosopher King, Frederick II, now the bitter enemy of France. The last thing the Encyclopedists needed was to appear opposed to the interests of the State. With their undeniable self-righteousness, as well as their courageous campaign for new ideas, they had made themselves scores of enemies already, and these enemies now scented blood. Pamphlets rushed off the presses, intrigues fluttered to and fro between Paris and Versailles, disappointed *littérateurs* and conservative clerics everywhere whetted their knives, ready to impale the smug band of *philosophes* who were threatening to ruin France and the Catholic faith with their corrosive views and insufferable self-satisfaction.

Seeing that the *Encyclopédie* was headed for possible disaster, Voltaire, who governed the Europe of the mind by correspondence, did what came naturally to him: he sent out a hectic stream of denials, declarations of solidarity, moral hectoring, good counsel, flattery, and helpful advice. For two months, from December to February 1758, the letters between Paris and Geneva must have made the Postmaster General consider buying extra horses for the overcharged route.

Seen through the prism of Voltaire's letters, the great crisis of the *Encyclopédie* and his role in it become as palpable as a love story in a Richardsonian correspondence novel. Obviously aware of the seriousness of the problem, Votaire fired off epistles in all directions, assuaging, ridiculing, dissembling, and generally having fun without becoming too involved:

> To M. Bertrand [a *philosophe*]
> Lausanne, 27 December
>
> I have finally read the article *Geneva* in the *Encyclopédie* that caused such a storm ... I find the Genevois very lucky to have nothing but such piffling problems, while people are strangling one another from Canada to the Oder river.

> To M. Vernes [in Geneva]
> Lausanne, 29 December
>
> Finally, if somebody orthodox or heterodox accuses me of
> having had the least part in the article *Geneva*, I beg of you to
> give truth its glory. I was the last to have heard of this affaire.
> I only want peace, and I wish it for all my brothers, be they
> monks, curates, ministers, seculars, regulars, Trinitarians, Unit-
> arians, Quakers, Moravians, Turks, Jews, Chinese, etc., etc., etc.

The very same day, after his letter to the Genevan theologian,
and after stating again that he had had nothing to do with the
article, Voltaire shows a less enthusiastic opinion of M. Vernes in a
letter to d'Alembert:

> Lausanne, 29 December
>
> My dear and prodigious *philosophe*, I have just read your excel-
> lent article *Geneva*. I think that the City Council owes you
> solemn thanks . . . they threaten to engage the magistrates to
> solicit the Royal Court in order to force you to retract, but the
> Court will not be mixed up with these Huguenots . . . Vernes,
> that Vernes convicted of theft of manuscripts . . . has he not
> printed, in some *Catechism*, which he has given me and which
> I threw into the fire, has he not printed, I say, that *revelation
> can have its uses*? Have you not heard him say twenty times that
> he does not regard Jesus Christ as God?

On 8 January Voltaire went a step further by writing to d'Alembert that all editors should resign their jobs if they could not work
'free of calumny', to which d'Alembert, who had been reluctant
in his collaboration for some time, answered with an enthusiastic
outpouring:

> Paris, 11 January
>
> I have received your two last letters almost at the same time,
> my very dear and illustrious *philosophe*, and I make haste to
> reply to them. Some days ago, I received a letter from Doctor

Tronchin, writing to me in the name of the pastors com-
plaining about me ... My response was simple, if M. Tronchin
will communicate it to you, and I flatter myself that you will
find it reasonable and measured. I told the ambassador that I
did not say a single word in the article *Geneva* that would make
it seem that the Genevan pastors *are not Christians* ...

Whether the work will be continued or not I do not know,
but I am certain that it will not be me who carries it on. I will
communicate to M. de Malesherbes and to the booksellers that
they can look for a successor ... I am exhausted by the tiresome
vexations of all sorts which this work brings us. The odious
and infamous satires published against us, which are not only
tolerated, but protected, applauded, ordered by those who
hold power; the sermons, or rather the alarm bells rung against
us in Versailles, in the presence of the King ... this new and
intolerable inquisition against the *Encyclopédie* by which we are
given new censors, the least reasonable and most absurd, worse
than those one could find in Goa; all these reasons, and others,
oblige me to give up this work for ever.

While d'Alembert was more than ready to throw in the quill,
Diderot was still ploughing on and had already made clear that he
would not consider abandoning his work or breaking his contract
with the booksellers. Voltaire, who had meanwhile become convinced that this would be the most high-minded course of action,
now addressed himself to Diderot:

Can it be true, monsieur, that while you are rendering a service
to humankind, which you enlighten, those who believe themselves born to blind should be allowed to publish libels against
you and those who think like you? What!

Are you not tempted to declare that you suspend the *Encyclopédie* until justice has been done to you? ... How I feel for you
that you are not writing your *Encyclopédie* in a free country!

Your admirer and partisan to the grave, the Free Swiss.

The 'Free Swiss' did not ration his flattery to Encyclopedists only,
and one of his next letters went to none other than Palissot, who

had made it his life's business to destroy the Encyclopedists and all
they stood for:

> Lausanne, 12 January
>
> Everything from you, Monsieur, will always be precious to me,
> and I impatiently await the *Lettres* which you have announced
> to me. If you come back to the land of the heretics, I will
> welcome you in Lausanne, better still than I did in Geneva.
> You will see a better setting here. I have a charming house
> here . . . I often talk about you with M. Vernes.

Diderot, meanwhile, had adopted his tried and tested tactic of
procrastination in the face of an apparent ally, Voltaire, whom he
was right not to trust. As his silence continued, Voltaire wrote to
him once again, insisting that the *philosophes* must not compromise.
Knowing that he had easier work with d'Alembert, he not only
continued to support his stance, but urged him to throw all caution
to the winds in his articles by exhorting him to 'Ban the trivial
morals which inflate some of your articles . . . Who forces you to
dishonour the *Encyclopédie* with all this tedium?' Courage and free
speech were easy to come by for a friend of kings living in Geneva.
Among the writers in Paris, only d'Alembert thought that he could
silence his critics by virtue of the simple fact (a common scientific
fallacy) that he had reason on his side. Voltaire, meanwhile, was
much more cautious for himself. He knew that some compromising
draft articles were still in Diderot's hands. He now wanted them
back, and was more than a little anxious at not having received an
immediate reply:

> To d'Alembert
> Lausanne, 13 February
>
> I have already told you that I have written to Diderot more
> than six weeks ago: firstly to ask him to encourage you about
> the article *Geneva* in case one tries to intimidate you; secondly
> to tell him that he has to present a united front with you, that
> he should quit together with you and will not take up the work

again without you . . . I have also written to him to return me
my letters, my article *Histoire*, the articles *Hauteur, Hautain,
Hémistiche, Heureux, Habile, Imagination, Idolatry*, etc. I can no
longer furnish a single word to the *Encyclopédie*.

I have no notion what could sanction his impertinence in
not having responded to me yet, but nothing can justify his
refusal to return my papers to me.

When Diderot's response finally came, it resonated with the
simple dignity he so loved in the figures he created in his plays. In
addition to this, however, the tone was cool and noncommittal, in
keeping with the arm's-length approach he had adopted towards
the Geneva master:

Paris, 19 February 1758

I ask you for forgiveness, Monsieur my dear master, for not
having written to you earlier. Whatever you may think, it is
nothing but negligence on my part.

You say that one treats us in an odious manner, and you are
right. You believe that I should be indignant, and I am. Your
opinion is that we should all quit the *Encyclopédie*, or that we
should go abroad, or that we should stay here and demand
justice. This is all very well, but it is illusory to want to achieve
this project elsewhere. There are the booksellers, who are working with us, the manuscripts which they have acquired but
which do not belong to us, and which we cannot use without
the plates. If we give up now, we turn our backs to the breach
in the wall and do exactly what the scoundrels, our persecutors,
want us to do. If you knew the joy with which they heard about
d'Alembert's desertion, and all the manoeuvres they deployed
to prevent him from returning!

So, what are we to do? The only thing suitable for the courageous: despise our enemies and go on; profit, as we have
done, from the imbecility of our censors. Would it be honest
to deceive the hopes of four thousand subscribers, and do we
not have a contract with the booksellers? If d'Alembert comes
back and we finish the work, are we not avenged? Ah, my dear
maître, where is the *philosophe* in you?

... there is another aspect to d'Alembert's desertion: he saw in it [the *Encyclopédie*] a means to gain honour, money, and the rest. As far as I am concerned, his desertion leaves me disconsolate and I will leave nothing untried to get him back ... After all this, you will believe that I am very attached to the *Encyclopédie*, and you would be wrong. My dear master, I am past forty, I am weary of all the trouble. I cry for peace, peace! from morning to evening. There is hardly a day during which I am not tempted to live in obscurity and to die in tranquillity in the depths of my home province. What does it matter to have been Voltaire or Diderot, and whether it is your three syllables or mine that stay? ... Adieu, my dear master, be well and love me.

Do not be angry with me, and please do not ask me to return your letters; if I were to send them back, I would never forget this slight. I no longer have your articles, they are in the hands of d'Alembert, as you know very well.

I am as ever, with attachment and with respect, Monsieur and dear master, etc.

The clash of temperaments between the two *philosophes* could hardly be clearer: Diderot regarded his continuation as an editor as a matter of principle, while Voltaire viewed the matter with the more detached, idealistic eyes of a wealthy man whose position (and exile) allowed him to write as he pleased, and of a slighted prince unused to being overlooked. Having finally received Diderot's letter, Voltaire was at a loss to understand how a great man, a man of the mind, could submit to the tyranny of commerce, and be exploited by people who were not his equals:

His duty to the booksellers! Is it seemly for a great man to depend on booksellers? It would be fitting for them to wait in his antechamber. This immense enterprise is going to earn him 30,000 *livres*! It should bring him 200,000 ... and, if they had honoured the little hole of Lausanne [i.e. Voltaire himself] with their confidence, I would have sent them a bill for 200,000 *livres* ...

The two months spanned by these exchanges were among the most fateful in the history of the *Encyclopédie*, and it became clear that the work would never be the same again. D'Alembert had remained firm in his resolution not to have anything to do with the work any longer – a decision that must have come as a relief after his long period of ambivalence – and the *Encyclopédie* had lost its most prestigious editor.

Diderot, however, had also remained firm in his resolution to continue the work, and to continue it in France. Despite Voltaire's enjoinders and manœuvrings, he had succeeded in maintaining his own line, though at the cost of annoying the work's most influential ally, whom he had always chosen to keep at arm's length. Voltaire was right to be stung by Diderot's tardiness. He might have been known as a bad keeper of appointments and a worse correspondent (though his letters to Sophie Volland and others close to him do not bear this out), but ignoring Voltaire for so long was certainly also a way of sending a message that needed no stagecoach. Voltaire was right to complain of the topics that had been 'abandoned' to him: Diderot, sensing that his famous colleague was pursuing his own interests, had kept him well away from the important and contentious topics, fobbing him off with headings like ELEGANCE, ESPRIT, FANTASIE, and GALANT, hardly solid fare for Europe's greatest thinker and controversialist. The editor's instinct had not let him down, as shown by Voltaire's imperious demands for the return of all manuscripts that might incriminate him and associate him with a failing project that might lose its protection from on high. In these circumstances, Diderot's office, which had been searched by police more than once, would simply be no safe place for Voltaire's finely spun heresies, and their author might lose both the protection of Mme de Pompadour and his own influence on Parisian literary life.

But Diderot's firmness won out, and four months later Voltaire approached the editor (perhaps through his factotum d'Argental) to ask whether the *Encyclopédie* would still be interested in his collaboration. In one of his few dated letters, Diderot – perhaps to make good his earlier tardiness and in order not to lose Voltaire's sympathy altogether – responded in the most flattering of tones:

Paris, 14 June, 1758

Whether I still want your articles, Monsieur and dear master? Could there possibly be any doubt? Would I not make the voyage to Geneva and ask for them on my knees if this was the price?

Choose; write. Send, and send often. I was not in a state to accept your offers earlier; my arrangement with the librarians [a modified contract] is hardly concluded. Now we have made a good contract together, just like the one between the devil and the peasant in the la Fontaine fable. The leaves are for me, the fruit for them, but at least the leaves are mine. This is what I have gained from the desertion of my colleague. Without doubt you know that he will continue to contribute mathematical articles. It was not for want of trying that he is not doing more.

M. d'Argental, who likes me well because he knows how attached I am to you, has given me the pieces you prepared for the eighth volume. Please accept my thanks. Above all, pardon my laziness. Love me, always, and believe that, when you no longer loved me, I preserved no less of the devotion and respect which I have always had and with which I will always be, Monsieur and dear master, your very humble and very obedient servant,

Diderot

The patriarch was assuaged, and the next letter from Délices, Voltaire's residence, was all sweetness and light. All troubles, anger, remonstration, and all thoughts of returning manuscripts and retracting any collaboration, were forgotten, though the great man's cunning and caution was still the same:

Délices, 26 June

Do not doubt, Monsieur, the honour and the pleasure I have when I have the occasion of contributing one or two bricks to

your great pyramid. It is a shame that, in everything regarding
metaphysics and history, one cannot speak the truth. The
articles that would be the most enlightening of all become
those that redouble public errors and ignorance. One is
obliged to lie, and then one is still persecuted for not having
lied enough. As for myself, I have so insolently spoken the
truth in *History, Imagination,* and *Idolater,* that I can only ask
you not to give them to the censor under my own name. They
might pass, if the author is not known.

The flutter of letters between Paris and Geneva had been entertaining enough for Voltaire; but the crisis of the *Encyclopédie*
continued to build, towards a conclusion far more serious than
wounded pride.

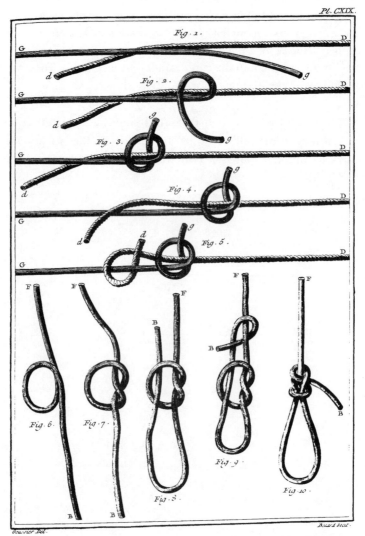

Pl. CXIX.

Fig. 1.

Fig. 2.

Fig. 3.

Fig. 4.

Fig. 5.

Fig. 6.

Fig. 7.

Fig. 8.

Fig. 9.

Fig. 10.

Boussier Del.

Bourd fecit.

Soierie, Nœud Tirant et Nœud Coulant, les différens temps de leur formation.

d d d d

FANATICISM

FANATICISM, s. m. (*Philosophie*) this is a blind and passionate zeal born out of superstition which causes actions that are ridiculous, unjust, & cruel; not only without shame and remorse, but with a sort of joy & contentment. *Fanaticism*, therefore, is superstition in action. *See* **SUPERSTITION**

Imagine an immense rotunda, a pantheon of a thousand altars; & in the middle of the dome, imagine a believer of every sect that has been or is still, at the foot of the divinity he honours in his way, in all the bizarre ways the imagination has been able to create . . . young maidens in tears mortify their still innocent flesh, trying to appease the demon of lustfulness with all the means likely to excite him; others, in a different posture altogether, solicit the approaches of the divinity: a young man, trying to neutralize the instrument of his virility, attaches to it iron rings of a weight proportional to its forces; another stops temptation at its source, by means of an inhuman amputation, and suspends over the altar the spoils of his sacrifice.

Watch them all coming out of the temple, & the divine fullness agitating them, will spread dread and illusion over the face of the earth. . . . The human mind, once having left the luminous ways of nature, will not find them again; it will err around truth, without meeting anything but glimmers mixing with false lights invested by superstition, only to put them out altogether in the depths of hell.

*This article by M. **DELEYRE**, author of the analysis of the philosophy of Chancellor Bacon*

Voltaire's letter of 26 June 1758 – like all others by him, a seismographic indication of how the *Encyclopédie* enterprise was perceived – shows that by the summer the crisis surrounding d'Alembert's GENEVA article seemed to have abated. D'Alembert had even seen fit, in his usual imperious manner, to demand that Malesherbes should stop the onslaught of satirical pamphlets against the Encyclopedists, especially after Fréron had made it his business to further the Cacouac idea with long reviews in his journal that revived all the particularly stinging parts of the parody. Malesherbes, however, would have none of it and reminded the Encyclopedist that the freedom of the press (limited as it was), which the *philosophes* claimed was of such a high value that it could not be valid only for them, or it would be just another kind of censorship.

Despite the encouraging signals from Geneva, however, the *Encyclopédie* was in a state of disarray. Having sworn that he would forever resign his post as editor, d'Alembert dithered for several months, effectively bringing work to a standstill. Volume eight was already on the presses, but could not be finished before the question of the editorship was settled. As documented in Diderot's correspondence, d'Alembert made the fullest possible use of the situation. He would give up for good (11 January); he might continue, but only under the right circumstances (28 January); he thought continuing was altogether impossible (8 February); he was firm in his resolution never to come back (26 February). Fearing for their investment, the booksellers now intervened, promising d'Alembert, and, in the event, Diderot as well, better terms if he agreed to continue with the work, even if he would only ensure that the mathematical section still carried his name.

By the summer, a new agreement was reached and d'Alembert had duly consented to undertake the writing of the mathematical and geometrical articles. In effect, this changed very little, though at least it made certain that no second GENEVA was likely to happen. D'Alembert had written very little outside his area of competence, and his one great exception had not been a success. The bulk of the editorial work had always fallen to Diderot; and so it was mainly the symbolic significance of d'Alembert's defection that had made the booksellers so keen to keep his name on the title-page.

Just as the Encyclopedists were trying to maintain a united front came the publication of an essay by Rousseau, *Lettre à M. d'Alembert*

sur les spectacles (Letter to M. d'Alembert on Stagecraft), which was
intended less to elucidate dramatic principles than to deliver a slap
in the face to his former friends – a public act of revenge.

It is hard to avoid feeling that there is a certain wilful contrariness
in the *Lettre sur les spectacles*. D'Alembert had written in favour of
the theatre, Voltaire was a dramatist already, and, most importantly,
Diderot had published one drama, *Le Fils naturel*, and was working
on another. Rousseau promptly, and predictably, took up a position
that was hostile to all theatre. Tragedy (Diderot's chosen form)
was to be condemned because it excited the emotions; comedy, because it ridiculed morality; actors, because they carry with them
immorality like dogs carry fleas.

Then, in a very personal side swipe, he lamented having lost his
Aristarchus, his faithful critic – Diderot – crushing what remained
of their long and close friendship by quoting from Ecclesiasticus:
'Although thou hast drawn a sword at a friend, despair not: for
there may be a returning. If thou hast opened a sad mouth, fear
not, for there may be reconciliation: except upbraiding, and
reproach, and pride, and disclosing of secrets, or a treacherous
wound: for in all these cases a friend will flee away.'[1]

Now it was Diderot's turn to be hurt at a publicly made accusation, a reply to his equally open assertion, two years earlier, that
'only the wicked man lives alone'. The salons were abuzz with the
delicious details (real and fictitious) of this rupture, some people
taking Diderot's side, others believing that he must have deserved
this rebuke since he made no efforts to defend himself. Diderot,
meanwhile, grieved silently for his lost friend, a grief evident from
one of the most curious documents by him to have survived, a
catalogue of all of Rousseau's misdemeanours, lies, and deceptions
in the affair, written as if to persuade himself that there really was
no possible friendship with this man. After rehearsing the entire
affair in all its stages, he resumes:

> He speaks badly about sentimental comedy because it is my
> genre. He pretends to be devout, because I am not; he drags
> the theatre through the mud because I said that I love this

profession. He says that he believed once one could have probity without religion, but that this is a prejudice and that he has come back [to religion], because he is despised by all who know him and especially by his friends, and he is delighted to make them look like rogues. It follows that this man is false, vain like Satan, ungrateful, cruel, hypocritical and wicked: all his apostasies from Catholicism to Protestantism and from Protestantism to Catholicism, without believing anything at all, prove this only too well.

One trait that has always offended me in his conduct towards me was the slight manner with which he treated me in the presence of others, and the signs of esteem and of docility he gave me in private; he squeezed me dry, he used my ideas, and he pretended to despise me.

In truth, this man is a monster . . .

He embraced me at the same time as writing against me.

He said that he hated all those he had reason to be grateful to, and he has proved it.[2]

For Diderot, the break with Rousseau was also a decisive break with his own past. The young man who lived in cafés and taverns, and who came home only occasionally even after he had married, the husband who always thought first about his books and about the next literary enterprise and then (if at all) about the money to feed his family, had been finally transformed when his daughter Angélique had been born in 1753. Her siblings had died young and, it appears, without causing too much grief to their father; but this girl and her welfare had assumed such an importance for him that, from then on, his attitude to life had no longer been the same. 'Oh Angélique, my dear child,' he wrote in a sudden outpouring of parental love in a letter to Sophie Volland. 'Parents are never really afflicted unless their children are the cause of it, and never really happy unless their children make them so.'[3]

He had marked this transition from literary gadfly to family man and responsible editor with symbolic acts, such as his trip to Langres and the reconciliation with his own father, and a new contract with his booksellers. In his plays also, to which he devoted most of his energies while the *Encyclopédie* was in abeyance, he had turned towards themes such as family and virtue. The rupture with Rousseau, who had emphatically rejected fatherhood several times and who had taken part as well in this life of weekly dinners until the small hours, hatching great plans and singing Italian arias, also marked a departure from Diderot's previous way of life, and much of what went with it.

The mature Diderot, the family man and author, had been working hard on his second play and was now ready to see it published. Before the drama could be printed, however, he found that his very name made the authorities jumpy. One censor was so unreasonably finickity that Malesherbes appointed a second, who promptly asked to be excused from editing the work of so contentious an author. A third candidate wrote to his superior, saying:

> I shall inform the publisher that I have had the honour of sending the work back to you, as being beyond my strength and my enlightenment to pass judgement on, which I confess to being true. But as I ask only for peace and comfort, and as I do not wish to have a quarrel with people who imagine themselves the sole possessors of all human reason, I dare to flatter myself that you will keep the word that you had the kindness to give me with them, for I am as apprehensive of them as I am of the theologians.[4]

The Encyclopedists were clearly becoming their own Church, with an influence that was not to be ignored, a faction not to be trifled with.

Le Père de famille, Diderot's new and revealingly named play, finally appeared with minor changes only. In its plot Diderot made a literary attempt to make peace with his father by rewriting the circumstances surrounding his own courtship of Toinette – but with some revealing differences. While the title character is patently the dignified and somewhat austere Diderot *père* transferred into the

kind of Paris bourgeois milieu that would have been utterly foreign
to him, his son, Saint-Albin, carries all the traits of Diderot himself.
The story, concerning the son of a respectable family who falls in
love with a poor but honest girl and the father who opposes the
marriage to the point of threatening a *lettre de cachet*, is based on
Diderot's own life, with the subtle variation that the virtuous girl
from a good but impoverished family has Toinette's background
but Sophie Volland's character. Here, the only thing that might
have prevented one of Mme Diderot's famous, and well-deserved,
fits of rage was the fact that she was not in the habit of reading
her husband's work.

The most delicate biographical question for the dramatist
Diderot was how to resolve the plot, whether to declare in retrospect
that father Didier was right in trying to prevent his son's marriage,
or whether finally to commit symbolic patricide by celebrating the
triumph of young love over parental authority. This, Diderot the
son could not bring himself to do, and so he settled for compromise. After drawing out for five acts a problem that was perfectly
clear in the first, it is suddenly revealed that Sophie, the poor but
virtuous girl, is in fact the father's niece: she is therefore of good
family and can marry the son after all, resolving the father–son
conflict in a sea of smiles. Any querying voice noting that this happy
end is somewhat incestuous is drowned out by the author's audible
sighs of relief.

The drama established its author as an artist in his own right.
Indirectly, however, it contributed to the impending catastrophe
that befell the *Encyclopédie*. To silence critics who cried plagiarism
once again, Diderot decided to translate the two Goldoni plays they
accused him of having copied so that the public could judge for
themselves. An ironic and all too obvious dedication, however,
which had probably been slipped into the proofs by a mischievous
Grimm, proved a costly mistake, as it antagonized the lover of one
of the ladies who were being riduculed, the Duc de Choiseul, Chief
Minister to Louis XV, one of the few friends the *Encyclopédie* had
at court.

This incident might have passed unnoticed had it not been for the publication in July 1758 of *De l'esprit* by Claude-Adrien Helvétius (1715–71), a philosopher and Encyclopedist. Pious and conservative readers were outraged by the book's argument that all human conduct was based on self-interest and egoism and, by implication, all morality on self-gratification, a model that left no space for nobility or righteousness, and not even the tiniest crack for God. If this opinion was widely accepted among the civilized French bourgeoisie, it was quite another proposition to publish it. 'He has upset everybody,' the society hostess Mme Deffand was heard to remark, 'by revealing what has been everybody's secret.'

Helvétius had the great fortune to possess a great fortune as well as excellent connections (he had been a *férmier général*, and his father had been the Queen's personal surgeon), and the ensuing tempest among the upholders of public morals and faith may have rattled his tiles but did not blow off the roof. Others, however, less solidly ensconced in wealth and position, were less fortunate. Even Helvétius had to sign retractions and resign an honorific post. The second of these public statements was so humiliating, wrote Grimm, that 'one would not be surprised to see a man escape to the Hottentots rather than sign a similar admission'.[5] Helvétius, though, obviously preferred humiliation in Paris to freedom in the African wilderness – a wise choice, as it turned out, because when the gusts of disgust had blown over he would trade on his reputation of persecuted sage for the rest of his life, and receive in his city *palais* royalty of the blood and of the mind. During his Paris stay, David Garrick naturally stayed *chez* Helvétius.

Despite, or because of, this storm, *De l'esprit* became extraordinarily popular and was re-edited twenty times within the year. It also quickly became the main target for pious outrage and tirades against the excesses of Enlightenment thinking, and in the attacks all *Lumières* came under fire. Helvétius, after all, supported penniless writers, received in his house the entire Encyclopedist clan, and was seen at their salons. Soon, religious and secular authorities formed a mighty chorus of condemnation. The Archbishop of Paris denounced the book on 22 November, the Pope on 31 January, the Paris *Parlement*, anxious not to be seen as contemptuous of

Church and Crown, soon followed suit with an investigation of all literature deemed 'dangerous, scandalous and licentious'.[6]

The speech given in front of the assembled parliamentarians on 23 January 1759 by the Public Prosecutor, Omer Joly de Fleury, is indicative of the strong sentiments the issue aroused against all writers whose orthodoxy was questionable – the very writers who had assembled under the banner of the *Encyclopédie*:

> Society, State, and Religion present themselves in front of this tribunal to bring their case. Their rights are violated, their laws ignored, impiety holds its head high . . . and licentiousness is increasing by the day. Humanity shudders, citizens are alarmed, one hears priests groan at the prospect of so many works . . . which will erase the foundations of our religion.
>
> In the shadows of a dictionary which assembles an infinity of useful and curious facts about the arts and sciences, one has admitted all sorts of absurdities, of impieties spread by all authors, embellished, augmented, and shockingly obvious . . .
>
> It is with grief that we are forced to conclude that there is a project formed, a society organized, to propagate materialism, to destroy religion, to inspire a spirit of independence, and to nourish the corruption of morals . . . Faith is useless, the existence of God doubtful, the creation of the world unproven, the universe formed of its own accord, the Messiah was a simple legislator, the progress of religion nothing but natural. The Scriptures are treated as fiction, the dogmas turned to ridicule, religion and fanaticism are synonymous, and Christianity inspires nothing but an insensible fury working for the destruction of Society.[7]

The scandal caused by a work of philosophy had rebounded on the *Encyclopédie*, which once more saw its existence in grave danger. Omer de Fleury warned the assembled company against the insidious effect of the cross-references (Diderot had only himself to blame for this), and it was decided that sales of the *Encyclopédie* were to be banned forthwith.

The hammer blow of a forcible suspension of the entire enterprise came just as the Encyclopedists believed they had left their greatest troubles behind them, and it proved a terrible shock. Not only had they played too open a game with articles like ENCYCLO-PÉDIE and GENEVA, they had also underestimated the force and determination of their opponents, who were by now well organized. In addition to scattered pamphlets and isolated attacks, there were now more effective works such as Abraham-Joseph de Chaumeix's *Préjugés légitimes contre l'Encyclopédie* (Legitimate Prejudices against the *Encyclopédie*), in eight volumes, published in 1758 and 1759, a hostile and close reading of the first seven volumes and their heretical potential. The *Encyclopédie*'s enemies on all sides, Jansenist and Jesuits, seemed to have closed ranks for one final assault.

The prohibition of sales, wrote Barbier, himself a member of the *Parlement*, in his journal, 'is seen as a declaration against the *philosophes* of this century, as much against M. Helvétius as against MM. Diderot and d'Alembert, editors of the *Encyclopédie*, and others who have worked at it, and who are now accused of wanting to introduce deism and materialism, and of endangering religion and state with their pernicious principles.'[8] Despite this menace, the mood among those working on the remaining volumes was defiant, even cheerful, and the general assumption was that a way would be found to iron out the present difficulties without too much loss of face for the *Parlement*. Grimm, on 15 February, made fun of Omer de Fleury's cumbersome rhetoric, and asked by what right he accused respected citizens of plotting against Church and Crown without the least proof. He then continued defiantly to his foreign subscribers:

> The *Parlement* has seized the affair [around *De l'esprit* and the *Encyclopédie*], and the enemies of philosophy are persuaded that they have won a great victory ... This immense work, regarded throughout Enlightened and learned Europe as the best enterprise and the greatest monument of the human mind, was supposed to succumb to superstition and envy. Finally, however, the opinion of the wisest prevailed in the *Parlement*. They were content to burn the book *De l'esprit* and

> several other little and very obscure works ... we are still bar-
> barians. The same decision has named commissaires, theo-
> logians and lawyers, to examine the offending articles in the
> *Encyclopédie*. It is said that, when these commissaires have done
> their report ... the *Parlement* will publish a rebuke of several
> articles and will demand of the publishers to publish it at
> the head of the eighth volume ... Thus the enemies of the
> *Encyclopédie*, despite their number and rank, have failed in their
> great project, which was to wrest it from M. Diderot's hands,
> to profit from his immense work, and to have it continued by
> the Jesuits.[9]

If the assumption among the Encyclopedists was that the entire
trial and investigation was nothing but a face-saving exercise, they
were to be sorely disappointed. The Chancellor, angry at Diderot
over a presumed insult to two aristocratic ladies at court, decided
for once to give the *Parlement* the spoils it was asking for by sacrificing the *Encyclopédie*. Rumours about this were flying thick and fast,
as d'Alembert wrote to Voltaire on 24 February: 'As for Diderot,
he is still set on continuing the *Encyclopédie*, but the Chancellor, I
am assured, has other ideas and will take away the *privilège* of the
work, thus giving Diderot some peace despite himself.[10]

On 8 March, the Royal Council condemned the *Encyclopédie*,
arguing that 'the advantages to be gained from such a work for the
arts and sciences can never compensate for the irreparable damage
inflicted on morality and religion'.[11] With this edict, any hope of
finding a diplomatic solution with the *Parlement* also vanished. This
looked terribly like the end, and a hundred, even fifty, years earlier
it would have been. For a while it looked as if Diderot might be
arrested again as the ringleader of a conspiracy seen as the most
dangerous since Damiens had raised his knife against the King.

Police agents were dispatched to Diderot's house to search for
and confiscate all papers pertaining to the *Encyclopédie*, only to find
the shelves empty and the office in a room above Diderot's flat in
the rue Taranne suspiciously orderly. The documents had vanished
and the officers could do nothing but report this to their superiors.
The papers had been stored in the safest place in the kingdom

(excepting, perhaps, the King's private bedroom): in the office of the Director of the Book Trade, Lamoignon de Malesherbes, who had been warned of the raid and had sent his own agents to salvage the tens of thousands of manuscripts and page proofs waiting to be published. Nobody would come to look in his office, the Chief Censor assured Diderot.[12]

Diderot was determined to plough on, to finish the work and discharge his obligation to the booksellers. He was a man of his word, he had glorified simple virtue in his writings, and he was not going to duck out of his commitment to courage and perseverance now, even though to have done so would have been sympathetically understood by many. To plan what was to happen next, the main parties concerned in the enterprise assembled for an extended dinner at the house of one of the booksellers, Le Breton, one evening in late March or April 1759. In a letter to Grimm, Diderot told him about the meeting in some detail:

> D'Alembert had fixed the date, but by I do not know what misunderstanding, he was not there [at the beginning of the dinner]. We finally sat down at four o'clock in the evening. We were cheerful. We drank, we laughed, we ate; and as the evening went on the real issue of the night finally asserted itself. I explained the project of completing the manuscript. I cannot tell you with what impatience my dear colleague [the late arrival, d'Alembert] listened to me. He finally set off with the puerile impetuosity you know in him, treated the booksellers like valets, the continuation of the work as madness, and while doing so threw at me all manner of upsetting things, which I took very calmly.
>
> He indulged in a good deal of violent derision, I remained conciliatory and tranquil. It is certain that the *Encyclopédie* has no more decided enemy than this man. It was no longer a question of getting him to work on as an editor again. The proposition made to him was no more than an indispensable politeness, which he had the foolishness to resist. He finally, and reluctantly, agreed to look after his section for another two years.

Your friend the Baron [Holbach], guess what kind of a face
he made during these discussions? He was in torments. Every
stupid word of d'Alembert's made me tremble that Holbach
might finally blow his top and start to shout at him. He, however, contained himself, and I was very happy indeed about
his digression. The Chevalier [de Jaucourt] did not say a word.
He kept his head lowered and he seemed stunned. D'Alembert,
having mumbled, sworn, and jumped about, finally left, and
nobody has mentioned a single word about him since.

When we were finally free of the little fool, we returned to
the topic that had brought us together. We examined all the
options; we made arrangements; we encouraged each other;
we swore to see the enterprise through; we decided to work
on the following volumes with the same liberty as on the first,
even if that would mean we would have to print in Holland;
and finally we separated.[13]

One can see, almost taste, the scene: a group of friends and associates, united against the powers that be, drinking, joking, and eating
in defiance of the threats of the next morning and the police spies
outside the doors, all interrupted by the furious d'Alembert. He
had been certain that he would be rid of the project and even
hoped to cut a nobly tragic figure, only to find that all those present
were set on continuing the work, thus adding danger to inconvenience. One can hear his shrill voice (which he was famous for)
cursing and insulting everyone within earshot, with the equally
argumentative Baron d'Holbach hardly able to contain himself and
de Jaucourt, quiet, scholarly, and no doubt shaken by recent events,
sitting by in utter disbelief.

For Le Breton and his three colleagues there was more at stake
than noble principles: not only had they invested considerable sums
in the enterprise in salaries, books bought, engravings made, in
printers and binders, in enormous amounts of expensive paper and
other items, they also held in trust the subscription money of
some four thousand subscribers. The conflicts between Jesuits and
Jansenists, between King and *Parlement,* and between various literary
factions and salons, were so much hot air to them as far as the

conduct of their business was concerned. For them, the work had been a commercial enterprise from the very beginning, and they were not going to let ideological quarrels prevent them from recouping their investment. As matters stood, they owed each subscriber 72 *livres*, a sum of 288,000 *livres* (equivalent to £2.3 million today) in all, not counting what they owed to printers and suppliers. In addition to this, and more gallingly, they had as yet hardly touched the commercial potential of a project with which they had been bound up for fourteen years, and which they had already seen through three major crises.

What followed was a quiet arrangement – an imperceptible but revolutionary turn of events that was to change the course of intellectual history. Officially, the project of the *Encyclopédie* was dead, and the booksellers were ordered, by edict of *Parlement* dated 21 July 1759, to refund to the subscribers the moneys owed in completion of their contractual obligations, and to close all accounts. The edict, however, had a rider, permitting them to supply the volumes of illustrations, which had been promised all along, instead of cash payments. For these volumes of plates, and for them only, a new *privilège* was issued on 8 September. There was another, strictly confidential and unwritten part to this arrangement, which expressed itself in a curious case of official blindness on the part of a state equipped with innumerable spies, police forces, internal security agencies, information vendors, rumour mongers, bigoted priests, literary rivals and general busybodies. For another six years, and behind 'closed and bolted doors', Diderot and de Jaucourt would prepare not only eleven volumes of plates, but also the remaining ten volumes of text, to be published at an opportune moment.

It is hard to overstate how extraordinary this toleration was. There were still some people in powerful positions who were friendly to the *Encyclopédie*. Malesherbes was the most immediate and devoted protector of the enterprise, whilst Abbé Bernis of the High Council was a powerful influence at Versailles. Mme de Pompadour, however, had become markedly more critical towards the *Encyclopédie*, which she now regarded as potentially destabilizing for the State.

There was Voltaire, who could be counted on to praise from afar, and also to do exactly as he pleased, and there was the general mantle of protection that came with the social position of Mme d'Épinay, the wife of a *fermier général*, of Baron d'Holbach, the Chevalier de Jaucourt, and various other members of the salon circuit. There was public opinion – a force to be reckoned with – and there was Grimm's considerable influence in foreign courts, which might have been more beneficial had not France been at war with the most significant of them, that of Frederick the Great.

Pitted against this extended but loose network were solid blocks of power: the King, who detested intellectuals and who was plunged into a depression after the defeat at Rossbach, thus being more than ever under the influence of his Jesuit confessor; the better part of the Versailles Court that saw itself ridiculed and its legitimacy questioned by the urban upstarts; the entire Church, and particularly the Jesuits, for reasons of pride and dogma; the theologians of the Sorbonne; the *Parlement*, which was overwhelmingly Jansenist and which also represented the French judiciary; and even the Pope himself, who had condemned the work and ordered every Catholic on pain of excommunication to ensure that any copies of the blasphemous work in their possession be burned by a priest. For different reasons, and in different ways, every branch of spiritual and temporal power, from the King right down to the magistrates, and from the Pope to the humblest curate, had good reason to hate the *Encyclopédie* and to see it stopped.

Any one of these opponents might have been enough to suppress the work and, at the very least, exile its authors for life: while the crisis of 1759 was taking its course, writers, printers, and free-thinkers (often Protestants or simply people who happened to talk too loudly in public) were imprisoned, sent to the galleys, and even hanged for much less than the sheer scale and depth of the *Encyclopédie* project. The Bastille was full of intellectuals, and cities like Amsterdam and Geneva, Berlin and London harboured enough exiles to support flourishing French-language publishing ventures turning out journals and books, often reimported into France in herring vats and bales of straw.

The single most important cause of the *Encyclopédie*'s survival, and of those working on it, contained the germ of the coming century, of the industrial revolution, and of the end of aristocratic rule. It was not a question of tolerance, nor of prestige, nor even intrigue: it was the down-to-earth, bourgeois calculation that there was simply too much money bound up in the enterprise to allow it to migrate to Holland or Prussia, which it certainly would have done had the State flexed its muscle. With thousands of livelihoods and hundreds of thousands of *livres* in the balance, economic factors carried the day and allowed work to continue under the eyes of all, but officially unseen by any of the authorities.

It was the survival of this final crisis that made the *Encyclopédie* invincible, and turned its exponents into the intellectual power of the day. Grimm had been right. All the powers in France had tried and failed to break it, and it now emerged as the most powerful of them all. It was also an indication, unseen at the time, that the age of capital was dawning, and that questions of true religion, of dogma, of respect for authority, even of royal power, could be subjugated to the higher interest of economic wellbeing if this was judged necessary.

Ann. Carac. Inv.   Benard Sculp.

Architecture, Cariatides.

HIDE, DISSEMBLE, DISGUISE

* HIDE, DISSEMBLE, DISGUISE (*Gram.*), terms pertaining to our conduct towards others when it is important to us that they are mistaken about our thinking & about our actions, which they do not know. One *hides* what one does not want to be seen; one dissimulates what is obvious; one disguises what one wants to be perceived as something else than it is
... One *hides* by silence: one *dissembles* by actions; one *disguises* by words. One is apparent in the *conduct*; the other in the *discourse*. One could say that the *dissimulation* is a lie in action.

With the *Encyclopédie* officially prohibited and declared heretical, the lives of those involved in writing it necessarily changed. They went on writing, of course, and the activity in and around Diderot's office, assiduously overlooked by the police spies, was as intense as ever.

After the dinner at which d'Alembert had given such a spectacular demonstration of his flaring temper, David l'aîné had been delegated by his fellow booksellers to arrange the details of the further work. He and Diderot agreed that there should be seven more volumes of text[1] (in fact there were to be ten), and that payment should be made on delivery of the manuscript, not on publication, as before. A publication date was, after all, not foreseeable. One name missing in these arrangements is that of the Chevalier de Jaucourt, who was in fact taking over most of the work. Neither Diderot nor the booksellers thought it necessary to include him in the payments, and Diderot had added mockingly in his letter to Grimm that 'the many copyists were groaning under the Chevalier' when Malesherbes's warning about the imminent raid was delivered.[2]

The relationship between Diderot and de Jaucourt was never close and was, it seems, overshadowed by a rather patronizing dislike on Diderot's part. Only three mentions of the Chevalier appear in Diderot's letters – all condescending in describing him as indefatigable and humourless. There is no flood of witty and warm letters by the Chevalier's own hand to defend him and bear witness to his character, so his articles have to serve as testimony. The indifference and mockery on Diderot's part, however, were almost certainly caused by a rare instance of pettiness. The provincial cutler's son who had seen no more of the world than his home town and the capital, and who had had to fight for his very existence, simply seems to have mistrusted a man from an ancient family who was widely travelled and spoke several languages, an independent scholar able to rely on his personal wealth to whom all doors and all careers were open but who yet chose to stay at home writing, dictating, compiling, and researching. Having surrounded himself with brilliant friends who shared his uncertain circumstances, such as Grimm and Rousseau, Diderot found it difficult to take the measure of a man who did not seek company, did not attend salons, who rarely let his wit sparkle around the dinner table, who came from a world of wealth and Protestant reserve, and who did not need to work.

It was the mistrust of a revolutionary for someone who had taken up the struggle not out of necessity, but out of the simple conviction that it was the right thing to do. His Huguenot background certainly gave de Jaucourt ample reason to see the France of his day through the eyes of an outsider; but he himself had never known persecution, and had always been able to do what he wanted. For all his apparent indifference to the circumstances of his birth, he was an aristocrat in the best sense of the word, and Diderot, whose every step had been haunted by his modest origins, by poverty, disapproval, and censorship, could not look at his new co-editor (though he was never graced with this title officially) without a certain measure of resentment and uncertainty.

Other Encyclopedists, notably Grimm, took Diderot's lead and looked down on de Jaucourt's 'merciless compiling'. This accusation against him, however, seems a deliberate misjudgment of the Chevalier's subjugation of his own very exacting standards to the paramount need of finishing the *Encyclopédie*. He wrote, within about ten years, 14,000 articles, 1,400 per year (fewer for some volumes, many more for others) or 120 per month, at least four articles a day, all of which had to be researched (with the aid of several secretaries paid out of his own pocket), written, and revised, on topics as different as PYGMÉES and PYRENEES, RÉDEMPTION and ESCLAVAGE (Slavery).

In the Chevalier's literary sweatshop there was simply no time for great refinement and the sophisticated *aperçus* so characteristic of his contributions to earlier volumes, written in easier times. The quality of these articles was often uneven. Some are written with great passion, immense erudition, and wicked humour, while others are plodding and obviously cobbled together, often, as Grimm remarked uncharitably, from the most mediocre sources; but the *Encyclopédie* simply had to be finished very fast or not at all, which meant a clear choice between doing the best that could be done with limited means, or seeing the entire enterprise fail.

De Jaucourt had already proven that he was a careful scholar with a penetrating mind. Had he not subjugated his own standards to the demands of finishing a work that seemed increasingly threatened from all sides, the *Encyclopédie* would not have been accomplished. De Jaucourt may not have been the most thrilling socialite, the greatest *galant* of Paris, or the most original mind; but he was exactly what the *Encyclopédie* had needed badly from the outset: a passionate man convinced of the importance of the enterprise (to which he sacrificed a good part of his fortune and many years of his life), wealthy and well-connected enough to keep trouble at bay and have the time to devote to the work, immensely diligent, and endowed with a truly encyclopedic knowledge of literature, languages, science, and history. The upright embodiment of

Weber's Protestant work ethic and the very image of the *honnête homme* who so fascinated Diderot, the discreet Chevalier soon became the project's engine, the new editor of a work that Diderot had come to regard as a burden.

In de Jaucourt's hands, the *Encyclopédie* assumed a different character. There were still the earnest definitions (many of which he wrote himself) and the enlightened diatribes (many of these by Diderot, though unsigned), as well as some decidedly cheeky contributions, such as Diderot's not very pious ILLAPS: 'a kind of contemplative ecstasy which is reached by degrees, and during which the exterior senses are numbed & the inner organs are set ablaze, are agitated, and put into a very tender & sweet state, hardly different from the state succeeding the possession of a much-loved & highly-esteemed woman'. But de Jaucourt was a man of quiet but strong conviction, and the reduction of polemical incendiary devices in the text is proportional to its increased use-fulness as a work of reference: there may be a little less wicked (though by now predictable) rhetoric, but the factual information is more reliable. Because of this loss of polemic charge, and the absence of some of the more famous authors who now preferred not to write for the *Encyclopédie*, it is often said that the last ten volumes are not as good as the first seven. But this very much depends on the perspective. To a modern eye in search of wit and provocation, there is less to be found here; but for an eighteenth-century person actually seeking an answer to a question, and to that question only, the Chevalier's scientific approach was almost certainly a relief after Diderot's unpredictable ramblings and unexpected diatribes.

It was not only the shift from Diderot to de Jaucourt that changed the nature of the *Encyclopédie*. Another formerly very active author, the Abbé Morellet, wrote later: 'As the *Encyclopédie* was suppressed . . . I no longer felt obliged to work for it, because of the disgrace this suppression brought on a man of my station who continued, in spite of the Government, to cooperate in a work forbidden for attacking authority and religion.'[3] Many others had felt the same way, and the number of collaborators had shrunk dramatically as contributors found work on the *Encyclopédie* simply too risky. They included highly productive and named collaborators such as the royal gardener Antoine-Joseph d'Argenville, the physician Arnulphe d'Aumont, the engineer Jacques-Nicolas Bellin, the architect Jacques-François Blondel, the naturalist Louis-Jean-Marie Daubenton, the watchmaker Jean-Baptiste Le Roy, the grammarian César Chesneau Dumarsais, the anatomist Pierre Tarin, the lawyer François-Vincent Toussaint, and the amateur painter and official Claude-Henri Watelet – all of these chose to leave what appeared to be a sinking ship, and it must be assumed that articles by these authors included in volumes eight to eighteen were submitted before the crisis.

Among the few contributors who continued to work were the famous lawyer Boucher d'Argis, the Baron d'Holbach, and the surgeon Antoine Louis, though it is possible that other regular contributors continued to write under the cloak of anonymity. Even among those continuing to write for the *Encyclopédie*, however, the balance had altered dramatically. While Diderot had supplied nearly two thousand articles for the first volume, the last six volumes were to have no more than sixty-six signed articles by his hand (others appeared anonymously and are impossible to attribute with certainty), with only four in volume sixteen, to which alone de Jaucourt personally contributed 2,494 articles.[4]

As a result of these resignations and of the practice of identifying contributors by a one-letter signature at the end of their articles, as well as frequent anonymous articles (even by the editor himself), it is impossible to say how many authors were still writing for the *Encyclopédie*, especially as many of the signed articles had been submitted before 1759. It appears, however, that only a handful of active collaborators remained, and that de Jaucourt shouldered the greatest workload.

Now that the only officially sanctioned part of the *Encyclopédie* was the sequence of plates illustrating the arts and crafts, it was therefore here that the anti-Encyclopedist campaign, by now well coordinated and effectively managed, decided to hit next by accusing the work of plagiarism even before the first volume of the plates appeared. The persecutor was once again Fréron's *Année Littéraire*, which in November 1759 published what it declared to be comprehensive proof that the 'marvel of the *Encyclopédie*', the plates, had all or mostly been plagiarized from an earlier work by the scholar René Antoine Ferchault de Réaumur, who had died two years earlier and who had devoted the greater part of his career to an illustrated description of trades and crafts for the Académie des Sciences. Réaumur's work was unfinished and unpublished, which made the accusation all the more dangerous as it was difficult to verify.

Fréron had procured a letter from one Pierre Patte, an architect and a disgruntled former employee of one of the booksellers, who had paid him to trace drawings and to verify details. Patte now wrote to Fréron, informing him that the booksellers and the authors had saved themselves the trouble and the cost of going around workshops all over France by procuring the engravings already finished:

> According to this plan, M. Diderot, the same M. Diderot who in his conversation and his writings runs down M. de Réaumur on every occasion, looked up M. Lucas, who has engraved the greatest part of the work of the industrious Academician, and at the price of ten *louis* and some fine promises in regard to the new enterprise of the plates for the *Encyclopédie* . . . pulled proofs of what he had done; the same thing was done in respect to some other engravers employed by M. de Réaumur, in such a way that soon all the engravings of our Academician were assembled.[5]

Scenting blood, another literary journal, the *Observateur Littéraire*, published a (fictitious?) interview with Diderot, in which he said, responding to the question of why Patte had been sacked, 'this Monsieur is too clever a man and too honest a man'. The journalist remarked that cleverness and honesty are not usually reasons for dismissal, to which Diderot supposedly replied, 'True, but we are very strange people.'[6] This cryptically nonsensical rejoinder does not have a very Diderotian ring to it, but subscribers who did not know him had to take the journalist's word for it.

Now under considerable public pressure (the plates were, after all, the one supposedly ideologically unproblematic and genuinely new element that still kept the enterprise afloat), the booksellers divulged that they did indeed have proof copies of some of Réaumur's engravings in their possession, though not in order to plagiarize them, but only for consultation. They offered to submit all the plates they possessed for inspection, and on 14 December 1759 six members of the Académie des Sciences visited Briasson's print shop in order to compare and evaluate the plans. In their research for their report to the Académie, they did indeed make an interesting discovery, though a very different one from that instigated by Fréron.

Of the thousand plates that Diderot had claimed were already finished as he was writing in volume five of the *Encyclopédie*, only 'a small number' actually existed, along with many hundreds of partly finished engravings and drawings of details, as well as entire drafts. On the question of the Réaumur plates, the committee stated that they had been shown some forty proofs, of which 'only two or three appear to us, by some points of resemblance, to have served for a model for such plates of the publishers as deal with the same subjects'.[7] While they stated that they were by no means certain that the publishers had shown them all the illustrations they had, they had received from them an assurance that they would not copy anything and would be happy to have any member of the Académie verify that nothing had been copied.

While the attacks on the *Encyclopédie* could be met with reasonable proof and continuous resistance, the constant strain was beginning to show on Diderot. In February 1758 he had already informed his father that he needed an 'iron health'[8] to withstand the stresses he was being subjected to, and since then his constitution had slowly been eroded. A stomach ailment, probably an ulcer, had plagued him since 1757, and while working on his article ENCYCLOPÉDIE he had been obliged to go on a milk diet, which was as humiliating as the symptoms of his complaint were disagreeable. After the crisis, his state had been aggravated by suspicions about those close to him. Holbach, observing his friend's poor general state, had invited him to his new country seat at Grandval, but Diderot had complained to Grimm that he did not dare accept the offer of a man 'so despotic and so changeable'.[9]

In this situation, Diderot repeatedly turned for consolation to the only two people he still fully trusted, Sophie Volland and Grimm. He wrote long letters to both of them, full of longing for a simple and harmonious life, for friendship, and for calm. Grimm being in Geneva on business, Diderot wrote to both him and Sophie frequently, in great detail and with great intimacy. In these letters (the greatest part by far of Diderot's surviving letters from 1759 and later), Diderot talks more directly and with less artifice than anywhere else.

The letters to Sophie Volland are long and tender elegies, brightened at times by comical, often burlesque stories of the goings-on at Grandval, Holbach's estate, where Diderot had finally agreed to spend some time away from Paris and its concerns, and safe from Toinette's temper. Fleeing from his wife, and only rarely able to be with his mistress and truly intimate friend, Diderot's emotions soared in his letters on wings of unfulfilled desire – describing curious figures in the air.

There is a constant ambiguity in these letters, in which he speaks of 'my Sophie' as being 'man and woman, as it pleases her', only to continue to her in the very next sentence, 'Oh, how much I miss him, my friend Grimm, because he indulges my flights of fancy . . . how I miss our sweet meals together, during which our souls opened and we described and praised our absent friends! What warmth of expression, of sentiments and of ideas! What enthusiasm! How happy we were to talk about them! How happy they would have been to hear us speak! Oh my Grimm!'[10]

To Diderot's enthusiastic soul, it often seemed as if Grimm and Sophie merged into one single, adored person, desired and respected, the very image of the perfect lover, venerated with the eroticism of all-embracing affection, all the burning purity of generous love. 'I love Grimm,' he wrote to Sophie on 24 September 1759. 'In other circumstances my heart would be bound up in the sole thought of going to find him and embrace him; with what impatience would I not wait for this dear man! Now I hardly think of it. It is you, it is you alone who occupies my thoughts. You obliterate everything in my heart and in my mind.'[11]

Diderot's relationship with Sophie was all the more complex because, to her considerable jealousy, he also paid his compliments to her sister, Mme Legendre, in what seems to have become a constantly shifting *ménage à trois*, platonic or otherwise, with Diderot simply unable to restrain his incorrigibly social temperament and Sophie, too, showing more than the usual affection for her sister. 'Tell her,' he wrote to his lover, 'that I am not just anyone; that nothing will change my feelings for you ... tell her that I am assured the greatest consideration in posterity ... tell her that I have reached the age at which one's character no longer changes ... tell her how much I would be flattered, how happy you would be to hold, to smell, to look at her and me, me and her.'[12]

Despite these assurances of warm feelings beyond the conventional, Sophie was always at the heart of Diderot's emotional life, of hundreds of letters, and of his waking dreams: 'Come, my Sophie, come. I feel my heart grow warmer. The tenderness that is your embellishment will appear on this face. It is there. Ah! That you are not by my side to taste its joys! You would be so happy if you could see me now! How these eyes are moist, these looks, my entire expression is at your command.'[13]

To the ardent lover's exasperation, his beloved's mother disapproved of the fact that a married man of a certain notoriety and without any fortune had taken to courting her daughter. He, in return, had few kind words for her: 'Your mother's soul is sealed with the seven seals of the Apocalypse. On her forehead is inscribed *Mystery*. I once saw two sphinxes at Marly, and they reminded me of her.'[14]

Amid these delicious imaginings and epistolary games came the news Diderot had feared for some time, as he reported in an uncharacteristically short and direct letter to Grimm:

9 June, Paris 1759

The last blow I could receive has fallen; my father is dead. I do not know when or how. I had promised myself to let myself be called to his bedside for his last moments. I am certain that he thought of it, but that there was no time. I have seen neither my father nor my mother die. I do not hide from you that I see this as a curse from heaven.

Adieu, my friend . . . You will give him your tears, will you not? Shed some for your unhappy friend as well.

Adieu, dear Grimm; you know me; judge my state. The other blows do not prepare for this one.

Adieu. Adieu.[15]

Diderot the son, whose career had never been without aspects of filial rebellion, had lost the one person who was unwaveringly and toweringly present throughout his life, whom he had adored, disobeyed, avoided, longed to be reconciled with, tried to make proud, and doted on. The effects of this age-old transition towards the front line of Camus's 'ultimate solidarity' – death – were immediate:

At the age of twenty, drunken on my reputation, growing in force day by day, and believing that I had in me the germ of an eternal existence, I would have flown towards all this work and would not have known rest nor sleep until they were finished. Today, as the eagles of youth are carrying me no longer through the air, I am on the surface of the earth, I weigh heavily, I am growing numb, I feel it, and every time I want to fling myself at the task at hand, I ask myself *quid tibi prodest aerias tentasse domos, animoque rotundum percurrisse polum morituro?* [What good is it to have attained celestial heights and to have run the length of the firmament with a mortal soul? (Horace, *Odes*, I, xxviii, 4–6)] I understand my feelings of inertia and of inadequacy, which are growing, to be contempt and disdain for philosophy, and your enchanting words can fool me only for an instance.[16]

At forty-six, Diderot, having just lost his father, was for the first time in his life feeling gravity pulling him down, and mortality encroaching on his unquenchable enthusiasms.

While Diderot the son was grieving, Diderot the Encyclopedist was ailing. He continued 'encyclopedizing like a galley slave'[17] only because he had a contractual obligation towards the booksellers' subscribers, and a moral one to his family and supporters. The playwright Diderot, however, was suddenly thriving, with successful performances of his plays not only in France, but also in Germany. He was also working on a new play, the *Commissaire de Kent* (of which he would eventually despair).

Despite the laudatory mentions of performances of *Le Père de famille* in Grimm's journal, however, Diderot had little opportunity to enjoy his success. Instead, he had to go to Langres to arrange the details of his inheritance with his beloved sister and his brother Didier, a conservative priest who detested Denis and everything he stood for. Their father had worked hard and accumulated considerable wealth. When everything was divided up, it was agreed that the two other siblings should keep the paternal house and furnishings and that the remaining assets were to be divided between the three. As a result, Diderot found himself in possession of property and rents that meant, for the first time in his life, he was now in a position of some financial comfort.

As ever, trying to escape the yoke of the *Encyclopédie*, Diderot now took to writing essays on the annual art exhibition at the Louvre for Grimm's *Correspondance littéraire*, and retreated once more to Holbach's house at Grandval, leaving the Chevalier de Jaucourt to continue the encyclopedia work on his own. He did this with a great sense of relief and very little bad conscience, writing to Sophie in November 1760: 'My colleagues have done hardly anything at all. I have no idea when I will get out of this galley. If I believe the Chevalier de Jaucourt, he intends to keep me on it for another year. That man has been surrounded by four or five secretaries for six or seven years, reading, dictating, working thirteen to fourteen hours a day, and this situation has not yet begun to bore him.'[18] He neglected to add that, while the Chevalier had very little time

to be bored, both the *Encyclopédie* and Diderot's own activities were
by now dependent on him to a large extent.

At Grandval, Diderot recovered some of the levity and peace he
had been missing since the beginning of the encyclopedia's crisis
three years earlier. Here he was surrounded by like-minded people,
could talk freely, play cards and go for long walks, have long dinners
with friends, and write quietly and to his heart's content. The one
painful absence during these happy visits was Sophie, to whom he
wrote long, longing letters. The contentment of these tranquil days
is almost palpable:

> I have been given a small apartment separated from the others
> and very quiet, very friendly, and very warm. Here, between
> Horace, Homer, and the portrait of my friend [Sophie], I
> spend hours reading, meditating, writing, and sighing. It is my
> occupation from six o'clock in the morning onwards until one
> o'clock. At one thirty I am dressed and go down to the salon,
> where I usually find all the guests assembled. Sometimes the
> Baron comes to visit me, very tactfully. If he sees me occupied,
> he waves at me and leaves. If he finds me idle, he sits down
> and we talk. The mistress of the house has no ceremonial
> obligations, and neither does anybody else. One is in her
> house, and in one's own.[19]

On his return to Grandval in October, he told Sophie about an
exchange he had had with d'Alembert at a salon. The conversation,
which Diderot assured Sophie was recorded 'almost word by word',
had surprised him. D'Alembert had remarked that, as a result of
Diderot's visits to Langres and Grandval, work on the encyclopedia
must have slowed down considerably. Not wanting to be goaded,
or to nourish any notion d'Alembert might have that the work could
not be finished without the eminent scientist's active involvement,
Diderot assured him that he had been making up for lost time:

> *You have advanced much then?* – Much. My articles on philosophy
> are all done; and they are neither the least difficult nor the
> shortest. Most of the others are already drafted. – *I see that it*

is time to go to work myself! – Whenever you want. *– Whenever the booksellers want. I have been to see them. I have made reasonable propositions. If they accept, I will work on the Encyclopédie as before. If not, I will cut all links for good. That would not be good for the work; but they can't ask me for more. –* Whatever you choose to do is fine by me.

At this point d'Alembert had finally admitted that things had become more difficult for him as the King of Prussia was no longer paying his pension. D'Alembert needed money, and his outburst at the editors' dinner was seemingly forgotten. Not by Diderot, however. Asked what he thought of the terms d'Alembert had proposed to the booksellers, Diderot reported himself as answering: 'I think that if you had made this proposal six months ago instead of foaming at the mouth with rage, they would have accepted immediately. Now that they have good reason to be disgusted at your behaviour, things are different.'

When he was unwise enough to ask Diderot to explain, d'Alembert had heard all the things his former colleague must have been mulling over in his mind for many months. He had a contract with the booksellers, Diderot had reminded him, and he had no right to ask for other conditions now. If he had ever done more than required, it was not their task to repay him for things done out of friendship to his collaborators or out of self-esteem. Be this as it may, d'Alembert had happily accepted *ex gratia* payments even while not doing any work, and had seen fit to travel to see the King of Prussia during the first great crisis of the *Encyclopédie*, when he had been needed in Paris. He had been disdainful of the economic imperatives underlying the work, had vaingloriously endangered the entire enterprise (with his Geneva article), and had then retreated in a sulk, leaving everyone else to pick up the pieces. It was a shameful business, Diderot had told him. Now it was d'Alembert's turn to be angry. Had Diderot really thought his proposal was serious? Diderot had replied that, serious or not, the booksellers would be none too keen to deal with d'Alembert again, and so the two men had parted.

Pl. I.

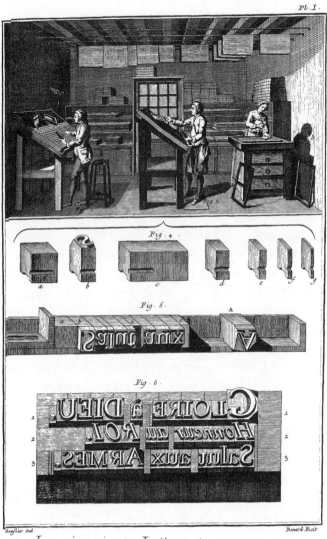

Imprimerie en Lettres, L'Operation de la Casse.

MÉTIER

MÉTIER, s. m. (*Gram.*) this is the name one gives to those occupations which require the use of the hands & which are limited to a certain number of mechanical operations, all of which have the same goal, & which the worker repeats continuously. I do not know why this word is thought of in such bad terms; we owe to the *métiers* all objects necessary in life. Those who take the trouble to go into the workshops will find usefulness & good sense everywhere. In antiquity, those who invented *métiers* were deified; but later centuries have thrown into the mud those who perfected these pursuits. I leave it to those with a sense of justice to determine whether it is reason or prejudice that makes us think so little of people who are so essential. The poet, the philosopher, the orator, the minister, the soldier, the hero – they all would be naked & without bread without the artisan whom they all despise.

During his frequent stays at Grandval, Diderot amused himself by reading and writing articles about philosophers such as Hobbes, Locke, and Machiavelli (listed not under their names but as systems of thought), and on non-Christian or non-Occidental philosophical traditions, especially those of Judaism, Islam, Confucianism, and Buddhism. The resulting articles, such as JAPON, PHILOSOPHIE DE; JUIF; PERSE (Persia, unsigned); and SARACENES (unsigned), often show a remarkable insight into the culture concerned, at least judged by the works available to Diderot. The culture best known to Christian Europe was, of course, Judaism, and it is an irony of history, as well as a considerable misjudgement, that

Diderot and other Encyclopedists (none of whom was as well informed about this tradition as the Abbé Mallet had been) have been called anti-Semites because of their articles in the *Encyclopédie.*

Judaism was well studied, and the articles by Abbé Mallet show a thorough familiarity not only with biblical but also with rabbinical writings, which are often given as direct sources. Articles by him are generally accurate and to the point; Diderot, on the other hand, clearly knew no Hebrew and had significantly less understanding of Jewish traditions, taking his information exclusively from secondary works such as the *Historia critica philosophiae* by the German Johann Jacob Bruckner,[1] which he used as reference for many of his philosophical articles, and particularly Jacques Basnage's *Histoire des Juifs.*[2] The one authority he did not consult, and which was directly under his nose, was represented by the rabbinical scholars of Paris.

What Diderot had to say about Jews was often unflattering, but quite consistent with the thinking of the Enlightenment. In so far as the Jews adhered to an ancient religion that was in so many ways contrary to eighteenth-century conceptions of rational behaviour, he could write about their 'fanaticism' as damningly as he did about Muslims or Hindus, and as he could not write about Catholicism: 'Everybody knows that the *Jews* never passed for a wise people. It is certain that they have no contact with the exact sciences and that they are grossly mistaken in all counts relying on such knowledge,' he wrote in JUIF.

As a community living outside the realm of secular education (the first 'secular' Jewish philosopher, Moses Mendelssohn, was only just beginning to attract attention in the 1760s, and was writing in German) and largely governed by the precepts of a revealed religion very close to Christianity, the Jews offered an ideal opportunity for implicit criticism of the origins and beliefs of the Church. 'Diderot and his colleagues,' writes Arthur Wilson, 'because of this dialectical necessity, were unfair to the Jews, unfair in the first place because they were insufficiently informed.'[3] In this spirit, Diderot was only too happy to write:

It will not be useless to warn the reader that one ought not to
expect to find among the Jews either accuracy in their ideas,
or exactitude in their reasoning, or precision in their style –
in a word, nothing that ought to characterize a sound doctrine
of philosophy. On the contrary, there is to be found among
them only a confused mixture of the principles of reason and
of revelation, an affected and often impenetrable obscurity,
principles that lead to fanaticism, a blind respect for the authority of the doctors and of antiquity – in a word, all the defects
indicative of an ignorant and superstitious nation.[4]

These were high words from a man unfamiliar with the Jewish
tradition, but one cannot help but suspect that Diderot was really
writing about something altogether closer to home: but for the
one mention of 'Jews', it seems to be a perfect description of the
Diderotian conception of Catholic tradition and philosophy, with
its mixture of reason and revelation and its 'blind respect' for the
doctors of antiquity. Displacement of criticism was, after all, an
established principle for the *Encyclopédie*. By ostensibly attacking
the Jews and their 'fanatical' beliefs, Diderot was in fact writing
against the priests and Catholic theology.

The civil situation of Jews in Europe, on the other hand, was a
matter of great concern for the Encyclopedists. De Jaucourt reflected that, 'if one thinks of the horrors the Jews have tasted from
the time of J.C. . . . & which were repeated so often by Christian
states, one is astonished that they still exist'. Despite their sensible
rules about marriage, divorce, and their 'sober and abstinent life,
their work and their daily routine' – all laudable practices that
Christian countries should, by implication, learn to emulate – Jews
had been consistently persecuted and bled for money by every
Christian monarch who found himself out of pocket:

In France, it was not forgotten to treat the Jews the same way;
they were thrown into prison, were pilloried, sold, accused of
magic, of sacrificing their children, of poisoning wells; they
were chased out of the kingdom and then allowed back for
money, & even in times during which they were tolerated,

they were distinguished from other inhabitants by shameful markings.

Diderot himself expressed positive sentiments when he claimed Moses for the cause of the *philosophes* ('What a historian! What a legislator! What a philosopher! What a poet! What a man!') in his long and serious, though at times confused, article on Jewish philosophy, which attempted to sum up Jewish thought from biblical times over the Talmudic period and through the Middle Ages up to the eighteenth century.

As for the Jews of his own time and their social condition, it can safely be said that Diderot had little interest in them one way or the other. In contrast to de Jaucourt, himself a member of a religious minority and a tireless defender of the oppressed, he had little to say about Jews. In his letters there is no more than a single contemporary reference to them, the surprised mention that the Jews he had seen in Russia 'were not as sullen [*maussades*] as they had been described' – an admission of his total ignorance on the matter. There were no Jews in Langres during his childhood, and his time in Paris had not brought him into contact with any. It was only later, during his trip to Russia, that he was to meet the Jewish community leader Isaac de Pinto in Amsterdam and to have the opportunity of being introduced into the Jewish world by him. The fact, however, that Diderot did not himself make the *Encyclopédie* into a vehicle for passionate philo-Semitic polemics is not indicative of hatred towards Jews; indeed, articles on topics used elsewhere as opportunities for anti-Jewish agitation expressed a largely positive attitude towards them. Joachim Faiguet de Villeneuve's USURE, for example, illustrates that in their own social context before the Exile, the Jews had no need of usury, that their society was much less corrupt than eighteenth-century France, and that it was Christian oppression that forced the Jews to become moneylenders. As the main editor, Diderot often tolerated views differing from his own or from one another, but not a single article in the work argued for discrimination against Jews, while several authors, from Faiguet to de Jaucourt, argued strongly for a compassionate, historical understanding of their situation and, by implication, for their legal integration into society.

With Diderot writing fewer and fewer articles, his work on the plates continued apace, and the first volume of illustrations appeared in early 1762. In accordance with the arrangement reached with the Chief Censor after the crisis of 1757, the title made no reference to the forbidden *Encyclopédie*, although the appearance, binding, and layout were identical.

The world described in these plates has a very particular beauty. The graceful idealization of airy and well-lit workshops, with healthy and able-bodied people cheerfully going about their tasks, gave an image that was often far removed from the dirty, cramped, and sometimes dangerous conditions encountered in real life.

It was not, however, very far removed from Réaumur's illustrations for the Académie des Sciences – not half as far, in fact, as the first commission had concluded. The *Encyclopédie* had indulged in wholesale theft, not only of the general layout, but also in the depiction of many of the individual processes, implements, and machines. The illustrations, after all, had been lying unused for more than half a century (shocked into action, the Academicians were to publish them from 1761 onwards), and it appears that the plates had to be published in a hurry to keep the *Encyclopédie* afloat and the subscribers satisfied. In the event, Diderot's assertion that he had personally visited hundreds, if not thousands, of workshops to interview tradesmen seems to have referred to nothing more than an ambition, despite the fact that Goussier made several extended to visits to Burgundy, the Champagne, and the Loire region, where he researched, among others, paper mills, an organ builder, and an iron smelter.

It was immediately realized that all was not well. In the Academy itself, these findings were the subject of virulent debate. 'Imagine,' wrote an exasperated Diderot to Sophie at the end of February 1760, 'the day before yesterday . . . Lebreton abducted me to work at his workshop from eleven in the morning until eleven at night.

It is still that damned business of the plates. The commissaires of the Academy have reverted to their initial judgment [that the plates had been plagiarized]. They tore one another's eyes out at the Academy. Yesterday they were at one another's throats like fishwives.'[5]

Surprisingly, this tumultuous debate and the emergency shift put in by Diderot and Le Breton are the last one hears of the accusation of plagiarism. Why had the commission chosen to accept Diderot's version of events at all, and why did they drop it again? Embarrassment may have been one reason. The Académie des Sciences had been commissioned to publish a comprehensive description of the *arts et métiers* by Louis XIV's minister Colbert in 1675, and so far not a single illustration had appeared. Making too much noise about the Encyclopedists was bound to attract attention to the Academy's flexible conception of time. On the other hand, the *Encyclopédie*'s illustrations promised to break a deadlock that had partly been the reason for the long delay: it had seemed desirable to systematize knowledge, but making this knowledge public risked giving away valuable economic secrets to rival nations. Publishing the entire work in a handful of copies destined only for the royal libraries was not viable, and so the enterprise had simply stalled. If, however, the trade secrets of France were made public by someone else, nobody would be able to blame the Académie later.

Diderot may not actually have visited all the workshops, but his task as editor was still immense. Even if many of the Academy's plates could be used as templates, techniques had advanced over seventy-five years, and everything had to be checked and updated. Moreover, only a small number of crafts were already fully illustrated, while for others there were only preparatory drawings, and some had been neglected altogether. In these cases, Diderot commissioned craftsmen to submit their own descriptions and illustrations, only to be inundated by an enormous amount of material:

> I remember one artist, who, after I had told him exactly what
> I needed to know about his métier (or so I thought), brought
> me, instead of the requested single sheet of writing and half

page of illustration about the technique of wallpaper hanging, ten or twelve enormously crowded plates and three thick folio booklets, enough to fill one or two volumes.

Another one, whom I had given the same exact parameters as the first, brought me a little catalogue of words without definition, without explication, without illustrations, and assured me that there was nothing more to his art, despite his craft being one of the most complex concerning the machines used, the different steps applied, and the objects made. He thought that the rest could not be described at all.[6]

Bringing order into this chaos was Diderot's real role; and while his countless visits to workshops are certainly fictional, he was nevertheless obliged to have some processes and machines explained to him directly where the explanations supplied were incomprehensible or ambiguous.

The plates of the Académie des Sciences only covered some crafts, and other sources were used for different topics such as mathematics, the military, anatomy, botany and zoology, draughtsmanship, or architecture. Many of them were the most authoritative works available at the time, such as Versalius, Albini, and James (whom Diderot had translated at the beginning of his career) on anatomy, Buffon on zoology, the fashionable London master Angelo on fencing, works by Annibale Carracci on drawing and architectural decoration, and Guérninière's famous equestrian illustrations for horsemanship.[7] They all formed the great quarry from which illustrations were redrafted and re-engraved, making the eleven volumes containing some 2,500 plates not so much an original work as a great survey of what was already in existence. At the time, this did not detract from its value, as it was the fact that these different subjects were brought together that made it an important and distinctive survey. Never before had it been possible to consult so many areas of human endeavour and nature outside a major library. Now, every subscriber (and every subscriber to later editions and pirated printings) found them all assembled in a relatively manageable form.

Today, these illustrations, astonishing in their variety and accuracy, are also the most poignant reminder of a world caught and recorded just before everything was turned upside-down. The world of craftsmanship and manufacture in these plates would be swept away within a single lifetime, and when Diderot's daughter Marie-Angélique wrote her memoirs of him (she died in 1824), most of these occupations were already remnants of another age, and rows of machines in large factories had taken the place of men and women in workshops. Many tradesmen had been ruined by this mechanized competition, and the poor had been transformed into the proletariat. The Revolution had been and gone, and another, far greater one was growing its first saplings in the minds of intellectuals and of the workers in the twilight world of the factories.

In the plates of the *Encyclopédie*, none of this, though it was so near in time, seems even a distant possibility. It is a universe ordered according to enlightened hope, to a trust in reason, to virtue, and to ingenuity. Its taboos and preoccupations are remarkably different from those of the succeeding century. Women are not consigned to the home, but are shown at work in professions they commonly exercised. What differentiation between the sexes was made in the work is shown clearly in the plate ART D'ÉCRIRE (Art of Writing).

The proper posture for writing is illustrated using a man and a woman as examples. The man is sitting asymmetrically, lightly supporting himself with his left arm, the left foot placed further forward under the table for proper balance in what is a comfortable writing position for someone expecting to write regularly and at length. The female example, however, is all symmetry and elegance, her pose perfectly centred, the head held high and well coiffed, the feet modestly kept back and just visible under the voluminous skirts, both hands in the same position; a posture that might lend itself to writing a quick note to a lover or perhaps a letter to *maman*, but certainly not a substantial treatise on geometry.

Despite these subtle but important differences between the graphic representation of the sexes, this is not a prudish world. Already the text shows a robust, eighteenth-century approach to human sexuality, much more so than many later encyclopaedias.

PL. II

Art d'Ecrire .

Benard Fecit .

Under CLITORIS, for instance, readers could not only find an anatomical description but also learn that 'this is an extremely sensitive part & the principal seat of the woman's pleasure, one reason why some people also call it *aestrum Veneris,* the sting of Venus'. GÉNÉRATION speaks generously of human desires and the 'fever' accompanying the act itself, while JOUISSANCE (Orgasm) throws all scientific caution to the wind by asking 'Is there an object more worthy of our pursuit, one whose possession & *jouissance* can make as happy, as those of a being thinking & feeling like you,

Art d'Ecrire.

imbued with the same ideas, feeling the same heat, the same trans-
ports, and who bears his tender & delicate arms towards you, who
envelops you & whose caresses are followed by the existence of a
new being?' PUBERTÉ, in its turn, is described long and lovingly
and introduced as 'the age in which nature renews itself & during
which it opens the source of sentiment, the time of pleasures, of
graces & of loves', before delineating the physical changes occur-
ring in boys and girls.

   Like the text, the anatomical plates leave nothing to the imagina-

tion and pay particular attention to the reproductive organs, while
the anatomical peculiarities of hermaphrodites are given the most
loving and lavish treatment. Freakish exceptions, however, were
not usually emphasized, contrary to the taste manifest in contemporary cabinets of natural curiosities, which positively revelled
in monstrous foetuses, Siamese twins, and calves with two heads.
The hermaphrodites are curious and lonely outcasts in the otherwise orderly universe of the *Encyclopédie*'s plates. Displaying and
describing human bodies was important not only with a view to
explaining the workings of a secular world; it would also have been
of central concern to de Jaucourt, who had begun working on the
Encyclopédie after his own medical dictionary had been lost in a
shipwreck, and who saw his work as a continuation of this earlier
enterprise. There were, however, political implications, too: everyone had a body, after all, from the King himself to the starving
rural poor.

The plates were inhabited by ordinary people. Of the thousands
of faces populating these sheets, not a single one is recognizable
as a portrait of a nobleman, of a great general, or even of a man
of genius. This is collective humanity at work, even if it did consist
of anonymous, neat, and able-bodied men and women in the flower
of their years. Their very anonymity made them universal, their
presence demonstrated that their value lay in their productivity, in
their skill, and their hard work. The printer's block displayed in
one of the illustrations of the printing trade might declare 'Glory
to God, Honour to the King, Salute to Arms', but the worlds of
faith and of the aristocracy were rendered irrelevant by their
absence from what was represented, and by the very preponderance
of everyday folk.

While a grand total of twenty-seven heraldic plates gave insight
into the coats of arms and family trees of the great and the good,
there were forty-two on watchmaking, forty-six on the production
of mirrors, fifty-one on carpentry, and eighty-one on forging metals.
For every coat of arms of a ruling house, there was a kind of nail,
or a horse shoe, and more than likely several carpenter's joints to
redress the balance. The utilitarian principles of the editors were

applied to the natural world as well as to society: under the heading MINÉRALOGIE one finds thirty-three pages of illustrations of different minerals, followed by eighty-four illustrations on mining tools, techniques, and machinery.

Ideological points could be made silently, but the silence and serenity reigning in the plates were themselves part of the Encyclopedic fiction, a blueprint for a better world, and their relationship with reality was tenuous at times. Not only is the printer's composition room clean and quiet, with three contented and well-dressed workers in a spacious room taking lead letters from the large trays in front of them and fixing them in their place, the press room itself is equally a model of Cartesian organization. To the left, a printer is blackening the type while his young apprentice carefully puts in place a new sheet of paper. To the right, a 'bear', as the press operators were called on account of their physical strength, shuts a press, stepping on a wedge to give him extra grip. A journeyman in the back of the room is preparing the ink. Apart from the two imposing presses and one table, there are only a few reams of paper on the shelves; otherwise the room is as clean and untouched as it had been the moment it was built.

The printers themselves must have found this image of their trade vaguely comical. The press room was notorious for its noise, stench, and dirt. Black ink and its constituent parts, soot and linseed oil, clung to hands, hair, and clothes; the pervading odour of oil and of the urine used to wash the leather blackening pads in the evening mingled with the smell of the sweat of journeymen operating the heavy presses, whose deafening clanging, rasping, and groaning was the cause of constant complaints to the authorities, and whose crushing weight often caused terrible injuries to the operators. In addition to this, space was scarce in the crowded Faubourg Saint Antoine where most printers (the legitimate ones, at least) were plying their trade, so the presses and the people working them were crammed together in conditions so infernal that printing journeymen regarded themselves as a hardened, secret brotherhood, a society with its own rules and laws. None of this is conveyed in the decorous plates of the *Encyclopédie*, whose editors were intimately aware of all these facts, having worked with their printers for some two decades.

This was not an oversight. It would not have been sensible to portray the printers as a band of sweaty rabble-rousers, and the printers themselves would certainly have objected. More importantly, however, it was the declared aspiration of the Encyclopedists to put an end to the trades being universally despised and to install them in their rightful place as immensely ingenious and industrious practitioners of 'applied science'. A chaotic and dirty print shop did not fit this image. Skilled physical activity as displayed in the *Encyclopédie* was always beautiful, organized, clean, and as admirable as any human endeavour could be.

Accuracy was a point of pride in all the illustrations and can hardly ever be faulted; indeed, some of them are so precise in their descriptions that they have been used to reconstruct entire manufacturing processes. When, in 1796, the newly opened and European-style College of Military Engineering in Constantinople accepted the necessity for reform in order to construct better artillery, they found everything they needed to know about cannon manufacture in a copy of the *Encyclopédie* that had made its way to the Ottoman capital.[8]

Despite their general reform-mindedness, the Encyclopedists did not pay a great deal of attention to new and emerging technologies. INOCULATION defends a new and promising method of combating infectious illnesses and the articles on clockmaking are at the cutting edge of their craft, but in other areas of knowledge there is no such forward thinking. In writing his large articles PAPETERIE and FORGES, Goussier was obviously unaware of innovations such as the Hollander pulping mill (already in use in Belgium) and especially of coke-smelted iron, which had been pioneered in England and was to revolutionize iron and steel production. Nowhere, however, is the historical limitation (today part of the *Encyclopédie*'s value and charm) more obvious than in this short article:

> * **FIRE** (*pump*) *Hydraul. & Mechanical Arts*: The first of these was constructed in England; several engineers have been

occupied in its perfection & simplification by degrees. One may regard Papin as its inventor: for what does one do if one constructs a *fire pump*? One adapts the body of an ordinary pump to the machine by Papin. *See his work*, the *article* **DIGESTEUR** & especially the *preceding article*.

What follows is the long and detailed description of a steam pump used in Austria to pump water. The 'fire pump' described in the short initial paragraph, however, was much more than a playful connection between Papin's primitive steam-driven piston and a water pump: it was to become the unquestioned economic ruler of the nineteenth and early twentieth centuries; the engine of the revolution that turned manufacture into large-scale industry, towns into sprawling metropolitan landscapes, and the rural poor into the urban proletariat; that drove railways across Europe and the world, and after which nothing was as it had been before: it was, of course, the steam engine.

Pl XXX.

Martinet Del.   *Benard Fecit*

Histoire Naturelle.

Fig. 1. L'AUTRUCHE. Fig. 2. LE CASOAR. Fig. 3. LE PELICAN. Fig. 4. LE FLAMANT.

PHOENIX

PHOENIX, s. m. (*Hist. nat. fabul.*) a miraculous bird that, according to popular thought, lives several centuries & when dying produces out of the marrow of its bones a small larva which will form a new *phoenix*.

The Egyptians ... have a bird they believe holy, but I have only ever seen pictures of it. It is not seen frequently in Egypt either, as it, if you believe the people of Heliopolis, appears only five times in five centuries, and only if its father is dead. They say it is as big as an eagle, has a beautiful crest on its head, the feathers around its head are golden, the others purple, a tail of white and beige feathers, and eyes as brilliant as the stars.

Despite official opposition, the encyclopedia enterprise continued. It even flourished in its quasi-secrecy. The young men with grand ideas who had set out on the project more than a decade earlier had matured and weathered many storms. They had gained important allies, from Voltaire to the King of Prussia, and Grimm's *Correspondance littéraire* had made them famous at courts throughout Europe. In Paris, their meetings at Holbach's salon and elsewhere had become recognized as the apex of the capital's intellectual life.

Against the odds, the Encyclopedists had become fashionable, even powerful; they constituted the intellectual avant-garde of their day, their well-deserved reputation gilded further by the brilliant aura of martyrdom. Far from being neutralized by the Paris *Parlement*, the *Encyclopédie* had become fashionable. It was quite chic to be called an Encyclopedist, and the hostesses of the capital's grand salons fought to have them attend their *soirées*. Foreign monarchs wanted Encyclopedists at their courts, fashionable young men from England and Germany sought introduction to their salons and their houses (visits detested by the otherwise gregarious Diderot); in short, the Encyclopedists became all the rage, especially since they were still heartily disapproved of by Jesuits and Jansenists alike – forces that were widely seen as having outlived their political usefulness. For while it had almost been the undoing of the entire *Encyclopédie* to be detested by these two powerful ecclesiastical factions, the very fact of being opposed to them eventually made the Encyclopedists the only faction standing for progress and openness, for a spirit of inquiry and criticism. For those looking for an ideological affiliation outside the Church, the Encyclopedists became an obvious choice.

Despite their new public standing, however, the problems of the *Encyclopédie* were far from over, and the task of keeping the project on track still depended almost entirely on de Jaucourt and Diderot. For Diderot, there had never been such a clash between personal and public needs. Having finished the first volume of plates (ten more were to appear, in addition to the volumes of letterpress), his instinct was to get the work done before retreating from grand public involvement and from politics, to take stock, and to enjoy what personal happiness he could find with his daughter, with Sophie, and among his friends.

At Grandval, he read English novels in the original, and also the anonymous Celtic 'Ossian' poems, which enchanted him and which he, along with most contemporaries, assumed to be authentic historical texts (they were later discovered to be forgeries). His own literary projects occupied him, too, though in secrecy. Having had more than his fair share of confrontations with censorship and persecution, he had resolved to write the things closest to his heart with complete honesty – and never publish them.

In 1760, he had already finished the manuscript of a novel, *La Religieuse* (The Nun), describing the fate of a young woman forced to take religious vows and attempting to flee the convent in which she has found unhappiness and depravity. This 'depravity' was dramatized in the form of mildly lesbian scenes, which have given the book an unexpected and posthumous popularity as a classic of erotic writing. For Diderot, though, whose own sister was a nun and who had at one point been imprisoned in a monastery for a month or so, the predicament of the young nun was far beyond titillation, and the erotic scenes between the nuns served to illustrate the unnatural condition of celibacy.

He had also begun work, in secret, on what was to become one of his literary masterworks: *Le Neveu de Rameau* (Rameau's Nephew). This relation of the famous composer Rameau did exist: a mediocre musician living mainly on his uncle's reputation. In the novel, which is really one long dialogue, Diderot, or *MOI* (I), meets the nephew, or *LUI* (HE), in the garden of the Palais-Royal and interrogates him about his life. The nephew cheerfully tells all about his life as a parasite in Paris, living off the rich, the stupid, and the credulous, feigning high principles wherever necessary, but despising everybody and everything. Unsurprisingly, the description of the grand houses frequented by the nephew gives the author ample opportunity to describe a whole rogues' gallery, including all those (named) adversaries who had made his own life miserable.

In these works written for the drawer, Diderot found his literary voice, even if the public had to wait until well into the nineteenth century to discover this for themselves – another reason for Diderot's curiously meagre literary reputation. *Le Neveu de Rameau* is symptomatic: it appeared first in German, in 1805, translated from a handwritten copy by Goethe, who greatly admired Diderot. The first French edition, badly mutilated, appeared in 1823, and the first edition from the original manuscript not until 1891. Thus Diderot's contemporaries never read its elegant and immediately engaging opening passage: 'Come sun or rain, it is my habit to go for a walk at the Palais-Royal around five o'clock in the evening. It is I who you always see dreaming on d'Argenson's bench. I talk with myself about politics, about love, about beauty, and philosophy. I abandon my mind to its libertine self. I leave it to its own devices, following the first wise or silly idea that presents itself.'[1]

Rameau's nephew himself is an indictment of all that is wrong

in Paris society, which can always be relied upon to work on baseness
and greed:

> I can reach happiness through the vices natural to me, which
> I have acquired without work and conserve without effort,
> which square with the morals of my nation, and follow the
> taste of my protectors because they mirror their little needs.
> Virtue would disturb this and accuse them from morning to
> evening, and I would be a curious case if I allowed myself to
> be tormented like a damned soul just in order to make myself
> into something I am not; to give myself a character that is not
> mine, and qualities which may be very laudable, this I don't
> dispute, but which would cost me a good deal to acquire, to
> practise, and which would bring me nothing, and perhaps
> worse than nothing: the ridicule of the rich among whom
> paupers like me make their livelihood. People praise virtue,
> but hate it, flee it, because it is icy cold, and in this world one
> has to keep one's feet warm.[2]

Clearly, Diderot saw himself as just such a curious case, aspiring to
something that was hard to attain, valued only in theory, and liable
to leave its few devotees out in the cold.

Unable to publish, and seeking to escape both his wife and the
'galley' of his work on the encyclopedia (which still cost him most
of his time), Diderot was only too happy to spend time at Grandval,
at La Chevrette, and wherever else he could find peace and congenial company. He adored losing himself in trivial entertainments,
and his letters to Sophie brim with descriptions of domesticity,
silliness, and inconsequential conversations. In 1759 he had written
to her about a boisterous evening's entertainment at Holbach's
country seat, during which the formidable Mme d'Aine, the mother
of the Baron's second wife and a generously proportioned lady of
a certain age, surprised the local curate by jumping astride his lap,
so that the little man almost vanished under her many billowing
skirts. The curate put up a decent show of resistance, protesting,
wriggling and flailing around underneath his heavy charge, but in
doing so caused his own soutane to push up towards his neck so

that he was almost naked. So comical was the situation that nobody in the room could keep from laughing, including Mme d'Aine:

> The lady laughed, more and more loudly, and then even more, holding her sides and finally lolling all over the Abbé and crying 'Mercy, mercy, I can't hold it any longer, everything will go; Abbé hold still!' And the Abbé, who had not understood what was going on and why he should not move soon found himself inundated by a deluge of tepid water, which ran right into his shoes, and it was now his turn to cry: 'Help, help, I am drowning!' All we could do was not to choke with laughter. Mme d'Aine, still in the saddle, called her chambermaid: 'Anselme, Anselme, pull me off this priest. And you, Abbé, my little Abbé, be consoled, you didn't miss a drop.'[3]

The one thing plaguing Diderot, even in the company of friends, was his chronic stomach ailment, not helped by his fondness for food and wine. 'I am a glutton,' he wrote about a particular dinner. 'I ate an entire pie, and then three or four peaches. Ordinary wine; Malaga wine, and a great cup of coffee. I returned at one o'clock at night. I could not close an eye. I had the very finest sort of indigestion and spent the entire day drinking tea.'[4] Sophie and her sister did not approve of his impending tubbiness, but he found himself unable to fight it: 'I am getting round like a ball. Mme Legendre, how you will detest me! My stomach is fighting with difficulty against the buttons of my waistcoat, indignant at its inability to overcome this obstacle, especially after dinner.'[5] But over-eating was not the real problem, and he wrote to de Jaucourt's friend, the eminent Dr Tronchin, a long and dejected letter about his stomach cramps and various digestive disorders, which the physician, it seems, could not alleviate.

As the year passed, Diderot's mood changed for the worse. He was depressed by the treadmill of his work, by Sophie's absence, by his domestic situation, by the political situation at large: 'Ah! Dear friend, where is the serenity I had last year? Mme d'Holbach is still delicate, Mme d'Aine still cheerful, the Baron still mad . . . but I have lost the brush I used to paint them for you,'[6] he complained to Sophie, with an almost audible sigh, in October 1760. The continuing work was made worse by the publishers' stinginess towards him and other contributors. 'Where was I these last beautiful days?' he wrote to his lover in September 1761. 'I was locked up in a very dark apartment, using up my eyes by collating the illustrations with their explanations, and I will work myself stupid for those men who would not give me as much as a glass of water if they no longer had any need of me.'[7]

Seen through the prism of these letters, Diderot's mood continued to darken. 'I will not leave Paris this autumn,' he wrote in October 1761. 'My troubles are chasing one another. I wear out my eyes over plates bristling with ciphers and letters, and, in the middle of this painful work, my thoughts are bitter with injuries, persecutions, the torments, the affronts that will result from it all.'[8] For the time being, the nobility of his work undertaken in the service of humanity had paled before humanity's lack of interest, even enmity, towards it. Diderot felt bitter, and sorry for himself. The mood of the other workhorse of the *Encyclopédie*, Louis de Jaucourt, is impossible to ascertain: while Diderot sought refuge in his letters and in his private literary works, the Chevalier found it in work alone, and his fourteen-hour days writing and collating articles left him no time to write letters or socialize.

With his immediate circumstances weighing heavily on Diderot's thoughts, political life in France was once more thrown into turmoil by the case of Jean Calas, a Protestant from Toulouse who was falsely accused of killing his son to prevent his conversion to Catholicism. Calas was found guilty, broken on the wheel, and strangled. The case brought into sharp focus the religious hysteria that could still so easily be whipped up in the country (a Protestant minister, François Rochette, had been hanged for preaching in Toulouse in February); but it also showed that there was now increasing revulsion against such medieval conceptions of faith and justice. A national subscription, in which even the King himself participated, was organized for the executed man's widow. Even Voltaire supported her cause. Diderot was touched by this gesture of his wily ally, whom until now he had only known to serve his own interests.

'You are astonished about the atrocity of the Toulouse judgment,'
he wrote to Sophie,

> But the priests had already buried the son as a martyr and if
> they had absolved the father they would have had to dig the
> so-called martyr out again and drag him through the mud
> ... It is Voltaire who has written for the unhappy family. Oh!
> My friend, what a wonderful use of genius! This man must
> have a soul after all, a sensibility that is revolted by injustice
> and which is attracted to virtue. For who are the Calas to him?
> Why should he be interested in them? Why should he interrupt
> the work he loves for their defence? If there were a Christ, I
> assure you that Voltaire would be saved.[9]

There seems to be more than a note of regret in these lines that
it was Voltaire, and not Diderot himself, who had had the resolve
to spring to the defence of someone innocently accused – and that
Voltaire was working on something that he loved, which made an
interruption seem like a sacrifice.

An air of inescapable domesticity began to characterize the cottage
industry of Diderot, de Jaucourt, and their handful of assistants
and correspondents toiling over the plates and the remaining ten
volumes of text. Diderot himself had to nurse his wife Toinette
through a long illness. She began hallucinating and suffering from
terrible fevers, which eventually turned out to be dysentery. Despite
the fact that they had not spoken for weeks and had been taking
their meals in separate rooms, Diderot looked after his Toinette
with every possible sign of devotion, reporting events to Sophie 'in
great haste' (a recurring phrase during this period). 'The symptom
that scares me most,' he admitted to his lover, 'is her gentleness,
her patience and silence, and, what is worse, a return of friendship
and confidence towards me.'[10]

Diderot seemed to relish the idea of retreat into the private
sphere during this period, even if it was partly forced upon him.
His letters are filled with reports about acquaintances and friends

(Grimm, Mme d'Épinay, the Holbachs, and Louise d'Épinay's jealousy towards Grimm, who showed too much attention to Baroness Holbach), about unfortunate neighbours he helped as well he could, and questions about Sophie and her sister. Among more than a hundred pages of letters, the Calas affair and the expulsion of the Jesuits merit no more than a few paragraphs.

Drawing Diderot out of these domestic concerns was a succession of foreign visitors to the Paris salons, in many of whom Diderot took a lively interest. As travel between Britain and France had become possible again after the end of the Seven Years War, many notable British figures now made their way to Paris, where they were greeted and lionized by the Anglophile intelligentsia. Diderot had begun his career as an English translator, and he still wrote elegant letters in English (one of which is preserved) and read English authors such as Richardson, whom he adored and on whose death he had written a moving eulogy.

In 1762, Diderot found a congenial and much admired colleague in the English novelist Laurence Sterne, whom he met in Holbach's salon and who later sent him a copy of *Tristram Shandy*, one of the inspirations for Diderot's own discursive fictional masterwork, *Jacques le fataliste*. Sterne himself was much impressed by his welcome, writing to a friend: 'What makes these men truly entertaining and desirable is, that they have the art, notwithstanding their wits, of living together without biting or scratching – an infinitude of gaiety & civility reigns among them – & wh[ich] Is no small art, Every man leaves the Room with a better Opinion of his own Talents than when he entered.'[11] Not everyone was so enamoured of the salons. Horace Walpole, who hated philosophers, predictably detested the talkative Frenchmen and their gatherings at Holbach's house, commenting tartly on their being 'so overbearing and so underbred' and on how they bothered him with absurd scientific ideas about early deluges, and other nonsense. He much preferred the Jesuits, he wrote.[12] A young and earnest Scottish traveller, Sir James Macdonald, meanwhile, found himself somewhat overwhelmed by the spectacle of Diderot in full conversational flight:

Diderot is noisy and talkative, and somewhat fond of a Dispute;
he is certainly very learned, and very conscious of his own
knowledge – he would be a better philosopher and a more
agreeable companion if he did not make philosophy a matter
of Party, and treat subjects of the gravest nature and which
require a cool examination too much like the head of an
opposition.[13]

In March 1763, John Wilkes came to Paris, followed in October
by David Hume, a secretary at the British Embassy, and David Garrick, who fascinated the salons with his dramatic skills. Diderot
wrote about him at length, eventually drawing on their meetings
to write his *Paradoxe sur le comédien* (Paradox of the Actor), an
investigation of the art of acting and the importance of being
unemotional and in control even when portraying the greatest
passions. Diderot describes an impromptu performance given by
Garrick in 1758 in answer to the opinion that acting depended on
words:

He took a cushion: 'Messieurs, I am the father of this child.'
Then he opened a window, took the cushion, threw it in the
air and kissed it, caressed it and imitated all the little things a
father does when amusing his child; but the moment came
when the cushion, or rather the child, slipped from his hands
and fell out of the window. Then Garrick took to miming a
father's despair . . . The spectators were so gripped by motions
of dismay and terror so violent that most of them could not
bear it and left the room.[14]

In September 1762, just as Diderot seemed to have settled into
a new routine of work on the *Encyclopédie*, with occasional periods
of respite in the salons and the country houses of his friends and
acquaintances, he received a nasty reminder that he was still under
the watchful eye of the authorities. True to a vow taken when he
himself had been poor, Diderot was always trying to help writers
and artists who did not know where their next meal would come
from. One of these, a man called Glénat, had appeared at his house

and asked whether there might be any copying or other work for him to earn a little money. Diderot had been only too happy to help, and even recommended him to Grimm, Mme d'Épinay, and Holbach for further work. When Diderot was asked whether he knew someone reliable to copy out a work on religious and political matters written by an anonymous acquaintance, he had no hesitation in giving the dangerous manuscript to Glénat. The result was as prompt as it was surprising. The manuscript was passed on to the Lieutenant of Police: the penniless copyist was in fact a police spy. Diderot went to the Lieutenant, a college acquaintance of his, to protest, only to find that the official burst out laughing when the writer made his earnest representation. He left, swearing not to be taken in so easily again:

> All those who come to me in the future with dirty and worn cuffs, holes in their stockings and in their shoes, the hair flat and dishevelled, their overcoat torn, or dressed in a bad black habit fraying at the seams, with faces and voices speaking misery and honesty, will from now on seem to me to be emissaries of the Lieutenant of Police, crooks sent to observe me.[15]

Another intrusion on Diderot's quiet routine was an offer that might have been flattering, but which revived unwelcome associations with the great crisis three years earlier. In April, Count Shuvaloff, the Russian Ambassador to Paris, had approached Diderot with an offer from the Tsarina, Catherine II, to finish the *Encyclopédie* in St Petersburg, with a guarantee of financial security and other tempting conditions. Diderot turned down the offer; but after Tsar Peter III was dethroned by Catherine two months later, she returned to the idea of inviting Diderot to St Petersburg, in which she was supported by Voltaire, who put pressure on his fellow *philosophe* to leave France.

Diderot stood his ground. 'No, dear and very illustrious brother,' he told Voltaire, 'we will go neither to Berlin nor to Petersburg to finish the *Encyclopédie*; and the reason is that at this very moment it is being printed here and the proof sheets are under my eyes.

But hush!'[16] Dated 29 September, the letter is a strong indication that the Encyclopedists had taken the suppression of the Jesuits on 6 August as a signal to redouble their efforts and to publish as soon as possible.

In October, Diderot demonstrated once more that, despite his workload, he still had time for quixotic intellectual projects. 'This is how my days are going at the moment,' he had written to Sophie. 'You will see that they are hardly less difficult than yours. My head is heated by an important question which occupies me constantly. It follows me through the streets. It distracts me in society. It interrupts me during the most essential tasks. It robs me of my sleep at night.'[17] This seemingly essential and overwhelming question was, quite literally, the squaring of the circle, to which Diderot believed he had found the mathematical solution that had eluded the greatest minds for millennia. Stubborn in his mathematical amateurism (he had published some competent mathematical articles some fifteen years earlier, but had done no work in the area since), he spent many days and nights on working out his theory. But just as he was on the point of publishing it, a kind soul tactfully pointed out a central flaw in his argument and he was persuaded to put the idea aside.

Unfortunately, only one of Diderot's letters has survived from 1763 and only a few between January and November 1764, and so much of the work leading up to the publication of the final volumes of the *Encyclopédie* remains undocumented. However, this allows one of the peripheral figures to re-enter the spotlight: Friedrich Grimm, the reluctant Encyclopedist (Diderot had persuaded him to contribute a handful of articles to the final volumes) and editor of the *Correspondance Littéraire*. Since his return from military duties, everything had seemed to be going well for him after the city of Frankfurt made him its Ambassador in Paris in 1759. Two years later, due to his own lack of circumspection, some letters of his criticizing the French conduct of the war had fallen into the hands of the French Foreign Ministry. With the help of influential friends, he had avoided being deported, but his diplomatic status had been revoked. In 1762 he had managed to become the unofficial representative of the Duchy of Saxe-Gotha, but no formal appointment was to come his way for another thirteen years.

Despite the mishap in 1761, Grimm had made a good living for himself as an international fixer, arranger of princely marriages, correspondent on the arts and other matters, supplier of Parisian wigs to dumpy duchesses in provincial Germany, and in any other role that might be asked of him by his aristocratic clients. Occasionally, though, he would strike out on his own, as in the case of a family for whom he acted as patron on their journey to Paris in 1763. He introduced the family in the *Correspondance littéraire* as follows:

> Real prodigies are so rare that it is worth talking about them when one sees one of them. A music master by the name of Mozart has just arrived from Salzburg with the two prettiest children in the world. His daughter, aged eleven, plays the harpsichord brilliantly . . . Her brother, who will be seven next February, is a phenomenon so extraordinary that one has difficulty believing what one sees with one's own eyes and hears with one's ears . . .
>
> The children of M. Mozart have excited the admiration of all those who have seen them. The [Habsburg] Emperor and the Empress have showered presents upon them, and the courts of Munich and Mannheim extended the same welcome to them. What a pity that people are so ignorant of music in this country.[18]

Grimm was happy to act as host and protector to the Mozarts and did his utmost to show them off in the most fashionable places. (On Mozart's catastrophic second journey to Paris in 1778, however, his erstwhile patron complained of his lack of worldliness, and they parted in anger.)

As work on the *Encyclopédie* drew towards its end, external events once again began to impinge directly on the project, though this time to its advantage. They centred on Father Antoine de Lavalette of Martinique, a Jesuit missionary who was to change the history of his order, as well as that of the *Encyclopédie*.

Stationed in the Carribbean, Lavalette, against all the rules of his order, had set up a very profitable trading operation in coffee, sugar, spices, and indigo, all of which relied on slavery. The riches of iniquity might help the cause of salvation, as the Gospel said, and Father Lavalette had taken the Saviour at his word. After learning about his dealings, however, his superiors in Paris had taken as dim a view of his theological reasoning as of his commercial enterprise. They summoned him to France, told him to behave himself, and sent him back. But the reprimand had had little effect. On his return, finding his business in a bad way, he had defrauded merchants in Marseilles and Nantes of considerable sums of money to tide over his trading mission, which had resulted in his being sued in France.

It was at this point, in 1759, that his Paris superiors had begun to suspect that the Lavalette case might be more serious than they had thought, and they immediately sent an envoy to bring the situation under control. But luck was not on their side. The envoy died at sea; a second envoy broke his leg on the eve of his departure; and a third was captured by pirates. When the fourth envoy arrived in Fort-de-France in 1762, he mounted an inquiry and sent back both a devastating report and the errant Father Lavalette, who promptly repented, made a full confession, and declared that 'among the first Superiors of the Company there was no one who authorized, or advised, or sanctioned the kind of commerce in which I engaged'.[19]

But the damage had been done. It was not the issue of slavery that outraged the French courts (slavery was, after all, enthusiastically and quite legally practised by French merchants); it was the fraud perpetrated by Lavalette that exercised the judges at Marseilles, where the suit had been brought. They eventually ruled that the Jesuit order itself should be held liable for the monies owed, which with interest and penalties totalled some five million *livres* (approximately £40 million in today's terms). This not only threatened to ruin the Jesuits financially; the court case now motivated the *Parlement* in Paris to settle old scores with their long-time adversaries. When the Jesuits appealed against the judgment to the Paris court, the *Parlement,* bastion of the Jansenist intelligentia, saw to it that not just an individual dishonest priest but the entire Jesuit order was put on trial. The ruling handed down on 6 August 1762 declared that the order had committed every possible offence, spiritual and temporal, against Church, morals and laws, and decreed the immediate closure of all Jesuit institutions as well as the abolition of the Society in France. The main enemies of the *Encyclopédie* were now neutralized, and the booksellers could finally dare to publish the work they had been preparing for just such a moment.

On the eve of the completion of the grand project of the *Encyclopédie,* however, its editors felt anything but triumphant. The formerly close friends who had begun the project had grown apart and were now following their own trajectories. D'Alembert, whose scientific career had lost its impetus, was concentrating on his work in the academies and was becoming a *de facto* scientific administrator, while continuing to correspond and publicize himself in as energetic and bellicose a fashion as ever. Rousseau had just published his *Contrat social* as well as his two novels *La Nouvelle Héloïse* and *Émile,* which were condemned by the authorities (and defended by Diderot) and necessitated his fleeing, first to Neuchâtel, and then to Berne. When he was ordered to leave Berne, David Hume offered him asylum in England, only to find his paranoia and misanthropic outbursts so difficult to live with that he was glad to see Rousseau return to France, having quarrelled with just about all his British admirers. Without the collaboration of their former friends, and of many who had once worked for the *Encyclopédie* but had found it impossible to continue after the crisis of 1759, the Encyclopedists had shrunk to a little group of core workers: Diderot, de Jaucourt, and Goussier, as well as some faithful satellites, such as Dalimaville, Naigeon, Grimm, and Holbach, who were still devoted to the cause. Having weathered political storms and ideological battles aplenty, the *Encyclopédie,* it seemed, was finally coming into harbour, battered, perhaps, but still afloat.

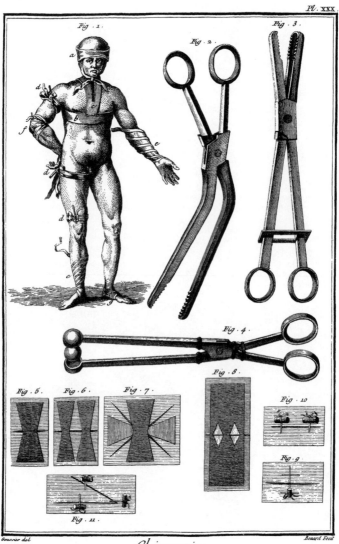

Pl. XXX.

Fig. 1.

Fig. 2.

Fig. 3.

Fig. 4.

Fig. 5.

Fig. 6.

Fig. 7.

Fig. 8.

Fig. 10.

Fig. 9.

Fig. 11.

Gousier del.

Benard Fecit

Chirurgie.

MUTILATION

MUTILATION, s. f. (*Gramm.*) is what one calls the cutting off of an essential part of a whole. One *mutilates* an animal by depriving it of one of its limbs; a work by suppressing parts of it. All the ancient authors were mutilated for the use of the youth educated in colleges, for fear that they would learn an ancient language which it is not essential to learn & thus corrupt the innocence of their morals. One *mutilates* a picture, a machine, &c.

   MUTILATION, s. f. *in Law and in Medicine*, is the cutting off of a member or external part of the body, such as the nose, the ears, or other. In criminal matters, one inflicts hardly any punishment that does not go along with the *mutilation* of limbs.

(A)

In the summer of 1764, almost all the articles had been written, manuscripts sent to the printers, and proof sheets revised. Most of the volumes were now prepared and ready to go to press. Finally, Diderot sighted land, and a life beyond the years of drudgery.

He worked mainly at home, having long avoided going to Le Breton's workshop in case he found himself being invited to the bookseller's home or country house, which he wanted to avoid at all costs: 'At three I am at Le Breton's. I will work there until seven, or half past. Whether the work is done or not, I will get out fast. I don't want these people to invite me for dinner and I have sworn not to eat there any more ... because they are greedy and put too much importance on such a silly dinner for me to accept it at this

price.'[1] When Diderot was finally obliged to call at the workshop
in order to check something in the proofs, a terrible surprise was
in store for him. Grimm takes up events:

> Printing of the work was almost as its end, when M. Diderot
> found it necessary to consult one of his great articles in philos-
> ophy under the letter S [SARACENS, OR ARABS], which he
> found entirely mutilated. He was confounded; and in an
> instant he understood the enormity of what the printer had
> done: he [Diderot] immediately looked up the finest articles
> by himself or by his best aides, and found almost all of them
> in the same disorder, the same vestiges of an absurd murder
> that had ravaged everything. This discovery put him in a state
> of frenzy and despair I will never forget.[2]

Unknown to Diderot, or to anybody else, Le Breton and one of his
workers had taken it upon themselves to protect their investment
and to censor any articles in the last ten volumes, by cutting or
changing the proofs, that they judged too daring or too critical of
Church and State; they had also burned the original manuscripts
to make restitution of the offending material impossible. What
remained, wrote Grimm, were the best articles 'in a fragmented
and mutilated state, robbed of everything that made them precious,
without even the connections between these scraps and these skel-
etons that had been hacked to pieces'.[3]

  Beside himself with rage and despair, Diderot consulted Grimm,
wondering whether this was the moment to abandon the entire
project. Grimm counselled against it, and eventually Diderot
accepted his advice: he would see through what he now considered
a work that was entirely spoiled. Before he could confront Le Breton
again, however, he set out his indictment against him in a long
letter:

12 November 1764

> Do not think it is my wish, monsieur; it is not for you that I
> come back. You have stabbed me in the heart, and seeing you
> will only drive in the dagger more deeply. It is also not because

of any attachment to the work, which I cannot but despise entirely in its present state . . .

I submit to the solicitation of M. Briasson [Le Breton's colleague]. I cannot but feel pity for your associates, who are caught by the treason you have committed, and who may be its victims along with you. You have deceived me in a cowardly manner for two successive years. You have massacred, or had massacred by a brute beast, the work of twenty honourable men who have dedicated their time as well as their talents and their sleep to you for nothing, for love of the good and of truth, and in the hope of seeing their ideas appear and collecting for them a little consideration which they merit so well, and of which your injustice and ingratitude has deprived them.

Think about what I am predicting to you: as soon as your book is out, they [the contributors] will seek out the articles they have written and when they see the injuries you have done to them with their own eyes, they will not contain themselves but will cry out aloud. The cries of MM. Diderot, de Saint-Lambert, Turgot, d'Holbach, de Jaucourt and others, all so respectable and so little respected by you, will be repeated by the multitude. The subscribers will say that they paid for my work, and that it is almost yours you are giving them. Friends, enemies, associates, will lift up their voices against you. The book will be seen as a flat and miserable rhapsody . . . A small part of your edition will sell slowly, and the rest will be pulped. . . .

So, this is the result of twenty-five years of work, of anxiety, of expenditure, of dangers, of mortifications of all kinds! An inept, an Ostrogoth, destroys it all in an instant. I speak of your butcher, of him, whom you have charged with dismembering us. In the end it turns out that the greatest damage we suffered, that disdain, shame, discredit, ruin, derision come to us from the principal proprietor of the affair![4]

Diderot had, he wrote to Le Breton, 'wept with rage in front of you, I wept with grief at home, in front of your associate M. Briasson, in front of my wife, my child, and my servant . . . I shall bear this wound until I die.'[5] He was convinced that two decades of work had been undone and destroyed.

Diderot's version has long been accepted, and the last volumes of the *Encyclopédie* consequently regarded as being of lower quality than their predecessors. In fact, they contain as many subversive articles as the first seven. The extent and nature of Le Breton's 'butchery' of the last ten volumes was an object of guesswork until 1933, when a Berlin bookseller offered an entire set of the *Encyclopédie* for sale. An *ex libris* label marked the set as having belonged to the Tsar's general staff. What made it unlike any other, however, was the fact that it had originally been Le Breton's personal set. Most importantly, there was an additional volume, consisting of blank pages bound exactly like the rest, into which had been pasted a historian's dream: 284 pages of proofs taken from the last ten volumes of the *Encyclopédie* and containing evidence of alterations undertaken on forty-four articles, and of the complete deletion of three others. Le Breton, a careful man, had obviously tried to shore up his reputation, and that of the encyclopedia he was trying to sell, against lawsuits, such as the one for breach of contract that was indeed to be brought against the *Encyclopédie* by one of its subscribers.

It is impossible to be certain that the Berlin volume contains a complete record of changes and deletions in the last ten volumes. Le Breton might have collected only a selection of deleted articles in the volume; if so, it is likely that the selection showed him in a favourable light – there was, after all, nobody who could possibly prove him wrong. In view of the extent of the articles contained in this paste book, however, and of the articles that survived Le Breton's censorship to be published in the last ten volumes, many of which are highly critical and far from anodyne, it is likely that the bookseller and his assistant were less systematic than they might have been, deleting and changing occasional articles, and that the Berlin volume does indeed present the great bulk of the changes.

Judging from Le Breton's paste book, Diderot had, in his shock, greatly exaggerated the extent of the mutilation of the articles.[6] Still, the damage was real: de Jaucourt's article TOLÉRANCE, 418 lines of it, had been cut out in its entirety, almost certainly because of its robust opinions about religious and political persecution, written, one must remember, at a time when Protestant pastors in France were still being hanged merely for preaching:

> A sovereign may have political reasons whether or not to receive strangers of this religion or that in his dominion; he can make his own religion, which he believes to be the best one, dominant. Those are the attributes of his power. But he cannot force the consciences of his subjects, nor deprive them of the reasons for their nonconformity with the dominant religion, rights which these subjects have both as human beings and as citizens.

Little wonder Le Breton was unhappy about this. Apart from two articles that had been cut as a whole, most changes concerned individual words or sentences: Diderot's remarks in LUXURE (Lust) – 'In the Christian religion, lust is one of the seven deadly sins; imagine how many damned there must be, if the slightest sin in this category is damning' – had been censored by removing the subversive speculation appended to the simple statement. Diderot's article PYRRHONIENNE (dealing with philosophical doubt) had come in for some heavy butchering, particularly where it mentioned the *Encyclopédie*'s great forerunner, the Protestant Pierre Bayle, and wrote of the Edict of Nantes (1685): 'At that time the most unheard-of vexations were carried out against members of the Reformed religion; France was made Catholic by ruining her; by violating the most sacred laws of humanity and by dishonouring religion, the extirpation of a heresy was carried forward. This is what Bayle demonstrated.'[7] Another article by Diderot, THÉO-LOGIEN, had had the following paragraph deleted, a swipe at Catholic doctrine and Jansenism at the same time:

> It is shameful that philosophers should often be in a position to give theologians lessons in tolerance and humanity. It is shameful that these men [theologians], whose science is full of difficulties, mysteries, and incomprehensibilities, and would agree that people have no faith in their teachings save by God's

special grace, should have employed fire and sword, and would
be employing them today, if the sovereign would let them.

In the equally censored article on Socratic philosophy, Diderot tries
on the mantle of Socrates for size, casting Jean-Jacques Rousseau
in the role of the savage and misanthropic Timon. After delineating
Socratic philosophy by borrowing generously from Brucker's work,
which had so often been useful to the *Encyclopédie*, Diderot suddenly
steps out of his role as objective summarizer: 'Oh, Socrates! I
resemble you very little; but at least you make me weep with admiration and joy.' No admiration is wasted on the burghers of Athens
and on their treatment of the sage and its historical lessons: 'The
ignominy which has settled upon those who found him guilty
should encourage every philosopher to speak the truth boldly, and
should make those worldly people who so readily condemn the
conduct of philosophers and who blame in us what they admire in
Socrates, more logical and more circumspect.' But Le Breton would
not have it, and it was cut.

According to the evidence contained in the Berlin volume, some
twelve thousand words, or forty pages of modern print, had been
altered or deleted, out of ten volumes totalling some nine thousand
pages. What remained, though, was ample material for waving the
flag of the *philosophes*, and of the Enlightenment.

The *avertissement* to volume eight began with an ode to virtue
and perseverance that was richly merited:

> Permit me to bring to the public attention all our able &
> courageous helpers! But if we had to mention only one, let us
> at least thank him with the dignity he deserves. He is M. le
> Chevalier de Jaucourt.
>
> If we were able to cry the cry of a sea hand when he sees
> land after a dark night that has kept him suspended between
> sky and earth, it is to M. le Chevalier de Jaucourt that we owe
> it. What has he not done for us over these last years? With
> what constancy has he not refused all the tender and forceful
> solicitations which tried to prize him away from us? Never has
> someone made a fuller and more absolute sacrifice of his rest,

his self-interest & his health. He has been ceaselessly at work,
only satisfied with himself if he could save others some trouble.
But what is missing in this eulogy can be found on every page
of this work: not one of them would not speak of the variety
of his knowledge & the width of his references!

Despite these words, it is notable that Diderot does not find it
necessary to praise the genius, the great mind, the profound philosopher – qualities he had seen so abundantly in other friends. He
did not see the Chevalier in these terms, and could not bring
himself to say better of him than that he was the most upright of
men, and had saved others trouble; for the rest, de Jaucourt's
articles would have to say what he himself would not.

Perhaps the Chevalier was not (despite Voltaire's estimation) a
great original mind; but his sheer workload and intellectual humil-
ity command respect. The author of 17,266 articles altogether,
he wrote 15,039 of them between the crisis of autumn 1759 and
publication in 1765 – an average of more than eight articles per
day.

Diderot, to his credit, appreciated the extent of de Jaucourt's
contribution. He had never been an intimate friend of the
Chevalier's, and looked down on his frantic working life, which he
seems to have deemed unworthy of a truly *bel esprit*. At the same
time, he was aware that without de Jaucourt he would never have
been able to afford any respite from his own work on the *Encyclopédie*, and that he owed to de Jaucourt his time at Grandval as well
as his many hours spent writing his novels and his art criticism.

The booksellers proved utterly pragmatic, as glad to have the
Chevalier as they were reluctant to pay him. He had offered his work
freely, after all, and they obviously felt no obligation whatsoever to
reward him for his generosity. The account books of the associated
booksellers show that they did send him books he needed free
of charge, amounting to a grand total of 2,749.69 *livres* (some
£22,000) over nine years. The permanent secretaries whom de
Jaucourt employed for research, excerpting, and copying of
materials, however, also needed to be paid, but it had been left to

the Chevalier himself to do this. Being a wealthy man, he found it possible to pay for some years, but finally the cost of a small publishing operation that brought him nothing but free books began to bite into his finances. In 1761, as related by Grimm, one of the booksellers was ready to come to his aid:

> Not only did M. Le Chevalier de Jaucourt, who, according to M. Diderot, contributed most to finishing this immense work, never get any compensation for his efforts, but he even found himself obliged to sell a house he had in Paris in order to be able to pay the salary of the three or four secretaries whom he had employed continuously for ten years. The pleasant part of this affair is that it was the bookseller Le Breton who bought this house with the money which the work of the Chevalier de Jaucourt had put into his pocket. It is said that Le Breton found the Chevalier de Jaucourt to be a very honourable man.[8]

It was a beautiful deal: de Jaucourt had almost ruined himself by working for nothing for the booksellers, who now bought a house from him (using, as Grimm pointed out, income from his work) so that he could continue to earn them money; in other words, Le Breton got out of de Jaucourt not only the publication of a dictionary that made him millions, but also a house, all for the expense of a few books.

The Chevalier, it seems, was so devoted to his work that hardly anything else mattered. He had been far from content with the role of 'merciless compiler' in which he had been seen by Grimm and others. As he increasingly found himself in the role of main editor of the work, he imposed his own priorities and style, reversing or subverting some of the conventions of the work, a fact that is all the more ironic as subversion had been one of the primary purposes of the *Encyclopédie*. Less ideologically inflexible than his fellow Encyclopedists, de Jaucourt believed, for example, that it was important to include the biographies of great men. This, however, was one of the things d'Alembert had loudly forsworn to do, and so de Jaucourt had found a diplomatic if impractical solution, leaving the original editors their pride and the work an appearance of continuity, while doing exactly as he pleased: biographical entries were included, but listed under the birthplace of the person in question. In the article VOORHOUT, for example, it took the Chevalier de Jaucourt just twenty-five words to come to his primary objective, the life of his teacher, the great Dr Boerhaave, to whom he was to devote another 3,877 words, none of which had anything to do with the Dutch village, its history, geography, or economy. Many biographical articles functioned like this: the life of Newton can be found under the heading WOLSTROPE.

De Jaucourt compiled a great number of articles from sources that he often did not acknowledge, on a huge range of subjects: Medicine (his area of academic specialization) and within it Anatomy, Surgery, Pharmacy; Philosophy; Literature, Grammar, and Mythology; Games (an excellent article on chess); History and Geography (and, by sleight of hand, Biography); Hydraulics; Zoology and Botany; Music and Architecture; Artillery; Numismatics; Painting; Law and Politics; Theology; and Economics. While there were some subjects he did not write about (among them Logic, Mechanics, Military Strategy, Navy, and Falconry), hardly any topic seemed beyond his readiness to do his best if there was no other contributor at hand and an article needed to be written. As a result, the articles are often hastily written, copied in part from other works, and undistinguished, as might be expected from a medical doctor writing about areas of knowledge in which he had no special expertise or interest.

In these pieces de Jaucourt employed a curious mixture of borrowing, outright theft, and exact attribution, without apparently following any single method. Often one finds a direction to the reader to 'see on this topic' followed by a specific author and work, or phrases such as 'I cannot enumerate the points here. Readers eager to be convinced of the truth of what I say will find the facts described in the following authors, followed by a long appended list of authors and titles. Among the authors used by de Jaucourt were Montesquieu and Voltaire for politics (particularly the former, whom the Chevalier venerated) and Montaigne, who appears again and again as the gold standard for compassionate and shrewd understanding of history and of human nature. Other sources include previous dictionaries such as those by Chambers and Bayle, and specialist works such as Brucker on philosophy, also much plundered by Diderot.[9]

In articles on subjects he could write about with some confidence, de Jaucourt may be less original than Diderot, and less wickedly elegant than Voltaire, but he was nevertheless a forceful writer and the quintessential Enlightenment Man: sceptical and humanistic, rational and moderate in all things. His opposition to slavery, one of the most lucrative trading interests in the French colonies, also fired his prose. Unable to condemn it openly, he contemptuously wrote in NEGRES (*Commerce*):

> One tries to justify this commerce, which is odious and against natural law, by saying that the slaves usually find the salvation of their souls along with their loss of liberty; that Christian instruction along with their productivity in sugar, tobacco and indigo, sweetens all that seems inhuman in a commerce in which men are buying and selling others as if they were beasts to be used for the cultivation of the fields.

If he was disgusted with the slave trade, religious fanaticism, under which his Protestant ancestors had suffered and which had forced him to seek his education abroad under an assumed name, roused his especial ire. Usually moderate in his choice of words, he preferred irony rather than diatribe, as in the case of the siege of La Rochelle in which French Protestants were exterminated by Richelieu's forces: 'It is astonishing how many millions the clergy furnished for the taking of this town, & with what joy they advanced the money ... Of fifteen thousand persons who were in the city, only four thousand survived this terrible disaster. What a strange power religion has over men!'

It is in these religious pieces especially that de Jaucourt emerges as a man of strong convictions and persuasiveness: whenever he could escape the role of the compiler, he did so with eloquence and dignity. PRESSE, for instance, is a vigorous defence of free speech, whilst other headings speak for themselves: PRÉJUDICE, SUPERSTITION, TOLÉRANCE, ZÈLE, *de religion* (*Christianisme*). His article INQUISITION is both a well-documented history of the institution (still in force outside of France, and finding clear contemporary parallels in cases like that of the unfortunate Calas) and a passionate indictment of religious intolerance: 'The son can witness against his father, the wife against her husband, the brother against his brother: finally the accused is obliged to be his own accuser and to guess & confess to a crime which is announced to him and of which he knew nothing.' Here even the gentle de Jaucourt raises his voice to a rhetorical storm:

> A priest is charged with its execution; a monk vowed to charity
> & gentleness, who lets people suffer the most cruel tortures
> in vast and profound prisons. It is also a theatre mounted in
> a public place, where the condemned are led to be butchered
> behind a procession of monks & other men of the cloth. They
> sing, they celebrate mass, then they kill men. An Asian arriving
> in Madrid on the day of such an execution would not know
> whether this is an entertainment, a religious holiday, a sacrifice,
> or butchery & yet it is all these at once. The kings, whose mere
> presence suffices to pardon the criminal, take part in these
> spectacles on a chair lower than the inquisitor's & watch as
> the victims expire in the flames. Montezuma is reproached for
> sacrificing prisoners to his gods; what would he have said, had
> he ever seen an *auto-da-fé*?

Other authors, too, contributed material that Le Breton must have overlooked or, less likely, simply not understood. Even after the bookseller had taken his scissors to it, SARACÈNES, the article that led Diderot to discover what had happened in November 1764, still contained some astonishing lines (as well as lovingly spun-out passages on Muslim theology) that were all too easily applicable to the *ancien régime*: 'Mahomet was so convinced of the incompatibility of *philosophie* and religion that he decreed the death penalty for all those practising the liberal arts: it is the same conviction for all times and all peoples that causes reason to be decried.'

If there were critical notes in SARACÈNES, other writers had gone considerably further. In an anonymous piece on INSTINCT, the surgeon Charles Le Roy virtually abolished the distinction between humans and animals by arguing against Descartes's notion that all animals are soulless automatons, thus undermining the very conception of man as the crown of creation. Naigeon used a tried and tested Encyclopedist stratagem in his article UNITARIANS, in which the ostensible description of the sect and its beliefs ends up, as if by chance, supplying excellent arguments against fundamental Catholic doctrines such as the Trinity, original sin, grace, predestination, the sacraments, heaven and hell, the divinity of Christ, and of God himself.

Baron d'Holbach, always loath to beat about the bush, made one of the period's most stinging attacks on France's absolute monarchy in his unsigned article REPRÉSENTANT. In a country in which the last monarch had famously remarked that he *was* the State, the piece began with the words: 'In a despotic state the chief of the nation is all, the nation nothing.' Holbach goes on to draw up a representative political system in which people's emissaries with different backgrounds and opinions 'oppose ventures of a power which would become abusive if it had no limit'. He scoffs at that 'pretentious nobility which arrogates to itself the right to speak exclusively in the name of the nation & will always regard its fellow citizens like vanquished slaves'. In France, seen against a backdrop of continuous conflict between Crown and regional *parlements*, the nobility, and a bourgeoisie that was still struggling to find its political voice, the following passage was especially resonant and was saved from the censor's pen only by its use of the past tense:

> Under the feudal government, the nobility & the clergy held the exclusive right of speaking for the entire nation, and of being their only *representatives*. The people, made up of those cultivating the land, the inhabitants of cities and rural areas, the manufacturers – in one word, the most numerous, most industrious and most useful part of society, did not have the right of speaking for itself; it was forced to accept without a

murmur the laws a few grandees had hatched out together
with the sovereign.

In a wise monarchy, Holbach argues, it is in the sovereign's interest
to have his people represented, or ultimately face the outcome of
oppression: 'A suffering people will attach itself instinctively to
those who have the courage to speak for them . . . ambitious cheats
who seduce the masses by persuading them that they are working for
their cause & who topple the State under the pretext of defending
it.' Only twenty-three years later, this was exactly what happened.

Deeply disillusioned with the *Encyclopédie*, Diderot nevertheless continued his work. His thoughts, though, were already elsewhere and,
preparing for the future, he was now ready to cut himself off from
his Encyclopedist past. He had long been worried about the fact
that his daughter Angélique, now nine years old, might not have
a sufficient dowry, and so he had resolved to sell his working library,
the only thing of value he possessed. Most of the collection had
been acquired through his work as editor, and he apparently cared
little for it, as long as 'Homer and Horace will stay with me'.[10] He
had offered it to collectors over the years, but none of them had
been willing to pay the price he was asking. Diderot finally decided
to ask Grimm's help by proposing the sale of his library to a foreign
ruler who had already shown interest in him, Tsarina Catherine II.
Not only did she jump at the chance to acquire with the library a
connection to one of Europe's leading progressive minds, she did
so in truly imperial style, paying Diderot, on top of the 15,000 *livres*
he had asked, an additional 1,000 *livres* per year for the upkeep
and development of the library, which was to remain at his disposal
until his death. More than this: when it was brought to her attention
by her ambassador to France that she had neglected to pay the
pension to Diderot and that the *philosophe* was still waiting for his
money, she paid him for the next fifty years in advance, declaring
that she did not want to be so forgetful another time. 'At the turn
of the century,' she decreed, 'further arrangements will be made.'[11]

His connection with Catherine the Great was to last for years, and eventually he could no longer find excuses for delaying a trip to St Petersburg to pay homage to his patroness.

Closer to home, Diderot, nostalgic, perhaps, for the days of easy friendship with his erstwhile collaborators, did his best to mend his relationships with Rousseau and d'Alembert. Rousseau, who came to Paris in December, would not even see him, but d'Alembert, who was ill, was more amenable to a restitution of friendship with his old co-editor. Always a curious mixture of vanity and modesty, d'Alembert, who had ascended the heights of the French academic establishment, was still living with his foster mother. During the summer of 1765, Diderot took to visiting him often. 'D'Alembert is in a terrible state,' he reported to Sophie. 'His indigestion is terrible; he has sent for Bouvart, who has bled him. I hear he is tormented by a colic which will not get better and is threatening to take him from us at any moment.'[12]

During one of his visits, Diderot had a confrontation with another member of the Encyclopedist circle, the Abbé Morellet, who also came regularly and who had had the opportunity of witnessing Toinette Diderot trying to cheer up the mathematician by telling him more domestic gossip than he had ever wished to hear. Morellet, who was famous as a mimic, now took it upon himself to entertain the assembled guests with his none too flattering imitation of Mme Diderot. Her husband, who could easily have written another encyclopedia about his wife's character and foibles, was not amused and asked the Abbé to listen to him for a few minutes without interruption. There were four rules to comedy, Diderot told him. First, that it was never a good idea to ridicule even the most ridiculous in front of their nearest and dearest; second, that every joke had its limits; third, that every joke had its place; and fourth, that anyone forgetting the first three rules was 'liable to get himself flaming well thrown out of the window. The Abbé, without answering me, gave me his hand in friendship and as a gesture of apology.'[13]

Diderot's refuge in friendship and company from the troubles of the *Encyclopédie* was wholehearted, and had the usual results. 'Do I suffer?' he wrote to Sophie:

More than ever, and I deserve it. I ate like a wolf cub, and drank like our friend M. Gascon when the dinner is particularly good. I have drunk wines of all sorts; an incredibly perfidious melon was waiting for me; and do you think that it was possible to resist an enormous iced cheese? And then the liqueurs; and then coffee; and then abominable indigestion which kept me up all night, and which caused me to spend the entire morning between the tea pot and another vessel, which it would not be decent to name. Thank God, now I am purged for ten years; and perhaps this débâcle will bring on rheumatism, which will awaken my gout if it pleases me; for, if my chest is well, I feel a stinging in my left hand, which is devilishly painful.[14]

At fifty-two, Diderot, the former youthful rebel and stubborn man of honour, was no longer a youngster with auburn curls falling on strong shoulders – above a strong constitution.

As the publication date moved closer, an honour-saving deal with the Government had to be found, resulting in the following advertisement in the Paris press in January 1766:

> Samuel Fauche, bookseller in Neuchâtel in Switzerland, advises the public that he has finished printing the *Encyclopédie*, the manuscripts for which he had been able to acquire after the publication of the first seven volumes printed in Paris. This continuation [of the *Encyclopédie*] begins with tome viii and contains ten volumes. Those who have the seven first volumes of the works and who desire to procure the rest are asked to present themselves at the Paris print shops with a writ proving that they have subscribed to the work, and the ten new volumes will be delivered in folios to the carrier of this document for the sum of approximately 200 *livres*. This formality is absolutely essential as the volumes have been produced in exactly the same number as the original seven, and preference will be given to the subscribers over all others.[15]

The publisher, Samuel Fauche of Neuchâtel, did exist, but it is not clear whether he had any idea of his nominal implication in the great project. Despite his name on the title-page, all the volumes

had been printed by Le Breton in Paris, using a work-force of fifty
full-time employees in his workshops.

Malesherbes, who had had to resign as Director of the Book
Trade in 1763 when his father, the Chancellor Guillaume de
Lamoignon, was disgraced, had been replaced in his post by the
Lieutenant of Police (the very one who had sent a spy into Diderot's
house), a man glorying in the name of Antoine Raymond Jean
Gualbert Gabriel de Sartine, Comte d'Alby (1729–1801). Sartine
was a curious figure, a Spaniard who stood under the direct protection of the King and who had been allowed to buy the office of
Lieutenant of Police at the age of twenty-nine, after the King had
exceptionally reduced the cost of the office from 250,000 *livres*
(some £2 million), to 100,000 *livres* (£800,000) in order to allow
his protégé to purchase it. He was well disposed towards the Encyclopedists and their enterprise, as well as to Enlightened thinking
in general. At the same time, however, his administration of the
police force was carried out with great efficiency, and Sartine prided
himself on being informed about everything going on and everyone
working and writing in Paris.

The Encyclopedists and their publishers had worked out with
Sartine an elaborate scheme designed to satisfy both the subscribers
and the all-important appearances the State had to maintain
towards the Church and the *Parlement* of Paris. In essence, the
agreement allowed the *Encyclopédie* to appear and to go on sale as
long as the French capital was in no way implicated in the affair.
This had necessitated the borrowing of Fauche's name, as well as
the stipulation that subscribers could arrange to have their copies
delivered to them from a point outside of Paris. Parisian subscribers
were, by implication only, allowed to transport their books into the
city at their own risk, after having had them sent to an address in
the provinces.

It was thus that, somewhere in an anonymous barn outside the
gates of Paris from 29 March to 23 April 1766, the last ten volumes
of the great *Encyclopédie* were shipped to their recipients. Like the
last volume to have appeared before the crisis of 1759, they were
printed in an edition of 4,000 copies. They were VIII: H–ITZEHOA;

IX: JU–MAMIRA; X: MAMELLE–MYVA; XI: N–PARKINSONE; XII: PAR-
LEMENT–POLYTRIC; XIII: POMACIES–REGGIO; XIV: REGGIO-
SEMYDA; XV: SEN–TCHUPRIKI; XVI: TEANUM–VÉNERIE; and,
finally, XVII: VÉNÉRIEN–ZZUÉNÉ.

Twenty years after having begun as a modest translation from
the English, the *Encyclopédie,* the greatest publishing project undertaken up to this time, was finished. The last volumes were not
revised, printed, and delivered until 1772; but the battle was over,
the war had been won. Producing the volumes of illustrations was
simply a chore that had to be completed, while the Encyclopedists
themselves began to go their separate ways.

Diderot especially lost no time in putting the *Encyclopédie* behind
him. To him, the work was ruined. The volumes represented the
waste of most of his working life for a project that he saw as having
brought him nothing but persecution, treachery, ridicule, boredom, and constant fear of arrest. When the work was finished, he
did not shed a single tear. He did, though, interrogate himself on
his own life and began a lengthy correspondence about posterity
with the sculptor Falconet, who had gone, on Diderot's recommendation, to St Petersburg in order to work on a great equestrian
stature of Tsar Peter the Great. Among all the preoccupations in
Diderot's letters to Falconet and to Sophie, to Garrick in London,
and to a young actress, Mlle Jodin, in Warsaw, there is not a single
mention of his two decades' work as an Encyclopedist.

While Diderot was doing his best to forget what he considered
a terrible disaster, Le Breton did what he could to extract fame
and fortune from the *Encyclopédie.* To achieve this, he could not
resist personally delivering several sets of the *Encyclopédie* to selected
influential courtiers at Versailles. He had specifically been asked
not to deliver any copies to Paris or Versailles to avoid antagoniz-
ing an Assembly of the Clergy. Afterwards, it had been signalled
to the booksellers that they could do what they wanted, though for
the time being Paris was to be excluded from deliveries. But Le
Breton thought it unnecessary to wait. He was soon to find out
that, while the agreement with Sartine had been designed to save
face, appearances nevertheless had to be kept up. Le Breton had

overstepped the mark by venturing directly into the lion's den. On 23 April, the bookseller was invited into the Bastille and incarcerated there. This, too, was nothing but a face-saving exercise and the entrepreneur, who was not interrogated and who had been allowed books, writing materials, and a servant while in prison, was released a week later. The *Encyclopédie* had reached its completion, not with a bang, but with a whimper.

Pl. II.

figure 1.re

fig. 2.

Benard Fecit.

Antiquités.

POSTERITY

POSTÉRITÉ, s. f. (*Gram.*) this is the collection of men who will come after us. Honourable men and great people of all walks of life, look towards *posterity*. He who only values the moment is cold, incapable of enthusiasm, whose projects will only cost him his fortune, his peace, & his life. Regnier said: *just judgment of posterity*, I call you as a witness; & by talking he manifested what is at the bottom of the soul of all those who compare their works to the recompense their century will give them.

Now the *Encyclopédie* was finished and published, Diderot looked back on all the years of work with a bitterness and disappointment that would never leave him. Having wasted his life on a work he now considered almost entirely bad, having seen how little had remained of the ambitious dreams of his young days, he was now obsessed with the question of how he would be remembered after his death. Posterity became an obsession, in letter after letter written to his friend Falconet. 'Dying is the common destiny of us all,' he wrote on 27 January 1766, 'dying in glory is the privilege of the virtuous man, his sweetest recompense.'[1] The dead, however, he had to admit, were just as dead whether or not they had made history. Diderot regarded the chance of being remembered as an honourable man as the only thing he could rescue from a life thrown away, not on women and drink, but on definitions of exotic plants and common workmen's tools: 'Oh posterity, holy and sacred, support of the unhappy and oppressed; you who is just, you who is not corrupted, who avenges the honourable man, who unmasks the hypocrite, who condemns the tyrant; constant, consoling, never abandoning me. Posterity is to the philosopher what heaven is to the religious man.'[2]

Diderot's introspection was to be rudely interrupted by yet another legal case that shook France and almost convinced him and his friends to flee abroad overnight, a case all the more remarkable as it was a direct backlash against the rising influence of the *philosophes* and the opinions they had spread through the *Encyclopédie* and other writings.

The train of events had begun during the night of 8 to 9 August 1765, when a wooden crucifix placed on the Pont-Neuf in Abbeville, a little town in Picardie, was damaged with slashes from a sabre or hunting knife. It was assumed that drunken soldiers were guilty of this act of vandalism. The Bishop of Amiens, responsible for Abbeville and known for his conservative opinions as well as his hatred of the new philosophy, took the mutilation of the crucifix as an occasion to reinforce the faith of his diocese. He took part in several processions to the crucifix and instituted a general manhunt for the perpetrators of the sacrilege, who were, however, nowhere to be found. At this point, public procedure became intertwined, as is so often the case, with personal revenge: a man by the name of Belleville informed the authorities that a young wastrel of his acquaintance could well have been the evildoer, as he had often seen him engaged in blasphemous acts and remembered specifically having once seen the young libertine failing to take off his hat to a religious procession. He neglected, however, to tell the judges that he was also in love with the young man's aunt, and that her nephew had warned him off her in no uncertain terms.

The young man who now found himself in the spotlight of the official investigation and accused of blasphemy was Jean-François le Fèvre, Chevalier de la Barre, the son of an impoverished noble family. He was nineteen years old. During the trial, some hundred and twenty witnesses came forward. Nobody had seen or heard anything specific, but they all thought they remembered something:

singing libertine songs, calling St Mary Magdalene a whore, genu-
flecting mockingly to a philosophical book, asking a pious woman
whether she had bought a plaster-cast image of a saint in order to
be close to a man, and other such stories. More damaging than all
of these, however, was the fact that the police had found in the
young man's lodgings a copy of Voltaire's *Dictionnaire philosophique
portatif*, a work generally judged highly dangerous to morals, Crown,
and Church. Further incriminating evidence came from de la
Barre's 'accomplice', a boy of fifteen.

The judges of Abbeville considered the case, which no longer
had anything to do with the defacing of the crucifix, a crime, for
which the young Chevalier, as it happened, had an alibi. Finally
they delivered their judgment. De la Barre and his accomplice
should 'make honourable amends'. The sentence specified the
nature of these amends: they should have their tongues ripped out
with pincers, their right hands amputated in front of the main gate
of the church, and then be burned alive on the market place 'over
a small fire'. As de la Barre's co-accused had succeeded in saving
himself by crossing the channel to England, the Chevalier alone
was to face this ordeal.

A sentence of such severity had to be endorsed by the region's
high court, in this case the Paris *Parlement*; and so de la Barre was
transported to the capital, where his defence was placed in the
hands of M. Le Fèvre d'Ormesson, a respected lawyer and distant
relative, who had to adopt a strategy for the boy's defence. He felt
sure that the *Parlement* would never endorse a sentence as monstrous as this and that it was therefore unnecessary to solicit public
sympathy for his client by the common practice of printing sentimental pamphlets and handing them out in the street – effectively
an attempt to blackmail the High Court judges to let him off or
face the fury of the population. This, however, d'Ormesson thought
would also blacken the name of a boy with a fine army career in
front of him, and it was better to let justice take its course quietly.

But D'Ormesson had fatally misjudged the situation, and the
climate of the day. The judgment was endorsed, though modified:
the Chevalier was to be beheaded and his corpse burned (together

with the *Dictionnaire philosophique*), after having been tortured by
crushing of his legs so that he might name possible accomplices.
The sentence was carried out on 1 July in Abbeville, by five
executioners imported from Paris for the occasion. 'This is what it
takes to decapitate a rash and badly brought up child in the middle
of France and of the eighteenth century,' commented Grimm bit-
terly. 'In the countries of the Inquisition he would have got away
with a month's imprisonment and a reprimand.'[3]

There was no doubt that the sentence, in its extreme cruelty
(and, as Voltaire pointed out, unlawfulness), was a sentence against
the author of the *Dictionnaire philosophique* and those of like mind
as much as against the unfortunate teenager. The exiled philosopher once again implored Diderot to save himself before a similar
fate befell him. Once more, Diderot refused, replying:

> I am not lying to you, as you can see; my soul is full of alarm
> ... I hear a voice joining yours, saying to me: Flee, flee! How-
> ever, the most stupid and least comprehensible inertia holds
> me back, and I stay. I have at my side a woman of advanced
> years [Toinette was fifty-six], who could be torn away from her
> parents, her friends, and her little living room only with the
> greatest of difficulty, and I am the father of a young daughter
> whom I owe an education; I also have friends. Should I leave
> all of these, who were always there to console me during the
> unhappy times of my life, the honest witnesses to my actions;
> what would I do with my existence?[4]

Diderot was too tired to flee, to start again elsewhere, in faraway
Russia or in Holland. Obstinacy won out over reasoned caution in
the face of a spectacular demonstration that the Encyclopedist spirit
of Enlightened tolerance might have been victorious in the polite
salons of the capital, but not beyond them.

Diderot's inertia did not prove lethal after all, and, despite wide-
spread rumours in Paris, the de la Barre case was not used as a
prelude for a witch hunt of the *philosophes*. Indeed, most of them
lived to a ripe old age. Diderot himself lived and wrote for another
nineteen years, without ever giving the world the great work all his

friends thought him capable of, the one creation that would prove his genius. He continued to write art criticism for Grimm's *Correspondance littéraire* and to write essays; most importantly of all, he received friends, attended dinners, and gave other people ideas they would never have been capable of without him. In 1773, when Catherine the Great had finally badgered him into visiting her in St Petersburg, he set off on the long journey, going via northern Germany and Holland but avoiding Prussia and Frederick the Great, whom he had never liked or trusted. His stay at the Russian Imperial Court (during the winter of 1773–4) was unhappy, and overshadowed by the sniping of courtiers jealous to see the inelegant and thoroughly uncourtly Frenchman supping with their Tsarina every evening, holding her in his spell with his conversation and his ideas.

He was never to change his mind about the *Encyclopédie*. When a bookseller named Panckoucke approached him for a revision of the work in 1768, while the volumes of plates were still being printed and distributed, Diderot, who did not like the entrepreneur, described their meeting to Sophie:

> That little Panckoucke, inflated with the arrogance of a true *parvenu* and believing he can exploit me as he apparently does with some poor devils whom he makes earn their bread with great hardship when they are obliged to work on his imbecilities, that little man thought it a good idea to solicit me. He had no luck at all. I let him go on as much as he wanted, then I got up brusquely, took him by the hand, and told him: 'Monsieur Panckoucke, wherever in the world it is, in the street, in church, in a brothel, one always should be honest and polite. Even more so when one speaks to a man who is no more patient than I am, and if one does so in his own house. Go and f*** yourself, you and your project. I do not want to work for it . . . Now have the goodness to get out of here and leave me in peace.'[5]

Not only did the upstart manners of an ambitious young bookseller irritate Diderot, but the censorship that had been imposed by Le

Breton had coloured his view of the entire enterprise, which he now thought to be thoroughly deficient:

> We did not have the time to take great pains in the choice of our contributors. Among some excellent men there were others that were weak, mediocre, or altogether bad. This is why the work is so mixed in quality and one finds a schoolboy's attempt next to a piece by a master; an idiocy neighbouring something sublime; a page written with force, purity, warmth, and judgement, reason, elegance, opposite one that is poor, miserly, flat, and miserable.[6]

Diderot's memory was poisoned by what had happened, and even his personal associations now seemed to be coloured by this bitter tint. About his collaborators, he wrote:

> They were a detestable race of workers who, not knowing anything and assuming that they knew everything, sought to distinguish themselves by a universality that could make one despair, as they threw themselves at everything, ruined every-thing, spoiled everything, and took their enormous sickle to the harvest of others. The *Encyclopédie* was a pit into which these rag pickers threw an infinity of things that were badly observed, half digested, good, bad, detestable, true, false, uncertain, and always incoherent and disparate.[7]

Despite such devastating judgements, Diderot eventually came to support Panckoucke and wrote a memoir to the Chancellor arguing in favour of a new edition of the *Encyclopédie*, predictably perhaps, by exaggerating the faults of the old. The Chancellor did not agree and refused to permit a rewritten version to be published (the old one having presented headaches aplenty). He did, though, authorize a reprint of the work, and Panckoucke bought the publi-cation rights and the original copper plates of the engravings from Le Breton and his associates. He eventually published an *Encyclo-pédie méthodique* based on the *Encyclopédie* by Diderot and d'Alembert, but organized according to subject matter. It began to appear in

1778 and was finally finished in 1832, thirty-three years after Panckoucke's death. It comprised 202 volumes. Even he was to find out that publishing an encyclopedia was no easy task. In 1770, when he had finished printing the first three volumes, he had to stand by while they were seized by the police and entombed in the Bastille (a fate that he himself, at least, escaped), to be released six years later and after a good deal of behind-the-scenes negotiation and bribery.

In 1776–7, Le Breton himself had published a five-volume *Supplément au Dictionnaire raisonné* in which he had corrected errors and filled gaps in the original edition, though without the participation of the original Encyclopedists. The *Encyclopédie* had made him a very wealthy man. Grimm had been right when he wrote that the associated booksellers had

> left M. Diderot all the glory, all the dangers, all the persecution, while keeping for themselves all the money coming from 4,300 subscriptions. The pay to M. Diderot for this immense work which absorbed half of his life was 2,500 *livres* for every one of the seventeen volumes of text, and the sum of 20,000 *livres* paid in bulk, while it brought to the booksellers millions. The *philosophe* was enough of an imbecile to be duped by their avarice, and his friends did not have enough influence on him to make him determined to get a better deal out of them.[8]

The question of whether the booksellers did in fact earn millions was addressed on the occasion of a law suit that Diderot must have cursed as yet another nuisance arising from the *Encyclopédie*, but which he eventually supported, partly, no doubt because of his anger against Le Breton. The suit was brought in 1770, by a group of subscribers, led and inspired by Pierre Joseph François Luneau de Boisjermain (1732–1801 or 1802), who argued that the final cost of the *Encyclopédie* was more than double the 280 *livres* originally proposed and therefore constituted a breach of contract. The suit would drag on until 1778. Luneau was also a late subscriber (his order had been placed in 1767), which further complicated the calculation of his claim. What makes his small-mindedness valuable is that, to support their suit, he and his partisans furnished a considerable corpus of material about the subscribers, the printing of the work, and the profits made by the booksellers; as a result, this document has become one of the primary sources on the economics of the *Encyclopédie.*

In 1771 Luneau estimated that the booksellers had expended 1,158,958 *livres*, 3 *sous* and 6 *deniers* (roughly £9.3 million) on the production of the plates, author's wages, paper, binding material, printing and production of the books, as well as miscellaneous expenses. In 1767, four years earlier, the bookseller Briasson himself had put the amount at 1,039,642 *livres*, 7 *sous* and 3 *deniers* (£8.3 million), which allows one to suspect that Luneau's accurate estimation was based not only on fine accountancy but that he also had inside information, which in turn implies that his profit estimates are also a reliable guide. Luneau put the total takings of the booksellers at 3,500,000 *livres* (£28 million) for the subscription fees, plus 230,000 *livres* (£1.8 million) for the sale of the copper plates to Panckoucke, putting the total takings at 3,730,000 *livres*, leaving, minus expenses, a net profit of 2,571,042 *livres*, roughly equivalent to £20.5 million. This was a very decent return on their investment, considering that most of the work (apart from the actual printing and distribution) was done by Diderot and his co-workers. Before the money came rolling in on a large scale between 1765 and 1766, however, the publishers found themselves sufficiently embarrassed for funds to borrow 12,000 *livres* from the Chevalier de Jaucourt and to sign an agreement with Diderot, on 8 August 1761, in which they agreed to pay the 30,000 livres they owed him as an annuity of five per cent of the overall sum.[9] When the work was finally finished, the Chevalier was surprised to discover that the booksellers did not think it necessary to give him a complimentary set.

Grimm, it seems, was right to be cynical about the booksellers' 'grandeur' towards de Jaucourt, and about their stance towards their main editor. Over the twenty-five years of his work, Diderot earned a grand total of between 60,000 and 80,000 *livres* (£500,000 to £750,000). At 2,800 *livres* a year on average, his income had put him somewhere between a professor at the Sorbonne and a provincial lawyer. After publication of the *Encyclopédie*, and mainly thanks to the generosity of Catherine the Great, his income was sufficient to enable him to invest 70,000 *livres* with a *fermier général* and, in 1772, to give his daughter a dowry of 100,000 *livres*; but despite his celebrity throughout Europe, he was never independently wealthy. A professional writer who had never sought an official position or a stipend, and who, until late in his life, had never enjoyed the benefits of a patron, Diderot was one of a new race of authors who decided to maintain their creative and intellectual independence at the cost of their financial security.

While the editor made a decent living from an indecent amount of work and harassment, the booksellers (two of whom, David l'aîné and Durand, died at the time of publication) had done very well indeed, and the *Encyclopédie* proved a success that none of them could have imagined. Even while the editorial work was going on, pirate editions were being prepared in England, Italy, and Germany, and after the printing of the Paris folio, several reprints appeared: Leghorn (1770–9, folio), Geneva (apparently printed partly in Neuchâtel and Lyon, 1777–81, quarto), and Lausanne and Berne (1778–82, octavo). The quarto edition was prepared by a renegade monk who promised not only to correct the mistakes of the *Encyclopédie*, but also to purge it of impieties and to rewrite passages to please Protestants. Voltaire, who had a fine sense for knowing on which side his bread was buttered, eventually abandoned the Paris booksellers' direct heir, Panckoucke, and declared that the quarto edition was far superior.

The continuing skirmishes over the completed *Encyclopédie*'s commercial potential form a curiously unheroic postscript to an heroic story. Competing publishers waged veritable trade wars trying to force one another out of the marketplace by all available means, including defamation, lies, buyouts, and unlikely alliances. In addition to the complete, reorganized or augmented reprints, innumerable selections and concise editions appeared in several languages.

Despite the mutedness of the last chapter in the history of the original *Encyclopédie*, the fact that it had been published in its entirety was an important signal, and even though the administration during the last years of Louis XV's reign actually grew more repressive, his successor, Louis XVI, was already a child of the Encyclopedic spirit, and Encyclopedists like Turgot and Malesherbes (who merits this title despite not having written for the *Encyclopédie*) played an important role in his government. The Encyclopedic spirit, it seemed, was becoming the dominant way of thinking. The careful, reformist, and tolerant approach to all political problems seemed to suit the King, who was unwilling to take sweeping action and tried to stay clear of the menacing waves of popular malcontent and political power struggles that were eventually to bury him, and with him an entire world. Post-revolutionary France was a different country altogether, and the *Encyclopédie* proved to have been the last great documentation of the customs, the tools, the thoughts, the aspirations, and the limitations of Europe before 1789.

The Revolution had no time for the generosity of spirit that marked Encyclopedist thought. The values espoused by the Encyclopedists, which had once seemed likely to dominate for decades, were swiftly crushed by Europe's first, though short-lived, totalitarian regime. When the monarchy was restored, the Encyclopedists were seen as sowers of unrest, rebellion, and impiety. The *Encyclopédie* was consigned to oblivion, a state only occasionally disturbed by academics and collectors of rare books. The plates, with their strange ethereal grace, conquered the public imagination sufficiently to secure for themselves an independent life in omnibus volumes devoted to individual métiers or walks of life, or as decorations on the walls of offices, clubs, and living-rooms; but the *Encyclopédie* itself seemed altogether too long, too difficult, too remote to be accorded much space beyond its historical significance. It became the kind of monument everyone has heard about but few have ever seen, like an Inca pyramid or a rare cave painting.

As for the Encyclopedists themselves, they fared surprisingly well. Busy as it was, eating its children, the Revolution did not devour the members of the group, who managed to survive despite the fact that their writings contained more than enough material to earn them a place on Dr Guillotine's newfangled but admirably efficient contraption. At least fifty-six Encyclopedists were still alive in 1789,[10] many of them still actively involved in their professions.

During the Reign of Terror, only one of the contributors to the *Encyclopédie*, Antoine Allut, author of articles on glass production, was executed as an 'enemy of the People', on 25 June 1794, while five others, Menuret, Lezay-Marnésia, Necker, Boufflers, and Grimm, emigrated, and at least one, Condorcet, went into hiding. The Abbé Morellet, now the director of the Académie Française, opposed the new government's stance towards his institution, which was closed by official order in 1793. Only one Encyclopedist, Alexandre Deleyre, author of ÉPINGLE [Pin], became an active revolutionary and voted, as a deputy in the National Convention, for the death of the King. Malesherbes, the saviour of the *Encyclo-pédie* on many occasions, came to his own death after defending the King – not out of ideological conviction, but out of a feeling that justice must be done. He was executed on 22 April 1794.

Most of the Encyclopedists who were still actively pursuing their professions during the Terror sought to take refuge in their work and avoided getting mixed up in politics, though they often had to prove the ideological reliability of their work. Goussier was employed by the Bureau of Designers of the Committee of Public Safety and dreamed up weapons for the new regime; Berthoud single-mindedly followed his passion for chronometers, which happened to be useful for the Navy; Jean-Baptiste Le Roy (who refused to change what was a very unfortunate surname) researched the manufacture of cannons; Desmarest occupied himself with the production of paper money and the preservation of the national heritage, much of it in the shape of furniture and works of art formerly owned by the King and the aristocracy; and Daubenton inspected and rewrote books for schools – and publicly dissected a rhinoceros that had died in the menagerie at Versailles.

*   *   *

And what of the main protagonists: what of Diderot, d'Alembert, Grimm, Rousseau, Mme d'Épinay, de Jaucourt, and Voltaire?

Having retired early from his Encyclopedic duties, Jean Lerond d'Alembert lived perhaps the happiest years of his life after the work had been published. He shared an apartment with a young woman, Julie Lespinasse, whom he loved deeply and passionately. After breaking with Julie's former protectress, Mme Deffant, he helped his friend establish a salon of her own, in which he himself was the leading intellectual light. Eventually, her salon even received an official Encyclopedist sanction from the *Correspondance littéraire*. Grimm included it in a (not very funny) satirical sermon allegedly given at the 'Grande Synagogue de la rue Royale', Holbach's town house, contrasting the simple but engaging salon of Julie Lespinasse with the more august, more prestigious, but also rather more intimidating one of Mme Geoffrin:

> Sister de Lespinasse lets you know that her fortune does not allow her to offer lunch or dinner, but that she has none the less great pleasure in receiving those brothers who want to go there to digest. The [Encyclopedic] Church has charged me with announcing that, to visitors with spirit and merit, beauty and fortune are of no account.
>
> Mother Geoffrin lets you know that she renews the prohibitive rules and laws of the previous years, and that it will be no longer tolerated to talk in her presence of internal affairs, of external affairs, of affairs of the Court, of town affairs, of northern affairs, of southern affairs, affairs of the Orient or the Occident; not of politics and not of finances, not of peace, of war, of religion, or of government, of theology or of metaphysics, of grammar or of music, nor, in general of any subject ... The Church acknowledges that silence on these subjects is not its strong point, but promises to obey in so far as it is constrained to do so by physical violence.[11]

Julie was obviously a success, and her salon added to d'Alembert's scientific glory. He himself never accepted Frederick the Great's offer to head the Prussian Academy of Sciences, or Catherine the

Great's to become preceptor of her son with a salary of 100,000 *livres*: he preferred to be financially insecure at home to being rich where he felt out of place. When Mlle Lespinasse fell ill and died in 1776 (her immortal dying words being 'Am I still alive?'), d'Alembert was beside himself with grief, and was even more distraught when he learned from her correspondence that she had had a passionate affair with a military officer while living with him. He was fortunately never to find out that this had not been the only affair she'd had. He himself died, embittered and isolated, on 29 October 1783.

Jean-Jacques Rousseau had perhaps the most famous life of all those involved in the *Encyclopédie* and is considered, not entirely accurately, the most seminal thinker of them all. Unsurprisingly, his stay with Hume in England had ended in catastrophe, and in 1767 he was back in France leading an unhappy, itinerant existence, constantly beset by pathological suspicions, constantly alienating those trying to help him. In 1770, he returned to Paris, still with Thérèse, to a small furnished apartment in an inexpensive hotel. As he had done a decade earlier, he lived from copying music, and wrote in whatever time was left to him, including the *Confessions*, his imaginative autobiography in which he railed against all his former friends. With its curious combination of candour and slander, of almost ritual self-castigation and self-aggrandizement, it caused a sensation in literary Paris when he read it publicly in various salons. He was by now convinced of the existence of a universal conspiracy against him. He died suddenly on 2 July 1778 in Ermenonville, on the property of another of his benefactors, having never seen any of his former friends again. His unexpected death may have been suicide.

The Chevalier de Jaucourt continued to lead a constant and measured life. Liberated from the immense task of writing all day and every day, he once more turned towards his friends, especially Theodore Tronchin, who was now living in Paris. Later in his life, at some point after 1771, he moved to Compiègne, into a house in the Street of the Turning Cat, behind the city hall.[12] Little is known about his old age and it is impossible to say why he chose to move to Compiègne, to which he was drawn neither by family connections nor, it seems, by other ties. His finances being very satisfactory (he had acquired a share in the *Encyclopédie* and left a substantial amount of money in his will), despite his Encyclopedic sacrifices, it may be the case that he simply craved the quiet of a small provincial town in order to pursue his passions: to read and to make notes. He died on 3 February 1780, aged seventy-six years, as quietly as he had lived.

Voltaire could not resist meddling with the further editions of the *Encyclopédie*. He hardly travelled any more, preferring instead to let everyone come to Ferney to see him, in the greatest place of cultural pilgrimage before the Weimar of the ageing Goethe. The enormous cult that developed around him reached fever pitch when he came to Paris in 1778, where he was celebrated in a manner that left no superlative unabused. It seemed as if all life in the capital was in abeyance: 'The cocksureness of the Encyclopedists has halved, the Sorbonne is trembling, the *Parlement* keeps silent, all men of letters are moved, all of Paris only wants to throw itself at the feet of the idol.'[13] He died there on 30 May.

Amid all the public clamour and reverence, Voltaire met one man who was cordial but in no way overawed by him: Denis Diderot, who had refused to make the pilgrimage to Ferney, as he had refused to take the *Encyclopédie* abroad, but who had wanted to set eyes on the man with whom his own life had been intertwined for more than thirty years.

The relationship between the two men had always been uneasy, and was marked by Diderot's suspicions about Voltaire's motives. He admired the great patriarch, but he did not like him, a fact borne out by a letter of recommendation Diderot had been asked to write to his fellow *philosophe* two years before Voltaire came to Paris. 'Monsieur,' the letter began, omitting the 'dear Master' used in earlier letters, 'people are convinced that you like me and esteem me, and that a note by my hand is a very good recommendation to you. I never disillusion them and never refuse to write these notes.'[14] Hardly a sign of a cordial relationship. Unfortunately, no record of their only meeting survives.

Grimm and Madame d'Épinay continued to be lovers, though their friendship was constantly overshadowed by his diplomatic journeys and his attention to foreign princesses, first and foremost Catherine the Great. Diderot, who had given up his moral disapproval of Louise d'Épinay, became a frequent guest at her country house, where he spent many weeks together with her and Grimm in a strictly platonic (at least from his point of view) *ménage à trois*. In 1762, the lady presiding over this philosophical idyll suddenly found herself ruined when she learned that her husband, from whom she had lived separated for thirteen years, had been deprived of his position as *fermier général* and with it of his bountiful and only source of income. She left La Chevrette and moved into a house in the faubourg Monceau, together with her mother and her daughter. For the summer, she maintained a cottage in the country. Grimm lived close by and spent most evenings with her. Thanks to him, the modest salon in the suburbs became a social hub, at which foreign ambassadors and Encyclopedists were frequent guests. It was his way of compensating her for his long and frequent absences. Her own compensation was her friendship with the Abbé Galiani, a connection Grimm had little reason to be jealous of as the diplomat, whose observations of French life in his letters had often been dangerously close to espionage, was banned from France and the friendship could only be played out in letters. When Louise d'Épinay's fragile health finally collapsed in 1779, she at least had the pleasure of seeing that she was, after all, more important to her long-time companion than his diplomatic ambitions, and he stayed at her side until her death on 15 April 1783.

Grimm's own career had never resulted in the regular diplomatic post he seems to have dreamt of for so long, but was, in the end, more distinguished than that of any ambassador. His editorship of the *Correspondance Littéraire* had made him the official voice of France, its culture and its most advanced opinions, throughout Europe, and his journal had become a useful propaganda tool on behalf of the Encyclopedists. In addition to his post as unofficial representative of Saxe-Gotha, he came to an arrangement with the

Landgravine of Hesse-Darmstadt, who promised, in return for his accompanying her young son on a European tour, to obtain for him the title of Baron of the Holy Roman Empire, which she duly did. The newly created Baron de Grimm had come a long way from the young man who had arrived in Paris and had implored his German friends not to use any kind of title on letters addressed to him.

In 1773, his diplomatic work had taken him to the court of Catherine the Great in St Petersburg, where he crossed paths with Diderot. Catherine offered Grimm a position at her court, but he declined, preferring instead to become her councillor of state – effectively her freelance representative in Paris. This gave him all the liberty he wanted in return for some interesting (and often well-paid) assignments, while also being able to continue working as Minister Plenipotentiary of the Duke of Saxe-Gotha in Paris. Having spent almost a year in St Petersburg from 1776 to 1777, he returned to the French capital wealthy and with excellent connections.

But Grimm's new prestige and responsibilities came at the price of weakening his earlier friendship with many of the Encyclopedists, including Diderot, who wrote (though probably did not send) a letter to him in 1781, which read:

> My friend, I no longer recognize you. You have become, per-
> haps unwittingly, one of the best disguised, but also one of the
> most [dangerous?] anti-*philosophes*. You live among us, but you
> hate us . . .
>   My friend, be the favourite of the Greats, serve them, I am
> all for it, as your talents and your age allow you to do with the
> greatest dignity; but be not their apologist, neither in your
> mind nor in your heart.[15]

Diderot's appeal fell on deaf ears as Grimm's political stance hardened. He regarded the Revolution as an unmitigated calamity that would be likely to take France back to the dark ages; but he continued his diplomatic work, travelling to Germany from Paris, until he was finally obliged to leave the capital for good in 1792. Before leaving, he copied from his correspondence with Catherine the Great any sympathetic references to Louis XVI and his family and saw to it that these excerpts were sent to the King in prison. He was officially declared an *émigré* in 1793 and was thus stripped of all his possessions that were still in the country, the loss of a small fortune. The now homeless baron lived, partly on diplomatic duty, in several German cities, a shadow of his former self. In 1798 he resigned his work for Catherine and moved to Germany. Goethe met him in the following year and found him witty and convivial, but also blind and full of bitterness against the Revolution. He died, forgotten, on 19 December 1807, aged eighty-four, a relic from a bygone age.

The second German among the Encyclopedists, the Baron d'Holbach, positively erupted with publications after the *Encyclopédie* had come to an end. His works, robustly atheistic treatises and defences of materialist ethics and social systems, such as *Le Christianisme dévoilé* (Christianity Unveiled, 1761 and 1766), the celebrated *Système de la Nature* (1770), *Le Système social* (1773), and *La Morale universelle* (The Universal Moral Code, 1776), were all published anonymously but nevertheless gave him a name as a considerable thinker in his own right. Despite his combative rhetoric, he was not in favour of a general uprising as the solution to France's problems, and put his faith in the reformist intentions of the young King Louis XVI. During the last years of his life he ceased publishing but remained involved in the intellectual life of his adopted country. Fearing a revolution, he had the good fortune of dying just in time, on 21 January 1789.

'My teeth are packing up; my eyes are refusing service at night; and my legs have become very lazy, multiplying the endless use of walking sticks. Still, I am cheerful; I do not feel either improvement or deterioration up where it counts, for the time being.'[16] At sixty-three, Diderot felt an old man. The journey to Russia, three years earlier, 1,500 miles by coach each way, had taken its toll on his health. Portraits from the period, one painted by Dimitri Levitskii during the stay in St Petersburg, the other a bust by Pigalle, show him tired, almost puzzled that age has caught up with his volcanic energy. Not one of all the known portraits, incidentally, shows Diderot with a wig or with his collar done up. Diderot cultivated the air of the working man, or, to be more precise, he hated all ceremony and frippery, and even in the portraits, some painted by first-rate masters like Fragonard and Van Loo, there is a degree of awkwardness, as if he is not quite sure why exactly he should hold still and stare into the visionary middle distance for so long, when there are more important things to do, and more beautiful subjects to paint. Only one rendering, a terracotta bust by Houdon, seems to do justice to the man Diderot, to his alert mind, the deep honesty of his character, and his reflective nature.

He was not short of work during his last few years. His criticism of the annual exhibition of paintings at the Louvre had become a regular and arduous task (the essays often grew into small books), and with Mme d'Épinay he had filled in for Grimm in his diplomatic absences at the *Correspondance littéraire*. In addition to all this, he had written essays, criticism, and fiction of his own. He had been declared a national treasure, courted by princes and celebrated by all, but was deeply ill at ease with it. More than ever, he found that he was his father's son: simple and honest, not cut out for the treacherously brilliant, waxed parquets of the elegant world.

In his usual, personable way, he gave voice to his uneasiness in an essay, *Regrets sur ma vieille robe de chambre ou avis à ceux qui ont plus de goût que de fortune* (Regrets about my Old House Coat, or Advice to all those who have more taste than fortune).

> Why haven't I kept it? It was made for me; I was made for it. It followed every fold of my body without embarrassing it; I was a true picture, and beautiful. The other one, tight, starched, makes me into a mannequin. My old robe knew no situation too lowly to offer its services, for indigence is almost always officious: if a book was covered by dust, one of its corners would offer itself to clean it. If thick ink refused to flow from

my plume, it offered its flank. One could see on it traces of
long stripes testifying to the frequent service it had given me.
These long stripes announced the man of letters, the writer,
the working man. At present, I look like a rich fop; no one
knows who I am.[17]

Diderot had been offered a complete refurbishment of his study,
as well as a new house coat, by Mme Geoffrin, but somehow the
noble garment, with its silk collar and sumptuous folds, came to
symbolize to him everything that made him uncomfortable about
being a famous man:

> My old coat was at one with the other bric-à-brac around me.
> A chair with a straw seat, a wooden table, a piece of wallpaper
> from Bergamo, a fir shelf supporting some books, some smoky
> prints without frames, stuck to the wallpaper at odd angles,
> between them three or four plaster casts, all of which formed
> the most harmonious impression of indigence together with
> my house coat.
>
> Now everything is out of tune. No longer an ensemble, no
> more unity, no more beauty.[18]

Enfolded in the stiff glory of his new coat, intimidated by damask
wall hangings, and perched like a stranger on the shiny morocco
leather of his replacement chair, 'Denis *le philosophe*' no longer felt
the honest working man he had always understood himself to be.
In this situation, he found himself compelled to utter a prayer to
the gods, declaiming that he was not corrupted ('the luxury is still
new and the poison has not yet done its work'), and asking them
to take everything away from him should he yield to the temptations
of his new surroundings – all except one painting, without which,
he admitted, life would not be worth living.

The drawers of Diderot's new desk were bulging with works he
could not publish, and which would only see the light of day after
his death, sometimes well into the nineteenth century. *Le Neveu de
Rameau* and *La Religieuse* had been joined by another novel, *Jacques
le fataliste*, and by several long essays, another play, *Est-il bon? Est-il*

méchant?(Is He Good, Is He Wicked?), and his best philosophical work, in which he gave his metaphysical ideas a cloak of fiction, *Le Rêve de d'Alembert* (D'Alembert's Dream) – imagined conversations between Diderot himself, the sick d'Alembert, who is at times delirious (allowing Diderot to play with ideas about perception), and other people present at his bedside.

If Diderot's most important work remained hidden in his sumptuous office, he did continue to publish (mainly in the *Correspondance littéraire*) and to correspond. The focus of his life, though, seems to have turned inwards. Having been forced to take a vivid interest in politics and the opinions of the Pope, the King, and his ministers, of cardinals, bishops, and foreign monarchs, he genuinely relished being able to spend time with his daughter, to look after her education, and to revive his attentions to Sophie and her sister. As much as Grimm needed the attention of the great and the good, Diderot was profoundly indifferent to it; he had other concerns. The erotic tension underlying much of his work, even a philosophical essay such as *Le Rêve de d'Alembert*, continued to keep him on edge. His letters to Sophie were now habitually addressed to her *and* her sister, an indication, perhaps, that he was equally intimate with both. Whatever the complexion of their relationship, the tone of the letters changed in character around 1769, and grew shorter: the protestations of longing, the evocations of warm embraces and closeness, make way for the conversations of old friends, even if, on Diderot's side, there often remained an element of wooing.

One reason for the change in his relationship with the Volland sisters may lie in the fact that they were not the only beloved creatures Diderot wrote letters to during this year. He had fallen in love with a certain Mme de Maux, and was trying to juggle his interest in all three women, only to lose them all. Mme de Maux soon vanished, leaving her ardent admirer shattered and disappointed, while the sisters seemed to drift into an ever further emotional distance: some letters from Diderot to them exist from his Russian journey, but after this the affair between them seems to have atrophied. As if living love by proxy, Denis now threw himself into the marriage preparations of his teenage daughter and saw to it that she got a thorough sex education from a Mlle Biheron, who constructed anatomical wax models. He was a proud father, enjoying every step of his daughter's intellectual development, the advancement of her piano playing, and the setting of her character. His excitement over Angélique's impending marriage, however, was soon soured by the personality of the groom he himself had chosen when the couple had still been children. The young M. Vandeul proved so determined to make money that he was not too worried about the methods he employed, often sailing dangerously close to the law, a particular horror to a father-in-law who worshipped at the altar of honesty and virtue. Undoubtedly, too, his anxiety about the bridegroom's character was a cloak for Diderot to hide his fears of losing his daughter and being left alone with Toinette once and for all. Women were very much on his mind in these years, a fact that found its literary expression in the essay *Sur les femmes.*

An essay with a title so uncompromisingly pragmatic, written by a man of the eighteenth century, cannot but give rise to misgivings. In fact, this short essay seems as much a result of his bafflement with women as of acute insight into their position in society. It is a text of subtle contradictions, conjuring up an image of women somewhere between his own wife in her more terrifying moments and Sophie Volland at her Athenian best, written by a man who stood in (often uncomprehending) awe of the other sex. There is the conventional Diderot, who believes that women feel more deeply than men but are rarely capable of systematic work: 'I have seen women carry love, jealousy, superstition, anger, to an extent to which a man would never be capable.'[19] There is also, however, the carefully observant Diderot, who notes that most women are in a state of bondage to their husbands, that most of them are sexually unfulfilled and have never 'felt the extreme of voluptuousness' due to male ignorance of their needs, and that the fate awaiting most of them is little short of terrifying: 'Neglected by her husband [Diderot knew all about that], left by her children, nothing in society, religious devotion becomes her only rescue. In almost all instances, the cruelty of civil law has united against women with the cruelty of nature. They have been treated like imbecile children.

No kind of iniquity may not be inflicted upon a woman in the most civilized nations of the world.'[20]

The essay culminates in the statement that the symbol of women should be the seal from the Apocalypse inscribed MYSTERY; but then Diderot, having snared the reader, drives on to a conclusion that is far from the conventions of his time. He translates the simple sentence 'I love you' when uttered by a man to a woman as: 'If you want to sacrifice your innocence and your morals; lose the respect you have for yourself and others have for you; walk with eyes down-cast in society, at least until, by having got used to your state, you have the cheek to show yourself; renounce every honourable position in society; make your parents die with grief, and give me a moment's pleasure, I would be greatly obliged.'[21] Women may be a mystery, but part of this mystery, the author implies, has been created by the men who denied them education and forced them to make up by perception and intuition what they could not learn methodically from books.

After Angélique's marriage (Toinette had forbidden her husband to invite any of his friends), Diderot's domestic situation was bleak: 'I am alone, I am devastated to be alone, and I feel nothing but this,'[22] as he wrote to Grimm ten days after the ceremony. His journey to Russia a year later may have been in part a flight from this loneliness. After his return, he spent his last years working on projects he had begun earlier, revising earlier pieces, and pub-lishing only occasionally. His collaboration in Abbé Raynal's *Histoire des Européens dans les deux Indes* (History of the Two Indies) was the only major literary project intended for publication that he tackled, a work in which he, under the cloak of anonymity, polemicized hotly against despotism, slavery, and colonial rule. It is possible that Diderot did not want to compromise his daughter's happiness by causing a scandal with another book that would be suppressed and publicly burned; but perhaps he had simply lost the will to fight. When his little granddaughter, seeing a bump on his head, asked him one day whether he also bumped his nose on doors, he laughed and thought to himself that he had, in fact, done little else all his life.

As old age closed in on the *philosophe*, he received news that the
Society of Antiquaries of Scotland in Edinburgh had elected him
an honourable member. He answered their invitation in English,
the language with which he had begun his career:

> Your letter came very seasonably to make me amends fort
> [*sic*] past sufferings, and to give me firmness against those to
> come. I cannot forget the persecutions I have suffered in my
> own country but with that painfull remembrance, I shall place
> that of the marks of esteem I have receiv'd from foreign
> nations.[23]

Diderot had survived most of his generation, most of his friends
and foes. D'Alembert and Mme d'Épinay died in 1783; Rousseau
and Voltaire were already gone, as were de Jaucourt, Hume, Garrick, Mme Geoffrin, Le Breton, and the old enemy of the *Encyclopédie*, Fréron. Sophie Volland died on 22 February 1784. With
Holbach and Grimm the only ones still active, Diderot's world was
contracting. His health began to give way in 1783. Surrounded by
his family, he died quite suddenly around noon on 31 July 1784,
while having lunch. As his daughter relates, his last moments on
earth were a scene of domestic discord: 'He ate a soup, some boiled
mutton, and a chicory; he took an apricot; my mother wanted to
prevent him from eating it. "But how the devil do you think this
could harm me?" He ate, leaned his elbow on the table to reach
for some little cherry compote, and gave a little cough. My mother
asked him something. As he did not answer, she raised her head,
and saw that he was no more. His internment presented only few
problems.'[24]

The last sentence was a tactful allusion to the fact that the family
had been afraid that Diderot might share the same fate as Voltaire,
who had died in the same parish and whose corpse, having been
refused a Christian burial in Paris, had to be smuggled out of the
capital sitting in his own coach. Diderot, however, had mollified
the local curate before his death, and his burial at Saint-Roch in
Paris was held with all honours. His daughter, Mme Vandeul, even

hired fifty priests to be present, a privilege her father would presumably have gladly done without.

As arranged with Catherine the Great when she had purchased his library, copies of Diderot's manuscripts, as well as some originals, were sent to St Petersburg together with his books. A much larger corpus stayed in the possession of his daughter. In the newly conservative climate of the July monarchy, the descendants of the *philosophe*, particularly Angélique's freshly ennobled son, grew increasingly embarrassed about their scandalous and impious ancestor and refused to have his manuscripts published, or even conserved properly, until the death of Albert de Vandeul in 1911. For more than a century, Diderot's entire French literary estate lay in the attic of Château d'Orquevaux, some twenty miles from Paris, where rain, moisture, and mice almost finished off what pious hands had not already burned.

Having been subject to mutilation from the elements as well as from family censorship, Diderot's *œuvre* was only finally inventoried and edited after the Second World War. His reputation as a great novelist and essayist never recovered from this period of enforced silence. The last of his works, an essay entitled *La mystification*, was not published until 1954. Having forfeited his career as a philosopher in order to be released from prison, his greatest fear had always been that he would only be remembered for having edited the *Encyclopédie*. To an extent this fear was justified – even today, his novels are read much less frequently than those of his contemporaries Sterne and Voltaire. Still, he should not have tormented himself. The great *Encyclopédie* of Diderot and d'Alembert may not have been the monument its premier editor wanted for himself, but it still shines as a brilliant beacon, a turning-point in history: the moment when new ideas carried the day over bigotry and orthodoxy. The Encyclopedists could not have wished for a finer memorial.

BIBLIOGRAPHY

Adams, David J., 'Formey continuateur de l'*Encyclopédie*', in *Recherches sur Diderot et sur l'Encyclopédie (RDidE)*, Paris, October 1992, vol. 13, pp. 117–29.

Affiches annonces avis diverses, May–Decembre 1751, Paris, 1751.

Albertan, Christian, 'Les Journalistes de Trévoux, lecteurs de l'*Encyclopédie*', in *Recherches sur Diderot et sur l'Encyclopédie (RDidE)*, Paris, 1992, vol. 13, October 1992, pp. 107–16.

Almanach des Parisiens en faveur des étrangers et des personnes curieuses, [Paris, 1781], reprinted Saint-Étienne, 2001.

Anonymous [attributed to Diderot or to Morellet], *Mémoire pour Abraham Chaumeix, contre les prétendus philosophes Diderot & d'Alembert: ou réfutation par faits authentiques des calomnies qu'on répand tout les jours, contre les Citoyens zélés qui ont eu le courage de relever les erreurs dangereus de l'Encyclopédie*, Amsterdam, 1759.

Arrêts de la Cour de Parlement, portant condamnation de plusieurs livres et autres ouvrages imprimés. Extrait des Registres du Parlement du 23 janvier 1759, Paris, 1759.

Arti, scienze e lavoro nell'età dell'Illuminismo: la filosofia dell'Encyclopédie, Diderot, D'Alembert, Marmontel, Quesnay, Deleyre, introduced and tr. Paolo Quintili, Rome, 1995.

Avezac-Lavigne, Charles, *Diderot et la société du baron d'Holbach (1713–1789)*, Geneva, 1970.

Badinter, Élisabeth, *Émilie, Émilie – l'ambition de la femme au XVIII* siècle*, Paris, 1983.

——, *Les passions intellectuelles*, 2 vols, Paris, 1999, 2002.

—— and Robert Badinter, *Condorcet: Un intellectuel en politique*, Paris, 1988.

Barbier, Edmond-Jean-François, *Chronique de la Régence et du règne de Louis XV, 1718–1763*, 8 vols, Paris, 1857.

Barni, Jules, *Histoire des idées morales et politiques en France au dix-huitième siècle*, Paris, 1865.

Barthes, Roland, Robert Mauzi and Jean-Pierre Seguin, *L'Univers de l'Encyclopédie*, Paris, 1964.

Bayle, Pierre, *Dictionnaire historique et critique*, 2 vols, Rotterdam, 1697.

Becq, Annie (ed.), *L'Encyclopédisme: actes du colloque de Caen, 12–16 janvier 1987*, Paris, 1991.

——, *Lumières et modernité: de Malebranche à Baudelaire*, Caen, 1994.

——, 'L'Encyclopédie: Le Choix de l'ordre alphabetique', in *Recherches sur Diderot et sur l'Encyclopédie (RDidE)*, Paris, October 1995, vols 18–19, pp. 133–7.

Belin, J. P., *Le mouvement philosophique de 1748 à 1789*, Paris, 1913.

Benrekassa, Georges, *Le langage des Lumières*, Paris, 1995.

Bertrand, Joseph, *D'Alembert*, Paris, 1889.

Berr, Henry, *L'Encyclopédie et la pensée du XVIIIe siècle*, [Paris], 1951.

Boilleau, Anne-Marie, *Liaison et liaisons dans les lettres de Diderot à Sophie Volland*, Paris, 1999.

Bonnefon, Paul, 'Diderot prisonnier à Vincennes', in *RHLF*, vi (1899), pp. 200–24.

Bonnet, Jean-Claude, *Diderot, textes et débats*, Paris, 1984.

Broglie, Louis de, *Un mathématicien homme de lettres: d'Alembert*, Paris, 1952

Bretonne, Restif de la, *Les Nuits de Paris*, ed. Daniel Baruch, in *Paris le Jour, Paris la Nuit*, Paris, 1990.

Caille, Jean de la, *Description de la ville et des fauxbourgs de Paris*, Paris, 1714.

Calot, Frantz, *Port-Royal et le Jansénisme*, Paris, n.d.

Cazes, André, *Grimm et les Encyclopédistes*, Paris, 1933, reprinted 1970.

Chagniot, Jean, *Paris au XVIIIe siècle*, Paris, 1988.

Chaumieux, A. J., *Préjugés légitimes contre l'Encyclopédie, et Essai de réfutation de cet ouvrage*, 8 vols, Brussels Paris, 1758–9.

Chaudon, Louis M., *Dictionnaire anti-philosophique*, Avignon, 1767.

Chouillet, Anne-Marie (ed.), *Les Ennemis de Diderot. Actes du colloque organisé par la Société Diderot. Paris, Hôtel de Sully, 25–26 Octobre 1991*, Paris, 1993.

Chouillet, Jacques, *Denis Diderot–Sophie Volland: un dialogue à une voix*, Paris, 1986.

Claudon, F. T., *Le Baron d'Holbach*, Paris, 1835.

Clement XIII, Pope, *Damnatio et prohibitio operis in plures Tomos distributi cujos est titulo: Encyclopédie*, n.p., 1759.

Cognet, Louis, *Le Jansénisme*, Paris, 1961.

Collé, Charles, *Journal historique 1748–1772*, 3 vols, Paris, 1868.

Collison, R., *Encyclopaedias: Their History Throughout the Ages*, London, 1964.

Contat, Nicolas de, *Anecdotes Typographiques*, in Philippe Minard, *Typographes des Lumières*, Seyssel, 1989.

Corday, Michel, *La vie amoureuse de Diderot*, Paris, 1928.

Cottret, Monique, *Jansénismes et Lumières – Pour un autre XVIIIe siècle*, Paris, 1998.

Cranston, Maurice William, *Philosophers and Pamphleteers: Political Theorists of the Enlightenment*, Oxford and New York, 1991.

Crocker, Lester G., *The Embattled Philosopher: A Biography of Denis Diderot*, London, 1955.

Cushing, Max Pearson, *Baron d'Holbach: A Study of Eighteenth-Century Radicalism in France*, New York, 1914 (this edition is available as a Project Gutenberg e-book).

Daoust, Joseph, *Encyclopédistes et Jésuites de Trévoux (1751–1752)*, Paris, 1952.

Damiron, Jean-Philibert, *Mémoires sur les encyclopédistes*, 6 vols, reprinted Geneva, 1968.

Darnton, Robert, *The Business of Enlightenment: A Publishing History of the Encyclopédie 1775–1800*, Cambridge, Mass., and London, 1979.

——, *The Great Cat Massacre and Other Episodes in French Cultural History*, London, 1984, 2001.

——, *The Literary Underground of the Old Regime*, Cambridge, Mass. and London, 1982.

—— (introd.), 'Les Metamorphoses de l'*Encyclopédie*', in *Recherches sur Diderot et sur l'Encyclopédie (RDidE)*, Paris, April 1992, vol. 12, pp. 19–23.

Delaye, Jacques, *Louis XV et Damiens*, Paris, 1986.

Désers, Léon, *Le Chevalier de La Barre, la légende et la réalité*, Paris, 1922.

Diderot, Denis, *Œuvres*, ed. Laurent Versini, 5 vols, Paris, 1994–7.

——, *Œuvres*, ed. André Billy, Paris, 1951.

——, and Jean d'Alembert (eds), *Encyclopédie ou Dictionnaire raisonné des sciences, des arts et des métiers, par une Société de Gens de lettres*, 28 vols, Paris, 1751–72.

Diderot et l'Encyclopédie, exposition commémorative du deuxième centenaire de l'Encyclopédie, exhibition catalogue, Bibliothèque Nationale, Paris, 1951.

Didier, Beatrice, 'Les Femmes et la diffusion des Lumieres', in

Marie-Laure Girou-Swiderski and John Hare (eds), *Man and Nature: L'Homme et la nature*, II, Edmonton, 1988, pp. 23–52.

Doig, Kathleen Hardesty 'L'Encyclopédie methodique et l'organisation des connaissances', in *Recherches sur Diderot et sur l'Encyclopédie (RDidE)*, Paris, April 1992, vol. 12, pp. 59–69.

Donato, Clorinda, and Robert M. Maniquis (eds), *The Encyclopédie and the Age of Revolution*, Boston, 1992.

Ducros, Louis, *Les Encyclopédistes*, Geneva, 1967.

Dulac, Georges (ed.), *Ferdinando Galiani, Louise d'Épinay – Correspondance 1769–1770*, Paris, 1992.

Dupont-Chatelain, M., *Les Encyclopédistes et les Femmes*, Paris, 1911.

Duprat, Pascal, *Les Encyclopédistes, leurs travaux, leurs doctrines et leur influence*, Paris, 1865.

Emery, Monique, and Pierre Monziani (eds), *Jean d'Alembert, savant et philosphe, portrait en plusiers voix*, Paris, 1989.

Encyclopédie ou Dictionnaire raisonné des sciences des arts et des métiers par une société de gens de Lettres, 17 vols text, 11 vols illustrations, Paris, 1751–1772.

L'Encyclopédie et la pensée du XVIIIe siècle Paris, Revue de syntèse, special issue, Paris, 1951.

Épinay, Louise d', *Les contre-confessions – Histoire de Madame de Montbrillant*, 3 vols, ed. Élisabeth Badinter, Paris, 1989.

——, *Mémoires*, 2 vols, Paris, 1865.

Falk, H., *Les privilèges de librairie sous l'ancien régime*, Geneva, 1970.

Fischer, Jean-Louis, 'L'Encyclopédie presente-t-elle une pre-science des monstres?' in *Recherches sur Diderot et sur l'Encyclopédie (RDidE)*, Paris, April 1994, vol. 16, pp. 133–52.

Fontenay, Elisabeth de, *Diderot ou le matérialisme enchanté*, Paris, 1981.

Furbank, P. N., *Diderot: A Critical Biography*, New York, 1992.

Garnot, Benoît, *Le Peuple au siècle des Lumières: échec d'un dressage culturel*, Paris, 1990.

Gaxotte, Pierre, *Paris au XVIIIe siècle*, Paris, 1968.

Gay, Peter, *Enlightenment: An Interpretation. The Rise of Modern Paganism*, New York, 1966.

Genlis, Mme de, *Les dîners du Baron d'Holbach, etc.*, Paris, 1822.

Gillot, Hubert, *Les Jésuites contre l'Encyclopédie (1751–1752)*, Bulletin de la société historique et archéologique de Langres, 1951.

Gordon, Douglas H. and N. L. Torrey, *The Censoring of Diderot's Encyclopédie and the Reestablished Text*, New York, 1947.

Gougy-François, Marie, *Les Grands Salons Féminins*, Paris, 1965.

Grand, Serge, *Ces bonnes femmes du XVIIIᵉ siècle*, Paris, 1926.

Grimm, Friedrich Melchior, *Correspondance inédite*, Munich, 1972.

——, *Correspondance inédite de Grimm et de Diderot et recueil de lettres, poésies, morceaux et fragments retranchés par la censure impériale en 1812 et 1813*, Paris, 1829.

Grimm, Friedrich Melchior, Denis Diderot and Louise d'Épinay, *Correspondance littéraire, philosophicuqe et critique depuis 1753 jusqu'en 1790*, 15 vols, Paris, 1829.

Grimsley, Ronald, *Jean d'Alembert (1717–83)*, Oxford, 1963.

Grosclaude, Pierre, *Malesherbes témoin et interprète de son temps*, Paris, 1961.

——, *Malesherbes et l'Encyclopédie*, Paris, 1951.

——, *Un audacieux message: L'Encyclopédie*, Paris, 1951.

Haechler, Jean, *L'Encyclopédie: les combats et les hommes*, Paris, 1998.

——, *L'Encyclopédie de Diderot et de . . . Jaucourt: Essai biographique sur le chevalier Louis de Jaucourt*, Paris, 1995.

Hankins, Thomas L., *Jean d'Alembert. Science and the Enlightenment*, New York, 1990.

Harth, Dietrich and Martin Raether, *Denis Diderot oder die Ambivalenz der Aufklärung. Heidelberger Vortragsreihe zum Internationalen Diderot-Jahr 1984*, Würzburg, 1987.

Hellegouarc'h, Jacqueline, *L'Esprit de société – Cercles et salons au XVIIIᵉ siècle*, Paris, 2000.

Heller, Lane Murch, 'Diderot's Friend Melchior Grimm', abstracted in Dissertation Abstracts, vol. 19 (1959), no. 7, p. 1740, also microfilm (positive), Ann Arbor, Mich., University Microfilms [1959].

Hillairet, Jacques, *Connaissance du vieux Paris*, Paris, 1959.

Hubert, René, *D'Holbach et ses amis*, Paris, 1928.

——, *Rousseau et l'Encyclopédie*, Paris, n.d.

Kafker, Frank A. (ed.), *Notable Encyclopedias of the Seventeenth and Eighteenth Centuries*, Oxford, 1981.

——, and Gisele Loriot-Raymer (tr.) 'Les Traductions de l'Encyclopédie au XVIIIᵉ siecle: Quelle fut leur influence?', in *Recherches sur Diderot et sur l'Encyclopédie (RDidE)*, Paris, April 1992, vol. 12, pp. 165–73.

Kafker, Frank A., and Serena L., *The Encyclopedists as Individuals: A Biographical Dictionary of the Authors of the Encyclopédie*, Oxford, 1988.

——, *The Encyclopedists as a Group: A Collective Biography of the Authors of the Encyclopédie*, Oxford, 1996.

Kley, Dale K. van, *The Damiens Affair and the Unravelling of the Ancien Régime 1750–1770*, Princeton, New Jersey, 1984.

Koseki, Takeshi, 'Diderot et le confucianisme: Autour du terme Ju-kiao de l'article *Chinois (Philosophie des)', in *Recherches sur Diderot et sur l'Encyclopédie (RDidE)*, Paris, April 1994, vol. 16, pp. 125–31.

Kreiser, B. Robert, *Miracles, Convulsions and Ecclesiastical Politics in Early Eighteenth-Century Paris*, Princeton, 1978.

Idée de l'Oeuvre des Secours Selon les sentiments de ses légitimes Défenseurs, En France, [n.p.], 1781.

Ladd, E., 'Helvétius and d'Holbach. La Moralisation de la Politique', in *Journal of the History of Ideas* 23 (1961), pp. 221–38.

Laignel-Lavastine, Maxime, *Les Médecins collaborateurs de l'Encyclopédie*, Paris, 1951.

Leca-Tsiomis, Marie, *Écrire l'Encyclopédie: Diderot, de l'usage des dictionnaires à la grammaire philosophique*, Oxford, 1999.

Lepape, Pierre, *Diderot*, Paris, 1991.

Leroy, Maxime, *L'Encyclopédie et les Encyclopédistes*, Paris, 1951.

Le Roy Ladurie, Emmanuel, *L'Ancien Régime*, 2 vols, Paris, 1991.

Lesure, François (ed.), *Querelle des gluckistes et des piccinistes*, Genève, 1984.

Liger, L., *Le Voyageur Fidele – Le guide des voyageurs dans la ville de Paris*, Paris, 1715.

Louette, Patricia, 'Madame de Tencin (1682–1749). Quelques aspects de la singularité féminine chez Mme de Tencin: les coulisses de la vertu', in Shirley Jones Day (ed.), *Writers and Heroines: Essays on Women in French Literature*, Berne, Berlin, Frankfurt, New York, Paris, and Vienna, 1999

Lough, John, *The Contributors to the 'Encyclopédie'*, London, 1973.

——, *The Encyclopédie*, Geneva, 1989.

——, 'Helvétius and Holbach', in *Modern Language Review*, 33 (1933), pp. 360–84.

——, 'Le Breton, Mills et Sellius', in *Dix-huitième Siècle*, i (1969), pp. 276–87.

——, 'Louis, Chevalier de Jaucourt (1704–1780). A Biographical Sketch', in *Essays Presented to C. M. Girdlestone*, Newcastle upon Tyne, 1960.

——, 'Luneau de Boisjermain v. the Publishers of the Encyclopédie', in *Studies on Voltaire and the Eighteenth Century*, 23 (1963), pp. 115–77.

Marie, Catherine-Laurence, *Les Convulsionnaires de Saint-Médard – miracles, convulsions et prophéties à Paris au XVIIIᵉ siècle*, Paris, 1985.

Mason, Amelia Gere, *The Women of the French Salons*, New York, 1891.

Mason, John Hope, *The Irresistible Diderot*, London and New York, 1982.

Mass, Edgar, and Peter-Eckhard Knabe, *L'Encyclopédie et Diderot*, Cologne, 1985.

Masson, Pierre-Henri, *Madame de Tencin*, Paris, 1909 .

May, Louis Philippe, 'Histoire et sources de l'*Encyclopédie d'après le registre de délibérations et de comptes des éditeurs et un mémoire inédit*', Paris, 1938 ; also in *Revue de Synthèse*, 1938.

Mercier, Louis Sébastien, *Tableau de Paris*, (2 vols, Neuchâtel, 1782–88) in *Paris le Jour, Paris la Nuit*, ed. Michel Delon, Paris, 1990.

Michel, Marie-José (ed.), *Jansénisme et Paris. 1640–1730*, Paris [n.d.].

Minard, Philippe, *Typographes des Lumières*, Seyssel, 1989.

Morellet, André, Abbé, *Mémoires de l'abbé Morellet*, ed. Jean-Pierre Guicciardi, Paris, 2000.

[Morellet, André], *Mémoire pour Abraham Chaumeix, contre les prétendus philosophes Diderot et d'Alembert*, Amsterdam [Paris], 1759.

Morley, John, *Diderot and the Encyclopaedists*, 2 vols, London, 1923.

Morris, Madeleine F., *Le Chevalier de Jaucourt, un ami de la terre*, Geneva, 1979.

Mortier, Roland, and Raymond Trousson (eds), *Dictionnaire de Diderot*, Paris, 1999.

Naumann, Manfred: 'Holbach und das Materialismusproblem in der französischen Aufklärung', in Werner Krauss and Hans Mayer (eds), *Grundpositionen der französischen Aufklärung*, Berlin, 1955, pp. 83–128.

Naigeon, Jacques-André, *Mémoires historiques et philosophiques sur la vie et les ouvrages de Diderot*, Paris, 1821.

Naville, Pierre, *D'Holbach et la philosophie scientifique au XVIIIᵉ siècle*, Paris 1943.

Nemeitz, J. C., *Sejour de Paris, c'est à dire, Instructions de fidèles pour les voiageurs de conditions, comment ils se doivent conduire, s'ils veulent faire un bon usare de leur temps & argent, durant leur Séjour à Paris*, Leiden, 1727.

O'Dea, Michael, 'Rousseau contre Rameau: Musique et nature dans les articles pour l'Encyclopédie et au-dela', in *Recherches sur Diderot et sur l'Encyclopédie (RDidE)*, Paris, October 1994, vol. 17, pp. 133–48.

Pallisot de Montenoy, Charles, *Petites lettres sur les grands philosophes*, Paris, 1757.

——, *Les Philosophes, comédie en trois actes en vers*, Paris, 1760.

——, *La Dunciade*, Chelsea, 1764.

Perey, Lucien and Gaston Maugras, *L'Abbé F. Galiani – Correspondance*, Paris, 1881.

Pinault, Madeleine, 'Les Metamorphoses des planches de

l'Encyclopédie: Quelques Exemples', in *Recherches sur Diderot et sur l'Encyclopédie* (*RDidE*), Paris, April 1992, vol. 12, pp. 99–112.

Pons, A. (ed.), *Encyclopédie ou Dictionnaire raisonné des Sciences, des Arts et des Métiers, 1751–1772*, Paris, 1963.

Proust, Jacques, *Diderot et l'Encyclopédie*, Paris, 1967.

——, 'La Documentation technique de Diderot dans l'*Encyclopédie*', in *Revue d'histoire littéraire*, 1957.

——, 'Diderot, l'Académie de Pétersbourg et le projet d'une *Encyclopédie* russe', *Diderot Studies XII*.

——, *L'Encyclopédie*, Paris, 1965.

——, *L'Encyclopédie de Diderot et de d'Alembert, planches et commentaires*, Paris, 1985.

——, 'L'image du peuple au travail dans les planches de l'Encyclopédie,' in *Images du peuple au dix-neuvième siècle*, Paris, 1973.

Rapp, Sigrid Mann, *Das Werk des Enzyklopädisten Louis de Jaucourt*, Inaug. Diss, Tübingen, 1965.

Recueil des miracles opérés au tombeau de M. De Paris Diacre, Paris 1731.

Roche, Daniel, *Les Français et l'Ancien Régime*, 2 vols, Paris, 1993.

——, *Les Républicains des Lettres, gens de culture et Lumières au XVIIIe siècle*, Paris, 1988.

——, *La France des Lumières*, Paris, 1993.

——, *Histoire des choses banales. Naissance de la Société de consommation, XVIIIe–XIXe siècle*, Paris, 1997.

——, *Le Peuple de Paris. Essai sur la culture populaire au XVIIIe siècle*, 2nd edn, Paris, 1998.

—— and V. Ferrone, *Le Monde des Lumières*, Paris, 1999.

—— and G. Chabaud, J.-F. Dubost, S. Juratic, M. Milliot, and J. M. Roy, *La Ville promise. Mobilité et accueil à Paris (fin XVIIe–début XIXe siècle)*, Paris, 2000.

——, 'Lumières et engagement politique: la coterie d'Holbach dévoilée', in *Annales E.S.C.*, XXXIII/4, 1978, pp. 720–8.

——, 'Lumières et maçonnerie', in *Histoire de la Franc-Maçonnerie en France*, Toulouse, 1981, pp. 97–116.

——, 'L'eau, du XVIe au XIXe siècle', in *Bulletin de la Société d'Histoire Moderne et Contemporaine*, no. 13, 1982, pp. 137–142.

Rogister, John, *Louis XV and the Parlement of Paris, 1737–55*, Cambridge, 2002.

Rousseau, Jean-Jacques, *Les Confessions*, 2 vols, Paris, 1998.

Russell, Terence M., and Ann-Marie Ashworth, *Architecture in the*

Encyclopédie of Diderot and d'Alembert: The Letterpress Articles and Selected Engravings, Aldershot, 1993.

Roussin, Philippe (ed.), *Critique et affaires de blasphème à l'époque des Lumières*, Paris, 1998.

Ru, Veronique Le, *Jean Le Rond d'Alembert philosophe*, Paris, 1994.

Scherer, Edmond, *Melchior Grimm: L'homme de lettres, le factotum – le diplomate*, (1887) reprinted Geneva, 1968.

Schmitt, Eric-Emmanuel, *Diderot ou la philosophie de la séduction*, Paris, 1997.

Schwab, Richard N., 'The Extent of the Chevalier de Jaucourt's Contribution to Diderot's *Encyclopédie*', in *Modern Language Notes*, 1957.

——, 'Un Encyclopédiste huguenot: le chevalier de Jaucourt', *Bulletin de la Société de l'Histoire du Protestantisme français*, 1962.

——, W. Rex and John Lough, *Inventory of Diderot's Encyclopédie*, Geneva, Banbury and Oxford (*Studies on Voltaire and the Eighteenth Century* 80, 83, 85, 91, 93, 223), 1971–86.

Selg, Anette and Rainer Wieland (eds), *Die Welt der Enzyklopädie*, Frankfurt, 2001.

Shackleton, R., 'The *Encyclopédie* and Freemasonry', in *The Age of Enlightenment: Studies Presented to Theodore Besterman*, Edinburgh, 1967.

Simowitz, Amy Cohen, *Theory of Art in the 'Encyclopédie'*, Ann Arbor, Mich., 1983.

Smiley, Joseph Royall, *Diderot's Relations with Grimm*, Urbana, 1950.

Steegmuller, Francis, *A Woman, a Man, and Two Kingdoms: The Story of Madame D'Épinay and the Abbé Galiani*, New York, 1991.

Stewart, Philip 'Illustration encyclopediques: De la Cyclopaedia à l'*Encyclopédie*', in *Recherches sur Diderot et sur l'Encyclopédie (RDidE)*, Paris, April 1992, vol. 12, pp. 71–98.

Storez, Isabelle, *Le Chancelier Henri François d'Aguesseau, monarchiste et libéral*, Paris, 1996.

Thelliez, Berthe, *L'Homme qui poignarda Louis XV – Robert François Damien (1715–1757)*, Paris, 2002.

Trousson, Raymond, *Jean-Jacques Rousseau – Mémoire de la critique*, Paris, 2000.

Vandeul, Angélique de, *Diderot, mon père* (1787), reprinted Strassbourg, 1992.

Venturi, Franco, *Le Origini dell'Enciclopedia*, Florence, 1963.

——, *La Jeunesse de Diderot, 1716–1753*, Paris, 1939.

Vidal, Daniel, *Miracles et convulsions jansénistes au xviiie siècle – le mal et sa connaissance*, Paris, 1987.

Viguerie, Jean de, *Histoire et dictionnaire du temps des Lumières*, Paris, 1995.

Vissiere, Jean-Louis, *La Secte des Empoisonneurs – Polemiques autour de l'Encyclopédie de Diderot et d'Alembert*, Aix-en-Provence, 1993.

Voltaire, *Correspondance*, ed. Theodore Besterman, 107 vols, Geneva, 1953–66.

——, *Histoire du Parlement de Paris par M. l'abbé Big*, Amsterdam, 1769.

Vovelle, Michel (ed. and intro.), *Mourir autrefois: attitudes collectives devant la mort aux XVIIe et XVIIIe siècle*, Paris, 1990.

Williams, E. N., *The Ancien Régime in Europe: Government and Society in the Major States 1648–1789*, London, 1970, 1999.

Wilson, Arthur M., *Diderot*, Oxford, 1972.

——, 'Why Did the Political Theory of the Encyclopedists Not Prevail?: A Suggestion', in *French Historical Studies*, vol. 1, no. 3 (Spring, 1960), pp. 283–94.

Young-Mock, Lee, 'Diderot et la lutte parlementaire au temps de l'*Encyclopédie* (deuxième partie)', in *Recherches sur Diderot et sur l'Encyclopédie*, April 2001, vol. 30, pp. 93–126.

NOTES

BN   Bibliothèque Nationale
Corr. litt. Correspondance littéraire

1 On the library of Assurbanipal, and other cuneiform compendia,
   see *Tous les savoirs du monde*, pp. 27ff. See also Jean Bottéro,
   Mésopotamie: l'écriture, la raison et les dieux, Paris, 1987; Antoine
   Cavigneaux, 'Lexikalische Listen', in *Reallexikon der Assyriologie*, vi,
   Berlin and New York, 1980–3, pp. 609–41; K. R. Veenhof, *Cuneiform
   Archives and Libraries*, Istanbul, 1986.
2 Ibid., p. 35.
3 On Pliny and other Roman encyclopedists, see P. Howe, 'In defense
   of the encyclopedic method. On Pliny's preface to the Natural
   History', in *Latomus* XLIV (1983), pp. 561–76; R. French and F.
   Greenaway (eds), *Science in the Early Roman Empire. Pliny the Elder, his
   Sources and Influence*, London, 1986; H. L. Bonniec, *Bibliographie de
   l'Histoire Naturelle de Pline l'Ancien*, Paris, 1946.
4 See Jonathan Spence, *The Memory Palace of Matteo Ricci*, London,
   1985.
5 On Chinese encyclopedias in general, see J.-P. Diény, 'Les
   encyclopédies chinoises', in *L'encyclopédisme*, pp. 195–200.
6 On Islamic encyclopedism, see Mounira Chapoutot-Remadi,
   'L'encyclopédie arabe au xe siècle', in *L'encyclopédisme*, pp. 37–47; Al
   Samman, Tarif, 'Arabische Enzyklopädie und Bibliographie' in *Die
   Arabische Welt und Europa: Ausstellung der Handschriften- und
   Ikunabelsammlung der Österreichischen Nationalbibliothek, 20. Mai–16.
   Oktober 1988*, ed. Tarif Al Samman and Otto Mazal, 219–24, Graz,
   ADEVA, 1988; J. V. Hammer-Purgstall, *Über die Encyklopädie der
   Araber, Perser und Türken*, Wien, 1857; Charles Pellat, 'Les

encyclopédies dans le monde arabe', *Cahiers d'histoire mondiale* 9 (1966), 631–58.

7 Isidore's work is well discussed in Carmen Codoner, 'De L'Antiquité au Moyen Age: Isidore de Séville' in *L'Encyclopédisme*, pp. 19–36; also Ernest Brehaut, *An Encyclopedist of the Dark Ages: Isidore of Seville*, New York, 2001.

8 See *Toutes les Savoirs du Monde*, p. 57.

9 On the medieval encyclopedic culture, see also E. D. Sylla, *The Cultural Context of Medieval Learning*, Dordrecht, 1975; Maria Teresa Fumagalli Beoni-Brochieri, *Le Enciclopedie medievali*, Torino, 1981.

10 The school of Saint-Victor was perhaps the most important encyclopedic movement of the Middle Ages. See Jean Longere, *L'abbaye Saint-Victor de Paris au Moyen Âge*, Brepols, 1991.

11 For a more detailed description and for further literature, see Philipp Blom, *To Have and to Hold: An Intimate History of Collectors and Collecting*, London, 2002.

12 The etymology of the word is a matter of some dispute, especially since there is only one classical reference for the Greek form of the word, Quintillian's *Institutio Oratoria* (I, x, 1). The original Greek *enkiklios* appears to mean 'what is current, popular, in daily usage', while the Latin author already translates it as 'the realm of teachings'. *Paideia* were things taught to children, or simply subjects taught. A brief discussion of this can be found in *Tous les savoirs du monde*, p. 19.

13 Ibid.

14 A good overview of Bacon and Leibniz is Walter Tega, 'Encyclopédie et untié du savoir de Bacon à Leibniz', in *L'encyclopédisme*, pp. 69–96. The encyclopedic thought of Leibniz is of great importance, but cannot be discussed here. See Couturat, Louis, *La Logique de Leibniz d'apres des documents inédits*, Paris, 1901.

15 The classic analysis of this is Leon Bernard's beautifully written *The Emerging City*, a pleasure in itself.

16 An unrivalled account of living conditions in eighteenth-century Paris is Daniel Roche's *Le peuple de Paris*.

17 Roche, p. 289.

18 Frank A. Kafker (ed.), *Notable Encyclopedias of the Seventeenth and Eighteenth Centuries: Nine Predecessors of the Encyclopédie*, Oxford, 1981, p. 8. For an exhaustive general introduction to the topic, see also Robert Collison, *Encyclopedias: Their History Throughout the Ages*, New York and London, 1966.

19 It is hardly surprising that the Encyclopedists sympathized strongly

with a man who had not only been a forerunner for their own
adventure but had also been a critical mind committed to serious
enquiry, flirting with atheism, and living in exile in the Netherlands.
Unable to declare their admiration openly, they were reduced to
admiring mentions in articles within the *Encyclopédie*, such as in
ANALYSE, where his work is called 'a model of impartiality' (which
it certainly was not), and, in a lengthy passage devoted to his
writings in ATHÉE, which lauds the 'force and clarity ... vivacity and
subtlety' of his consideration of atheism and his defence of the
faith, a welcome ploy for the article's author, the less than orthodox
abbé Yvon, to explore the ins and outs of arguments against
religion. Bayle was a fascinating figure indeed. See J.-M. Gros,
'Bayle: de la tolérance à la liberté de conscience', in *Les fondements
philosophiques de la tolerance*; Hrg. Y. C. Zarka, F. Lessay, J. Rogers,
Paris, PUF, 2002, vol. 1, SS. 295–311; R. C. Bartlett, 'On the Politics
of Faith and Reason: The Project of Enlightenment in Pierre Bayle
and Montesquieu', *Journal of Politics*, 1 (2001), pp. 1–28; I. Dingel,
'Zwischen Orthodoxie und Aufklärung. Pierre Bayles
Historisch-Kritisches Wörterbuch im Umbruch der Epochen',
Zeitschrift für Kirchengeschichte, 110 (1999), pp. 229–46; T. M.
Lennon, *Reading Bayle*, Toronto, 1999.

20 See Jean Macary, 'Les dictionnaires universels de Furetiere et de
Trévoux, et l'esprit encyclopédique moderne avant l'Encyclopédie'
in *Diderot Studies*, XVI (1973), pp. 145–58. The history of
encyclopedias of the period is very authoritatively analyzed in Frank
Kafker's *Notable Encyclopedias of the Seventeenth and Eighteenth Centuries*.

21 There is surprisingly little research on this important and ambitous
work. See Bernhard Kossmann, 'Deutsche Universallexika des 18.
Jahrhunderts. Ihr Wesen und ihr Informationswert, dargestellt am
Beispiel der Werke von Jablonski und Zedler', in *Börsenblatt für den
Deutschen Buchhandel* 24/89 (1968), pp. 2946–69.

22 Chambers, *Cyclopaedia*, p. 1.

Paris, 1739

1 Reliable estimates of the population of Paris are hard to come by,
especially as city borders were not always clearly defined and the
numbers of citizens permanently resident in the city and of people
seeking a livelihood there and drifting in and out as beggars,
domestic servants, seasonal workers, day labourers, etc., are likely to

have differed considerably. In 1806, the first official census put the number of inhabitants at 580,609. For the preceding century, contemporary estimates vary between 436,000 for 1714 (Dénombrement Fiscal) and 800,000 for the following year (de Fleury). It is likely, however, that during the eighteenth century the population steadily increased from some 560,000 in the 1740s to around 650,000 just before the Revolution, when state terror and lack of food supplies caused many to flee abroad or to the provinces and the population of the city fell by some 100,000. See Roche, *Le peuple de Paris*, pp. 27–34.

2 J. C. Nemeitz, *Sejour de Paris, c'est à dire, Instructions de fidéles pour les voiageurs de conditions, comment ils se doivent conduire, s'ils veulent faire un bon usage de leur temps & argent, durant leur Séjour à Paris*, Leiden, 1727, pp. 53–4.

3 Mercier, *Tableau de Paris*, p. 55.

4 This case is recounted in Leon Bernard's excellent *The Emerging City*, pp. 36–7.

5 Cardinal Richelieu, in Boris Porchnev, *Les soulèvements populaires en France de 1623 à 1648*, Paris, 1963, p. 559.

6 This enumeration of competences is from Bernard, *The Emerging City*, p. 44.

7 Mercier, *Tableau de Paris*, p. 57. Mercier may overestimate the number of water carriers, but the basic situation was exactly as he described. See also Simon Lacordaire, *Sources et fontaines de Paris*, Paris, 1979.

8 Nemeitz, *Sejour à Paris*, pp. 475–6.

9 Ibid., p. 440.

10 Ibid., p. 408.

11 Mercier, *Tableau de Paris*, p. 47.

12 Nemeitz, *Sejour à Paris*, p. 116.

13 Ibid., p. 117.

14 Mercier, *Tableau de Paris*, p. 46.

15 Ibid., p. 118.

16 Mercier, *Tableau de Paris*, p. 199.

17 Some data here is from Darnton, etc., on numbers of book trade.

18 N. Contat, quoted in P. Minard, *Typographes des Lumières*, p. 150.

Friendship

1 Mercier: *Tableau de Paris*, p. 32.

2 James Boswell, *Life of Samuel Johnson, LL.D.*, Oxford, 1904, p. 206.

In a rare act of literary kindness by the city fathers, the street was renamed Milton Street in 1830. For Darnton on Grub Street, see Darnton, *The Literary Underground of the Old Regime, The Great Cat Massacre*, etc.

3 Nemeitz, *Séjour à Paris*, p. 139.

4 Denis Diderot, *Jacques le fataliste*, quoted in Wilson, p. 20.

5 Diderot's Paris school career is, in fact, unclear. There are indications for both the Collège Louis-le-Grand and the Collège de Harcourt, as well as for two others, the Collège de Bourgogne and the Collège de Beauvais. Arthur Wilson thinks that it is unlikely Diderot attended only one school. He might have changed, or spent most of his time at one to attend some lectures at another. In view of his Jesuit upbringing in Langres, Diderot's extreme piety around 1727, which made him try to run away and join the Jesuits, the fact that his father took him to Paris himself, and in view of the ideological compatibility between the Jesuit Collège Louis-le-Grand and the Jansenist Collège de Harcourt, it is highly probable that Diderot initially entered a Jesuit establishment in Paris; it is extremely unlikely that he went to the Collège de Harcourt with the blessing of his Jesuit teachers. The nineteenth-century French historian of philosophy Damiron, incidentally, thinks that Diderot *père*'s aversion to the Jesuits made him enter his son at the Collège de Harcourt immediately. It may, however, be the case that the Diderot's sympathies began to wander from one faction to the other during his schooling, and that his attending the Collège de Harcourt (for which his daughter is the principal witness) is the expression of this change of heart, whether it was actually full-time membership or not. See Louis-François Marcel, 'Diderot écolier', *RHLF*, xxxiv, pp. 396–9; Ralph Bowen, 'The Education of an Encyclopedist', *Teachers of History: Essays in Honor of Laurence Bradford Packard*, Ithaca, NY, 1954, pp. 33–9; Wilson, *Diderot*, pp. 25–6, 725; Jean-Philibert Damiron, *Mémoires sur Diderot*, 6 vols, 1852–7, i, p. 7.

6 For an authoritative treatment of Jansen and the beginnings of Jansenism, see William R. Newton, *Port-Royal and Jansenism: Social Experience, Group Formation, and Religious Attitudes in 17th-Century France*, 3 vols, Michigan, 1974.

7 Naigeon, *Mémoires*, p. 8.

8 Vandeul, *Diderot*, pp. 11–14; this translation is in Wilson, *Diderot*, p. 28.

9 Diderot, *Œuvres*, iv, p. 1407; this translation is in Wilson, *Diderot*, p. 30–1.

10 Ibid., v, p. 83, tr. PB.

11 Rousseau, *Confessions*, p. 28, tr. Mallory.

12 Diderot, *Œuvres*, iv, pp. 730–1. Actually, Diderot spent twenty-six years on the *Encyclopédie*.

13 Diderot, *Œuvres*, v, pp. 12–13.

14 Vandeul, *Diderot, mon père*, p. 23.

15 Ibid., translation in Furbank, *Diderot*, p. 42.

16 Joseph Bertrand, *D'Alembert*, p. 9.

17 Ibid., p. 29.

18 This kind of word game is very probably exactly how the young François Marie Arouet chose his pen name, Voltaire: *Arovet LI*eune.

19 Reference Flaubert

20 A.-T., I, p. 16

21 Quoted in Furbank, *Diderot*, p. 28.

22 Diderot, *Oeuvres*, i, p. 20.

23 Ibid., p. 21.

24 Ibid., p. 37.

25 Rousseau, *Confessions*, p. 118.

26 Marmontel, quoted in Damiron, *Mémoires sur d'Alembert*, p. 12–13.

Project

1 *Mémoire pour Pierre-Joseph François Luneau de Boisjermain, Suscripteur de l'Encyclopédie*, Paris, 1771, pp. 8–9. As John Lough points out (*The Encyclopédie*, p. 11), there is no surviving copy of the original court summons.

2 *Mémoires secrets pour servir à l'histoire de la République des Lettres en France de 1762 jusqu'à nos jours*, London, 1777–89, 36 vols, iii, p. 198.

3 Louis-Gabriel Michaud, *Biographie universelle ancienne et moderne*, Paris, 1843, 45 vols, vol. xxx, p. xxx ; this quote originally from Meusnier de Querlon.

4 Mills to the Revd Thomas Birch, quoted in F. Venturi, 'Le Origini dell'Enciclopedia in Inghliterra', *Itinerari*, 1954, pp. 217–18.

5 This is the opinion of Arthur Wilson in his magisterial Diderot biography (p. 78). It is quite possible that Diderot became involved at this early stage. He was, after all, already known as a translator from the English and had published one translation with Briasson, one of Le Breton's future partners in the enterprise.

6 *Mémoire pour Pierre-Joseph François Luneau*, pp. 5–6.

7 *Mémoire pour André-François Le Breton . . . Contre le Sieur Jean Mills, se disant Gentilhomme Anglais*, Paris, 1745, p. 2.

8 The contractual details of the publication of the *Encyclopédie* are collected in L. P. May's 'Histoire et sources de l'*Encyclopédie*'. See also Lough, *The Encyclopédie*, p. 13.

9 Marie Jean Antoine Nicolas de Caritat Condorcet, 'Eloge de M. l'abbé de Gua', in *Œuvres de Condorcet*, ed. A. Condorcet O'Connor and M. F. Arago, Paris, 1847–9, 12 vols, iii, pp. 241–58.

10 Jacques André Naigeon, *Mémoires sur la vie et les Œuvres de Diderot*, Paris, 1823, p. 45.

11 Quoted in L. P. May, pp. 18–20.

12 L. P. May, 'Histoire et sources', p. 18.

13 *Lettres de M. de Voltaire, avec plusieurs pièces de différents auteurs*, The Hague, 1738, p. 60–2. On Ramsay himself, see also Daniel Ligou, 'Le chevalier de Ramsay, précurseru de l'*Encyclopédie* ou aventurier religieux', in Anne Becq (ed.), *L'Encyclopédisme*, pp. 169–182.

14 Condorcet, 'Eloge', pp. 247–8. This translation is taken from Arthur Wilson, *Diderot*, p. 79.

15 Quoted in Morley, *Diderot and the Encyclopédie*, p. 73.

16 Quoted by P. Bonnefon, 'Diderot prisonnier à Vincennes', in *Revue d'Histoire littéraire de la France*, vi (1899), p. 203, translation in Furbank, *Diderot*, p. 47.

17 The alphabetical order was one of the most hotly contested characteristics of the *Encyclopédie*. See Jean Ehrard, 'De Diderot à Panckoucke: duex pratiques de l'alphabet' (pp. 243–52) and Charles Porset, 'L'*Encyclopédie* et la question de l'ordre: réflexions sur la lexicalisation des conaissances au xviii^c siècle' (pp. 253–65), both in Anne Becq, *L'Encyclopédisme*.

18 Rousseau, *Confessions*, ii, p. 119.

19 On the plates in the *Encyclopédie*, see Madeleine Pinault, *Les planches de l'Encyclopédie*, Paris, 1972. Also by the same author: 'Sur les planches de l'*Encyclopédie*' in Anne Becq (ed.), *L'Encyclopedisme*, pp. 355–64.

20 Chrétien-Guillaume Lamoignon de Malesherbes, *Mémoire sur la liberté de la presse*, Paris, 1814, p. 89, translation in Wilson, *Diderot*, p. 82. In his *Diderot* (p. 81), Arthur Wilson is of the opinion that the meeting is likely to have taken place in early 1748, as Diderot was obviously chosen to represent the *Encyclopédie*. If one is to believe Malesherbes that d'Aguesseau sent for Diderot, however, it seems more likely that the meeting took place earlier.

21 Location of the privilege. The mention of Harris indicates that John Harris's *Lexicon technicum or a Universal English dictionary of arts and sciences* (London, 1736) was originally intended to deliver further articles.

22 Bibliothèque Nationale, MSS, Fr. 22191, fo. 22, translation in Wilson, *Diderot*, p. 82.

23 Maurice Tourneux, *Un Factum inconnu de Diderot*, Paris, 1901, p. 40, translation in Wilson, *Diderot*, p. 82.

Prison

1 Diderot, *Œuvres*, i, p. 141.

2 Wilson, *Diderot*, p. 97.

3 Diderot, *Œuvres*, i, p. 169.

4 Diderot, *Œuvres*, v, p. 13.

5 Ibid. p. 15.

6 Diderot, *Œuvres*, v, p. 17.

7 Ibid.

8 L. P. May, *Documents nouveaux*, p. 52.

9 Bibliothèque de l'Arsenal, Archives de la Bastille 11671, f. 8.

10 Diderot, *Œuvres*, v, pp. 20–1.

11 Bonnefon, 'Diderot prisonnier', p. 216, translation in Wilson, p. 108.

12 Bonnefon, ibid., pp. 217–18.

13 Rousseau, *Confessions*, p. 120.

14 Ibid., pp. 124–5.

15 Ibid., p. 124.

16 Ibid., p. 126.

17 *Corr. litt.*, p. 53.

18 Ibid., p. 55.

19 J. H. S. Formey, *Souveniers d'un Citoyen*, Berlin, 1789, 2 vols, ii, pp. 365–6.

20 For the treatment of writers during this period, see Lepape, *Diderot*, p. 88.

Philosophe

1 Rousseau, *Confessions*, ii, p. 135.

2 J. W. von Goethe, *Autobiography*, tr. J. Oxenford, 2 vols, Chicago, 1975, ii, p. 106.

3 Rousseau, *Confessions*, ii, p. 151.

4 *Corr. litt.*, pp. 17–19.
5 Wilson, *Diderot*, p. 119.
6 Diderot, *Œuvres*, v, p. 159.
7 Ibid., p. 163.
8 *Corr. litt.*, p. 160.
9 Lough, *The Encyclopédie*, p. 20.
10 Diderot, *Prospectus*, quoted in Wilson, *Diderot*, pp. 4–5.
11 Ibid., pp. 6–7.
12 *Encyclopédie*, ame, fo.
13 Diderot, *Œuvres*, i, p. 42.

Controversy

1 All the following quotes are in *Annonces affiches et avis divers*, May–December 1751, Paris, 1751, pp. 101–5.
2 Diderot, *Œuvres*, v, p. 22.
3 *Journal de Trévoux*, 1 February 1751, p. 577.
4 *Discours Preliminaire.*
5 Psalms 14:1, 53:1.
6 On this scholastic dispute, see Nicholas Wolterstorff, 'In Defense of Gaunilo's Defense of the Fool', in C. Stephen Evans and Merold Westphal, (eds), *Christian Perspectives on Religious Knowledge*, Grand Rapids, MI, 1993.
7 *Encyclopédie*, i.
8 Ibid., i, p. xxxiii.
9 Venturi, *Origini*, 57, 59–60, translation in Wilson, *Diderot*.
10 Diderot, *Œuvres*, v, p. 26.
11 Coyecque, *Inventaire de la collection Anisson*, i, pp. xcvii–xcviii.
12 BN, Fr. 22139, fo. 94.
13 *Journal de Trévoux*, November 1751, pp. 2419–57.
14 Ibid., March 1752, p. 468n.
15 Pierre Clément, *Cinq Années Littéraires*, Berlin, 1755, iii. pp. 164–5.

Play of Nature

1 There is very little biographical material on Louis de Jaucourt, and not even a portrait has survived. By far the best biography is Jean Haechler's *L'Encyclopédie de Diderot et . . . Jaucourt*, from which this information is taken.
2 BPUG Arch., Tr. 210, p. 7.
3 Ibid.

4 Ibid.
5 L. de Neufville, *La vie de Mr Leibniz*, Amsterdam, 1734, p. 57.
6 Boswell, *Life of Johnson*.
7 AN, 86 AP6, p. 39.
8 BPUG, Arch. Tr., pp. 211, 265.
9 Voltaire, *Correspondance*, tome II, pp. 830, 837.
10 Raymond de Montmort, 28 December 1738, Archives Micheli, Jussy & Voltaire, C. 6919.
11 Durcos, *Les Encyclopédistes*, p. 123. This beautiful story is also cited in Wilson, *Diderot*, p. 145.
12 *Corr. litt.*, p. 86.
13 *Journal de Sçavants*, September 1751, pp. 625–6, translation in Arthur Wilson, *Diderot*, p. 152.
14 Quoted in Lough, *The Encyclopédie*, p. 32.
15 See Frank Kafker, *The Encyclopedists as a Group*, p. 87.
16 Camille Daux, 'Une Réhabilitation: l'Abbé Jean-Martin de Prades', in *Science Catholique*, xvi (1901–2), pp. 1025–39, 1095–1109, this quotation p. 1097.
17 *Mandement de Monseigneur l'Evéque de Montauban, portant condamnation d'une these*, Montauban, 1752, p. 3, translation in Wilson, *Diderot*, p. 156.
18 *Nouvelles Ecclesiastiques*, 27 February 1752, p. 35.
19 D'Argenson, *Journal et mémoires*, 7 vols, vii, p. 110, this translation in Wilson, *Diderot*, p. 160.
20 Grimm, certainly no impartial observer, was convinced of it, but others, including Edmond Barbier, believed the same. See also Cazes, *Grimm*, p. 66.
21 Barbier, v, p. 151.
22 Malzesherbes, *Mémoire sur la liberté de la presse*, p. 90.
23 Ibid., p. 91.
24 BN MSS, Fr. 22177, fo. 54, translation in Wilson, *Diderot*, p. 159.
25 D'Argenson, *Journal et mémoires*, vii, pp. 106, 122 ; Barbier, *Journal*, iii, p. 355.
26 Barbier, v, p. 153, January 1752.
27 *Corr. litt.*, ii, 15 November 1753, p. 298.
28 D'Argenson, *Journal et mémoires*, vii, pp. 223–4.
29 Voltaire, *Correspondance*, ed. Moland, xxxvii, p. 471–2, 24 August 1752.
30 Formey, *Souvenirs d'un Citoyen*, ii, p. 49.
31 Diderot, *Œuvres*, i, p. 552.

The War of Fools

1 Morellet, *Mémoires*, i, p. 134.
2 Naigeon, quoted in Cushing, *Baron d'Holbach*, p. 14.
3 Morellet, *Mémoires*, Paris, 1821, pp. 128–9.
4 Ibid., p. 150.
5 Ibid., pp. 150–1.
6 Rousseau, *Confessions*, ii, pp. 152–3.
7 Rousseau, *Confessions*, ii, pp. 172–3
8 Grimm, *Petit prophète*, p. 7.
9 Denise Launay (ed.), *La Querelle des Bouffons*, 3 vols, Paris, 1973, iii, pp. 2216–17, translation in Cranston, *Jean-Jacques*, p. 278.
10 Launay, *La Querelle*, i, pp. 678–9.
11 Rousseau, *Confessions*, ii, p.163.
12 R. A. Leigh (ed.), *Correspondance complète de Jean-Jacques Rousseau*, Geneva, Banbury and Oxford, 1965, pp. 197–8.
13 Rousseau, *Confessions*, ii, p. 154.
14 Marmontel, *Œuvres complètes*, Paris, 1819, i, p. 200.
15 Rousseau, *Confessions*, ii, pp. 176–7.
16 D'Holbach, published in the *Journal de Paris*, Supplement to No. 336, 2 December 1789, pp. 1567–8, translation in Wilson, *Diderot*, p. 182.

Encyclopédie

1 The most thorough and authoritative analysis of the social composition of the Encyclopedists is still Jacques Proust's *Diderot et L'Encyclopédie*, on which the following is based.
2 See Proust, *Diderot et l'Encyclopédie*, p. 23.
3 Some authors, notably John Lough (*Encyclopédie*, pp. 274–7, *passim*), have attacked the Encyclopedists for being weak on political thought because of their constant recourse to earlier authorities. This view seems strangely unhistorical. Surely it was, given the conditions of the time, a very cunning strategem to disseminate and elaborate the theories of thinkers who might not otherwise have been so widely read and at the same time protect the *Encyclopédie* from further criticism by hiding behind these revered authorities. Any other course of action would have been almost suicidal.
4 Wilson, *Diderot*, p. 235.
5 Sébastien Vauban, *Projet d'une dîme royale*, Paris, 1707.
6 On this debate as held outside the *Encyclopédie*, see Henry Higgs,

The Physiocrats – Six Lectures on the French Economistes of the 18th Century, London, 1897.

Love of the Sexes

1 Mme d'Épinay, *Histoire de Madame de Montbrillant*, p. 99. The situation surrounding Mme d'Épinay's autobiographical novel is somewhat clouded. It was edited in the early nineteenth century and published in 1818 under the title *Mémoires de Madame d'Épinay*, presumably to cash in on the fashion for memoirs. This edition, though, was a heavily edited version of her own epistolary novel. The names she had changed were changed back to the original protagonists and some of the letters were taken out altogether and linked with explanatory passages so that the result cannot be said to be the work of Mme d'Épinay at all. A version faithful to the original manuscript only appeared in 1951.

2 Mme d'Épinay, original source?, quoted in Steegmuller, *A Woman, a Man*, p. 6.

3 Mme d'Épinay, *Mémoires de Mme Montbrillant*, i, p. 290.

4 Mme d'Épinay, *Les moments heureux*, 1758.

5 Mme d'Épinay, *Mémoires de Mme Montbrillant*, i, p. 733.

6 Ibid., p. 731.

7 Mme d'Épinay, *Historie de Mme de Montbrillant*, ii, pp. 650–1.

8 The question whether or not Grimm got into a sword fight defending the honour of a lady he had only met socially is by no means easy to resolve. If he already felt more than a passing interest in Mme d'Épinay, perhaps for the first time when speaking up for her as one of his drinking companions chose to slander her, it is possible that he indeed drew his sword to appear as a knight in shining armour and found himself facing a man who is described as 'an officer in foreign service' and who would certainly have killed him if he had been less drunk. Grimm himself was known for his use of a quill rather than the epée; but, on the other hand, his pining for Mlle Fel (from which he had only just recovered) shows that he went to considerable lengths where his own emotions were concerned.

The mere fact that none of the other writers attest to the episode is not in itself sufficient proof that it did not take place: many documents from this period are lost. Of the more than 1,400 pages of Diderot's correspondence, for instance, only four letters fall into the winter 1752–3. Two of these are to his family and one to Mme de Pompadour, neither of them would have been particularly interested in a quarrel between two young men, in itself hardly a rare occurrence, and neither of them constituted an audience with whom Diderot would have discussed personal questions such as the problems of a close friend unknown to them. Rousseau does not mention the duel, but he himself is hardly a reliable witness. It is true that the author of the only source, Mme d'Épinay, might have invented the incident to portray Grimm as chivalrous and daring on her behalf; but the very fact that it seems so little in character with what we know of Grimm may itself be an indication that the episode was unlikely to have been invented. Also, it is not at all in the spirit of the novel, which portrays the heroine as suffering and virtuous, even to imply that she might have stolen a note of debt in order to relieve the financial burden on her profligate husband, and thus on herself. A final indication is that it was indeed around this time that Mme d'Épinay began to see Grimm not only as a witty dinner guest but also as a possible companion and lover. See also Steegmuller, *A Woman, a Man and Two Kingdoms*, p. 30.

9 It is not known why Raynal decided to abandon his journal, but the *Anecdotes historiques* (Amsterdam, 3 vols, 1753) must have been a considerable drain on his time and energy. The book came out before he handed over the editorship (Grimm reviewed it in his first edition), but it may be that Raynal wanted to concentrate on other projects. Seemingly in two minds about the journal, he continued it once again for ten months in 1754–5, but found that by this time Grimm's *Correspondance littéraire* had cornered the market.

10 *Corr. litt.*, ii, p. 3, November 1750.

11 Ibid., ii, p. 86.

12 Ibid., ii, p. 101.

13 Scherer, *Grimm*, p. 39.

14 Rousseau, *Confessions*, ii, pp. 289–90.

15 Mme d'Épinay, *Mémoires*, ii, p. 675.

16 Ibid., p. 754.

17 Rousseau, *Confessions*, ii, p. 220.

18 Rousseau, *Œuvres complètes*, Paris, 1959, iii, p. 161.

19 See Furbank, *Diderot*, p. 119.

20 In fact, Diderot's thought and Kant's categorical imperative, 'Act as if the maxim of your action were to become through your will a

universal law of nature', lies in their idea of society. Kant, in his search for an *a priori* foundation of morality, presupposes the notion of 'good will' as an empirical truth, while Diderot's 'general will' is something close to the idea of a 'vox populi', the will of the many. Diderot, it seems, found it impossible to assume the existence of an isolated individual even in his philosophy.

21 Diderot, *Œuvres*, v, p. 412, 15 August, 1762.

22 Diderot, *Œuvres*, v, p. 42. The negotiations were eventually concluded and the new contract stipulated that Diderot should get 2,500 *livres* for each volume and 20,000 *livres* on conclusion of the project, a distinct improvement on the previous terms.

23 Marmontel, *Mémoires*, Clermont-Ferrand 1972, ii, pp. 306–7, translation in Wilson, *Diderot*, pp. 220–1.

Virtue

1 Fréron to Malesherbes, 21 March 1757; Étienne Charavanay, 'Diderot & Fréron', in *Revue des Documents Historiques*, iii, 1875–6, p. 160.

2 Rousseau, *Confessions*, ii, pp. 271–2.

3 Rousseau to Mme d'Épinay, 13 March 1757.

4 Diderot, *Œuvres*, v, pp. 63–4.

5 Rousseau, *Confessions*, ii, p. 258.

6 Rousseau, *Corr. Gén.*, iii, p. 120.

7 Rousseau, *Confessions*, ii, pp. 264–5.

8 Grimm to Mme d'Épinay, quoted in Steegmuller, *A Woman, a Man*, p. 34.

Regicide

1 *Pièces originales et procédures du procès fait à Robert-François Damiens, tant en la prévôté de l'Hôtel qu'en la cour du parlement*, Paris, 1757, p. 64.

2 Quoted in Kley, *The Damiens Affair*, p. 5.

3 Barbier, *Journal*, vii, pp 2–3.

4 *A Particular and Authentic Narration of the Life, Examination, Torture, and Execution of Robert Francis Damien* [sic], tr. Thomas Jones, London, 1757.

5 Quoted in Kley, *The Damiens Affair*, p. 34.

6 Ibid., p. 35.

7 *Pièces originales et procédures du procès, fait à Robert-François Damiens*, Paris, 1757.

8 Quoted in *Corr. litt.*, iii, p. 331, footnote.

9 *Lettres et autres pièces sur l'assassinat de Louis XV, année 1757*, Bibliothèque Municipale de Troyes, RR 479.

10 See Mme du Hausset, *Mémoires de la femme de chambre de Mme de Pompadour*, Paris, 1824.

11 For an engaging nineteenth-century interpretation of his, and other regicides', states of mind, see Emmanuel Régis, *Les Régicides dans l'historie et de présent*, Paris, 1890.

12 François Ravaisson, *Archives de la Bastille: documents inédits. [XVII].* *Règne de Louis XV: 1757 à 1762*, Paris, 1891, pp. 36, 139–41, 243–4, 351, 388, *passim*.

Geneva

1 Quoted in Delaye, *Louis XV et Damiens*, p. 249.

2 Diderot, *Œuvres*, v, p. 66.

3 Rousseau, *Confessions*, ii., p. 299.

4 Rousseau, *Corr. Gén.*, vi, p. 325, here quoted in Wilson, *Diderot*, p. 297.

5 Ibid., iii, pp. 136–43.

6 This letter has sometimes been called a forgery, but there is every reason to accept it as genuine. See Wilson's discussion of the controversy in *Diderot*, p. 765.

7 *Premier Mémoire*, in Vissiere, *La Secte des Empoisonneurs*, pp. 40–64.

8 Ibid., p. 43.

9 Ibid., p. 45.

10 Ibid., p. 53.

11 Diderot, *Œuvres*, v, p. 70.

12 See Raymond Naves, *Voltaire et l'Encyclopédie*, Paris, 1938, pp. 38–49.

Fanaticism

1 Ecclesiasticus, 22: 26–7.

2 Diderot, quoted in *Jean-Jacques Rousseau, mémoire de la critique*, p. 175.

3 Diderot, *Œuvres*, v, p. 262.

4 Piere-Nicolas Bonamy to Malesherbes, in Eugène Asse, 'Diderot et Voltaire, d'après les papiers inédits de la censure', *Cabinet Historique*, 1 (1882), p. 29, quoted in Wilson, *Diderot*, p. 316.

5 *Corr. litt.*, iv, p. 30.

6 Ibid.

7 *Arrests de la Cour de Parlement*, 1759, i, 2, p. 13.

8 Edmond Jean-François Barbier, *Chronique*, vii, pp. 126–130.

9 *Corr. litt.*, iv, pp. 80–1.

10 Voltaire, *Œuvres*, lvii, pp. 43–4.

11 *Arrêt du conseil d'Etat du Roi* . . . 8 March 1759, Paris, 1759, in BN MSS, Fr. 22177, fo. 324.

12 This story, attested by Diderot's daughter, Mme Vandeul, in her memoirs, is often thought to relate to the search of Diderot's office in 1752. A letter that appeared in 1931, however, in which Diderot writes to Grimm that it was necessary 'to save the manuscripts in the middle of the night . . . and to find them a shelter' (Diderot, *Œuvres*, v, p. 90, 1 May 1759), makes it more likely that his daughter, who was a child at the time and must have heard of the affair through stories, mistook the date, and that 1759 is the more likely year. See Wilson, *Diderot*, p. 339; Darnton, *The Business of Enlightenment*, p. 12.

13 Diderot, *Œuvres*, v, p. 89.

Hide, Dissemble, Disguise

1 Ibid., p. 90.

2 Ibid.

3 Ibid., p. 112.

4 Counting the contributions in the later volumes is a delicate question of judgement, as in many cases it depends on attribution. These numbers are taken from Haechler's very thoroughly researched *L'Encyclopédie de Diderot*, pp. 499–500.

5 *Année Littéraire*, vii, 1759, pp. 345–6, quoted in Wilson, *Diderot*, pp. 360–1.

6 *Observateur Littéraire*, v, 1759, p. 216, quoted in Wilson, *Diderot*, p. 361.

7 Registre de l'Académie des Sciences, 1759, fo. 817–18.

8 Diderot, *Œuvres*, v, p. 72.

9 Ibid., p. 94.

10 Diderot, *Œuvres*, v, p. 97.

11 Ibid., p. 159.

12 Ibid., p. 101.

13 Ibid., p. 100.

14 Ibid., p. 97. See also the following letter to Grimm, p. 99.

15 Ibid., p. 107.

16 Ibid., p. 118.

17 Ibid., p. 103.
18 Ibid., p. 316.
19 Ibid., p. 160.

Métier

1 Leipzig, 5 vols, 1742–67.
2 The Hague, 2 vols, 1706–11. Basnage was a Protestant theologian and very prolific writer, whose studies of Jewish sources were rather cursory.
3 Wilson, *Diderot*, p. 236.
4 This translation is in Wilson, *Diderot*, p. 237.
5 Diderot, *Œuvres*, v, p. 197.
6 Diderot, quoted in Proust, *Diderot et l'Encyclopédie*, p. 194.
7 For exact information on the titles of the works used, see Pinault, 'Sur les plances de l'*Encyclopédie*', in *L'Encyclopédisme*, pp. 355–62; Proust, *Diderot et l'Encyclopédie*, pp. 189–96, *passim*.
8 See Bernard Lewis, *The Muslim Discovery of Europe*, London, 2001 (1982), p. 237.

Phoenix

1 Diderot, *Œuvres*, Paris, 1951, p. 395.
2 Ibid., pp. 425–6.
3 Diderot, *Œuvres*, v, pp. 185–6.
4 Ibid., pp. 210–11.
5 Ibid, p. 176; Diderot to Sophie Volland, 20 October 1760.
6 Ibid., p. 256.
7 Ibid., p. 350.
8 Ibid., p. 359.
9 Ibid., p. 406.
10 Ibid., p. 453.
11 Quoted in A. H. Cash, *Laurence Sterne*, London, 1975, ii, p. 137.
12 Walpole to George Selwyn, 2 December 1765.
13 Sir James Macdonald of the Isles to Mrs Elizabeth Montagu, Paris, 11 April 1764, in Elizabeth R. Montagu, *Mrs Montagu, 'Queen of the Blues'*, ed. Reginald Blunt, 2 vols, New York, 1924, i, p. 97.
14 Diderot, *Œuvres*, v, p. 81.
15 Ibid., p. 441.
16 Ibid., p. 449.
17 Ibid., p. 458.

18 *Corr Litt.*, v, pp. 410–12.
19 Ibid, p. 273.

Mutilation

1 Diderot, *Œuvres*, v, p. 459.
2 Ibid., ix, pp. 208.
3 Ibid.
4 Diderot, *Œuvres*, v, pp. 487–9.
5 Ibid.
6 For a thorough analysis of the cuts and changes, see D. H. Gorden and N. L. Torrey, *The Censoring in Diderot's Encyclopédie: The Reestablished Text.*
7 Quoted in Wilson, *Diderot*, p. 475.
8 *Corr. litt.*, vii, p. 45.
9 For a thorough analysis of de Jaucourts borrowing and compiling practices, see Haechler, *L'Encyclopédie*, pp. 509–25.
10 Diderot, *Œuvres*, v, p. 395.
11 Quoted in Wilson, *Diderot*, p. 513.
12 Diderot, *Œuvres*, v, p. 508.
13 Ibid., p. 511.
14 Ibid., p. 494.
15 *Mémoire à consulter pour les Libraires associés à l'Encyclopédie*, Paris, p. 16.

Posterity

1 Diderot, *Œuvres*, v, p. 591.
2 Ibid., p. 606.
3 Ibid., vii, pp. 76–7.
4 Ibid., v, p. 702.
5 Ibid., pp. 967–8.
6 Diderot, *Réponse signifiée de M. Luneau de Boisjermain au Précis des Libraires associés à l'impression de l'Encyclopédie*, Paris, 1772, 10–13.
7 Ibid., p. 11.
8 *Corr. litt.*, ix, p. 207.
9 See Proust, *Diderot*, pp. 104–5.
10 Kafker, *The Encyclopedists as a Group*, p. 123.
11 *Corr. litt.*, viii, p. 438.
12 See Haechler, *L'Encyclopédie de Diderot et . . . de Jaucourt*, p. 554.
13 *Corr. litt.*, xii, p. 53.

14 Diderot, *Œuvres*, v, p. 1271.

15 Quoted in Kafker, *The Encyclopedists as Individuals*, p. 161.

16 Diderot, *Œuvres*, v, p. 1280.

17 Diderot, *Œuvres* (Gallimard), p. 943.

18 Ibid., p. 944.

19 Ibid., p. 949.

20 Ibid., p. 955.

21 Ibid., p. 957.

22 Diderot, *Œuvres*, v, p. 1126.

23 Quoted in Wilson, *Diderot*, p. 703.

24 Vandeul, *Diderot*, p. 52.

INDEX

233–4, 267; booksellers 39, 82, 102, 232–3, 237, 242–3, 272, 280, 289–90, 299, 309–10; clandestine writers 11; contributors xiv, xvi, 44, 95–8, 101, 108, 139–44, 192, 240–1, 289, 308; deteriorating relations between 205–7; editors xiv, xvi, 39–40, 41, 63–5, 111, 156, 238–40, 280, 290; enemies of 83–4, 98–9, 109–10, 114–15, 211, 227–30, 234, 241, 268, 272, 280; and Enlightenment rationalism 86–7, 228; influence of 225, 304, 312; reduced to small group 240–1, 280; reputation of 267–8; and Revolution 143, 312–13; Rousseau's relations with 223; social backgrounds xiv, 141–2; threats to xiii–xiv, 232; vow to continue 231–2; women 143, 160

GENERAL: announcements 82–3, 108, 297; banned xvi, 114, 116, 119, 228–9, 233, 237, 240; censorship 88–9, 111, 115, 119, 155, 213, 219, 222, 255; completion of 299–300; continues despite ban 233–5, 267; crisis in 211–17, 219, 222, 233–5; economics of 310–11; editorial policy 76, 90, 99, 116, 139–40, 145; enlarged concept of project 40, 43, 76; faults acknowledged by

Diderot 153–4; ignored by posterity 312; law suit against 75, 286, 309–10; pirate editions 110–11, 311; *privilèges* (licences) 38–9, 48, 89, 230, 233; *Prospectus* 37–8, 63, 73, 75–8, 83–4, 110; publication of volumes 89–90, 111, 136, 139, 204, 222, 277, 283, 297–9; purchase price 57–8, 75, 82–3; purpose of 76, 77, 140, 151, 290; quarto edition 311; reprints and later editions 43, 307–9, 311, 316; reviews and critiques 87, 109, 166; sales 110, 136; satires against 207–8, 213, 222; scale of xvi, 65, 144; shareholders in 39; subscribers 79, 82–3, 110, 232–3, 297–8, 309–10; supplement published by Le Breton 309; as translation of Chambers' *Cyclopaedia* xxv, 35–40, 45, 76

Encyclopédie méthodique 308–9
ENFER article 95–6
English encyclopedias xxiv–xxv
Enlightenment xiii, 30, 87, 227, 252; encyclopedias xxii–xxv
ÉPARGNE (Thrift) article 148
Epicurus 77
Épinay, Denis-Joseph d' 95, 161, 168, 317
Épinay, Louise-Florence d' 160–2, 204; appearance 162; autobiographical novel (*Mémoires de Madame de Montbrillant*) 160, 162–4, 168,